Kaplan Publishing are constantly finding new
ways to make a difference to your st
exciting online resources really do o
different to students looking for exa

G000241182

This book comes with free MyKaplan online resources so that
you can study anytime, anywhere. This free online resource is
not sold separately and is included in the price of the book.

Having purchased this book, you have access to the following online study materials:

CONTENT	ACCA (including FFA,FAB,FMA)		FIA (excluding FFA,FAB,FMA)	
	Text	Kit	Text	Kit
Electronic version of the book	✓	✓	✓	✓
Check Your Understanding Test with instant answers	✓			
Material updates	✓	✓	✓	✓
Latest official ACCA exam questions*		✓		
Extra question assistance using the signpost icon**		✓		
Timed questions with an online tutor debrief using clock icon***		✓		
Interim assessment including questions and answers	✓		✓	
Technical answers	✓	✓	✓	✓

* Excludes F1, F2, F3, F4, FAB, FMA and FFA; for all other papers includes a selection of questions, as released by ACCA

** For ACCA P1-P7 only

*** Excludes F1, F2, F3, F4, FAB, FMA and FFA

How to access your online resources

Kaplan Financial students will already have a MyKaplan account and these extra resources will be available to
you online. You do not need to register again, as this process was completed when you enrolled. If you are having
problems accessing online materials, please ask your course administrator.

If you are not studying with Kaplan and did not purchase your book via a Kaplan website, to unlock your extra online
resources please go to www.mykaplan.co.uk/addabook (even if you have set up an account and registered books
previously). You will then need to enter the ISBN number (on the title page and back cover) and the unique pass key
number contained in the scratch panel below to gain access.

You will also be required to enter additional information during this process to set up or confirm your account details.

If you purchased through Kaplan Flexible Learning or via the Kaplan Publishing website you will automatically receive
an e-mail invitation to MyKaplan. Please register your details using this email to gain access to your content. If you do
not receive the e-mail or book content, please contact Kaplan Publishing.

Your Code and Information

This code can only be used once for the registration of one book online. This registration and your online content will
expire when the final sittings for the examinations covered by this book have taken place. Please allow one hour from
the time you submit your book details for us to process your request.

Please scratch the film to access your MyKaplan code.

Please be aware that this code is case-sensitive and you will need to include the dashes
within the passcode, but not when entering the ISBN. For further technical support,
please visit www.MyKaplan.co.uk

ACCA

Applied Skills

Financial Reporting (FR)

EXAM KIT

British Library Cataloguing-in-Publication Data

A catalogue record for this book is available from the British Library.

Published by:
Kaplan Publishing UK
Unit 2 The Business Centre
Molly Millar's Lane
Wokingham
Berkshire
RG41 2QZ

ISBN: 978-1-78740-413-7

Acknowledgements

These materials are reviewed by the ACCA examining team. The objective of the review is to ensure that the material properly covers the syllabus and study guide outcomes, used by the examining team in setting the exams, in the appropriate breadth and depth. The review does not ensure that every eventuality, combination or application of examinable topics is addressed by the ACCA Approved Content. Nor does the review comprise a detailed technical check of the content as the Approved Content Provider has its own quality assurance processes in place in this respect.

Trade Marks

CONTENTS

Section

This document references IFRS® Standards and IAS® Standards, which are authored by the International Accounting Standards Board (the Board), and published in the 2018 IFRS Standards Red Book.

Features in this edition

In addition to providing a wide-ranging bank of exam-standard questions, we have also included in this edition:

- Details of the examination format.

- Examples of objective-test, objective-test case and constructed response questions that will form part of the examination format.

- Exam-specific information and advice on exam technique.

- An analysis of all of the recent published examinations.

- Our recommended approach to make your revision for this particular subject as effective as possible. This includes step-by-step guidance on how best to use our Kaplan material (study text, pocket notes and exam kit) at this stage in your studies.

- Enhanced tutorial answers packed with specific key answer tips, technical tutorial notes and exam technique tips from our experienced tutors.

You will find a wealth of other resources to help you with your studies on the following sites:

www.mykaplan.co.uk and www.accaglobal.com/students/

Quality and accuracy are of the utmost importance to us so if you spot an error in any of our products, please send an email to mykaplanreporting@kaplan.com with full details.

Our Quality Co-ordinator will work with our technical team to verify the error and take action to ensure that it is corrected in future editions.

INDEX TO QUESTIONS AND ANSWERS

INTRODUCTION

A number of the previous ACCA exam questions within this kit have been adapted to reflect updated standards, and the revised exam format. If changed in any way from the original version, whether due to updates in the IFRS® Standards or due to changes in exam format, this is indicated in the end column of the index below with the mark (A).

The specimen exam and September 2016 full examination is included at the end of the kit.

KEY TO THE INDEX

ENHANCEMENTS

We have added the following enhancements to the answers in this exam kit:

Key answer tips

All answers include key answer tips to help your understanding of each question.

Tutorial note

All answers include more tutorial notes to explain some of the technical points in more detail.

Top tutor tips

For selected questions, we 'walk through the answer' giving guidance on how to approach the questions with helpful 'tips from a top tutor', together with technical tutor notes.

These answers are indicated with the 'footsteps' icon in the index.

ONLINE ENHANCEMENTS

 Question debrief

For selected questions, we recommend that they are to be completed in full exam conditions (i.e. completed to time in a closed book environment).

In addition to the examiner's technical answer, enhanced with key answer tips and tutorial notes in this exam kit, online you can find an answer debrief by a top tutor that:

- works through the question in full

- points out how to approach the question

- shows how to ensure that the easy marks are obtained as quickly as possible, and

- emphasises how to tackle exam questions and exam technique.

These questions are indicated with the 'clock' icon in the index.

Online question enhancements and answer debriefs will be available on MyKaplan at

www.MyKaplan.co.uk

KAPLAN PUBLISHING

ANALYSIS OF PAST EXAMINATIONS

The table summarises the key topics that have been tested in recent Financial Reporting exams. A much wider range of topics will now be examined following the introduction of objective-test questions. The information from June 2015 onwards only relates to constructed response questions released by ACCA, as multiple-choice questions have not usually been published. For the September 2016 examination, following a change in the examination format, ACCA published the full examination. This will not be repeated for future sittings.

	Dec 2014	Jun 2015	Sep/ Dec 2015	Mar/ Jun 2016	Sep 2016	Dec 2016	Mar/ Jun 2017	Sep/ Dec 2017	Mar/ Jun 2018	Sep/ Dec 2018
Group financial statements										
Consolidated statement of profit or loss and other comprehensive income		✓				✓				
Consolidated statement of financial position			✓	✓		✓	✓	✓		✓
Consolidated SPL and SFP	✓									
Associates						✓				
Disposal									✓	
Single entity financial statements										
From trial balance	✓	✓	✓	✓	✓				✓	✓
Redraft					✓					
Statement of changes in equity		✓	✓						✓	✓
Statement of cash flows	✓									
Performance appraisal										
Ratios	✓	✓	✓	✓	✓	✓	✓	✓	✓	✓
Groups							✓	✓	✓	✓
Framework/IFRS										
IASB Framework	✓	✓			✓	✓				
Accounting principles/ substance	✓									
Not for profit/specialised entities	✓					✓				
IAS 2	✓								✓	
IAS 7	✓				✓					
IAS 8	✓				✓					✓
IAS 10		✓				✓				

IAS 12	✓	✓	✓	✓	✓	✓	✓			✓
IAS 16	✓	✓	✓	✓	✓	✓	✓		✓	
IAS 17/IFRS 16	✓	✓			✓					
IAS 20		✓			✓					
IAS 23		✓								
IAS 28							✓			
IAS 32/IFRS 7/ IFRS 9	✓	✓	✓	✓	✓	✓			✓	✓
IAS 33	✓	✓		✓	✓	✓				✓
IAS 36	✓	✓		✓	✓	✓				
IAS 37	✓	✓			✓					✓
IAS 38		✓	✓			✓				
IAS 40										
IAS 41		✓								
IFRS 3								✓		✓
IFRS 5	✓				✓	✓				
IFRS 10		✓			✓	✓	✓			✓
IFRS 13										
IAS 18/IAS 11/IFRS 15	✓	✓	✓	✓		✓			✓	✓

EXAM TECHNIQUE

Computer-based exams (CBE)

- Do not attempt a CBE until you have **completed all study material** relating to it.

- On the ACCA website there is a specimen Financial Reporting CBE. It is **ESSENTIAL** that you attempt this before your real CBE. You will become familiar with how to move around the screens and the way that questions are formatted, increasing your confidence and speed in the actual exam.

- Be sure you understand how to use the **software** before you start the exam. Ensure that you use the resources on the ACCA website to practise, **especially the CR workspace**. If in doubt, ask the assessment centre staff to explain it to you.

Time management

- The examination is 3 hours long.

- This equates to 1.8 minutes per mark, so you need to allow 36 minutes per Constructed Response (CR) question and an average of 3.6 minutes per objective-test (OT) question.

- Decide whether you want to attempt the OTs first, or after completion of the CR questions. Whichever you choose to do first, ensure that you leave enough time to tackle the remainder.

- Whatever happens, always keep your eye on the clock and **do not over-run on any part of any question**!

Objective-test questions

- **Do not skip any of the material** in the syllabus during revision.

- No credit for workings will be given in these questions. The answer will either be correct (2 marks) or incorrect (0 marks).

- Read each question **very carefully**, as the alternative answer choices will be given based on common mistakes that could be made in attempting the question.

- **Double-check your answer** before committing yourself to it.

- Answer **every** question – if you do not know an answer, you don't lose anything by guessing, but think carefully before you **guess**.

- Remember that there is **only one correct answer to a multiple-choice question**. After you have eliminated the ones that you know to be wrong, if you are still unsure, guess. Only guess after you have **double-checked** that you have only eliminated answers that are **definitely** wrong.

- If you get **completely stuck** with a question, choose your best answer, flag the question for review and **return to it later** if you have time.

- The objective –test question types are as follows:
  - **Multiple choice** – choose one answer from a number of given options
  - **Multiple response** – choose more than one an answer from a number of given options
  - **Fill in the blank** – type an answer into a box
  - **Drag and drop** – drag an answer and drop it into place
  - **Drop down list** – choose one answer from a drop down list
  - **Hot spot** – choose one point on an image
  - **Hot area** – choose an area in an image

Constructed Response questions

- There will be a computational financial statements preparation question and a written analysis question.

- **Computational questions** require the use of a standard format, e.g. statement of profit or loss and other comprehensive income. Be sure that you know all the formats thoroughly before the exam and use the layouts that you see in the answers given in this book and in model answers.

- It is essential to show all your workings in your answer.

- For the **written question** consider how to structure the response and lay it out so as to articulate the answer clearly.

- Stick to the question and **ensure that you explain the reasons** why the numbers have changed.

- Your response should have:
  - a clear structure
  - a brief introduction, a main section and a conclusion.

  It is better to write a little about a lot of different points than a great deal about one or two points.

- You should do everything you can to make things easy for the marker. Cross-reference answers to workings in computational questions and use headings and sub-headings in written answers.

EXAM SPECIFIC INFORMATION

THE EXAM

FORMAT OF THE EXAM

The exam will be in **THREE sections**, and will be a mix of narrative and computational answers. Section A will be 15 objective test questions, each worth 2 marks. Section B will consist of 3 objective case questions, each worth 10 marks and containing 5 questions. Section C will consist of two 20-mark questions

		Number of marks
Section A:	Fifteen 2-mark objective test (OT) questions	30
Section B:	Three 10-mark objective case questions	30
Section C:	Two 20-mark constructed response questions, covering the interpretation and preparation of financial statements for a single entity or a group	40
		———
		100

Note that the FR exam will have both a discursive and computational element. The questions will therefore include a mix of calculation-based and explanations-based questions.

PASS MARK

The pass mark for all ACCA Qualification examinations is 50%.

DETAILED SYLLABUS, STUDY GUIDE AND CBE SPECIMEN EXAM

The detailed syllabus and study guide written by the ACCA, along with the specimen exam, can be found at:

accaglobal.com/financial-reporting

KAPLAN'S RECOMMENDED REVISION APPROACH

QUESTION PRACTICE IS THE KEY TO SUCCESS

Success in professional examinations relies upon you acquiring a firm grasp of the required knowledge at the tuition phase. In order to be able to answer the questions, knowledge is essential.

However, the difference between success and failure often hinges on your exam technique on the day and making the most of the revision phase of your studies.

The **Kaplan study text** is the starting point, designed to provide the underpinning knowledge to tackle all questions. However, in the revision phase, poring over text books is not the answer.

Kaplan Online knowledge check tests help you consolidate your knowledge and understanding, and are a useful tool to check whether you remember key topic areas.

Kaplan pocket notes are designed to help you quickly revise a topic area, but you then need to practise questions. There is a need to progress to full exam standard questions as soon as possible, and to tie your exam technique and technical knowledge together.

The **ACCA CR Workspace** provides an essential practice area for you to become familiar with the software available on the examination day. Try and use this to practise Constructed Response questions where possible.

The importance of question practice cannot be over-emphasised.

The recommended approach below is designed by expert tutors in the field, in conjunction with their knowledge of the examiner.

The approach taken for the Applied Skills exams is to revise by topic area.

You need to practise as many questions as possible in the time you have left.

OUR AIM

Our aim is to get you to the stage where you can attempt exam standard questions confidently, to time, in a closed book environment, with no supplementary help (i.e. to simulate the real examination experience).

Practising your exam technique on exam standard examination questions, in timed conditions, is also vitally important for you to assess your progress and identify areas of weakness that may need more attention in the final run up to the examination.

In order to achieve this we recognise that initially you may feel the need to practise some questions with open book help and exceed the required time.

The approach below shows you which questions you should use to build up to coping with exam standard question practice, and references to the sources of information available should you need to revisit a topic area in more detail.

Remember that in the real examination, all you have to do is:

- attempt all questions required by the exam

- only spend the allotted time on each question, and

- get them at least 50% right!

Try and practise this approach on every question you attempt from now to the real exam.

EXAMINER COMMENTS

We have included some of the examiner's comments to the examination questions in this kit for you to see the main pitfalls that students fall into with regard to technical content.

However, too many times in the general section of the report, the examiner comments that students had failed due to poor time management where students had shown signs of 'spending too much time on an earlier question and clearly rushing the answer to a subsequent question'.

Ensure that you read the examiner's comments from recent exams on the ACCA website.

Good exam technique is vital.

ACCA SUPPORT

For additional support with your studies please also refer to the ACCA Global website.

THE KAPLAN FINANCIAL REPORTING REVISION PLAN

Stage 1: Assess areas of strengths and weaknesses

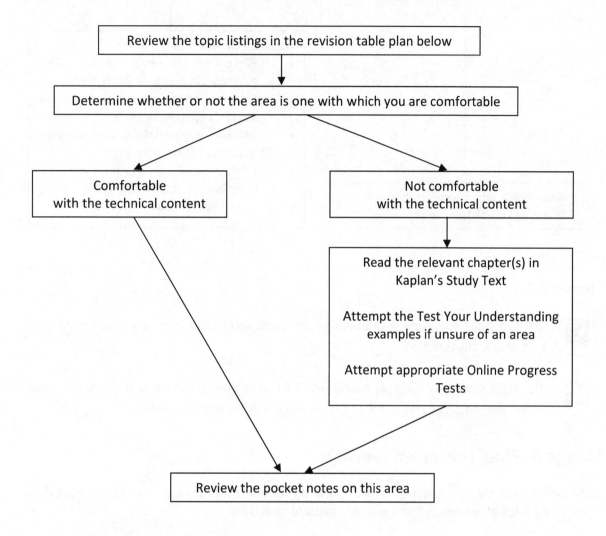

Stage 2: Practise questions

Follow the order of revision of topics as recommended in the revision table plan below and attempt the questions in the order suggested.

Try to avoid referring to text books, notes or the model answer until you have completed your attempt.

Try to answer the question in the allotted time.

Review your attempt with the model answer and assess how much of the answer you achieved in the allocated exam time.

Use the self-assessment box below to decide on your best course of action.

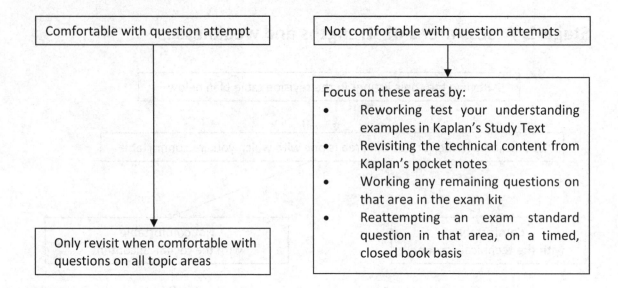

Comfortable with question attempt

Not comfortable with question attempts

Focus on these areas by:
- Reworking test your understanding examples in Kaplan's Study Text
- Revisiting the technical content from Kaplan's pocket notes
- Working any remaining questions on that area in the exam kit
- Reattempting an exam standard question in that area, on a timed, closed book basis

Only revisit when comfortable with questions on all topic areas

Note that:

 The 'footsteps questions' give guidance on exam techniques and how you should have approached the question.

 The 'clock questions' have an online debrief where a tutor talks you through the exam technique and approach to that question and works the question in full.

Stage 3: Final pre-exam revision

We recommend that you **attempt at least one three-hour mock computer-based examination** containing a set of previously unseen exam standard questions.

It is important that you get a feel for the breadth of coverage of the real exam without advanced knowledge of the topic areas covered – just as you will see on the real exam day.

Ideally this mock should be sat in timed, closed book, real exam conditions and could be:

- an online mock examination offered by your tuition provider and/or

- the examinations in the back of this exam kit (answered using ACCA CR Workspace) and/or

- the latest released examination Constructed Response questions (available shortly afterwards on MyKaplan with enhanced walk-through answers and a full tutor debrief). Ensure that you use the ACCA CR Workspace to attempt these.

KAPLAN'S DETAILED REVISION PLAN

Topic	Study Text Chapter	Pocket note Chapter	Questions to attempt	Tutor guidance	Date attempted	Self assessment
Consolidated statement of financial position	18/20	18/20	141–150 316–320 369, 373, 375, 376, 378, 383, 385	Practise the Kaplan 5 working approach. Ensure you get the easy marks available in the question from adding the parent and subsidiary assets and liabilities together.		
Consolidated statement of profit or loss and other comprehensive income	19/20	19/20	151–154 156–162 321–325 370, 372, 374, 377, 380, 382, 384	Watch the dates carefully – is there a mid-year acquisition? If so you have to time apportion the subsidiary company results when adding the parent and subsidiary together.		
Consolidated statement of profit or loss and other comprehensive income and statement of financial position	18-20	18-20	371, 379, 381	Set up your proformas first and get the easy marks by adding the parent and subsidiary results together – then complete the 5 standard statement of financial position workings before moving on to complete the statement of profit or loss.		
Disposal of subsidiaries	21	21	182–185 330 405	Ensure you familiarise yourself with the workings related to calculating a profit/loss on disposal.		

Topic	Study Text Chapter	Pocket note Chapter	Questions to attempt	Tutor guidance	Date attempted	Self assessment
Accounting standards:						
Non-current assets (IAS 16, IAS 20, IAS 23, IAS 38, IAS 40, IFRS 5)	2	2	1–22, 30–36 221–230 231–235 236–245	Be clear on initial recognition rules and subsequent measurement for property, plant and equipment, intangible assets and investment properties. Ensure you know the definition of borrowing costs and the three recognition and two derecognition criteria. Ensure you understand how to deal with assets held for sale.		
IAS 36	4	4	23–29 246–250	Learn the impairment test proforma and the cash generating unit write down rules.		
Framework	6/7	6/7	37–58	Learn the key definitions and be able to apply them to various situations		
IAS 2, IAS 8, IAS 41, IFRS 13	8	8	59–62 69–75 256–265	Each standard is relatively small, but it is key that you learn definitions and the specific rules relating to each.		

KAPLAN PUBLISHING

Topic	Study Text Chapter	Pocket note Chapter	Questions to attempt	Tutor guidance	Date attempted	Self assessment
IAS 32/IFRS 7/IFRS 9	9	9	87–96 276–285	Amortised cost is the core area of financial liabilities here. Make sure you can deal with loans issued at a discount & redeemed at a premium. You will also need an awareness of the categories of financial asset in accordance with IFRS 9 and the accounting treatment for them.		
IAS 21	10	10	97–101 286–288	Examine the initial and subsequent treatment, in addition to the rules for unsettled transactions.		
IFRS 15	11	11	102–114 291–300	Different revenue scenarios should be looked at, in particular where revenue is recognised over time.		
IFRS 16	12	12	76–86 266–275	Be sure that you are able to construct a liability table.		
IAS 12	13	13	115–118 289–290	Learn the definition of a temporary difference and practise its application.		
IAS 33	14	14	119–128 301–305	Learn the formula and apply to share issues.		
IAS 37, IAS 10	15	15	129–140 306–312	For IAS 37 the recognition rules are very clear – learn the 3 recognition rules. Learn the differences between adjusting and non-adjusting events.		

Topic	Study Text Chapter	Pocket note Chapter	Questions to attempt	Tutor guidance	Date attempted	Self assessment
Statement of cash flows	16	16	211–220 341–350 367–369	Learn the proforma. Start with calculations in questions 201, 203, and 204 before moving on to analysing cash flows in 221 and 226.		
Preparation of individual company financial statements	1, 23	1	351–366	You have to learn the accounting standards examinable first and then apply your knowledge to these recommended questions.		
Ratio interpretation	22	22	186–210 331–340 388–406	Learn the ratio calculations and practise identifying where you pull the information for the formula out of the financial statements.		

TECHNICAL UPDATE

There were no additions or amendments to the Financial Reporting syllabus from 2018 to 2019, other than to reflect the update to the Conceptual Framework.

Section 1

OBJECTIVE TEST QUESTIONS – SECTION A

CONCEPTUAL FRAMEWORK/INTERNATIONAL FINANCIAL REPORTING STANDARDS

1 IAS 16 *Property, Plant and Equipment* requires an asset to be measured at cost on its original recognition in the financial statements. EW used its own staff, assisted by contractors when required, to construct a new warehouse for its own use.

Identify whether the costs listed below should be capitalised or expensed.

	Capitalise	Expense
Clearance of the site prior to commencement of construction		
Professional surveyor fees for managing the construction work		
EW's own staff wages for time spent working on construction		
A proportion of EW's administration costs, based on staff time spent		

2 On 1 July 20X4, Experimenter opened a chemical reprocessing plant. The plant was due to be active for five years until 30 June 20X9, when it would be decommissioned. At 1 July 20X4, the costs of decommissioning the plant were estimated to be $4 million in 5 years' time. Experimenter considers that a discount rate of 12% is appropriate for the calculation of a present value, and the discount factor at 12% for five years is 0.567.

What is the total charge to the statement of profit or loss in respect of the decommissioning for the year ended 30 June 20X5?

A $453,600

B $725,760

C $800,000

D $2,268,000

3 An entity purchased property for $6 million on 1 July 20X3. The land element of the purchase was $1 million. The expected life of the building was 50 years and its residual value nil. On 30 June 20X5 the property was revalued to $7 million, of which the land element was $1.24 million and the buildings $5.76 million. On 30 June 20X7, the property was sold for $6.8 million.

What is the gain on disposal of the property that would be reported in the statement of profit or loss for the year to 30 June 20X7?

A   Gain $40,000

B   Loss $200,000

C   Gain $1,000,000

D   Gain $1,240,000

4 A manufacturing entity receives a grant of $1m towards the purchase of a machine on 1 January 20X3. The grant will be repayable if the entity sells the asset within 4 years, which it does not intend to do. The asset has a useful life of 5 years.

What is the deferred income liability balance at 30 June 20X3?

$_____ ,000

5 On 1 January 20X1 Sty received $1m from the local government on the condition that they employ at least 100 staff each year for the next 4 years. Due to an economic downturn and reduced consumer demand on 1 January 20X2, Sty no longer needed to employ any more staff and the conditions of the grant required full repayment.

What should be recorded in the financial statements on 1 January 20X2?

A   Reduce deferred income balance by $750,000

B   Reduce deferred income by $750,000 and recognise a loss of $250,000

C   Reduce deferred income by $1,000,000

D   Reduce deferred income by $1,000,000 and recognise a gain of $250,000

6 **Which of the following properties owned by Scoop would be classified as an investment property?**

A   A property that had been leased to a tenant but which is no longer required and is now being held for resale

B   Land purchased for its investment potential. Planning permission has not been obtained for building construction of any kind

C   A new office building used as Scoop's head office, purchased specifically in order to exploit its capital gains potential

D   A stately home used for executive training

7 During the current year an entity had in place $1 million of 6% loan finance and $2 million of 9% loan finance.

It constructed a new factory which cost $600,000 and this was funded out of the existing loan finance. The factory took 8 months to complete.

To the nearest thousand, what borrowing costs should be capitalised?

$_____ ,000

8 **Which of the following statements is correct?**

Statement 1 If the revaluation model is used for property, plant and equipment, revaluations must subsequently be made with sufficient regularity to ensure that the carrying amount does not differ materially from the fair value at each reporting date.

Statement 2 When an item of property, plant and equipment is revalued, there is no requirement that the entire class of assets to which the item belongs must be revalued.

	Statement 1	Statement 2
True		
False		

9 **Which TWO of the following items should be capitalised within the initial carrying amount of an item of plant?**

A Cost of transporting the plant to the factory

B Cost of installing a new power supply required to operate the plant

C A deduction to reflect the estimated realisable value

D Cost of a three-year maintenance agreement

E Cost of a three-week training course for staff to operate the plant

10 Tibet acquired a new office building on 1 October 20X4. Its initial carrying amount consisted of:

	$000
Land	2,000
Building structure	10,000
Air conditioning system	4,000
	16,000

The estimated lives of the building structure and air conditioning system are 25 years and 10 years respectively.

When the air conditioning system is due for replacement, it is estimated that the old system will be dismantled and sold for $500,000.

Depreciation is time-apportioned where appropriate.

At what amount will the office building be shown in Tibet's statement of financial position as at 31 March 20X5?

A $15,625,000

B $15,250,000

C $15,585,000

D $15,600,000

11   The following trial balance extract relates to a property which is owned by Veeton as at 1 April 20X4.

	Dr	Cr
	$000	$000
Property at cost (20 year original life)	12,000	
Accumulated depreciation as at 1 April 20X4		3,600

On 1 October 20X4, following a sustained increase in property prices, Veeton revalued its property to $10.8 million.

What will be the depreciation charge in Veeton's statement of profit or loss for the year ended 31 March 20X5?

$_____ ,000

12   **Which TWO of the following statements about IAS 20 *Accounting for Government Grants and Disclosure of Government Assistance* are true?**

A   A government grant related to the purchase of an asset must be deducted from the carrying amount of the asset in the statement of financial position.

B   A government grant related to the purchase of an asset should be recognised in profit or loss over the life of the asset.

C   Free marketing advice provided by a government department is excluded from the definition of government grants.

D   Any required repayment of a government grant received in an earlier reporting period is treated as prior period adjustment.

13   Smithson Co purchased a new building with a 50-year life for $10 million on 1 January 20X3. On 30 June 20X5, Smithson Co moved out of the building and rented it out to third parties on a short-term lease. Smithson Co uses the fair value model for investment properties. At 30 June 20X5 the fair value of the property was $11 million and at 31 December 20X5 it was $11.5 million.

What is the total net amount to be recorded in the statement of profit or loss in respect of the office for the year ended 31 December 20X5?

A   Net income $400,000

B   Net income $500,000

C   Net income $1,900,000

D   Net income $2,000,000

14 Gilbert took out a $7.5 million 10% loan on 1 January 20X6 to build a new warehouse during the year. Construction of the warehouse began on 1 February 20X6 and was completed on 30 November 20X6. As not all the funds were needed immediately, Gilbert invested $2 million in 4.5% bonds from 1 January to 1 May 20X6.

What are the total borrowing costs to be capitalised in respect of the warehouse?

$_____

15 Croft acquired a building with a 40-year life for its investment potential for $8 million on 1 January 20X3. At 31 December 20X3, the fair value of the property was estimated at $9 million with costs to sell estimated at $200,000.

If Croft Co uses the fair value model for investment properties, what gain should be recorded in the statement of profit or loss for the year ended 31 December 20X3?

$_____ ,000

16 **Which of the following CANNOT be recognised as an intangible non-current asset in GHK's consolidated statement of financial position at 30 September 20X1?**

A GHK spent $132,000 developing a new type of product. In June 20X1 management worried that it would be too expensive to fund. The finances to complete the project came from a cash injection from a benefactor received in November 20X1.

B GHK purchased a subsidiary during the year. During the fair value exercise, it was found that the subsidiary had a brand name with an estimated value of $50,000, but had not been recognised by the subsidiary as it was internally generated.

C GHK purchased a brand name from a competitor on 1 November 20X0, for $65,000.

D GHK spent $21,000 during the year on the development of a new product, after management concluded it would be viable in November 20X0. The product is being launched on the market on 1 December 20X1 and is expected to be profitable.

17 **Which of the following could be classified as development expenditure in M's statement of financial position as at 31 March 20Y0 according to IAS 38 *Intangible Assets?***

A $120,000 spent on developing a prototype and testing a new type of propulsion system. The project needs further work on it as the system is currently not viable.

B A payment of $50,000 to a local university's engineering faculty to research new environmentally friendly building techniques.

C $35,000 developing an electric bicycle. This is near completion and the product will be launched soon. As this project is first of its kind it is expected to make a loss.

D $65,000 developing a special type of new packaging for a new energy-efficient light bulb. The packaging is expected to reduce M's distribution costs by $35,000 a year.

18 **Which TWO of the following factors are reasons why key staff cannot be capitalised as an intangible asset by an entity?**

A They do not provide expected future economic benefits

B They cannot be controlled by an entity

C Their value cannot be measured reliably

D They are not separable from the business as a whole

19 Amco Co carries out research and development. In the year ended 30 June 20X5 Amco Co incurred total costs in relation to project X of $750,000, spending the same amount each month up to 30 April 20X5, when the project was completed. The product produced by the project went on sale from 31 May 20X5.

The project had been confirmed as feasible on 1 January 20X5, and the product produced by the project was expected to have a useful life of five years.

What is the carrying amount of the development expenditure asset as at 30 June 20X5?

A $295,000

B $725,000

C $300,000

D $0

20 Sybil has acquired a subsidiary Basil in the current year.

Basil has a brand which has been reliably valued by Sybil at $500,000, and a customer list which Sybil has been unable to value.

Which of these describes how Sybil should treat these intangible assets of Basil in their consolidated Financial Statements?

A   They should be included in goodwill.

B   The brand should be capitalised as a separate intangible asset, whereas the customer list should be included within goodwill.

C   Both the brand and the customer list should be capitalised as separate intangible assets.

D   The customer list should be capitalised as a separate intangible asset, whereas the brand should be included within goodwill.

21 Dempsey Co owns a pharmaceutical business with a year-end of 30 September 20X4. Dempsey Co commenced the development stage of a new drug on 1 January 20X4. $40,000 per month was incurred until the project was completed on 30 June 20X4, when the drug went into immediate production. The directors became confident of the project's success on 1 March 20X4. The drug has an estimated life span of five years and time-apportionment is used by Dempsey where applicable.

What amount will Dempsey charge to profit or loss for development costs, including any amortisation, for the year ended 30 September 20X4?

A $12,000

B $98,667

C $48,000

D $88,000

22 **Which of the following statements relating to intangible assets is true?**

	True	False
All intangible assets must be carried at amortised cost or at an impaired amount, they cannot be revalued upwards.		
The development of a new process which is not expected to increase sales revenues may still be recognised as an intangible asset.		

23 A division of an entity has the following balances in its financial statements:

	$
Goodwill	700,000
Plant	950,000
Building	2,300,000
Intangibles	800,000
Other net assets	430,000

Following a period of losses, the recoverable amount of the division is deemed to be $4 million. A recent valuation of the building showed that the building has a market value of $2.5 million. The other net assets are at their recoverable amount. The entity uses the cost model for valuing building and plant.

To the nearest thousand, what is the balance on the building following the impairment review?

A $2,300,000

B $2,500,000

C $2,027,000

D $1,776,000

24 A division of an entity has the following balances in its financial statements:

	$
Goodwill	700,000
Plant	950,000
Building	2,300,000
Intangibles	800,000
Other net assets	430,000

Following a period of losses, the recoverable amount of the division is deemed to be $4 million. A recent valuation of the building showed that the building has a market value of $2.5 million. The other net assets are at their recoverable amount. The entity uses the cost model for valuing building and plant.

To the nearest thousand, what is the balance on plant following the impairment review?

$_____,000

25 A vehicle was involved in an accident exactly halfway through the year. The vehicle cost $10,000 and had a remaining life of 10 years at the start of the year. Following the accident, the expected present value of cash flows associated with the vehicle was $3,400 and the fair value less costs to sell was $6,500.

What is the recoverable amount of the vehicle following the accident?

$_____

26 The net assets of Fyngle, a cash generating unit (CGU), are:

	$
Property, plant and equipment	200,000
Allocated goodwill	50,000
Product patent	20,000
Net current assets (at net realisable value)	30,000
	———
	300,000
	———

As a result of adverse publicity, Fyngle has a recoverable amount of only $200,000.

What would be the value of Fyngle's property, plant and equipment after the allocation of the impairment loss?

A $154,545

B $170,000

C $160,000

D $133,333

27 Which of the following is NOT an indicator of impairment?

A Advances in the technological environment in which an asset is employed have an adverse impact on its future use.

B An increase in interest rates which increases the discount rate an entity uses.

C The carrying amount of an entity's net assets is higher than the entity's number of shares in issue multiplied by its share price.

D The estimated net realisable value of inventory has been reduced due to fire damage although this value is greater than its carrying amount.

28 Riley acquired a non-current asset on 1 October 20X9 at a cost of $100,000 which had a useful life of ten years and a nil residual value. The asset had been correctly depreciated up to 30 September 20Y4. At that date the asset was damaged and an impairment review was performed. On 30 September 20Y4, the fair value of the asset less costs to sell was $30,000 and the expected future cash flows were $8,500 per annum for the next five years. The current cost of capital is 10% and a five year annuity of $1 per annum at 10% would have a present value of $3.79.

What amount would be charged to profit or loss for the impairment of this asset for the year ended 30 September 20Y4?

$_____

29 Metric owns an item of plant which has a carrying amount of $248,000 as at 1 April 20X3. It is being depreciated at 12.5% per annum on a reducing balance basis.

The plant is used to manufacture a specific product which has been suffering a slow decline in sales. Metric has estimated that the plant will be retired from use on 31 March 20X7.

The estimated net cash flows from the use of the plant and their present values are:

	Net cash flows	Present values
	$	$
Year to 31 March 20X5	120,000	109,200
Year to 31 March 20X6	80,000	66,400
Year to 31 March 20X7	52,000	39,000
	_____	_____
	252,000	214,600
	_____	_____

On 1 April 20X4, Metric had an offer from a rival to purchase the plant for $200,000.

At what value should the plant appear in Metric's statement of financial position as at 31 March 20X4?

$_____

30 As at 30 September 20X3 the value of Dune's property in its statement of financial position comprised:

Cost (useful life 15 years)	$45 million
Accumulated depreciation	$6 million

On 1 April 20X4, Dune decided to sell the property. The property is being marketed by a property agent at a price of $42 million, which was considered a reasonably achievable price at that date. The expected costs to sell have been agreed at $1 million. Recent market transactions suggest that actual sale prices achieved for this type of property in the current market conditions are 10% less than the price at which they are marketed.

At 30 September 20X4 the property has not been sold.

At what value should the property be reported in Dune's statement of financial position as at 30 September 20X4?

A $36 million

B $37.5 million

C $36.8 million

D $42 million

31 BN has an asset that was classified as held for sale at 31 March 20X2. The asset had a carrying amount of $900 and a fair value of $800. The cost of disposal was estimated to be $50.

According to IFRS 5 *Non-current Assets Held for Sale and Discontinued Operations*, which value should be used for the asset as at 31 March 20X2?

A $750

B $800

C $850

D $900

32 **According to IFRS 5 *Non-current Assets Held for Sale and Discontinued Operations* which of the following represent criteria for an asset to be classified as held for sale?**

(i)   Available for immediate sale in its present condition.

(ii)   Sale is highly probable.

(iii) The sale is expected to be completed within the next month.

(iv)   The asset is being marketed at a reasonable price.

A   All of the above

B   (i), (ii) and (iii)

C   (i), (ii) and (iv)

D   (ii), (iii) and (iv)

33 **According to IFRS 5 *Non-current Assets Held for Sale and Discontinued Operations* which of the following amounts in respect of a discontinued operation must be shown on the face of the statement of profit or loss?**

	Shown on the face of the statement of profit or loss	Not shown
Revenue		
Gross profit		
Profit after tax		

34 Rural has the following two lines of business that have been disposed of in the year:

Sector X operated in Country A. Rural has no other operations in Country A, and Sector X produced 0.5% of the total revenue of Rural.

Sector Y operated in the same country as the Rural head office. It sold a different product from the other components of Rural, and contributed 10% of the total revenue of Rural Co.

Which of these sectors, if either, should be disclosed as a discontinued operation in the current year?

	Discontinued operation Yes/No
Sector X	
Sector Y	

35 **What is the primary reason why discontinued operations are presented separately within financial statements?**

A   To show an accurate valuation of the business

B   To enhance the predictive nature of financial statements

C   To make the financial statements easier to understand

D   So the financial statements are verifiable

36 At 1 April 20X4, Tilly owned a property with a carrying amount of $800,000 which had a remaining estimated life of 16 years, and was carried under the cost model. On 1 October 20X4, Tilly decided to sell the property and correctly classified it as being 'held-for-sale'. A property agent reported that the property's fair value less costs to sell at 1 October 20X4 was expected to be $790,500 which had not changed at 31 March 20X5.

What should be the carrying amount of the property in Tilly's statement of financial position as at 31 March 20X5?

A $775,000

B $790,500

C $765,000

D $750,000

37 **Which of the following gives the best description of the objectives of financial statements as set out by the International Accounting Standards Board's (The Board's) Conceptual Framework for Financial Reporting?**

A   To fairly present the financial position and performance of an enterprise.

B   To fairly present the financial position, performance and changes in financial position of an enterprise.

C   To provide information about the financial position and performance of an enterprise that is useful to a wide range of users in making economic decisions.

D   To provide information about the financial position, performance and changes in financial position of an enterprise that is useful to a wide range of users in making economic decisions.

38 **The International Accounting Standards Board's Conceptual Framework for Financial Reporting defines a liability as:**

A   an amount owed to another entity

B   a present obligation of the entity to transfer an economic resource as a result of past events

C   expenditure that has been incurred but not yet charged to the statement of profit or loss

D   an obligation that may arise in the future

39 The International Accounting Standards Board's Conceptual Framework for Financial Reporting lists two fundamental qualitative characteristics of financial statements, relevance and faithful representation.

Place the qualities listed alongside the appropriate qualitative characteristic.

	Faithful representation	**Relevance**
Completeness		
Predictive value		
Neutrality		

40 The International Accounting Standards Board's Conceptual Framework for Financial Reporting identifies qualitative characteristics of financial statements.

Which TWO of the following characteristics are NOT fundamental qualitative characteristics according to the *IASB's The Conceptual Framework for Financial Reporting?*

A Relevance

B Reliability

C Faithful representation

D Comparability

41 **Match the element to the correct definition according to the International Accounting Standards Board's Conceptual Framework for Financial Reporting?**

Element	Definition
Expense	A present economic resource controlled by the entity as a result of past events
Liability	The residual interest in the assets of the entity after deducting all its liabilities.
Asset	A present obligation of the entity to transfer an economic resource as a result of past events
Equity	Decreases in assets or increases in liabilities, that result in decreases in equity, other than those relating to distributions to holders of equity claims

42 **Which of the following explains the value that relevant information contains?**

A Instructive value

B Fair value

C Confirmatory value

D Approximate value

43 Which of the following is an example of following the principle of faithful representation?

    A   Showing lease payments as a rental expense

    B   Being prudent by recording the entire amount of a convertible loan as a liability

    C   Creating a provision for staff relocation costs as part of a planned restructuring

    D   Recording a sale and repurchase transaction with a bank as a loan rather than a sale

44 The International Accounting Standards Board's Conceptual Framework for Financial Reporting defines an asset as:

    A   A resource controlled by an entity which is capable of generating independent cash flows.

    B   A present economic resource controlled by the entity as a result of past events.

    C   A resource owned by an entity as a result of past events, from which future economic benefits are expected.

    D   A resource capable of generating income for the entity.

45 Which of the following criteria need to be satisfied in order for an element to be recognised within the financial statements?

    (i)   It meets the definition of an element of the financial statements.

    (ii)   Recognition provides relevant information.

    (iii)   Recognition provides a reliable measure.

    (iv)   The element has fair value.

    (v)   Recognition provides faithful representation of the element.

    A   (i), (ii) and (v)

    B   (i), (iii) and (v)

    C   (i), (ii) and (iv)

    D   (i), (iii) and (iv)

46 Which description defines information that is relevant to users of financial information?

    A   Information that is free from error, bias and is a faithful representation of events

    B   Information that has been prudently prepared

    C   Information that is comparable from one period to the next

    D   Information that influences the decisions of users

47 Which description is most representative of the accounting framework used under IFRS Standards?

	True	False
It is a principles-based framework		
It is a legal obligation		

48 Which of the advantages below is/are likely advantage(s) of the global harmonisation of accounting standards?

	Advantage	Not advantage
Greater comparability between different firms		
Greater compatibility with legal systems		
Easier for large international accounting firms		

49 Which THREE of the following are advantages of applying a principles-based framework of accounting rather than a rules-based framework?

A It avoids 'fire-fighting', where standards are developed in responses to specific problems as they arise

B It allows preparers and auditors to deal with complex transactions which may not be specifically covered by an accounting standard

C Principles-based standards are thought to be harder to circumvent

D A set of rules is given which attempts to cover every eventuality

E It is easier to prove non-compliance

50 Which of the following is NOT a purpose of the International Accounting Standards Board's (the Board's) Conceptual Framework?

A To assist the Board in the preparation and review of IFRS Standards.

B To assist auditors in forming an opinion on whether financial statements comply with IFRS Standards.

C To assist in determining the treatment of items not covered by an existing IFRS Standards.

D To be authoritative where a specific IFRS Standard conflicts with the Conceptual Framework.

51 Financial statements represent transactions in words and numbers. To be useful, financial information must represent faithfully these transactions in terms of how they are reported.

Which of the following accounting treatments would be an example of faithful representation?

A Capitalising development costs as an intangible asset

B Including a convertible loan note in equity on the basis that the holders are likely to choose the equity option on conversion

C Continuing to recognise factored trade receivables sold with recourse

D Treating redeemable preference shares as equity

52 Faithful representation is a fundamental characteristic of useful information within the International Accounting Standards Board's Conceptual Framework for financial reporting.

Which of the following treatments applies the principle of faithful representation?

A   Reporting a transaction based on its legal status rather than its economic substance.

B   Excluding a subsidiary from consolidation because its activities are not compatible with those of the rest of the group.

C   Recording the whole of the net proceeds from the issue of a loan note which is potentially convertible to equity shares as a liability.

D   Allocating part of the sales proceeds of a motor vehicle to interest received even though it was sold with interest-free finance.

53 The International Accounting Standards Board's Conceptual Framework for Financial Reporting defines recognition as the process of incorporating within the financial statements an item which meets the definition of an element and satisfies certain criteria.

Which of the following elements should be recognised in the financial statements of an entity in the manner described?

A   As a non-current liability: a provision for possible hurricane damage to property for an entity located in an area which experiences a high incidence of hurricanes.

B   In equity: irredeemable preference shares.

C   As a trade receivable: an amount of $10,000 due from a customer which has been sold (factored) to a finance company with no recourse to the seller.

D   In revenue: the whole of the proceeds from the sale of an item of manufactured plant which has to be maintained by the seller for three years as part of the sale agreement.

54 Increasingly the International Accounting Standards Board is requiring or allowing current cost to be used in many areas of financial reporting.

Drexler acquired an item of plant on 1 October 20X2 at a cost of $500,000. It is being depreciated over five years, using straight-line depreciation and an estimated residual value of 10% of its historical cost or current cost as appropriate. As at 30 September 20X4, the manufacturer of the plant still makes the same item of plant and its current price is $600,000.

What is the correct carrying amount to be shown in the statement of financial position of Drexler as at 30 September 20X4 under historical cost and current cost? Select the correct value in each column.

Historical cost	✓	Current cost	✓
$300,000		$384,000	
$320,000		$600,000	

55 Tynan's year end is 30 September 20X4 and a number of potential liabilities have been identified.

Which TWO of the following should Tynan recognise as liabilities as at 30 September 20X4?

	Liability	Not a liability
The signing of a non-cancellable contract in September 20X4 to supply goods in the following year on which, due to a pricing error, a loss will be made.		
The cost of a reorganisation which was approved by the board in August 20X4 but has not yet been implemented, communicated to interested parties or announced publicly.		
An amount of deferred tax relating to the gain on the revaluation of a property during the current year. Tynan has no intention of selling the property in the foreseeable future.		
The balance on the warranty provision which relates to products for which there are no outstanding claims and whose warranties had expired by 30 September 20X4.		

56 **Which of the following items should be recognised as an asset in the statement of financial position of an entity?**

A   A skilled and efficient workforce which has been very expensive to train. Some of these staff are still employed by the entity.

B   A highly lucrative contract signed during the year which is due to commence shortly after the year-end.

C   A government grant relating to the purchase of an item of plant several years ago which has a remaining life of four years.

D   A receivable from a customer which has been sold (factored) to a finance company. The finance company has full recourse to the entity for any losses.

57 Comparability is identified as an enhancing qualitative characteristic in the International Accounting Standards Board's Conceptual Framework for Financial Reporting.

Which of the following does NOT improve comparability?

A   Restating the financial statements of previous years when there has been a change of accounting policy.

B   Prohibiting changes of accounting policy unless required by an IFRS Standard or to give more relevant and reliable information.

C   Disclosing discontinued operations separately in financial statements.

D   Applying an entity's current accounting policy to a transaction which an entity has not engaged in before.

58   **Which of the following criticisms does NOT apply to historical cost financial statements during a period of rising prices?**

    A   They contain mixed values, some items are at current values, some at out-of-date values

    B   They are difficult to verify as transactions could have happened many years ago

    C   They understate assets

    D   They overstate profits

59   **According to IAS 8 *Accounting Policies, Changes in Accounting Estimates and Errors*, how should a material error in the previous financial reporting period be accounted for in the current period?**

    A   By making an adjustment in the financial statements of the current period through the statement of profit or loss, and disclosing the nature of the error in a note.

    B   By making an adjustment in the financial statements of the current period as a movement on reserves, and disclosing the nature of the error in a note.

    C   By restating the comparative amounts for the previous period at their correct value, and disclosing the nature of the error in a note.

    D   By restating the comparative amounts for the previous period at their correct value, but without the requirement for a disclosure of the nature of the error in a note.

60   **Which of the following statements regarding IFRS 13 *Fair Value Measurement* is not true?**

    A   Level 1 inputs are likely to be used without adjustment.

    B   Level 3 inputs are based on the best information available to market participants and are therefore regarded as providing the most reliable evidence of fair value.

    C   Level 2 inputs may include quoted prices for similar (but not identical) assets and liabilities in active markets.

    D   Level 1 inputs comprise quoted prices in active markets for identical assets and liabilities at the reporting date.

61   **Which of these changes would be classified as 'a change in accounting policy' as determined by IAS 8 *Accounting Policies, Changes in Accounting Estimates and Errors*?**

    A   Increased the allowance for irrecoverable receivables from 5% to 10% of outstanding debts

    B   Changed the method of valuing inventory from FIFO to average cost

    C   Changed the depreciation of plant and equipment from straight line depreciation to reducing balance depreciation

    D   Changed the useful life of motor vehicles from six years to four years

62   In which TWO of the following situations can a change in accounting policy be made by an entity?

A   If the change is required by an IFRS Standard

B   If the entity thinks that a new accounting policy would be easier to report

C   If a new accounting policy would show more favourable results

D   If a new accounting policy results in more reliable and relevant presentation of events or transactions

63   According to the International Accounting Standards Board's Conceptual Framework for Financial Reporting which of the measurement bases below can be used by an entity for measuring assets and liabilities shown in its statement of financial position?

	Can be used	Cannot be used
Historical cost		
Present value		
Realisable value		

64   Which of the following statements is true about historical cost financial statements in times of rising prices?

A   Profits will be overstated and assets will be understated

B   The asset values will be overstated

C   Unrecognised gains will be recorded incorrectly

D   Depreciation will be overstated

65   Which of the following concepts aims to ensure that excess dividends are not paid in times of changing prices?

A   Going concern

B   Amortised cost

C   Faithful representation

D   Capital maintenance

66   Which of the following is a change in accounting policy and which a change in accounting estimate in accordance with IAS 8 *Accounting Policies, Changes in Accounting Estimates and Errors*?

	Change in accounting policy	Change in accounting estimate
Classifying commission earned as revenue in the statement of profit or loss, having previously classified it as other operating income		
Revising the remaining useful life of a depreciable asset		

67 **Which of the following would be a change in accounting policy in accordance with IAS 8** *Accounting Policies, Changes in Accounting Estimates and Errors***?**

A Adjusting the financial statements of a subsidiary prior to consolidation as its accounting policies differ from those of its parent.

B A change to reporting depreciation charges as cost of sales rather than as administrative expenses.

C Depreciation method changed to reducing balance method rather than straight line.

D Reducing the value of inventory from cost to net realisable value due to a valid adjusting event after the reporting period.

68 Isaac is an entity which buys agricultural produce from wholesale suppliers for retail to the general public. It is preparing its financial statements for the year ending 30 September 20X4 and is considering its closing inventory.

In addition to IAS 2 *Inventories***, which of the following IFRS Standards may be relevant in determining the figure to be included in its financial statements for closing inventories?**

A IAS 10 *Events After the Reporting Period*

B IAS 36 *Impairment*

C IAS 16 *Property, Plant and Equipment*

D IAS 41 *Agriculture*

69 **To which of the following items does IAS 41** *Agriculture* **apply?**

(i) A change in fair value of a herd of animals relating to the unit price of the animals.

(ii) Logs held in a wood yard.

(iii) Farm land which is used for growing vegetables.

(iv) The cost of developing a new type of crop seed which is resistant to tropical diseases.

A All four

B (i) only

C (i) and (ii) only

D (ii) and (iii) only

70 IAS 2 Inventories specifies expenses that should be included in year-end inventory values. **Which THREE of the expenses below are allowable by IAS 2 as expenses that should be included in the cost of finished goods inventories?**

A Marketing and selling overhead

B Variable production overhead

C General management overhead

D Factory management overhead allocated to production

E Cost of delivering raw materials to the factory

F Abnormal increase in overhead charges caused by unusually low production levels due to the exceptionally hot weather.

71 Neville has only two items of inventory on hand at its reporting date.

Item 1 – Materials costing $24,000 bought for processing and assembly for a customer under a 'one off' order which is expected to produce a high profit margin. Since buying this material, the cost price has fallen to $20,000.

Item 2 – A machine constructed for another customer for a contracted price of $36,000. This has recently been completed at a cost of $33,600. It has now been discovered that in order to meet certain health and safety regulations modifications at an extra cost of $8,400 will be required. The customer has agreed to meet half of the extra cost.

What should be the total value of these two items of inventory in the statement of financial position?

$_____

72 Mario has incurred the following costs in relation to a unit of inventory:

	$
Raw materials cost	1.50
Import duties	0.40
Direct labour	0.50
Subcontracted labour costs	0.80
Recoverable sales tax	0.20
Storage costs	0.05
Production overheads (per unit)	0.25

There was a problem with the first batch of items produced, so abnormal wastage costs of $0.10 per unit have also been incurred by Mario.

At what cost should Mario value this inventory in its financial statements?

A $3.50

B $3.45

C $3.80

D $3.70

73 On 30 September 20X4 Razor's closing inventory was counted and valued at its cost of $1 million.

This included some items of inventory which had cost $210,000 and had been damaged in a flood on 15 September 20X4. These are not expected to achieve their normal selling price which is calculated to achieve a gross profit margin of 30%.

The sale of these goods will be handled by an agent who sells them at 80% of the normal selling price and charges Razor a commission of 25%.

At what value will the closing inventory of Razor be reported in its statement of financial position as at 30 September 20X4?

$_____

74 Identify whether the following items would be accounted for under IAS 41 *Agriculture* or not.

	Accounted for under IAS 41 *Agriculture*	Outside the scope of IAS 41 *Agriculture*
Dairy cattle		
Milk		
Cheese		

75 Magna owned cattle recorded in the financial statements at $10,500 on 1 January 20X4. At 31 December 20X4 the cattle have a fair value of $13,000. If Magna sold the cattle, commission of 2% would be payable.

What is the correct accounting treatment for the cattle at 31 December 20X4 according to IAS 41 *Agriculture*?

A   Hold at cost of $10,500

B   Revalue to $13,000, taking gain of $2,500 to the statement of profit or loss

C   Revalue to $13,000, taking gain of $2,500 to the revaluation surplus

D   Revalue to $12,740, taking gain of $2,240 to the statement of profit or loss

76 During the year ended 30 September 20X4 Hyper entered into two lease transactions.

On 1 October 20X3, Hyper made a payment of $90,000 being the first of five equal annual payments under a lease for an item of plant. The lease has an implicit interest rate of 10% and the present value of the total lease payments on 1 October 20X3 was $340,000.

On 1 January 20X4, Hyper made a payment of $18,000 for a one-year lease of an item of equipment.

What amount in total would be charged to Hyper's statement of profit or loss for the year ended 30 September 20X4 in respect of the above transactions?

A $108,000

B $111,000

C $106,500

D $115,500

77 Z entered into a five year lease agreement on 1 November 20X2, paying $10,975 per annum, commencing on 31 October 20X3. The present value of the lease payments was $45,000 and the interest rate implicit in the lease was 7%.

What is the amount to be shown within non-current liabilities at 31 October 20X3?

A $26,200

B $28,802

C $37,175

D $36,407

78   IFRS 16 *Leases* permits certain assets to be exempt from the recognition treatment for right-of-use assets. Which of the following assets leased to an entity would be permitted to be exempt?

A   A used motor vehicle with an original cost of $15,000 and a current fair value of $700, leased for 24 months

B   A new motor vehicle with a cost of $15,000, leased for 24 months

C   A new motor vehicle with a cost of $15,000, leased for 24 months, to be rented to customers on a daily rental basis

D   A new motor vehicle with a cost of $15,000, leased for 12 months

79   On 1 January 20X3 Rabbit acquires a new machine with an estimated useful life of 6 years under the following agreement:

An initial payment of $13,760 will be payable immediately

5 further annual payments of $20,000 will be due, commencing 1 January 20X3

The interest rate implicit in the lease is 8%

The present value of the lease payments, excluding the initial payment, is $86,240

What will be recorded in Rabbit's financial statements at 31 December 20X4 in respect of the lease liability?

	Finance cost	Non-current liability	Current liability
A	4,123	35,662	20,000
B	5,299	51,539	20,000
C	5,312	51,712	20,000
D	5,851	43,709	15,281

80   **On 1 April 20X7 Pigeon entered into a five-year lease agreement for a machine with an estimated life of 7 years. Which of the following conditions would require the machine to be depreciated over 7 years?**

A   Pigeon has the option to extend the lease for two years at a market-rate rental

B   Pigeon has the option to purchase the asset at market value at the end of the lease

C   Ownership of the asset passes to Pigeon at the end of the lease period

D   Pigeon's policy for purchased assets is to depreciate over 7 years

81   On 1 January 20X4 Badger entered into a lease agreement to lease an item of machinery for 4 years with rentals of $210,000 payable annually in arrears. The asset has a useful life of 5 years and at the end of the lease term legal ownership will pass to Badger. The present value of the lease payments at the inception of the lease was $635,000 and the interest rate implicit in the lease is 12.2%. For the year ended 31 December 20X4 Badger accounted for this lease by recording the payment of $210,000 as an operating expense. This treatment was discovered during 20X5, after the financial statements for 20X4 had been finalised.

In the statement of changes in equity for the year ended 31 December 20X5 what adjustment will be necessary to retained earnings brought forward?

A $5,530 credit

B $132,530 credit

C $210,000 debit

D $Nil

82   Owl leases an asset with an estimated useful life of 6 years for an initial period of 5 years, and an optional secondary period of 2 years during which a nominal rental will be payable. The present value of the initial period lease payments is $87,000.

What will be the carrying amount of the right-of-use asset in Owl's statement of financial position at the end of the second year of the lease?

$_____

83   On 1 January 20X6, Sideshow sold a property for its fair value of $2 million, transferring title to the property on that date. Sideshow then leased it back under a 5-year lease, paying $150,000 per annum on 31 December each year. The present value of rentals payable was $599,000 and the interest rate implicit in the lease was 8%. The carrying amount of the property on 1 January 20X6 was $1.6 million and it had a remaining useful life of 20 years.

What entries would be made in Sideshow's statement of profit or loss for the year ended 31 December 20X6?

A   Profit on disposal of $280,200, depreciation of $95,840, finance cost of $47,920

B   Profit on disposal of $400,000, rental expense of $150,000

C   Profit on disposal of $400,000, depreciation expense of $95,840, finance cost of $47,920

D   Profit on disposal of $280,200, depreciation of $119,800, finance cost of $47,920

84   On 1 October 20X3, Fresco acquired an item of plant under a five-year lease agreement. The agreement had an implicit interest rate of 10% and required annual rentals of $6 million to be paid on 30 September each year for five years. The present value of the annual rental payments was $23 million.

What would be the current lease liability in Fresco's statement of financial position as at 30 September 20X4?

    A $19,300,000

    B $4,070,000

    C $5,000,000

    D $3,850,000

85   **Which of the following would not be included within the initial cost of a right-of-use asset?**

    A   Installation cost of the asset

    B   Estimated cost of dismantling the asset at the end of the lease period

    C   Payments made to the lessor before commencement of the lease

    D   Total lease rentals payable under the lease agreement

86   On 1 January 20X4, Stark entered into a sale and leaseback of its property. When it was sold, the asset had a carrying amount of $6 million and a remaining life of 10 years. Stark sold the asset for $7 million and leased it back on a 10 year lease, paying $1 million on 31 December each year. The lease carried an implicit interest rate of 7%.

What is the total expense that should be recorded in the statement of profit or loss for the year ended 31 December 20X4?

    $_____ ,000

87   Viking issues $100,000 5% loan notes on 1 January 20X4, incurring issue costs of $3,000. These loan notes are redeemable at a premium, meaning that the effective rate of interest is 8% per annum.

What is the finance cost to be shown in the statement of profit or loss for the year ended 31 December 20X5?

    A $8,240

    B $7,981

    C $7,760

    D $8,000

88 An entity issues 3,000 convertible bonds at the start of year 1 at par. They have a three year term and a face value of $1,000 per bond. Interest is payable annually in arrears at 7% per annum. Each bond is convertible at any time up to maturity into 250 common shares. When the bonds are issued the prevailing market interest rate for similar debt without conversion options is 9%. The relevant discount factors are shown below.

Discount factors	7%	9%
Year 1	0.933	0.914
Year 2	0.871	0.837
Year 3	0.813	0.766

How is this initially recorded between the debt and equity elements?

	Debt element	Equity element
A	$2,988,570	$11,430
B	$2,826,570	$173,430
C	$528,570	$2,471,430
D	$3,000,000	$Nil

89 For a debt investment to be held under amortised cost, it must pass two tests. One of these is the contractual cash flow characteristics test.

What is the other test which must be passed?

A   The business model test

B   The amortised cost test

C   The fair value test

D   The purchase agreement test

90 **What is the default classification for an equity investment?**

A   Fair value through profit or loss

B   Fair value through other comprehensive income

C   Amortised cost

D   Net proceeds

91 ABC purchased 10,000 shares on 1 September 20X4, making the election to use the alternative treatment under IFRS 9 *Financial Instruments*. The shares cost $3.50 each. Transaction costs associated with the purchase were $500.

At 31 December 20X4, the shares are trading at $4.50 each.

What is the gain to be recognised on these shares for the year ended 31 December 20X4?

$_____

92   DEF purchased 15,000 shares in KMH Co on 1 August 20X6 at a cost of $6.50 each. Transaction costs on the purchase amounted to $1,500.

At the year-end 30 September 20X6, these shares are now worth $7.75 each.

Select the correct gain and the place it will be recorded.

Gain
$17,250
$18,750

Where recorded
Other comprehensive income
Statement of profit or loss

93   **For which category of financial instruments are transaction costs excluded from the initial value, and instead expensed to profit or loss?**

A   Financial liabilities at amortised cost

B   Financial assets at fair value through profit or loss

C   Financial assets at fair value through other comprehensive income

D   Financial assets at amortised cost

94   On 1 October 20X3, Bertrand issued $10 million convertible loan notes which carry a coupon rate of 5% per annum. The loan notes are redeemable on 30 September 20X6 at par for cash or can be exchanged for equity shares. A similar loan note, without the conversion option, would have required Bertrand to pay an interest rate of 8%.

The present value of $1 receivable at the end of each year, based on discount rates of 5% and 8%, can be taken as:

	5%	8%
End of year 1	0.95	0.93
2	0.91	0.86
3	0.86	0.79

How much would be recorded in equity in relation to the loan notes?

$_____ ,000

95   Wonder issued $10 million 5% loan notes on 1 January 20X9, incurring issue costs of $400,000. The loan notes are redeemable at a premium, giving them an effective interest rate of 8%.

What expense should be recorded in relation to the loan notes for the year ended 31 December 20X9?

$_____ ,000

96 For each of the financial instruments below, match them to the appropriate accounting treatment.

Instrument
Convertible loan notes
Equity investments where the entity has an intention to hold long-term and has chosen to apply the alternative treatment
Financial liability, not held for trading
Equity investments (default position)

Treatment
Fair value through profit or loss
Amortised cost
Split accounting
Fair value through other comprehensive income

97 IAS 21 *The Effects of Changes in Foreign Exchange Rates* defines the term 'functional currency'.

Which of the following is the correct definition of 'functional currency'?

A   The currency in which the financial statements are presented

B   The currency of the country where the reporting entity is located

C   The currency that mainly influences sales prices and operating costs

D   The currency of the primary economic environment in which an entity operates

98 Sunshine is an entity with a reporting date of 31 December 20X1 and a functional currency of dollars ($). On 30 June 20X1, it purchased land from overseas at a cost of 30 million dinars. The land is an item of property, plant and equipment and is measured using the cost model.

Exchange rates are as follows:

	Dinars: $1
As at 30 June 20X1	3.0
As at 31 December 20X1	2.0
Average rate for year-ended 31 December 20X1	2.5

The fair value of the land at 31 December 20X1 was 32 million dinars.

What is the carrying amount of the land as at 31 December 20X1?

A $10 million

B $15 million

C $12 million

D $16 million

99 **In relation to IAS 21 *The Effects of Changes in Foreign Exchange Rates*, which of the following statements are true?**

(i) Exchange gains and losses arising on the retranslation of monetary items are recognised in other comprehensive income in the period.

(ii) Non-monetary items measured at historical cost in a foreign currency are not retranslated at the reporting date.

(iii) An intangible asset is a non-monetary item.

A All of the above

B (ii) and (iii) only

C (i) and (iii) only

D (i) and (ii) only

100 An entity took out a bank loan for 12 million dinars on 1 January 20X1. It repaid 3 million dinars to the bank on 30 November 20X1. The entity has a reporting date of 31 December 20X1 and a functional currency of dollars ($). Exchange rates are as follows:

	Dinars: $1
1 January 20X1	6.0
30 November 20X1	5.0
31 December 20X1	5.6

What is the total loss arising (to the nearest $000) on the above transactions in the year ended 31 December 20X1?

$_____,000

101 A manufacturing entity buys a machine (an item of property, plant and equipment) for 20 million dinars on 1 January 20X1. The machine is held under the cost model and has a useful life of 20 years. The entity has a reporting date of 31 December 20X1 and a functional currency of dollars ($). Exchange rates are as follows:

	Dinars: $1
1 January 20X1	2.0
31 December 20X1	3.0
Average rate for year-ended 31 December 20X1	2.5

What is the carrying amount of the machine as at 31 December 20X1?

A $9.7 million

B $9.6 million

C $9.5 million

D $6.3 million

102 Mango sold an item of maturing inventory to a bank on 1 January 20X3 for $500,000. At this date the inventory had cost $200,000 to produce but had a fair value of $900,000, which was expected to increase over the next 3 years. At the end of 3 years, Mango have the option to repurchase the inventory at $665,500, giving an effective interest rate of 10%.

What items should be recorded in the statement of profit or loss for the year ended 31 December 20X3?

A   Revenue $500,000, cost of sales $200,000

B   Profit on disposal $300,000

C   Deferred income $500,000

D   Finance cost $50,000

103 Repro has prepared its draft financial statements for the year ended 30 September 20X4. It has included the following transactions in revenue at the amounts stated below.

Which of these has been correctly included in revenue according to IFRS 15 *Revenue from Contracts with Customers*?

A   Agency sales of $250,000 on which Repro is entitled to a commission of 10%.

B   Sale proceeds of $20,000 for motor vehicles which were no longer required by Repro.

C   Sales of $150,000 on 30 September 20X4. The amount invoiced to and received from the customer was $180,000, which includes $30,000 for ongoing servicing work to be done by Repro over the next two years.

D   Sales of $200,000 on 1 October 20X3 to an established customer who (with the agreement of Repro) will make full payment on 30 September 20X5. Repro has a cost of capital of 10%.

104 Yling entered into a contract to construct an asset for a customer on 1 January 20X4 which is expected to last 24 months. The agreed price for the contract is $5 million. At 30 September 20X4, the costs incurred on the contract were $1.6 million and the estimated remaining costs to complete were $2.4 million. On 20 September 20X4, Yling received a payment from the customer of $1.8 million which was equal to the full amount billed. Yling calculates contract progress using the output method, on the basis of amount billed compared to the contract price.

What amount would be reported as a contract asset in Yling's statement of financial position as at 30 September 20X4?

$_____

105 CN started a three-year contract to build a new university campus on 1 April 20X4. The contract had a fixed price of $90 million. CN will satisfy the performance obligation over time. CN incurred costs to 31 March 20X5 of $77 million and estimated that a further $33 million would need to be spent to complete the contract.

CN measures the progress of contracts using work completed compared to contract price. At 31 March 20X5, a surveyor valued the work completed to date at $63 million.

Select the correct amounts to be shown in revenue and cost of sales in the statement of profit or loss for the year ended 31 March 20X5?

Revenue	Cost of sales
$63 million	$77 million
$57 million	$83 million

106 Locke sells machines, and also offers installation and technical support services. The individual selling prices of each product are shown below.

Sale price of goods $75
Installation $30
One year service $45

Locke sold a machine on 1 May 20X1, charging a reduced price of $100, including installation and one year's service.

Locke only offers discounts when customers purchase a package of products together.

According to IFRS 15 *Revenue from Contracts with Customers*, how much should Locke record in revenue for the year ended 31 December 20X1? Workings should be rounded to the nearest $.

$_____

107 Place the following steps for recognising revenue in order in accordance with IFRS 15 *Revenue from Contracts with Customers*.

Step		Correct order
Identify the separate performance obligations within a contract		
Identify the contract		
Determine the transaction price		
Recognise revenue when (or as) a performance obligation is satisfied		
Allocate the transaction price to the performance obligations in the contract		

108 BL entered into a contract with a customer on 1 November 20X4. The contract was scheduled to run for two years and has a sales value of $40 million. BL will satisfy the performance obligations over time.

At 31 October 20X5, the following details were obtained from BL's records:

	$m
Costs incurred to date	16
Estimated costs to completion	18
Progress at 31 October 20X5	45%

Applying IFRS 15 *Revenue from Contracts with Customers*, how much revenue and cost of sales should BL recognise in its statement of profit or loss for the year ended 31 October 20X5?

	Revenue	*Cost of sales*
A	$40 million	$15.3 million
B	$40 million	$34 million
C	$18 million	$16 million
D	$18 million	$15.3 million

109 Malik is a construction business, recognising progress based on work certified as a proportion of total contract value. Malik will satisfy the performance obligation over time. The following information relates to one of its long-term contracts as at 31 May 20X4, Malik's year-end.

	$
Contract price	200,000
Costs incurred to date	130,000
Estimated cost to complete	20,000
Invoiced to customer	120,000
Work certified to date	180,000

In the year to 31 May 20X3 Malik had recognised revenue of $60,000 and profit of $15,000 in respect of this contract.

What profit should appear in Malik's statement of profit or loss as at 31 May 20X4 in respect of this contract?

$_____

110 **Which of the following items has correctly been included in Hatton's revenue for the year to 31 December 20X1?**

A $2 million in relation to a fee negotiated for an advertising contract for Rees, one of Hatton's clients. Hatton acted as an agent during the deal and is entitled to 10% commission.

B $500,000 relating to a sale of specialised equipment on 31 December 20X1. The full sales value was $700,000 but $200,000 relates to servicing that Hatton will provide over the next 2 years, so Hatton has not included that in revenue this year.

C $800,000 relating to a sale of some surplus land owned by Hatton.

D $1 million in relation to a sale to a new customer on 31 December 20X1. Control passed to the customer on 31 December 20X1. The $1 million is payable on 31 December 20X3. Interest rates are 10%.

111 Sugar has entered into a long-term contract to build an asset for a customer, Hewer. Sugar will satisfy the performance obligation over time and has measured the progress towards satisfying the performance obligation at 45% at the year end.

The price of the contract is $8 million. Sugar has spent $4.5 million to date, but the estimated costs to complete are $5.5 million. To date, Hewer has paid Sugar $3 million.

What is the net liability that should be recorded in Sugar's statement of financial position?

$_____ ,000

112 Ratten commenced a contract to build an asset for a customer in the year ended 30 September 20X4. The contract price was agreed at $1.5m, and the total expected costs of the contract are $800,000. Ratten will satisfy the performance obligation over time.

The following figures were correctly recognised in the profit or loss account for the year ended 30 September 20X4:

	$000
Revenue	450
Cost of sales	(240)
Profit	210

The following figures are also relevant in relation to this contract:

	20X4 $000	20X5 $000
Costs incurred to date	325	575
Work certified to date	450	1,050

Ratten recognises progress on the basis of work certified compared to contract price.

What should Ratten include in its statement of profit or loss for the year ended 30 September 20X5 for cost of sales in respect of the contract?

A $320,000

B $250,000

C $560,000

D $240,000

113 Sawyer entered into a contract to construct an asset for a customer during the year, and identified the performance obligation as one which is satisfied over time. Sawyer recognises progress towards completion using an output method, based on work certified compared to contract price. The following information is relevant to the contract.

	$
Contract price	1,000,000
Costs incurred to date	530,000
Estimated cost to complete	170,000
Work certified to date and invoiced	600,000

What is the value of the contract asset to be recorded in Sawyer's statement of financial position?

A $110,000

B $100,000

C $190,000

D $150,000

114 Hindberg is a car retailer. On 1 April 20X4, Hindberg sold a car to Latterly on the following terms:

The selling price of the car was $25,300. Latterly paid $12,650 (half of the cost) on 1 April 20X4 and will pay the remaining $12,650 on 31 March 20X6 (two years after the sale). Latterly can obtain finance at 10% per annum.

What is the total amount which Hindberg should credit to profit or loss in respect of this transaction in the year ended 31 March 20X5?

A $23,105

B $23,000

C $20,909

D $24,150

115 Tamsin Co's accounting records shown the following:

	$
Income tax payable for the year	60,000
Over provision in relation to the previous year	4,500
Opening provision for deferred tax	2,600
Closing provision for deferred tax	3,200

What is the income tax expense that will be shown in the statement of profit or loss for the year?

A $54,900

B $67,700

C $65,100

D $56,100

116 The following information has been extracted from the accounting records of Clara Co:

	$
Estimated income tax for the year ended 30 September 20X0	$75,000
Income tax paid for the year ended 30 September 20X0	$80,000
Estimated income tax for the year ended 30 September 20X1	$83,000

What figures will be shown in the statement of profit or loss for the year ended 30 September 20X1 and the statement of financial position as at that date in respect of income tax?

Statement of profit or loss	Statement of financial position

Options:

$75,000
$80,000
$83,000
$88,000

117 Hudson has the following balances included on its trial balance at 30 June 20X4.

	$	
Taxation	4,000	Credit
Deferred taxation	12,000	Credit

The taxation balance relates to an overprovision from 30 June 20X3.

At 30 June 20X4, the directors estimate that the provision necessary for taxation on current year profits is $15,000.

The carrying amount of Hudson's non-current assets exceeds the tax written-down value by $30,000. The rate of tax is 30%.

What is the charge for taxation that will appear in the statement of profit or loss for the year to 30 June 20X4?

A $23,000

B $28,000

C $8,000

D $12,000

118 Holmes has the following balances included on its trial balance at 30 June 20X4:

	$	
Taxation	7,000	Credit
Deferred taxation	16,000	Credit

The taxation balance relates to an overprovision from 30 June 20X3.

At 30 June 20X4, the directors estimate that the provision necessary for taxation on current year profits is $12,000. The balance on the deferred tax account needs to be increased to $23,000, which includes the impact of the increase in property valuation below.

During the year Holmes revalued its property for the first time, resulting in a gain of $10,000. The rate of tax is 30%.

What is the charge for taxation that will appear in the statement of profit or loss for the year to 30 June 20X4?

A $9,000

B $12,000

C $23,000

D $1,000

119 Garfish had profits after tax of $3 million in the year ended 31 December 20X7. On 1 January 20X7, Garfish had 2.4 million ordinary shares in issue. On 1 April 20X7 Garfish made a one for two rights issue at a price of $1.40 when the market price of Garfish's shares was $2.00.

What is the basic earnings per share (to one decimal place) for the year ended 31 December 20X7, according to IAS 33 *Earnings Per Share*?

_____ cents.

120 On 1 January 20X4, Sam Co had 3 million ordinary shares in issue. On 1 June 20X4, Sam Co made a 1 for 3 bonus issue. On 30 September 20X4, Sam Co issued a further 1 million shares at full market price. Sam Co had profits attributable to ordinary equity holders of $2 million for the year ended 31 December 20X4.

What is the basic earnings per share figure for the year ended 31 December 20X4, according to IAS 33 *Earnings Per Share*?

A   47.1¢

B   52.2¢

C   56.8¢

D   50.0¢

121 During the year, Mac made a 1 for 3 rights issue at $1.60 when the market price was $2.20. Last year's EPS was 81 cents. There were no other issues of shares during the year.

What is the restated earnings per share figure for comparative purposes?

_____ cents.

122 Coral Co has net profit for the year ended 30 September 20X5 of $10,500,000. Coral has had 6 million shares in issue for many years. On 1 October 20X4 Coral issued a convertible bond. It had an initial liability element of $2,500,000, and the market interest rate for non-convertible instruments is 8%. The bond is convertible in five years, with 50 shares issued for every $100 nominal of convertible bond held. Coral Co pays tax at a rate of 28%

What is the Diluted Earnings per Share figure?

A   177.4¢

B   175.0¢

C   147.6¢

D   146.8¢

123 Isco's financial statements show a profit for the year to 31 December 20X5 of $2 million. On 1 January 20X5 Isco had 4 million shares in issue and made no further issues of shares during the year. At 31 December 20X5 there were 1 million outstanding options to buy shares at $3 each. For the year to 31 December 20X5, the average market value of Isco's shares was $5.

What is Isco's diluted earnings per share for the year ended 31 December 20X5?

A   50.0¢

B   28.6¢

C   45.5¢

D   43.4¢

124 Gromit Co has the following extract from its consolidated profit or loss account:

	$000
Profit for the period	2,800
Other comprehensive income: revaluation gain	500
Total comprehensive income	3,300
Profit for the period attributable to:	
Parent	2,250
Non-controlling Interest	550
	2,800
Total comprehensive income attributable to:	
Parent	2,600
Non-controlling interest	700
	3,300

What figure should be used as earnings by Gromit in its earnings per share (EPS) calculation?

$_____ ,000

125 Which TWO of the following do NOT need to be removed from an entity's net profit in a statement of profit or loss in order to calculate the earnings figure to be used in the earnings per share calculation?

A Redeemable preference share dividends

B Irredeemable preference share dividends

C Profit attributable to the non-controlling interest

D An error in expenses discovered after the financial statements have been authorised for issue

E Ordinary dividends

126 Aqua has correctly calculated its basic earnings per share (EPS) for the current year.

Allocate the items to the appropriate category.

Included within Diluted EPS calculation	Included within Basic EPS calculation

Options:

A 1 for 5 rights issue of equity shares during the year at $1.20 when the market price of the equity shares was $2.00
The issue during the year of a loan note, convertible into ordinary shares
The granting of directors' share options during the year, exercisable in three years' time
Equity shares issued during the year as the purchase consideration for the acquisition of a new subsidiary

127 Many commentators believe that the trend of earnings per share (EPS) is a more reliable indicator of underlying performance than the trend of the net profit for the year.

Which of the following statements supports this view?

A Net profit can be manipulated by the choice of accounting policies but EPS cannot be manipulated in this way.

B EPS takes into account the additional resources made available to earn profit when new shares are issued for cash, whereas net profit does not.

C The disclosure of a diluted EPS figure is a forecast of the trend of profit for future periods.

D The comparative EPS is restated where a change in accounting policy affects the previous year's profits.

128 On 1 October 20X3, Hoy had $2.5 million of equity shares of 50 cents each in issue.

No new shares were issued during the year ended 30 September 20X4, but on that date there were outstanding share options to purchase 2 million equity shares at $1.20 each. The average market value of Hoy's equity shares during the year was $3 per share.

Hoy's profit after tax for the year ended 30 September 20X4 was $1,550,000.

What is Hoy's diluted earnings per share for the year ended 30 September 20X4?

A   25.0¢

B   31.0¢

C   26.7¢

D   22.1¢

129 AP has the following two legal claims outstanding:

- A legal action claiming compensation of $500,000 filed against AP in March 20X4.

- A legal action taken by AP against a third party, claiming damages of $200,000, which was started in January 20X3 and is nearing completion.

In both cases, it is more likely than not that the amount claimed will have to be paid.

How should AP report these legal actions in its financial statements for the year ended 31 March 20X5?

Allocate the correct treatment against each of the cases.

Legal action against AP	Legal action by AP

Options:

Contingent Liability
Contingent Asset
Provision
Asset

130 Which of the following would require a provision for a liability to be created by BW at its reporting date of 31 October 20X5?

A   The government introduced new laws on data protection which come into force on 1 January 20X6. BW's directors have agreed that this will require a large number of staff to be retrained. At 31 October 20X5, the directors were waiting on a report they had commissioned that would identify the actual training requirements.

B   At the year-end BW is negotiating with its insurance provider about an outstanding insurance claim. On 20 November 20X5, the provider agreed to pay $200,000.

C   BW makes refunds to customers for any goods returned within 30 days of sale, and has done so for many years.

D   A customer is suing BW for damages alleged to have been caused by BW's product. BW is contesting the claim and at 31 October 20X5 the directors have been advised by BW's legal advisers that it is very unlikely to lose the case.

131 Using the requirements set out in IAS 10 *Events after the Reporting Period*, which of the following would be classified as an adjusting event after the reporting period in financial statements ended 31 March 20X4 that were approved by the directors on 31 August 20X4?

A   A reorganisation of the enterprise, proposed by a director on 31 January 20X4 and agreed by the Board on 10 July 20X4.

B   A strike by the workforce which started on 1 May 20X4 and stopped all production for 10 weeks before being settled.

C   The receipt of cash from a claim on an insurance policy for damage caused by a fire in a warehouse on 1 January 20X4. The claim was made in January 20X4 and the amount of the claim had not been recognised at 31 March 20X4 as it was uncertain that any money would be paid. The insurance enterprise settled with a payment of $1.5 million on 1 June 20X4.

D   The enterprise had made large export sales to the USA during the year. The year-end receivables included $2 million for amounts outstanding that were due to be paid in US dollars between 1 April 20X4 and 1 July 20X4. By the time these amounts were received, the exchange rate had moved in favour of the enterprise.

132 Target is preparing its financial statements for the year ended 30 September 20X7. Target is facing a number of legal claims from its customers with regards to a faulty product sold. The total amount being claimed is $3.5 million. Target's lawyers say that the customers have an 80% chance of being successful.

According to IAS 37 *Provisions, Contingent Liabilities and Contingent Assets*, what amount, if any, should be recognised in respect of the above in Target's statement of financial position as at 30 September 20X7?

$_____,000

133 ABC has a year end of 31 December 20X4. On 15 December 20X4 the directors publicly announced their decision to close an operating unit and make a number of employees redundant. Some of the employees currently working in the unit will be transferred to other operating units within ABC.

The estimated costs of the closure are as follows:

	$000
Redundancy costs	800
Lease termination costs	200
Relocation of continuing employees to new locations	400
Retraining of continuing employees	300

	1,700

What is the closure provision that should be recognised?

A $800,000

B $1,000,000

C $1,400,000

D $1,700,000

134   On 1 October 20X3, Xplorer commenced drilling for oil in an undersea oilfield. The extraction of oil causes damage to the seabed which has a restorative cost (ignore discounting) of $10,000 per million barrels of oil extracted. Xplorer extracted 250 million barrels of oil in the year ended 30 September 20X4.

Xplorer is also required to dismantle the drilling equipment at the end of its five-year licence. This has an estimated cost of $30 million on 30 September 20X8. Xplorer's cost of capital is 8% per annum and $1 has a present value of 68 cents in five years' time.

What is the total provision (extraction plus dismantling) which Xplorer would report in its statement of financial position as at 30 September 20X4 in respect of its oil operations?

A $34,900,000

B $24,532,000

C $22,900,000

D $4,132,000

135   **Which TWO of the following events which occur after the reporting date of an entity but before the financial statements are authorised for issue are classified as ADJUSTING events in accordance with IAS 10 *Events after the Reporting Period*?**

A   A change in tax rate announced after the reporting date, but affecting the current tax liability

B   The discovery of a fraud which had occurred during the year

C   The determination of the sale proceeds of an item of plant sold before the year end

D   The destruction of a factory by fire

136   Each of the following events occurred after the reporting date of 31 March 20X5, but before the financial statements were authorised for issue.

Identify whether the events would represent adjusting or non-adjusting events.

	Adjusting	Non-adjusting
A public announcement in April 20X5 of a formal plan to discontinue an operation which had been approved by the board in February 20X5.		
The settlement of an insurance claim for a loss sustained in December 20X4.		

137 In a review of its provisions for the year ended 31 March 20X5, Cumla's assistant accountant has suggested the following accounting treatments:

(i) Based on past experience, a $200,000 provision for unforeseen liabilities arising after the year end.

(ii) The partial reversal (as a credit to the statement of profit or loss) of the accumulated depreciation provision on an item of plant because the estimate of its remaining useful life has been increased by three years.

(iii) Providing $1 million for deferred tax at 25% relating to a $4 million revaluation of property during March 20X5 even though Cumla has no intention of selling the property in the near future.

Which of the above suggested treatments of provisions is/are permitted by IFRS Standards?

A (i) only

B (i) and (ii)

C (ii) and (iii)

D (iii) only

138 Identify whether the statements below are true or false:

	True	False
IAS 10 *Events After the Reporting Period* covers the period from the reporting date to the annual general meeting		
According to IAS 10 *Events After the Reporting Period*, any non-adjusting event should be disclosed as a note in the financial statements		

139 Fauberg owns a number of offices in country Y and is in the process of finishing its financial statements for the year ended 31 December 20X4. In December 20X4, country Y announced changes to health and safety regulations, meaning that Fauberg's air conditioning units will have to be replaced by 30 June 20X5.

This is estimated to cost Fauberg $500,000. Fauberg has a history of compliance with regulations and intends to do the work by June 20X5.

Which of the conditions for a provision will be met at 31 December 20X4?

	Yes/No
There is a present obligation from a past event	
A reliable estimate can be made	
There is a probable outflow of economic benefits	

140 **Which TWO of the following statements about provisions are true?**

A   Future operating losses cannot be provided for

B   Changes in provisions should be applied retrospectively, adjusting the prior year financial statements

C   Provisions should be accounted for prudently, reflecting the maximum that could possibly be paid out

D   Provisions should be discounted to present value if the effect of the time value of money is material

CONSOLIDATED FINANCIAL STATEMENTS

141 Petre owns 100% of the share capital of the following companies. The directors are unsure of whether the investments should be consolidated into the group financial statements of not.

Identify whether the following companies should be consolidated or not.

	Consolidated	Not to be consolidated
Beta is a bank and its activity is so different from the engineering activities of the rest of the group that it would be meaningless to consolidate it.		
Delta is located in a country where local accounting standards are compulsory and these are not compatible with IFRS Standards used by the rest of the group.		
Gamma is located in a country where a military coup has taken place and Petre has lost control of the investment for the foreseeable future.		

142 Tazer acquired Lowdown, an unincorporated entity, for $2.8 million. A fair value exercise performed on Lowdown's net assets at the date of purchase showed:

	$000
Property, plant and equipment	3,000
Identifiable intangible asset	500
Inventory	300
Trade receivables less payables	200
	4,000

How would the purchase be reflected in the consolidated statement of financial position?

A   Record the net assets at their above values and credit profit or loss with $1.2 million

B   Record the net assets at their above values and credit goodwill with $1.2 million

C   Ignore the intangible asset ($500,000), recording the remaining net assets at their values shown above and crediting profit or loss with $700,000

D   Record the purchase as a financial asset investment at $2.8 million

143 **Which of the following definitions is not included within the definition of control per IFRS 10 *Consolidated Financial Statements*?**

A   Having power over the investee

B   Having exposure, or rights, to variable returns from its investment with the investee

C   Having the majority of shares in the investee

D   Having the ability to use its power over the investee to affect the amount of the investor's returns

144 Pamela acquired 80% of the share capital of Samantha on 1 January 20X1. Part of the purchase consideration was $200,000 cash to be paid on 1 January 20X4. The applicable cost of capital is 10%.

What will the deferred consideration liability be at 31 December 20X2?

A $150,262

B $165,288

C $200,000

D $181,818

145 Philip acquired 85% of the share capital of Stanley on 1 October 20X1. The profit for the year ended 31 December 20X1 for Stanley was $36,000. Profits are deemed to accrue evenly over the year. At 31 December 20X1 Stanley's statement of financial position showed:

Equity share capital $200,000

Retained earnings $180,000

What were the net assets of Stanley on acquisition?

$_____ ,000

146 On 30 June 20X4 GHI acquired 800,000 of JKL's 1 million shares.

GHI issued 3 shares for every 4 shares acquired in JKL. On 30 June 20X4 the market price of a GHI share was $3.80 and the market price of a JKL share was $3.

GHI agreed to pay $550,000 in cash to the existing shareholders on 30 June 20X5. GHI's borrowing rate was 10% per annum.

GHI paid professional fees of $100,000 for advice on the acquisition.

What is the cost of investment that will be used in the goodwill calculation in the consolidated financial statements of GHI?

$_____ ,000

147 MNO has a 75% owned subsidiary PQR. During the year MNO sold inventory to PQR for an invoiced price of $800,000. PQR have since sold 75% of that inventory on to third parties. The sale was at a mark-up of 25% on cost to MNO. PQR is the only subsidiary of MNO.

What is the adjustment to inventory that would be included in the consolidated statement of financial position of MNO at the year-end resulting from this sale?

A $120,000

B $40,000

C $160,000

D $50,000

148 West has a 75% subsidiary Life, and is preparing its consolidated statement of financial position as at 31 December 20X6. The carrying amount of property, plant and equipment in the two companies at that date is as follows:

West $300,000

Life $60,000

On 1 January 20X6 Life had transferred some property to West for $40,000. At the date of transfer the property, which had cost $42,000, had a carrying amount of $30,000 and a remaining useful life of five years.

What is the carrying amount of property, plant and equipment in the consolidated statement of financial position of West as at 31 December 20X6?

$_____ ,000

149 **Which TWO of the following situations are unlikely to represent control over an investee?**

A   Owning 55% and being able to elect 4 of the 7 directors

B   Owning 51%, but the constitution requires that decisions need the unanimous consent of shareholders

C   Having currently exercisable options which would take the shareholding in the investee to 55%

D   Owning 40% of the shares but having majority of voting rights within the investee

E   Owning 35% of the ordinary shares and 80% of the preference shares of the investee

150 **Identify if the following will be recognised as part of the cost of an investment in a subsidiary.**

	Include in cost of investment	Do not include in the cost of investment
An agreement to pay a further $30,000 if the subsidiary achieves an operating profit of over $100,000 in the first 3 years after acquisition		
Professional fees of $10,000 in connection with the investment		

151 Peter acquires 80% of the share capital of Paul on 1 August 20X6 and is preparing its group financial statements for the year ended 31 December 20X6.

How will Paul's results be included in the group statement of profit or loss?

A   80% of Paul's revenue and expenses for the year ended 31 December 20X6

B   100% of Paul's revenue and expenses for the year ended 31 December 20X6

C   80% of Paul's revenue and expenses for the period 1 August 20X6 to 31 December 20X6

D   100% of Paul's revenue and expenses for the period ended 1 August 20X6 to 31 December 20X6

152 **Which of the following would result in an unrealised profit within a group scenario?**

A   A parent sells a building originally costing $800,000 to its subsidiary for $900,000. The subsidiary still holds this asset at the date of consolidation.

B   A parent sells a building originally costing $800,000 to its subsidiary for $900,000. The subsidiary has sold this asset before the date of consolidation.

C   A parent sells goods which originally cost $14,000 to its subsidiary for $18,000. The subsidiary has sold all of these goods at the date of consolidation.

D   A parent sells goods which originally cost $14,000 to an associate for $18,000. The associate has sold all of these goods at the date of consolidation.

153 Identify whether the following facts about impairment are true or false.

	True	False
Impairment will always be deducted in full from the parent's retained earnings		
Impairment will be apportioned between the parent and the non-controlling interest (NCI) when the NCI is valued at fair value		

154 Which of the following is not a condition which must be met for the parent to be exempt from producing consolidated financial statements?

    A   The activities of the subsidiary are significantly different to the rest of the group and to consolidate them would prejudice the overall group position

    B   The ultimate parent produces consolidated financial statements that comply with IFRS Standards and are publicly available

    C   The parent's debt or equity instruments are not traded in a public market

    D   The parent itself is a wholly owned subsidiary or a partially owned subsidiary whose owners do not object to the parent not producing consolidated financial statements

155 On 1 January 20X1, Branch purchased 75% of Leaf's 80 million shares. At this date, Leaf's retained earnings were $60 million. The consideration paid for Leaf was 2 Branch shares for every 3 Leaf shares purchased, plus a cash payment of $1 per purchased share. At the date of acquisition, the value of a Branch share was $2.50.

What is the consideration paid for Branch on 1 January 20X1?

$_____

156 STU has an 80% subsidiary VWX, which has been a subsidiary of STU for the whole of the current year. VWX reported a profit after tax of $600,000 in its own financial statements. You ascertain that at the year-end there was unrealised profit of $60,000 on sales by VWX to STU.

What is the non-controlling interest in VWX that would be reported in the consolidated statement of profit or loss and other comprehensive income of STU for the year?

$_____

157 Harry acquired an 80% holding in Style on 1 April 20X6. From 1 April 20X6 to 31 December 20X6 Style sold goods to Harry for $4.3m at a mark-up of 10%. Harry's inventory at 31 December 20X6 included $2.2m of such inventory. The statements of profit or loss for each entity for the year to 31 December 20X6 showed the following in respect of cost of sales:

Harry $14.7m

Style $11.6m

What is the cost of sales figure to be shown in the consolidated statement of profit or loss for the year to 31 December 20X6?

A $18,900,000

B $20,200,000

C $19,100,000

D $19,300,000

158 Heel acquired a 60% holding in Sock on 1 January 20X6. At this date Sock owned a building with a fair value $200,000 in excess of its carrying amount, and a remaining life of 10 years. All depreciation is charged to operating expenses. Goodwill had been impaired by $55,000 in the year to 31 December 20X6. The balances on operating expenses for the year to 31 December 20X7 are shown below:

Heel $600,000

Sock $350,000

What are consolidated operating expenses for the year to 31 December 20X7?

$_____ ,000

159 A acquired a 60% holding in B on 1 July 20X6. At this date, A gave B a $500,000 8% loan. The interest on the loan has been accounted for correctly in the individual financial statements. The totals for finance costs for the year to 31 December 20X6 in the individual financial statements are shown below.

A $200,000

B $70,000

What are consolidated finance costs for the year to 31 December 20X6?

A $215,000

B $225,000

C $230,000

D $250,000

160 Identify whether the following would affect the profit attributable to the non-controlling interest in the consolidated statement of profit or loss if the non-controlling interest is measured at fair value

	Affects the NCI share of profit	Does not affect the NCI share
Goodwill impairment		
The parent selling inventory to the subsidiary at a profit of $10,000, all of which remains in the subsidiary's inventory at the year end		
The subsidiary having an item of plant with a fair value of $500,000 above its carrying amount at acquisition, and a remaining life of 10 years		

161 AB has owned 80% of CD for many years. In the current year ended 30 June 20X3, AB has reported total revenues of $5.5 million, and CD of $2.1 million. AB has sold goods to CD during the year with a total value of $1 million, earning a margin of 20%. Half of these goods remain in year-end inventories.

What is the consolidated revenue figure for the AB group for the year ended 30 June 20X3?

$_____ ,000

162 Burridge bought 30% of Allen on 1 July 20X4. Allen's statement of profit or loss for the year shows a profit of $400,000. Allen paid a dividend to Burridge of $50,000 on 1 December 20X4. At the year end, the investment in Allen was judged to have been impaired by $10,000.

What will be the share of profit from associate shown in the consolidated statement of profit or loss for the year ended 31 December 20X4?

A $57,000

B $50,000

C $60,000

D $110,000

163 Beasant bought 30% of Arnie on 1 January 20X8, when Arnie had share capital of 100,000 $1 shares and $400,000 retained earnings. The consideration comprised one Beasant share for every 3 shares bought in Arnie. At the date of acquisition, Beasant's shares had a market value of $4.50 and Arnie's had a market value of $2. At 31 December 20X8, Arnie's net assets were $460,000.

What is the value of investment in associate shown in the consolidated statement of financial position as at 31 December 20X8?

A $8,000

B $33,000

C $63,000

D $123,000

164 Identify which concept each of the following transactions is applying

	Single entity concept	Going concern concept
Removing unrealised profits on group sales		
Removing intra-group balances		

165 Identify the correct treatments for the following investments in the consolidated financial statements of the Nicol group.

30% of the share capital of Hansen. The other 70% is owned by Lawro, another listed entity, whose directors make up Hansen's board.	Subsidiary
80% of the share capital of Kennedy, whose activities are significantly different from the rest of the Nicol group.	Associate
30% of the share capital of Bruce. The Nicol group have appointed 2 of the 5 board members of Bruce, with the other board members coming from three other entities.	Investment

166 Badger acquired 30% of Eagle on 1 July 20X3 at a cost of $5.5 million. Badger has classified Eagle as an associate undertaking. For the year ended 30 September 20X3, Eagle has reported a net profit of $625,000.

What is the value of the associate investment in the group statement of financial position of Badger as at 30 September 20X3?

A $5,546,875

B $5,500,000

C $6,125,000

D $5,968,750

167 Green is an associate undertaking of Purple. Purple owns 30% of the shares in Green, and has done so for many years.

During the year ended 31 December 20X4, Green made a net profit of $1.5 million. Green sold goods to Purple during the year with a value of $2 million, and half are still in Purple's inventories at year end. All the goods were sold at a margin of 30%.

Purple has recognised previous impairments in relation to its investment in Green of $225,000. In the current year, Purple wishes to recognise an additional impairment charge of $35,000.

What is the share of profit of associate to be shown in Purple's consolidated statement of profit or loss?

$_____ ,000

168   Which of the following statements regarding consolidated financial statements is correct?

    A   For consolidation, it may be acceptable to use financial statements of the subsidiary where the year-end differs from the parent by 2 months.

    B   For consolidation, all companies within the group must have the same year end.

    C   All companies within a group must have the same accounting policy in their individual financial statements.

    D   The profit made on all intra-group sales in the year must be removed from the consolidated financial statements.

169   'An associate is an entity over which the investor has significant influence' (IAS28, para 3).

Which TWO of the following indicate the presence of significant influence?

    A   The investor owns 330,000 of the 1,500,000 equity voting shares of the investee

    B   The investor has representation on the board of directors of the investee

    C   The investor is able to insist that all of the sales of the investee are made to a subsidiary of the investor

    D   The investor controls the votes of a majority of the board members

170   Consolidated financial statements are presented on the basis that the companies within the group are treated as if they are a single economic entity.

Which TWO of the following are requirements of preparing consolidated financial statements?

    A   All subsidiaries must adopt the accounting policies of the parent in their individual financial statements

    B   Subsidiaries with activities which are substantially different to the activities of other members of the group should not be consolidated

    C   All assets and liabilities of subsidiaries should be included at fair value

    D   Unrealised profits within the group must be eliminated from the consolidated financial statements

171   The Caddy group acquired 240,000 of August's 800,000 equity shares for $6 per share on 1 April 20X4. August's profit after tax for the year ended 30 September 20X4 was $400,000.

On the assumption that August is an associate of Caddy, what would be the carrying amount of the investment in August in the consolidated statement of financial position of Caddy as at 30 September 20X4?

    A $1,455,000

    B $1,500,000

    C $1,515,000

    D $1,395,000

172   On 1 January 20X4, Viagem acquired 80% of the equity share capital of Greca.

Extracts of their statements of profit or loss for the year ended 30 September 20X4 are:

	Viagem	Greca
	$000	$000
Revenue	64,600	38,000
Cost of sales	(51,200)	(26,000)

Sales from Viagem to Greca throughout the year to 30 September 20X4 had consistently been $800,000 per month.

Viagem made a mark-up on cost of 25% on these sales.

Greca had $1.5 million of these goods in inventory as at 30 September 20X4.

What would be the cost of sales in Viagem's consolidated statement of profit or loss for the year ended 30 September 20X4?

$_____ ,000

173   Pact acquired 80% of the equity shares of Sact on 1 July 20X4, paying $3 for each share acquired. This represented a premium of 20% over the market price of Sact's shares at that date.

Sact's equity at 31 March 20X5 comprised:

	$	$
Equity shares of $1 each		100,000
Retained earnings at 1 April 20X4	80,000	
Profit for the year ended 31 March 20X5	40,000	
	———	
		120,000
		———
		220,000
		———

The only fair value adjustment required to Sact's net assets on consolidation was a $20,000 increase in the value of its land.

Pact's policy is to value non-controlling interests at fair value at the date of acquisition.

For this purpose the market price of Sact's shares at that date can be deemed to be representative of the fair value of the shares held by the non-controlling interest.

What would be the carrying amount of the non-controlling interest of Sact in the consolidated statement of financial position of Pact as at 31 March 20X5?

A $54,000

B $50,000

C $56,000

D $58,000

174 Germane has a number of relationships with other companies.

In which of the following relationships is Germane necessarily the parent?

(i)   Foll has 50,000 non-voting and 100,000 voting equity shares in issue with each share receiving the same dividend. Germane owns all of Foll's non-voting shares and 40,000 of its voting shares.

(ii)   Kipp has 1 million equity shares in issue of which Germane owns 40%. Germane also owns $800,000 out of $1 million 8% convertible loan notes issued by Kipp. These loan notes may be converted on the basis of 40 equity shares for each $100 of loan note, or they may be redeemed in cash at the option of the holder.

(iii)   Germane owns 49% of the equity shares in Polly and 52% of its non-redeemable preference shares. As a result of these investments, Germane receives variable returns from Polly and has the ability to affect these returns through its power over Polly.

A   (i) only

B   (i) and (ii) only

C   (ii) and (iii) only

D   All three

175 Wilmslow acquired 80% of the equity shares of Zeta on 1 April 20X4 when Zeta's retained earnings were $200,000. During the year ended 31 March 20X5, Zeta purchased goods from Wilmslow totalling $320,000. At 31 March 20X5, one quarter of these goods were still in the inventory of Zeta. Wilmslow applies a mark-up on cost of 25% to all of its sales.

At 31 March 20X5, the retained earnings of Wilmslow and Zeta were $450,000 and $340,000 respectively.

What would be the amount of retained earnings in Wilmslow's consolidated statement of financial position as at 31 March 20X5?

$_____ ,000

176 IFRS Standards require extensive use of fair values when recording the acquisition of a subsidiary.

Which TWO of the following comments, regarding the use of fair values on the acquisition of a subsidiary, are correct?

A   The use of fair value to record a subsidiary's acquired assets does not comply with the historical cost principle.

B   The use of fair values to record the acquisition of plant always increases consolidated post-acquisition depreciation charges compared to the corresponding charge in the subsidiary's own financial statements.

C   Cash consideration payable one year after the date of acquisition needs to be discounted to reflect its fair value.

D   When acquiring a subsidiary, the fair value of liabilities and contingent liabilities must also be considered.

E   Patents must be included as part of goodwill because it is impossible to determine the fair value of an acquired patent, as, by definition, patents are unique.

177 **Identify whether the following statements are true or false**

	True	False
The profit made by a parent on the sale of goods to a subsidiary is only realised when the subsidiary sells the goods to a third party		
Eliminating intra-group unrealised profits never affects non-controlling interests		
The profit element of goods supplied by the parent to an associate and held in year-end inventory must be eliminated in full		

178 Johnson paid $1.2 million for a 30% investment in Treem's equity shares on 1 August 20X4.

Treem's profit after tax for the year ended 31 March 20X5 was $750,000. On 31 March 20X5, Treem had $300,000 goods in its inventory which it had bought from Johnson in March 20X5. These had been sold by Johnson at a mark-up on cost of 20%.

Treem has not paid any dividends.

On the assumption that Treem is an associate of Johnson, what would be the carrying amount of the investment in Treem in the consolidated statement of financial position of Johnson as at 31 March 20X5?

$_____ ,000

179 On 1 January 20X4, Pigagem acquired 80% of the equity share capital of Streca.

Extracts of their statements of financial position for the year ended 31 December 20X4 are:

	Pigagem	Streca
	$000	$000
Receivables	64,600	38,000

At 31 December 20X4, Streca recorded a payable to Pigagem of $3 million which did not agree to Pigagem's receivable balance due to $1 million cash in transit.

What is the value of receivables in the consolidated statement of financial position as at 31 December 20X4?

$_____ ,000

180 **Identify whether the following statements are true or false.**

	True	False
If a subsidiary is disposed of on the last day of the reporting period then its assets and liabilities must still be included in the consolidated statement of financial position.		
The gain or loss arising on the disposal of a subsidiary in the consolidated financial statements is recorded in other comprehensive income.		

181 Johanna acquired 100% of Sidney on 1 January 20X4, paying $5 million cash, including $200,000 professional fees. Johanna also agreed to pay $10 million on 1 January 20X6. Johanna Co has a cost of capital of 10%

Identify the components to be included within the calculation of goodwill for the acquisition of Sidney Co for the year ended 31 December 20X4.

Consideration

Cash consideration of $5 million

Cash consideration of $4.8 million

Deferred cash consideration of $8.3 million

Deferred cash consideration of $9.1 million

To be included in goodwill

182 The Garden group has a reporting date of 31 December 20X3. On 30 September 20X3, the group disposed of its 80% holding in the ordinary shares of Shed for $10 million in cash. The disposal of Shed constitutes a discontinued operation. The following information relates to Shed:

	$m
Goodwill at disposal	2
Net assets at disposal	9
Non-controlling interest at disposal	3

What should be recorded as the profit (or loss) on disposal in the consolidated statement of profit or loss for the year ended 31 December 20X3?

A Loss of $2 million

B Profit of $2 million

C Profit of $4 million

D Loss of $4 million

183 Wind purchased 80% of the ordinary shares of Snow for $4 million many years ago and holds the investment in its individual statement of financial position at cost. On 30 September 20X3, Wind disposed of its shares in Snow for $10 million in cash

What is the profit arising on the disposal of the shares that will be reported in Wind's individual statement of profit or loss for the year ended 30 September 20X3?

$_____

184 On 30 June 20X4, the Winter group disposed of its 70% holding in the ordinary shares of Spring for $9 million in cash. Winter originally purchased the shares for $6 million. At the acquisition date, the goodwill was $4.6 million, and has not been impaired. Spring's net assets at the disposal date were $5 million. The non-controlling interest in Spring at the disposal date was $3.1 million.

What is the profit arising on the disposal of Spring that will be recorded in the consolidated statement of profit or loss for the year ended 31 December 20X4?

$_____ ,000

185 On 30 June 20X4, the Tea group disposed of its 60% holding in the ordinary shares of Coffee for $15 million in cash. The non-controlling interest at the acquisition date was measured at its fair value of $2.2 million.

Coffee's net assets at the acquisition and the disposal date were $5 million and $8 million respectively. Goodwill arising on the acquisition of Coffee of $1 million had been fully impaired by the disposal date.

What is the profit arising on the disposal of Coffee that will be recorded in the consolidated statement of profit or loss for the year ended 31 December 20X4?

A   Profit of $10.0 million

B   Profit of $9.2 million

C   Profit of $10.4 million

D   Profit of $10.2 million

INTERPRETATION OF FINANCIAL STATEMENTS

186   Which of the following statements about a not-for-profit entity is valid?

A   There is no requirement to calculate an earnings per share figure as it is not likely to have shareholders who need to assess its earnings performance.

B   The current value of its property is not relevant as it is not a commercial entity.

C   Interpretation of its financial performance using ratio analysis is meaningless.

D   Its financial statements will not be closely scrutinised as it does not have investors.

187   Which of the following ratios is likely to be most relevant for a local charity?

A   Operating profit margin

B   Current ratio

C   Earnings per share

D   Return on capital employed

188 **Identify whether each of the following is a limitation of applying ratio analysis to published financial statements or not.**

	Limitation	Not a limitation
Different ways of calculating certain ratios exist		
Accounting policy choices can limit comparability between different companies		

189 The following information has been taken from Preston's financial statements:

Preston has inventory turnover of six times.

The year-end receivables collection period is 42 days.

Cost of sales for the year was $1,690,000. Credit purchases for the year were $2,150,000.

Preston's cash cycle at 31 December 20X7 was 68 days

All calculations should be made to the nearest full day, and the trading year has 365 days.

What is Preston's trade payables collection period as at 31 December 20X7?

_____ days

190 **Which TWO of the following explanations are unlikely to lead to an increase in receivables collection period?**

A   A new contract with a large customer has been won following a competitive tender

B   A large one-off credit sale has been completed just before the year end

C   The entity has recently expanded into a number of high street retail units

D   Difficult economic conditions have led to some customers struggling to pay on time

E   A website has been opened in the year for trade direct to the public

191 The following extracts of the financial statements of Wiggo have been obtained:

Revenue	$980,000
Cost of sales	($530,000)
Operating expenses	($210,000)

Equity	$600,000
Loan	$300,000
Deferred tax	$44,000
Payables	$46,000

What is the return on capital employed of Wiggo?

A   24.2%

B   25.4%

C   26.7%

D   50%

192 The following extracts of the financial statements of Wiggo have been obtained:

	20X5
Inventories	$130,000
Receivables	$80,000
Cash	$10,000
Loan repayable 20X8	$90,000
Deferred tax	$14,000
Payables	$70,000
Overdraft	$34,000

What is the quick ratio of Wiggo?

_____:1

193 **Which of the following items is unlikely to be considered a 'one-off' item which would impact the comparability of ratios?**

A   A new website selling direct to the public has meant that deliveries are now made to more diverse geographical areas, increasing delivery costs

B   A closure of a department has led to redundancies

C   Sale of surplus property leading to a profit on disposal

D   A storm in the year led to significant damage to the warehouse

194 **Which of the following is not a valid reason for a decrease in gross profit margin?**

A   A major customer renewed their contract during the year following a competitive tender process

B   New plant and equipment used in the manufacturing process has been purchased in the year, which has increased the depreciation expense

C   Delivery costs to customers have risen following an increase in the rates charged by couriers

D   A national recession has led to sales prices being cut in response

195 KRL manufactures pharmaceuticals, and is investigating a proposed takeover of another entity which is based overseas.

Identify which sources of information will be available for KRL to use in relation to the acquisition.

	Available to KRL to use	Not available to KRL to use
Details of the overseas country in which the target entity operates		
Recent financial statements of the entity		
Internal business plans of the takeover target		

196 Marcel has calculated that its current year Price Earnings (P/E) ratio is 12.6.

The sector average P/E ratio is 10.5

Which of the following would be an explanation of the difference between Marcel's P/E ratio and the sector average?

A   Marcel is seen as a less risky investment than the sector average, and there is higher confidence about the future prospects of Marcel.

B   Marcel is seen as a more risky investment than the sector average, however there is higher confidence about the future prospects of Marcel.

C   Marcel is seen as a less risky investment than the sector average, however there is low confidence about the future prospects of Marcel.

D   Marcel is seen as a more risky investment than the sector average, and there is low confidence about the future prospects of Marcel.

197 **Identify whether the statements about diluted earnings per share below are true or false.**

	True	False
It acts as a prediction of the future Earnings Per Share figure		
It discloses that Earnings Per Share could have been higher		

198 Apollo took out a new loan on 1 January 20X6. This loan carries an effective interest rate of 8%. The initial proceeds of the loan are $2.5m, which is after paying issue costs of $250k. The coupon rate on the loan is 6%. Apollo must keep to an interest cover ratio of 9 times under the arrangements made with the bank.

What operating profit must be maintained by Apollo in the year ended 31 December 20X6, in order to meet the minimum interest cover ratio specified by the bank?

A $1,350,000

B $1,800,000

C $450,000

D $1,980,000

199 Rodgers has just completed its financial statements for the year ended 30 June 20X6. It is reporting a net profit of $1,250,000 for the current year, and has $1 million of 50 cent shares in issue. The current market price of Rodgers' shares is $3.50.

What is the Price Earnings (P/E) ratio of Rodgers for the year ended 30 June 20X6?

_____ times

200 Puel has just completed its financial statements for the year ended 30 June 20X6. It has $1 million of 50 cent shares in issue, and the current market price per share is $3.50.

Puel has paid total dividends during the year ended 30 June 20X6 of $1,500,000.

What is the dividend yield (to one decimal place) for the year ended 30 June 20X6?

_____ %

201 Alco and Saleco are both food retailers. They are both showing a return on capital employed (ROCE) figure of 10% for the current year. Both companies have the same financial year end. Alco has reported a net profit (based on profit before interest and tax) of 25% and Saleco has reported a net profit of 2%.

What, if any, is the difference between these two companies, even though they are showing the same ROCE calculation?

A   The companies are identical

B   Alco operates at the high end of the market, and Saleco at the lower end

C   Alco operates at the lower end of the market, and Saleco at the high end

D   There is not enough information in the question to determine the difference

202 **Identify whether each of the following is a limitation of applying ratio analysis to published financial statements or not.**

	Limitation	Not a limitation
Financial statements often use historic cost, meaning that inflation is not taken into account		
Complex items may not fit into any accounting standards and therefore may be omitted from the financial statements		

203 Lepchem is a pharmaceutical business which was launched in September 20X1. Lepchem have been funded through bank loans and equity investment. Lepchem's aim is to develop new pharmaceuticals which could then be sold for a high margin. So far, Lepchem have not managed to successfully develop or sell any pharmaceuticals.

Which ratio is likely to be the most relevant for Lepchem for the year to 31 December 20X1?

A   Current ratio

B   Gross profit margin

C   Operating profit margin

D   Receivables collection period

204 **Identify whether the following criteria could be used to assess the performance of a not-for-profit entity.**

	Could be used to assess	Will not be used
The return given to investors		
The success in achieving the organisation's stated aims		
How well costs are being managed		

205 Which of the following measures is likely to be the least relevant to a property management business which rents out commercial properties?

    A   Non-current asset turnover

    B   Return on capital employed

    C   Average rent earned

    D   Inventory turnover period

206 Quartile is in the jewellery retail business which can be assumed to be highly seasonal. For the year ended 30 September 20X4, Quartile assessed its operating performance by comparing selected accounting ratios with those of its business sector average as provided by an agency. You may assume that the business sector used by the agency is an accurate representation of Quartile's business.

Which TWO of the following circumstances may invalidate the comparison of Quartile's ratios with those of the sector average?

    A   In the current year, Quartile has experienced significant rising costs for its purchases

    B   The sector average figures are compiled from companies whose year-end is between 1 July 20X4 and 30 September 20X4

    C   Quartile does not revalue its properties, but is aware that others in this sector do

    D   During the year, Quartile discovered an error relating to the inventory count at 30 September 20X3. This error was correctly accounted for in the financial statements for the current year ended 30 September 20X4

207 The following information has been taken or calculated from Fowler's financial statements for the year ended 30 September 20X4.

Fowler's cash cycle at 30 September 20X4 is 70 days. Its inventory turnover is six times.

Year-end trade payables are $230,000.

Purchases on credit for the year were $2 million.

Cost of sales for the year was $1.8 million.

What is Fowler's trade receivables collection period as at 30 September 20X4?

$_____ days

208 Trent uses the formula (year-end trade receivables/credit sales for the year) × 365 to calculate how many days on average its customers take to pay.

Which TWO of the following would NOT affect the correctness of the above calculation of the average number of days a customer takes to pay?

    A   Trent experiences considerable seasonal trading

    B   Trent makes a number of cash sales through retail outlets

    C   Revenue does not include a 15% sales tax whereas the receivables do include the tax

    D   Trent factors with recourse the receivable of its largest customer

209 At 31 March 20X5 Jasim had equity of $200,000 and debt of $100,000.

Which of the following transactions, considered separately, would increase Jasim's gearing?

A   During the year a property was revalued upwards by $20,000

B   A bonus issue of equity shares of 1 for 4 was made during the year using other components of equity

C   A provision for estimated damages was reduced during the year from $21,000 to $15,000 based on the most recent legal advice

D   An asset was acquired under a lease with a present value of lease payments of $23,000

210 **Which of the following current year events would explain a fall in an entity's operating profit margin compared to the previous year?**

A   An increase in gearing leading to higher interest costs

B   A reduction in the allowance for uncollectable receivables

C   A decision to value inventory on the average cost basis from the first in first out (FIFO) basis. Unit prices of inventory had risen during the current year

D   A change from the amortisation of development costs being included in cost of sales to being included in administrative expenses

STATEMENT OF CASH FLOWS

211 The following information is available for the property, plant and equipment of Fry as at 30 September:

	20X4	20X3
	$000	$000
Carrying amounts	23,400	14,400

The following items were recorded during the year ended 30 September 20X4:

(i)   Depreciation charge of $2.5 million

(ii)   An item of plant, with a carrying amount of $3 million, was sold for $1.8 million

(iii) A property was revalued upwards by $2 million

(iv)   Environmental provisions of $4 million relating to property, plant and equipment were capitalised during the year

What amount would be shown in Fry's statement of cash flows for purchase of property, plant and equipment for the year ended 30 September 20X4?

$_____ '000

212 At 1 October 20X4, BK had accrued interest payable of $12,000.

During the year ended 30 September 20X5, BK charged finance costs of $41,000 to its statement of profit or loss, including unwinding a discount relating to a provision stated at its present value of $150,000 at 1 October 20X4. The closing balance on accrued interest payable account at 30 September 20X5 was $15,000, and BK has a discount rate of 6%.

How much interest paid should BK show on its statement of cash flows for the year ended 30 September 20X5?

A $38,000

B $29,000

C $35,000

D $41,000

213 The following balances were extracted from N's statement of financial position as at 31 December.

	20X9	20X8
	$000	$000
Deferred taxation	38	27
Current tax payable	119	106

Extract from statement of profit or loss for the year ended 31 December 20X9.

	$000
Income tax expense	122

The amount of tax paid that should be included in N's statement of cash flows for the year ended 31 December 20X9 is:

$_____ ,000

214 Which item would be NOT be shown in a statement of cash flows using the indirect method?

A   Cash paid to employees

B   Cash paid to purchase machinery

C   Cash paid to shareholders as dividend

D   Cash paid to redeem loan notes

215 IAS 7 *Statement of Cash Flows* sets out the three main headings to be used in a statement of cash flows.

Which TWO of the items below would be included under the heading 'Cash flows from operating activities' according to IAS 7?

A   Tax paid

B   Purchase of investments

C   Loss on disposal of machinery

D   Purchase of equipment

216 During the year to 31 July 20X7 Smartypants made a profit of $37,500 after accounting for depreciation of $2,500.

During the year non-current assets were purchased for $16,000, receivables increased by $2,000, inventories decreased by $3,600 and trade payables increased by $700.

What was the increase in cash and bank balances during the year?

A $21,300

B $30,300

C $24,900

D $26,300

217 **Identify the correct treatment in the calculation of net cash from operating activities under the indirect method.**

	Add to profit before tax	Deduct from profit before tax
Decrease in trade receivables		
Increase in inventories		
Profit on sale of non-current assets		
Depreciation		

218 Butcher had the following balances in its statement of financial position as at 30 June 20X0 and 20X1:

	20X1	20X0
Share capital	$170,000	$150,000
Share premium	$105,000	$95,000
10% debentures	$170,000	$190,000

How much will appear in the statement of cash flows for the year ended 30 June 20X1 under the heading 'cash flows from financing activities'?

$_____ ,000

219 At 1 January 20X0 Casey had property, plant and equipment with a carrying amount of $180,000. In the year ended 31 December 20X0 Casey disposed of assets with a carrying amount of $60,000 for $50,000. Casey revalued a building from $75,000 to $100,000 and charged depreciation for the year of $20,000. At the end of the year, the carrying amount of property, plant and equipment was $250,000.

How much will be reported in the statement of cash flows for the year ended 31 December 20X0 under the heading 'cash flows from investing activities'?

A $75,000 outflow

B $125,000 outflow

C $135,000 outflow

D $50,000 inflow

220 At 1 January 20X0 Casey had government grants held in deferred income of $900,000. During the year, Casey released $100,000 to the statement of profit or loss. At 31 December 20X0, the remaining deferred income balance was $1,100,000.

Select the TWO amounts to be included in the statement of cash flows for Casey.

Amortisation of government grant	Receipt of grant
Increase of 100,000 to cash generated from operations	Cash received from grant $300,000 in investing activities
Decrease of 100,000 to cash generated from operations	Cash received from grant $100,000 in investing activities

Section 2

OBJECTIVE CASE QUESTIONS – SECTION B

CONCEPTUAL FRAMEWORK/INTERNATIONAL FINANCIAL REPORTING STANDARDS

The following scenario relates to questions 221–225

Flightline is an airline which treats its aircraft as complex non-current assets, accounted for under the historical cost model. The cost and other details of an aircraft are:

	$000	Estimated life
Interior cabin fittings – installed 1 April 20X5	25,000	5 years
Engine - installed 1 April 20X5	9,000	36,000 flying hours

In the year ended 31 March 20X9, the aircraft flew for 1,200 hours for the six months to 30 September 20X8.

On 1 October 20X8 the aircraft suffered a 'bird strike' accident which damaged the engine beyond repair. This was replaced by a new engine with a life of 36,000 hours at cost of $10.8 million.

Flightline's year end is 31 March 20X9.

---

221 **What is the depreciation to be charged in respect of the engine for the 6 month period to 1 October 20X8?**

$_____ ,000

222 **Which of the following explains the correct accounting treatment of the engine?**

A   Write off the damaged engine, capitalise the new engine and depreciate over 24,000 hours

B   Treat the $10.8 million as a repair to the damaged engine and continue to depreciate the engine as in the first 6 months

C   Capitalise $6 million to replace the damaged engine, expense the other $4.8 million

D   Write off the damaged engine, capitalise the new engine and depreciate over 36,000 hours

223 A wing was also damaged, but was repaired at a cost of $3 million. The accident also caused cosmetic damage to the exterior of the aircraft which required repainting at a cost of $2 million.

Identify the correct treatment for the $3 million repair costs to the wing and the $2 million repainting of the aircraft

	Capitalise	Expense
$3 million repair of the wing		
$2 million repainting of the exterior		

224 As the aircraft was out of service for some weeks due to the accident, Flightline took the opportunity to upgrade its cabin facilities at a cost of $4.5 million. This did not increase the estimated remaining life of the cabin fittings, but the improved facilities enabled Flightline to substantially increase the air fares on this aircraft.

What is the carrying amount of the cabin fittings as at 31 March 20X9?

A $8,600,000

B $8,000,000

C $5,000,000

D $7,250,000

225 The 'bird strike' accident represents an indication of impairment.

Complete the following sentence from the choice below.

The aircraft will be impaired if its _____ exceeds its recoverable amount.

Options: Replacement cost, Fair value less costs to sell, Carrying amount, Value in use

---

The following scenario relates to questions 226–230

Speculate owns two properties and uses fair value accounting where possible.

Property A: An office building used by Speculate for administrative purposes. At 1 April 20X2 it had a carrying amount of $2 million and a remaining life of 20 years. On 1 October 20X2, the property was let to a third party and reclassified as an investment property. The property had a fair value of $2.3 million at 1 October 20X2, and $2.34 million at 31 March 20X3.

Property B: Another office building let on a 12-month lease to a subsidiary of Speculate. At 1 April 20X2, it had a fair value of $1.5 million which had risen to $1.65 million at 31 March 20X3.

---

226 **What is the correct treatment when Property A is reclassified as an investment property?**

A   Take $350,000 gain to other comprehensive income

B   Take $350,000 gain to the statement of profit or loss

C   Take $400,000 gain to other comprehensive income

D   Take $400,000 gain to the statement of profit or loss

227 Which of the following models can Speculate use to account for investment properties in its individual financial statements?

(i) Cost model

(ii) Revaluation model

(iii) Fair value model

A (i) and (ii) only

B (i) and (iii) only

C (ii) and (iii) only

D All three

228 What is the total gain for investment properties to be included in Speculate's individual statement of profit or loss for the year ended 31 March 20X3? Enter your answer to the nearest dollar ($).

$ _____

229 In the individual and consolidated financial statements of Speculate, how would Property B be accounted for?

Individual	✓	Consolidated	✓
Investment property		Investment property	
Property, plant & equipment		Property, plant & equipment	
Within goodwill		Cancelled as an intra-group item	

230 What would the carrying amount of Property A be at 31 March 20X3 if Speculate used the cost model for investment properties?

A $1,950,000

B $1,900,000

C $2,185,000

D $2,182,051

The following scenario relates to questions 231–235

Apex received a $10 million 6% loan on 1 April 20X7. The loan will be redeemable at a premium which means the loan has an effective finance cost of 7.5% per annum. The loan was specifically issued to finance the building of a new store.

Construction of the store commenced on 1 May 20X7 and it was completed and ready for use on 28 February 20X8, but did not open for trading until 1 April 20X8.

231 How should the loan be treated in the financial statements of Apex for the year ended 31 March 20X8?

A Present value

B Fair value through other comprehensive income

C Fair value through profit or loss

D Amortised cost

232 Which TWO of the statements below regarding IAS 23 *Borrowing Costs* are correct?

A Borrowing costs must be capitalised if they are directly attributable to qualifying assets

B Borrowing costs should cease to be capitalised once the related asset is substantially complete

C Borrowing costs must be capitalised if they are directly attributable to non-current assets

D Borrowing costs may be capitalised if they are directly attributable to qualifying assets

E Borrowing costs should commence to be capitalised once expenditure is being incurred on the construction of the asset

233 How much should be recorded as finance costs in the statement of profit or loss for the year ended 31 March 20X8?

$_____ ,000

234 How much interest should be capitalised as part of property, plant and equipment as at 31 March 20X8?

$_____ ,000

235 Apex decided that not all of the funds raised were needed immediately and temporarily invested some of the funds in April 20X7, earning $40,000 interest.

How should the $40,000 be accounted for in the financial statements of Apex?

A Net off the amount capitalised in property, plant and equipment

B Taken to the statement of profit or loss as investment income

C Taken as other comprehensive income

D Deducted from the outstanding loan amount in the statement of financial position

The following scenario relates to questions 236–240

Shawler constructed a furnace on 1 April 20X3, causing significant environmental damage which must be repaired at the end of the asset's useful life of ten years. The present value of this is estimated to be $4 million. Shawler has a cost of capital of 8%.

On 1 October 20X3, Shawler received a government grant of $1.2 million relating to the cost of plant with a five year life. Shawler accounts for grants using the deferred credit method.

On 1 October 20X3, Shawler also acquired land for 12 million dinars. The land was used to construct a factory during the year. Shawler's functional currency is the dollar ($).

On 1 October 20X3 the exchange rate was 4 Dinars: $1. At 31 March 20X4 the exchange rate was 2 Dinars:$1 and the average rate for the year was 3 Dinars:$1.

---

236 **What is the total finance cost (to the nearest thousand) to be recorded in the statement of profit or loss in respect of the environmental damage caused by the furnace for the year ended 31 March 20X4?**

$_____ ,000

237 **What is the non-current liability in respect of the government grant to be shown in Shawler's statement of financial position as at 31 March 20X4?**

A $840,000

B $1,080,000

C $960,000

D $720,000

238 **What is the carrying amount of the land to be shown in the statement of financial position of Shawler as at 31 March 20X4? Give your answer to the nearest $000.**

$_____ ,000

239 The costs below are the costs associated with the construction of the factory.

Which of the following can NOT be capitalised?

A   Legal fees relating to the site purchase

B   Health and safety training for new construction workers

C   Direct labour costs associated with the construction

D   Costs of site preparation

---

240 In the following year it was discovered that Shawler had breached the conditions relating to the government grant and therefore the grant had to be repaid.

Which TWO of the following describe the correct accounting treatment to record the repayment of the grant?

A Remove all deferred income balances

B Record an expense in the statement of profit or loss

C Increase the cost of plant

D Make an adjustment to the prior year financial statements

The following scenario relates to questions 241–245

During the year Darby started research work on a new processor chip. Darby has a past history of being particularly successful in bringing similar projects to a profitable conclusion. In addition to this, Darby spent $200,000 training staff to use new equipment.

Darby also developed a new online platform during the year, spending $100,000 a month evenly from 1 February 20X5 to 31 October 20X5. Darby was unsure of the outcome of the project, but doubts were resolved on 1 May, following successful testing. The platform launched on 1 November 20X5 and was expected to last 5 years.

---

241 Darby's accounting assistant has read something which states that intangible assets are identifiable, non-monetary items without physical substance.

Which TWO of the following relate to items being classed as identifiable?

A Items must have probable future economic benefits

B Items must arise from legal or contractual rights

C Items must have a measurable cost

D Items must be separable

242 **Identify the correct accounting treatment for items below.**

	Capitalise	Expense
Training for staff		
Expenditure on processor chip		

243 **How much should be recorded in Darby's statement of profit or loss for the year ended 31 December 20X5 in relation to the development of the online platform?**

$_____ ,000

244 **Which of the facts relating to the online platform is correct?**

(i)   The online platform will be subject to annual impairment review due to the judgemental nature of the project.

(ii)   Once capitalised, the development costs should be held at fair value at each year-end.

(iii)   Depreciation on any plant used to develop the platform would be capitalised as part of the development costs.

A   (i) only

B   (ii) and (iii) only

C   (iii) only

D   (i) and (ii) only

245 Darby acquired a patent with a 10 year life for $500,000 on 1 January 20X5. On 31 December 20X5, management believed that the patent was less fully utilised than expected and determined the following information as part of their impairment review:

	$000
Potential sale proceeds of the patent	400
Estimated disposal costs	20
Value in use of the asset	480

What is the value of the impairment loss in the year ended 31 December 20X5?

A $70,000

B $30,000

C $20,000

D   Nil

The following scenario relates to questions 246–250

Aphrodite has a year end of 31 December and operates a factory which makes computer chips for mobile phones. It purchased a machine on 1 July 20X3 for $80,000 which had a useful life of ten years and is depreciated on the straight-line basis, time apportioned in the years of acquisition and disposal. The machine was revalued to $81,000 on 1 July 20X4. There was no change to its useful life at that date.

A fire at the factory on 1 October 20X6 damaged the machine, leaving it with a lower operating capacity. The accountant considers that Aphrodite will need to recognise an impairment loss in relation to this damage and has ascertained the following information at 1 October 20X6:

(1)   The carrying amount of the machine is $60,750.

(2)   An equivalent new machine would cost $90,000.

(3)   The machine could be sold in its current condition for a gross amount of $45,000. Dismantling costs would amount to $2,000.

(4)   In its current condition, the machine could operate for three more years which gives it a value in use figure of $38,685.

246   **In accordance with IAS 16 *Property, Plant and Equipment*, what is the depreciation charged to Aphrodite's statement of profit or loss in respect of the machine for the year ended 31 December 20X4?**

    A $9,000

    B $8,000

    C $8,263

    D $8,500

247   IAS 36 *Impairment of Assets* contains a number of examples of internal and external events which may indicate the impairment of an asset.

    In accordance with IAS 36, which TWO of the following would definitely NOT be an indicator of the potential impairment of an asset (or group of assets)?

    A   A reduction in Aphrodite's cost of capital

    B   Adverse changes in the economic performance of one or more assets

    C   A significant change in the technological environment in which an asset is employed making its software effectively obsolete

    D   The carrying amount of an entity's net assets being below the entity's market capitalisation

    E   An unexpected fall in the market value of one or more assets

248 **What is the total impairment loss associated with Aphrodite's machine at 1 October 20X6?**

    A $nil

    B $17,750

    C $22,065

    D $15,750

249 The accountant has decided that it is too difficult to reliably attribute cash flows to this one machine and that it would be more accurate to calculate the impairment on the basis of the factory as a cash-generating unit.

In accordance with IAS 36 *Impairment of Assets*, which TWO of the following are TRUE regarding cash generating units?

    A   A cash-generating unit to which goodwill has been allocated should be tested for impairment every five years.

    B   A cash-generating unit must be a subsidiary of the parent.

    C   There is no need to consistently identify cash-generating units based on the same types of asset from period to period.

    D   A cash-generating unit is the smallest identifiable group of assets for which independent cash flows can be identified.

    E   Assets in a cash-generating unit should never be impaired below their recoverable amount.

250 On 1 July 20X7, it is discovered that the damage to the machine is worse than originally thought. The machine is now considered to be worthless and the recoverable amount of the factory as a cash-generating unit is estimated to be $950,000.

At 1 July 20X7, the cash-generating unit comprises the following assets:

	$000
Building	500
Plant and equipment (including the damaged machine at a carrying amount of $35,000)	335
Goodwill	85
Net current assets (at recoverable amount)	250
	1,170

In accordance with IAS 36 *Impairment of Assets*, what will be the carrying amount of Aphrodite's plant and equipment when the impairment loss has been allocated to the cash-generating unit?

$_____

The following scenario relates to questions 251–255

Radar's directors made the following decisions during the year ended 31 March 20X3:

• it disposed of all of its outlets in country A

• it rebranded all of its outlets in country B to target the tourism market. The previous target market in country B had been aimed at business clients.

At a board meeting on 1 January 20X3, Pulsar's directors decided sell an item of plant, which had a carrying value of $4 million at 1 April 20X2 and a remaining life of 20 years. The plant is expected to sell for $3.9 million within 12 months.

A decision was also made to close down a regional office, which was communicated to the employees before the year-end. 50 employees would be retrained and kept within Radar at a cost of $100,000, the others took redundancy and will be paid $300,000.

$75,000 is to be spent on marketing materials directing customers of the existing factory to other production facilities operated by Radar.

251 **Which THREE of the following criteria need to be satisfied in order to recognise an asset as held for sale in accordance with IFRS 5 *Non-Current Assets Held for Sale and Discontinued Operations*?**

    A   Asset is no longer in use

    B   Asset is being actively marketed

    C   Sale of the asset has been agreed

    D   The plan to sell the asset is unlikely to be withdrawn

    E   Asset is likely to be sold within twelve months

252 **Identify whether the change in operations in countries A and B represent a discontinued operation in accordance with IFRS 5 *Non-Current Assets Held for Sale and Discontinued Operations*.**

    A   Only country A represents a discontinued operation

    B   Only country B represents a discontinued operation

    C   Both countries will be regarded as discontinued operations

    D   Neither country will be regarded as a discontinued operation

253 **At what value should the plant be held at 31 March 20X3 according to IFRS 5 *Non-Current Assets Held for Sale and Discontinued Operations*?**

    A $3,800,000

    B $3,900,000

    C $4,000,000

    D $3,850,000

254 **What provision should be recorded in relation to the office closure?**

    A $300,000

    B $475,000

    C $375,000

    D $400,000

255 On 30 June 20X3, before the financial statements were authorised for issue, the plant was sold at a loss of $100,000 and the redundancies were settled at $50,000 more than expected.

Identify whether each item represents an adjusting or non-adjusting event according to IAS 10 Events After the Reporting Period

	Adjusting event	Non-adjusting event
Disposal of plant		
Redundancy settlement		

The following scenario relates to questions 256–260

Tunshill has an item of plant with an estimated five-year life. The plant is wearing well and at 1 October 20X8 the production manager believed that the plant was likely to last 5 more years.

Tunshill wishes to change its method of inventory valuation from first-in/first-out (FIFO) to average cost (AVCO). The value of Tunshill's inventory at 30 September 20X9 (on the FIFO basis) is $20 million. However, on the AVCO basis it would be valued at $18 million. Tunshill's inventory at 30 September 20X8 was $15 million, but on the AVCO basis it would have been reported as $13.4 million.

Tunshill also has two items of inventory that require review. Item A cost $50 per unit. Tunshill has struggled to sell the item and has 2,000 units still in inventory. Tunshill has agreed a contract with a distributor to sell the items for $55 each, but will charge commission of 20%.

Item B relates to a one-off purchase of rare metal for a profitable contract costing $80,000. No work has yet been done, but after further costs of $20,000 it will be converted into a product and sold for an agreed price of $150,000. Since buying the metal, the cost price has fallen to $50,000.

256 **Which TWO circumstances are outlined in IAS 8 *Accounting Policies, Changes in Accounting Estimates and Errors* as acceptable reasons to change accounting policy?**

    A   To provide greater comparison with competitors

    B   If a change results in providing more reliable and relevant information to users

    C   If required by an International Financial Reporting Standard

    D   If tax law in a country changes

    E   To show the best possible results for the investors

257 **Fill in the blanks in the sentence below with the correct option.**

The change in useful life of the plant will be a change in accounting _____ and should be applied _____.

Options: Policy, Estimate, Error, Retrospectively, Prospectively, Prudently

258 **Which of the options below outline the correct treatment for the change in valuation method from FIFO to AVCO?**

A   Profit would be reduced by $400,000

B   Profit would be reduced by $2,000,000

C   Opening retained earnings would increase by $1,600,000

D   Opening retained earnings would decrease by $400,000

259 **At what value should item A be included in Tunshill's statement of financial position as at 30 September 20X9?**

$_____ ,000

260 **At what value should item B be included in Tunshill's statement of financial position as at 30 September 20X9?**

A $50,000

B $80,000

C $130,000

D $100,000

The following scenario relates to questions 261–265

Schrute owns a herd of cattle, which produce milk. Schrute then turns this into cheese.

On 1 April 20X5, Schrute purchased a flock of sheep for $100,000, which included transaction costs of $5,000. At 31 March 20X6, the flock was valued at $120,000. Every time animals are sold there is a 5% commission fee payable to the national farming agency.

Schrute uses the historical cost model and charges all depreciation as an operating expense.

In addition to this, Schrute uses a number of items of specialised farm machinery. This machinery cost Schrute $200,000 on 1 April 20X2 and has a 10-year useful life. At 31 March 20X6, there is only one supplier who still sells this machinery and the current price of new machinery is $300,000.

261 **Which of the following items held by Schrute will be accounted for under the provisions of IAS 41 *Agriculture*?**

    (i)   Herd of cattle

    (ii)   Milk

    (iii)   Cheese

    A   (i) only

    B   (ii) and (iii) only

    C   (i) and (ii) only

    D   All three items

262 **What gain should be taken to Schrute's statement of profit or loss for the year ended 31 March 20X6 in respect of the flock of sheep?**

    $_____

263 **Using current cost accounting, what is the value of the machinery at 31 March 20X6?**

    A $120,000

    B $180,000

    C $200,000

    D $300,000

264 At 31 March 20X6, a valuations expert informed the directors of Schrute that the property owned and used by Shrute for farming had significantly increased in value. This had been decided by looking at the price per square metre at similar properties in the area and concluded that this could be used to value Schrute's farm with no adjustments necessary.

Which of the following inputs within IFRS 13 *Fair Value Measurement* describes the method used to value the farm?

  A   Level 1 input

  B   Level 2 input

  C   Level 3 input

  D   Level 4 input

265 **If Schrute chooses to value the farm at the market value, which TWO of the following ratios will NOT be affected?**

  A   Current ratio

  B   Return on capital employed

  C   Gross profit margin

  D   Gearing

  E   Net profit (before tax) margin

The following scenario relates to questions 266–270

On 1 October 20X6 Fino entered into an agreement to lease twenty telephones for its team of sales staff. The telephones are to be leased for a period of 24 months at a cost of $240 per telephone per annum, payable annually in advance. The present value of the lease payments at 1 October 20X6 is $9,164.

On 1 April 20X7, Fino entered into an agreement to lease an item of plant from the manufacturer. The lease required four annual payments in advance of $100,000 each commencing on 1 April 20X7. The plant would have a useful life of four years and would be scrapped at the end of this period. The present value of the total lease payments is $350,000.

Fino has a cost of capital of 10%.

---

266 **Which of the following applies the principle of faithful representation to the above plant lease agreement?**

  A   Recording an annual rent expense in Fino's statement of profit or loss

  B   Expensing any interest on a straight-line basis over 4 years

  C   Recording an asset in Fino's statement of financial position to reflect control

  D   Record the $100,000 paid as a prepayment to be released over 4 years

267 How much would be charged to Fino's statement of profit or loss for the year ended 30 September 20X7 in respect of the telephones?

    A $4,800

    B $4,582

    C $4,364

    D $5,498

268 What would be the carrying amount of the right-of-use plant asset as at 30 September 20X7?

    $_____

269 What interest would be charged to Fino's statement of profit or loss for the year ended 30 September 20X7 in respect of the plant lease?

    A $12,500

    B $25,000

    C $17,500

    D $35,000

270 Applying the principles of IFRS 16 *Leases* to capitalise the plant and recognise the lease liability would have what impact upon the following ratios?

	Increase	Decrease
Return on Capital Employed		
Gearing		
Interest cover		

The following scenario relates to questions 271–275

On 1 January 20X6 Lotso entered into an agreement to lease new machinery under a 5 year lease, with $300,000 payable on 31 December each year. The asset has a useful life of 6 years, and ownership transfers to Lotso at the end of the lease. The interest rate implicit in the lease is 6% and the present value of the lease payments is $1,263,000.

On 1 January 20X6 Lotso sold its head office to a finance company, but continued to use the head office for the remainder of its 20-year estimated useful life under a lease agreement. The carrying amount of the head office on 1 January 20X6 was $10 million and the fair value of the asset and sale proceeds received on 1 January 20X6 were $11.5 million.

271 What would be the finance cost in respect of the machinery lease for the year ended 31 December 20X6?

    $_____

272   What current liability (to the nearest thousand) will be recorded in Lotso's statement of financial position as at 31 December 20X6 in relation to the machinery lease?

    A $300,000

    B $238,000

    C $1,039,000

    D $801,000

273   What is the carrying amount of the right-of-use machinery asset as at 31 December 20X6?

    A $1,039,000

    B $1,263,000

    C $1,052,500

    D $1,010,400

274   What would be the carrying amount of the head office at 31 December 20X6?

    A   Nil

    B $9,500,000

    C $8,075,000

    D $10,925,000

275   Identify if the statements below are true or false

Statement 1: In a sale and leaseback transaction, no profit will be recognised by the lessee.

Statement 2: In a sale and leaseback transaction, the sale proceeds will usually be treated as a loan to the lessee.

	True	False
Statement 1		
Statement 2		

The following scenario relates to questions 276–280

On 1 September 20X3, Laidlaw factored (sold) $2 million of trade receivables to Finease. Laidlaw received an immediate payment of $1.8 million. Under the factoring agreement any receivables not collected after four months will be sold back to Laidlaw.

On 1 October 20X2, Laidlaw sold some maturing inventory which had a cost of $4.5 million to a bank for its fair value of $5 million. Under the terms of the sale agreement Laidlaw has the option to repurchase the inventory after a period of ten years at a price of $7.4 million. At this date the fair value of the inventory is expected to be $11 million, and the repurchase price reflects an equivalent annual rate of interest of 4%

Laidlaw issued $10 million convertible loan notes on 1 October 20X2 that carry a nominal (coupon) interest rate of 5% per annum, and are redeemable on 1 October 20X5. A similar loan note, without the conversion option, would have required Laidlaw to pay an interest rate of 8%.

Relevant discount rates are shown below:

End of year		5%	8%
	1	0.95	0.93
	2	0.91	0.86
	3	0.86	0.79

276 **Which of the following is correct regarding Laidlaw's factoring of trade receivables for the year ended 30 September 20X3?**

    A $200,000 should be recorded as an administrative expense for the disposal of the receivables

    B   The receivables should be removed from the statement of financial position

    C   This represents a 'without recourse' factoring agreement

    D   The receipt of $1.8 million should be treated as a loan

277 **What amount should be recorded in equity (to the nearest thousand) in respect of the convertible loan notes issued by Laidlaw?**

    $_____000

278 **Which TWO of the following items should be recorded in Laidlaw's financial statements for the year ended 30 September 20X3 in respect of the maturing inventory sale?**

    A $200,000 finance cost

    B $50,000 release of deferred income

    C $5 million revenue

    D $5.2 million loan

    E $450,000 deferred income liability

    F $500,000 gross profit

279 Which of the following statements regarding the convertible loan notes is NOT true?

A   The convertible loan notes will affect gearing due to the liability component being different to the equity component

B   The equity amount will remain fixed until the date of conversion

C   The liability at 30 September 20X5 will be $10 million

D   5% interest will be charged to the statement of profit or loss as a finance cost

280 Applying the principle of split accounting to convertible loan notes is important to satisfy which of the following qualitative characteristics?

A   Faithful representation

B   Timeliness

C   Verifiability

D   Relevance

The following scenario relates to questions 281–285

The following trial balance extract relates to Howard at 30 September 20X5:

	$000	$000
Convertible loan notes – Liability component at 1 Oct X4 (note (i))		28,508
5% loan notes (note (ii))		10,000
Equity investments (note (iii))	6,000	

The following notes are relevant:

(i)   The convertible loan notes are 8% $30 million convertible loan notes issued on 1 October 20X4 at par. An equivalent loan without the conversion would carry an interest rate of 10%. Howard's finance director correctly split the instrument into its equity and liability components at 1 October 20X4, but has done nothing else.

(ii)   The 5% loan notes were issued at par of $10 million, but Howard incurred $400,000 issue costs. The loan notes have an effective interest rate of 8%.

(iii) The equity investments relate to 1 million shares in Kapoor, an unrelated entity. During the year, Kapoor paid a dividend of 10 cents per share. At 30 September 20X5 the fair value of each Kapoor share was $7.

281 Which of the items included in the trial balance extract will be classified as financial instruments?

A   Convertible loan notes and equity investments only

B   Loan notes and equity investments only

C   Convertible loan notes and loan notes only

D   All three items

282 What should the value of the liability element of the convertible loan note be at 30 September 20X5, to the nearest thousand?

A $28,508,000

B $28,389,000

C $28,959,000

D $30,000,000

283 What finance cost should be shown in the statement of profit or loss in respect of the loan notes?

$_____

284 What income should be recorded in the statement of profit or loss in relation to the equity investments?

A $600,000

B $1,100,000

C $1,600,000

D $1,000,000

285 Howard is uncertain of how to treat professional fees. For which of the following investments should professional fees be capitalised as part of initial value of the asset?

	Capitalised	Not capitalised
Fair value through other comprehensive income investments		
Fair value through profit or loss investments		
Amortised cost investments		

The following scenario relates to questions 286–290

Vance buys and sells goods in Kromits (Kr), but has a functional currency of dollars ($).

Vance purchased goods for Kr 10,000 on 1 September 20X1. At Vance's year-end of 31 December 20X1 this amount remains unpaid.

Vance sold goods on 1 September 20X1 for Kr 60,000. On 1 October 20X1 Vance received Kr 30,000. The remaining Kr 30,000 is unpaid at 31 December 20X1.

Vance's assistant accountant estimated the tax expense for the year ended 31 December 20X1 at $43,000. However, he had ignored deferred tax. At 1 January 20X1 Vance had a deferred tax liability of $130,000. At 31 December 20X1 Vance had temporary taxable differences of $360,000. Vance pays tax at 25%. All movements in deferred tax are taken to the statement of profit or loss.

Relevant exchange rates are:

1 September   Kr10:$1

1 October   Kr10.5:$1

31 December   Kr8:$1

Average rate   Kr9:$1

286   **What gain or loss should be recorded in the statement of profit or loss for the year ended 31 December 20X1 in relation to the payable recorded for the purchase of goods?**

    A   Loss of $111

    B   Gain of $111

    C   Loss of $250

    D   Gain of $250

287   **What gain or loss should be recorded in the statement of profit or loss for the year ended 31 December 20X1 in relation to the sale of goods?**

    A   Loss of $607

    B   Gain of $607

    C   Loss of $893

    D   Gain of $893

288   **Which of the statements below is/are true?**

Statement 1: The inventory purchased on 1 October 20X1 should be retranslated at the closing rate if the goods remain in inventory at 31 December 20X1.

Statement 2: The foreign exchange gains will be added to the revenue for the year.

	True	False
Statement 1		
Statement 2		

289 **What will be recorded as the tax expense in the statement of profit or loss for the year ended 31 December 20X7?**

$_____

290 Vance's assistant accountant has discovered that there is a debit balance on the trial balance of $3,000 relating to the over/under-provision of tax from the prior year.

What impact will this have on Vance's current year financial statements?

A   Increase the tax liability by $3,000 in the statement of financial position

B   Decrease the tax liability by $3,000 in the statement of financial position

C   Increase the tax expense by $3,000 in the statement of profit or loss

D   Decrease the tax expense by $3,000 in the statement of profit or loss

The following scenario relates to questions 291–295

Bailey constructs buildings for customers which can take many years to complete. Bailey has three contracts in progress at 30 September 20X7, which are detailed below. All of the contracts below began in the current year.

	Contract 1	Contract 2	Contract 3
	$000	$000	$000
Price	10,000	8,000	4,000
Costs incurred to date	(6,000)	(4,000)	(500)
Costs to complete	(1,000)	(6,000)	(2,000)
Progress	80%	60%	25%
Amount billed to date	7,000	3,000	1,000

291 **What revenue should be recorded (to the nearest thousand) in relation to contract 1?**

$_____ ,000

292 **What cost of sales should be recorded (to the nearest thousand) in relation to contract 2?**

A $4,200,000

B $9,400,000

C $5,640,000

D $6,800,000

293 **What should be recorded in the statement of financial position (to the nearest thousand) in relation to contract 3?**

A   Nil

B $500,000 contract liability

C $125,000 contract liability

D $3,000,000 contract asset

294 Bailey's assistant accountant is unsure about how to deal with a brand new contract where the progress and overall profit cannot yet be ascertained.

Which of the statements below is/are true?

Statement 1 – Where the progress and overall profit are unknown, no contract asset or liability can be recognised.

Statement 2 – Where the progress and overall profit are unknown, revenue should be recognised to the level of recoverable costs.

	True	**False**
Statement 1		
Statement 2		

295 Bailey's assistant has also enquired about changing the way of measuring the progress of contracts.

Complete the following to show how the change should be applied.

As a change in accounting _____ , applied _____ .

Options: prospectively, retrospectively, estimate, policy

The following scenario relates to questions 296–300

Creg sold and installed a large item of machinery for $800,000 on 1 November 20X7. Included within the price was a 2 year servicing contract which has a value of $240,000 and a fee for installation of $50,000.

Creg works as an agent for a number of smaller contractors, earning commission of 10%. Creg's revenue includes $6 million received from clients under these agreements with $5.4 million in cost of sales representing the amount paid to the contractors.

Creg sold a large number of vehicles to a new customer for $10 million on 1 July 20X7. The customer paid $990,000 up front and agreed to pay the remaining balance on 1 July 20X8. Creg has a cost of capital of 6%.

296 **How much should be recorded in Creg's revenue in its statement of profit or loss for the year ended 31 December 20X7 in relation to the large machinery sale?**

A $530,000

B $680,000

C $560,000

D $580,000

297 Creg's sales director is close to selling another large machine, offering free service, therefore selling the entire machine for $560,000. Creg never sells servicing separately.

How should this discount be applied in relation to the sale of the machinery?

Sales element	Discount applied	Discount not applied
Machine		
Installation		
Service		

298 **What adjustment needs to be made to revenue in respect of the commission sales?**

A Reduce revenue by $6 million

B Reduce revenue by $5.4 million

C Increase revenue by $600,000

D No adjustment is required

299 **How much should initially be recorded in revenue in respect of the sale of vehicles in the statement of profit or loss for the year ended 31 December 20X7? Answer to the nearest $000.**

$_____,000

300 On 31 December 20X7 Creg sold some maturing goods to a bank for $3 million. The estimated value of the goods at that date was $5 million, which is expected to keep rising. Creg keeps the goods on its premises and has the option to repurchase the goods on 31 December 20X9 for $3.63 million.

Which of the following outlines the correct treatment for the maturing inventory?

A Record a loss on disposal of $2 million in the statement of profit or loss

B Take $3 million to revenue, disclosing the repurchase option

C Leave the inventory in current assets, increasing in value as the goods mature

D Treat the $3 million as a loan with 10% compound interest accruing over the 2 years

The following scenario relates to questions 301–305

The profit after tax for Barstead for the year ended 30 September 20X7 was $15 million. At 1 October 20X6 Barstead had in issue 36 million equity shares. On 1 January 20X7 Barstead made a fully subscribed rights issue of one new share for every four shares held at a price of $2.80 each. The market price of the equity shares of Barstead immediately before the issue was $3.80.

The profit after tax for Cabott for the year ended 30 September 20X7 was $15 million. At 1 October 20X6 Cabott had in issue 43.25 million equity shares and a $10 million convertible loan note which has an effective interest rate of 8%. The loan note will mature in 20X8 and will be redeemed at par or converted to equity shares on the basis of 25 shares for each $100 of loan note at the loan-note holders' option. The loan interest is tax deductible. Cabott's tax rate is 25%.

The profit after tax for Dunstan for the year ended 30 September 20X7 was $12 million. On 1 October 20X6 Dunstan had 34 million shares in issue. On 1 February 20X7 Dunstan made a market issue of 3 million shares at full price. On 1 July 20X7 Dunstan made a bonus issue of one new share for every five shares held.

301 What is the basic earnings per share for Barstead for the year ended 30 September 20X7?

    A   41.7¢

    B   35.5¢

    C   33.2¢

    D   34.7¢

302 What is the diluted earnings per share for Cabott for the year ended 30 September 20X7?

    A   34¢

    B   35¢

    C   36¢

    D   33¢

303 What is the basic earnings per share for Dunstan for the year ended 30 September 20X7?

    A   26¢

    B   32¢

    C   28¢

    D   31¢

304 Which of the three companies will have to restate the prior year comparative earnings per share figure?

Company	Comparative restated	No restatement
Barstead		
Cabott		
Dunstan		

305 **Which, if any, of the statements below regarding diluted earnings per share is/are correct?**

Statement 1: Diluted earnings per share is a forecast of a future trend in profit, showing the expected earnings in the next period to improve the relevance of information for users.

Statement 2: Diluted earnings per share acts as a warning to shareholders and shows how the current earnings per share could fall based on items currently in existence.

	Correct	Incorrect
Statement 1		
Statement 2		

The following scenario relates to questions 306–310

On 7 January 20X5, Hermione was informed that it was being sued by an employee in respect of a workplace accident that took place in October 20X4. Legal advisors advise that Hermione is certain to lose the case. They have provided the following information:

Estimated pay-out	Probability of payment occurring
$1 million	30%
$2 million	60%
$3 million	10%

Hermione has sold 100,000 machines that are covered by a warranty agreement as at 31 December 20X4. If a machine develops a major fault then the average cost to Hermione of repairing it is $100. If a machine develops a minor fault then the average cost to Hermione of repairing it is $30. It is believed that 6% of the machines under warranty will develop major faults and that 8% will develop minor faults. The time value of money can be ignored.

On 15 December 20X4, the directors of Hermione decided to restructure the business and created a detailed and formal plan. On that date, an announcement was made to the employees who were informed that they would be made redundant in March 20X5. The directors estimate that the restructuring exercise will involve the following costs:

Type of cost	$m
Redundancy payments	1.2
Staff relocation	0.8
Investment in new systems	2.0

306 **Which of the following are outlined in IAS 37 *Provisions, Contingent Liabilities and Contingent Assets* as criteria required for recognising a provision?**

(i)　An entity has a present obligation from a past event.

(ii)　It is possible that an outflow of resources will be required.

(iii)　A reliable estimate can be made of the amount of the obligation.

A　(i), (ii) and (iii)

B　(i) and (ii) only

C　(i) and (iii) only

D　(ii) and (iii) only

307 **What amount should be recognised as a provision in respect of the workplace accident claim in the year ended 31 December 20X4?**

A   Nil

B $1.8 million

C $2 million

D $3 million

308 **What amount should be recognised as a warranty provision in the year ended 31 December 20X4?**

$_____ ,000

309 **What amount should be recognised as a restructuring provision in the year ended 31 December 20X4?**

A $1.2 million

B $2.0 million

C $3.2 million

D $4.0 million

310 The following situations have arisen in the year ended 31 December 20X4:

Situation 1: A law was introduced in November 20X4 requiring Hermione to fit new smoke filters in its factory by February 20X5 at an estimated cost of $500,000. By the reporting date, Hermione had not fitted the smoke filters.

Situation 2: The management accountant of Hermione has reliably forecast an operating loss of $4 million for the year ended 31 December 20X5.

Which, if any, of the situations require a provision to be recognised?

	Provision	No provision
Situation 1		
Situation 2		

The following scenario relates to questions 311–315

Promoil's financial statements for the year ended 30 September 20X8 were authorised for issue by its directors on 6 November 20X8 and the Annual General Meeting will be held on 6 December 20X8.

On 1 October 20X7, Promoil acquired an oil platform at a cost of $30 million. The estimated cost of removing the platform at the end of the asset's life on 30 September 20Y7 will be $15 million. The present value of $1 in 10 years using Promoil's cost of capital of 8% is $0.46.

On 12 October 20X8 a fire destroyed Promoil's largest warehouse. The carrying amount of the warehouse was $10 million. Promoil expects to be able to recover $9 million from its insurers and its going concern is not in doubt.

A single class of inventory held at another warehouse was valued at its cost of $460,000 and sold for $280,000 on 10 October 20X8.

311 There is no legal obligation for Promoil to remove the oil platform, but Promoil has a published environmental policy which it has a history of honouring.

Which of the following is correct regarding Promoil's proposed accounting treatment?

A   No provision should be recorded as there is no legal obligation

B   Promoil should recognise a provision as there is a constructive obligation

C   No provision should be made but a contingent liability should be recorded

D   If Promoil make a provision, the present value of the costs will be expensed in the statement of profit or loss for the year to 30 September 20X8

312 **If Promoil makes the provision, what liability (to the nearest thousand) will be shown in its statement of financial position as at 30 September 20X8?**

$_____ ,000

313 **Select the correct category for the events listed below in relation to IAS 10 *Events After the Reporting Period*.**

	Adjusting	Non-adjusting
Fire in the warehouse		
Sale of inventory		

314 On 18 November 20X8 the government announced tax changes which have the effect of increasing Promoil's deferred tax liability by $650,000 as at 30 September 20X8.

Which of the following is correct in respect of IAS 10 *Events After the Reporting Period* regarding the tax changes?

A   This is a non-adjusting event and no disclosure is required

B   This is an adjusting event

C   This is neither an adjusting or non-adjusting event

D   This is an adjusting event and the financial statements should be reissued

315 Promoil owns the whole of the equity share capital of its subsidiary Hamlet. Hamlet's statement of financial position includes a loan of $25 million that is repayable in five years' time. $15 million of this loan is secured on Hamlet's property and the remaining $10 million is guaranteed by Promoil in the event of a default by Hamlet. It is possible that Hamlet will be unable to repay the loan, but not likely.

How should this be treated in the financial statements of Promoil?

A   A contingent liability

B   A provision

C   Not included in Promoil's financial statements

D   A reduction to property, plant and equipment

CONSOLIDATED FINANCIAL STATEMENTS

The following scenario relates to questions 316–320

On 1 April 20X4 Penfold acquired 80% of Superted's equity shares in a share for share exchange. Penfold issued 2 shares for every 5 acquired in Superted. Penfold's share price on 1 April 20X4 was $5.30. The share exchange has not yet been recorded.

Extracts from the individual financial statements of Penfold and Superted as at 30 September 20X4 are shown below.

	Penfold	Superted
	$000	$000
Property, plant and equipment	345,000	141,000
Trade receivables	32,400	38,000
Equity shares of $1 each	170,000	15,000
Other components of equity (share premium)	6,000	2,000

(i) During the year, Penfold traded with Superted, and had a payable of $6 million at 30 September 20X4. Superted's receivable balance differed from this due to a $2 million payment from Penfold not being received until October 20X4.

(ii) Penfold measures the non-controlling interest at fair value. At the date of acquisition this was $7.2 million.

(iii) Superted made a profit of $24 million for the year ended 30 September 20X4.

(iv) Penfold sold an item of plant to Superted on 1 April 20X4 for $25 million when its carrying amount was $20 million. It had a remaining useful life of 5 years at this date.

(v) Penfold also owns 30% of Arnold, an unrelated entity. Penfold are not able to appoint any members of the board of Arnold as the other 70% is held by another investor who is able to appoint all members of the board.

316 **What will be reported as other components of equity on the consolidated statement of financial position as at 30 September 20X4?**

    A $31,440,000

    B $26,640,000

    C $28,640,000

    D $33,440,000

317 **What will be reported as receivables on the consolidated statement of financial position as at 30 September 20X4?**

    $_____,000

318 **What will be reported as non-controlling interest on the consolidated statement of financial position as at 30 September 20X4?**

    A $9,700,000

    B $9,500,000

    C $7,200,000

    D $9,600,000

319 **What will be reported as property, plant and equipment on the consolidated statement of financial position as at 30 September 20X4?**

$_____,000

320 **How should the investment in Arnold be recorded in the consolidated statement of financial position of Penfold?**

A   A subsidiary

B   An associate

C   A financial instrument

D   A contingent asset

The following scenario relates to questions 321–325

On 1 October 20X4, Popper purchased 70% of the share capital of Stopper. Popper agreed to pay $6 million on 30 September 20X6. Popper has a cost of capital of 8%.

Extracts from the statements of profit or loss for the year ended 31 March 20X5 for both Popper and Stopper are shown below.

	Popper	Stopper
	$000	$000
Cost of sales	(319,200)	(176,400)
Operating expenses	(50,610)	(33,120)

The following notes are relevant:

(i)   Since acquisition, Popper sold goods to Stopper totalling $1 million per month, making a margin of 20%. At the year end, Stopper held 30% of these goods.

(ii)   On acquisition, Stopper's net assets were equal to their carrying amount, with the exception of Stopper's head office, which had a fair value of $4 million in excess of its carrying amount and a remaining life at acquisition of 20 years. All depreciation is charged to operating expenses.

(iii)   At 31 March 20X5, goodwill is impaired by $600,000. Goodwill impairment is included within operating expenses. Popper measures the non-controlling interest using the fair value method.

321 **What liability (to the nearest thousand) should be recorded in respect of the deferred consideration in Popper's consolidated statement of financial position as at 31 March 20X5?**

$_____,000

322 **What is the cost of sales figure to be included in the consolidated statement of profit or loss for the year ended 31 March 20X5?**

A $402,600,000

B $401,760,000

C $395,760,000

D $396,400,000

323 What is the operating expenses figure to be included in the consolidated statement of profit or loss for the year ended 31 March 20X5?

A $67,970,000

B $67,670,000

C $67,570,000

D $67,870,000

324 Which of the items in the scenario would affect the profit attributable to the non-controlling interest?

A   Notes (i) and (ii) only

B   Notes (i) and (iii) only

C   Notes (ii) and (iii) only

D   Notes (i), (ii) and (iii)

325 Which, if any, of the following statements about fair values is/are correct?

Statement 1: Popper must include all of Stopper's assets, liabilities and contingent liabilities at fair value in the consolidated financial statements.

Statement 2: Professional fees associated with the acquisition of Stopper can be included within the goodwill because the non-controlling interest is measured at fair value.

	Correct	**Incorrect**
Statement 1		
Statement 2		

The following scenario relates to questions 326–330

On 1 January 20X5, Prunier acquired 80% of Sheringham's two million $1 ordinary shares. At this date, Sheringham had retained earnings of $4 million and a revaluation surplus of $2 million. Prunier had retained earnings of $10 million and a revaluation surplus of $5 million.

The fair value of Sheringham's net assets at acquisition were equal to their carrying amounts with the exception of Sheringham's property which had a fair value of $800,000 in excess of its carrying amount and a remaining life of 20 years.

At 31 December 20X5, Prunier and Sheringham both revalued their assets. Prunier's assets increased by a further $2 million while Sheringham's increased by $500,000. At this date, Prunier's retained earnings were $11 million and Sheringham's were $3.5 million.

326 What will the consolidated retained earnings be at 31 December 20X5?

A $11,432,000

B $10,560,000

C $11,368,000

D $10,568,000

327 What will be the other comprehensive income attributable to the parent for the year ended 31 December 20X5?

$_____ ,000

328 Identify whether or not the following items should be recognised as assets in the consolidated financial statements of Prunier.

	Recognised	Not to be recognised
Prunier's brand name, which was internally generated so not shown in Prunier's financial statements but has a fair value of $3 million		
A research project in progress, which was one of the main reasons Prunier purchased Sheringham and has a fair value of $2 million		
An intangible asset related to an encryption process which has now been deemed illegal. This is included within intangibles at $1.5 million		

329 Prunier has also owned 30% of Anderson for many years, and uses equity accounting to account for the investment. During the year Prunier sold $3 million of goods to Anderson at a mark-up of 20%. Anderson has a quarter of the goods left in inventory at the year end.

What is the value of the unrealised profit adjustment as at 31 December 20X5?

A $150,000

B $37,500

C $125,000

D $45,000

330 On 31 December 20X9, Prunier disposed of its entire holding of Sheringham for $9 million. At this date, the remaining goodwill was $1 million. The fair value of the non-controlling interest was $2.5 million and the fair value of the net assets (including the fair value adjustment) was $10.6 million.

What is the profit/loss on the disposal of Sheringham to be shown in the consolidated financial statements of Prunier?

A $100,000 loss on disposal

B $1,900,000 gain on disposal

C $5,100,000 loss on disposal

D $2,020,000 gain on disposal

INTERPRETATION OF FINANCIAL STATEMENTS

The following scenario relates to questions 331–335

LOP is looking to expand overseas by acquiring a new subsidiary.

Two geographical areas have been targeted, Frontland and Sideland.

Entity A operates in Frontland and entity B operates in Sideland. Both entities are listed on their local exchanges.

Figures for entities A, B and LOP are provided below for the last trading period.

	A	B	LOP
Revenue	$160m	$300m	$500m
Gross profit margin	26%	17%	28%
Profit from operations margin	9%	11%	16%
Gearing	65%	30%	38%
Average rate of interest expensed in profit or loss	4%	9%	8%
Price/Earnings (P/E) ratio	11.6	15.9	16.3

331 **Which of the following statements is a realistic conclusion that could be drawn from the above information?**

A   A appears to be benefiting from economies of scale.

B   B has lower operating expenses than A.

C   A has attracted a lower rate of interest on its borrowings than B because it's gearing level would suggest that is a lower risk to lenders than B.

D   Acquisition of either entity would lead to an improvement in LOP's gross margin due to the increased revenue that would be achieved.

332 **Which TWO of the following statements are true, based on the information provided?**

A   A would be a riskier investment than B because it has higher gearing.

B   A would give LOP greater benefit in terms of additional borrowing capacity.

C   The market is more confident about the future performance of B than LOP.

D   The market is more confident about the future performance of LOP than A or B.

E   LOP's P/E ratio would definitely fall if it acquired either A or B.

333 **Which of the following statements concerning the use of ratio analysis to make a decision about investing in A or B is FALSE?**

A   A and B may use different accounting standards when preparing their financial statements and this would reduce the comparability of their profit margins.

B   A and B may target different types of customer, meaning that comparison between the two is difficult.

C   A and B may apply different accounting policies, such as cost model v revaluation model for property, plant and equipment. This would reduce comparability of their gearing ratios.

D   A and B are listed on different stock exchanges which reduces comparability of their P/E ratios.

334 If LOP acquired B, it has assessed that combining the two companies would lead to an overall saving in cost of sales of $5 million.

If this was taken into account, what would be the gross margin of LOP combined with B to one decimal place?

_____%

335 Your assistant has raised concerns about B, having heard that they may have treated lease payments as operating expenses instead of capitalising the right-of-use assets as required by IFRS 16 *Leases*.

Which, if any, of the following statements is/are true in relation to this?

Statement 1: If B has incorrectly treated the leases, gearing will be overstated.

Statement 2: If B has incorrectly treated the leases, the average rate of interest calculated could be inaccurate.

	Correct	Incorrect
Statement 1		
Statement 2		

The following scenario relates to questions 336–340

Key figures from Franck's financial statements for the year ended 30 September 20X2 are shown below.

	$000
Revenue	9,400
Profit from operations	1,500
Share capital	15,000
Retained earnings	3,000
Loans	2,000

Franck has operated in the computer software industry for many years, gaining a reputation for steady growth. It is interested in acquiring Duik, which has recently been put up for sale. Extracts from Duik's financial statements can be seen below.

	$000
Revenue	1,200
Loss from operations	(600)
Share capital	24,000
Retained losses	(1,200)
Loans	4,000

336 **Calculate Franck's return on capital employed (based on profit from operations) without the acquisition of Duik to one decimal place.**

_____%

337 **What is the combined operating margin if Franck and Duik are combined?**

A   9.6%

B   19.8%

C   14.2%

D   8.5%

338 **Which, if any, of the following statements is/are correct?**

Statement 1: If Duik is acquired, gearing will increase.

Statement 2: If Duik is acquired, return on capital employed will decrease.

	Correct	Incorrect
Statement 1		
Statement 2		

339 **Which of the following is NOT a factor to consider in respect of Duik being a subsidiary of another entity?**

A   Sales or purchases between the parent and Duik may not be at market rates

B   Duik may get the benefit of shared assets with the parent

C   Duik's individual financial statements may contain errors

D   Loans made from Duik's parent may carry lower interest than market rates

340 **What other information is NOT likely to be available to Franck before entering into negotiations for the acquisition of Duik?**

A   A breakdown of dividends paid by Duik historically

B   Duik's statement of cash flows

C   A breakdown of Duik's upcoming projects which are in progress

D   The directors' report outlining the performance for the year

STATEMENT OF CASH FLOWS

The following scenario relates to questions 341–345

The assistant accountant of Cooper has started work on the statement of cash flows for the year ended 31 December 20X8, completing a draft of the cash generated from operations as shown below.

	$000
Profit from operations	3,500
Depreciation	4,600
Release of government grant	1,400
Profit on disposal of property	(3,700)
Increase in inventories	(400)
Decrease in trade and other receivables	(300)
Increase in trade and other payables	900
	————
Cash generated from operations	**13,400**
	————

In addition to this, the assistant has seen that the balance of property was $39.5 million at 1 January 20X8 and $29 million at 31 December 20X8. There were no additions of property in the year.

There was also a deferred income balance relating to government grants of $6 million at 1 January 20X8. The closing deferred income balance was $8 million.

341 **What method has Cooper's assistant accountant used to calculate the cash generated from operations?**

   A   Classification by function

   B   Classification by nature

   C   Indirect method

   D   Direct method

342 **In relation to the calculation of cash generated from operations, select the TWO cells which contain errors made by the assistant.**

	$000
Profit from operations	3,500
Depreciation	4,600
Release of government grant	1,400
Profit on disposal of property	(3,700)
Increase in inventories	(400)
Decrease in trade and other receivables	(300)
Increase in trade and other payables	900
Cash generated from operations	6,000

343 How much would be recorded in Cooper's statement of cash flows in relation to the sale of property?

A $9,600,000

B $2,200,000

C $3,700,000

D $5,900,000

344 What will be recorded as the receipt of government grants in the year?

$_____ ,000

345 Cooper's assistant accountant has been studying statements of cash flows and is unsure whether the information contained in the study material is true.

Which, if any, of the following statements is/are true?

Statement 1: Intangible assets will have no impact on the statement of cash flow as they have no physical substance.

Statement 2: A rights issue of shares will increase the cash flows from financing activities.

A   Statement 1 is correct

B   Statement 2 is correct

C   Both statements are correct

D   Neither statement is correct

The following scenario relates to questions 346–350

Extracts from Depay's financial statements for the year ended 30 September 20X2 are shown below.

Statement of profit or loss extract:	$000
Finance costs	(60)
Profit before tax	142
Income tax expense	(57)
Profit for the year	85

Statement of financial position extract:	20X2	20X1
	$000	$000
Retained earnings	900	940
5% loan notes	515	500
Deferred tax liability	150	125
Tax payable	30	40
Lease liabilities	300	310

The following information is relevant:

(i)   Depay disposed of some land during the year, which had a remaining revaluation surplus at disposal of $20,000.

(ii) $40,000 of the finance costs relate to the loan notes which are repayable at a premium, making the effective rate of interest 8%. The remaining interest relates to the lease liabilities.

(iii)   During the year, Depay received a dividend from a subsidiary.

(iv)   Depay acquired $70,000 of new assets under lease agreements during the year. Depay makes annual payments under leases on 30 September each year.

346   **What will be recorded in Depay's statement of cash flows under dividends paid?**

    A $145,000

    B $105,000

    C $40,000

    D $125,000

347   **What will be recorded in Depay's statement of cash flows under interest paid?**

    A $20,000

    B $25,000

    C $45,000

    D $60,000

348 **What will be recorded in Depay's statement of cash flows under tax paid?**

$_____

349 **Where should the dividend received be shown in Depay's statement of cash flows?**

A   Operating activities

B   Investing activities

C   Financing activities

D   It should not be recorded

350 **How much should be shown within financing activities in respect of lease liabilities repaid?**

$_____

Section 3

CONSTRUCTED RESPONSE QUESTIONS – SECTION C

Please note that the following icons will be used in this section

🖳 = word processing
▦ = spreadsheet

PREPARATION OF SINGLE ENTITY FINANCIAL STATEMENTS

351 CANDEL *Walk in the footsteps of a top tutor*

The following trial balance relates to Candel at 30 September 20X8:

	$000	$000
Leasehold property – at valuation 1 October 20X7 (note (i))	50,000	
Plant and equipment – at cost (note (i))	76,600	
Plant and equipment – accumulated depreciation at 1 October 20X7		24,600
Capitalised development expenditure – at 1 October 20X7 (note (ii))	20,000	
Development expenditure – accumulated amortisation at 1 October 20X7		6,000
Closing inventory at 30 September 20X8	20,000	
Trade receivables	43,100	
Bank		1,300
Trade payables and provisions (note (iii))		23,800
Draft profit before tax		59,100
Preference dividend paid (note (iv))	800	
Research and development costs (note (ii))	8,600	
Equity shares of 25 cents each		50,000
8% redeemable preference shares of $1 each (note (iv))		20,000
Retained earnings at 1 October 20X7		18,500
Deferred tax (note (v))		5,800
Leasehold property revaluation surplus at 1 October 20X7		10,000
	219,100	219,100

The following notes are relevant:

(i) **Non-current assets – tangible:**

The leasehold property had a remaining life of 20 years at 1 October 20X7. Candel's policy is to revalue its property at each year-end and at 30 September 20X8 it was valued at $43 million. Ignore deferred tax on the revaluation.

On 1 October 20X7 an item of plant was disposed of for $2.5 million cash. The proceeds have been treated as sales revenue by Candel. The plant is still included in the above trial balance figures at its cost of $8 million and accumulated depreciation of $4 million (to the date of disposal).

All plant is depreciated at 20% per annum using the reducing balance method.

Depreciation and amortisation of all non-current assets is charged to cost of sales.

(ii) **Non-current assets – intangible:**

In addition to the capitalised development expenditure of $20 million, further research and development costs were incurred on a new project which commenced on 1 October 20X7. The research stage of the new project lasted until 31 December 20X7 and incurred $1.4 million of costs. From that date the project incurred development costs of $800,000 per month. On 1 April 20X8 the directors became confident that the project would be successful and yield a profit well in excess of its costs. The project is still in development at 30 September 20X8.

Capitalised development expenditure is amortised at 20% per annum using the straight-line method. All expensed research and development is charged to cost of sales.

(iii) Candel is being sued by a customer for $2 million for breach of contract over a cancelled order. Candel has obtained legal opinion that there is a 20% chance that Candel will lose the case. Accordingly Candel has provided $400,000 ($2 million × 20%) included in administrative expenses in respect of the claim. The unrecoverable legal costs of defending the action are estimated at $100,000. These have not been provided for as the legal action will not go to court until next year.

(iv) The preference shares were issued on 1 April 20X8 at par. They are redeemable at a large premium which gives them an effective finance cost of 12% per annum. The finance assistant in Candel was uncertain how to deal with these. The dividend paid in the trial balance represents the debit side of the cash payment made during the year.

(v) The directors have estimated the provision for income tax for the year ended 30 September 20X8 at $11.4 million. The required deferred tax provision at 30 September 20X8 is $6 million.

Required:

(a) **Calculate the revised profit for the year, taking into account the items from notes (i) to (v).** **(8 marks)**

(b) **Prepare the statement of financial position as at 30 September 20X8.**

(12 marks)

Notes to the financial statements and a statement of changes in equity are not required.

(Total: 20 marks) ▦

352 PRICEWELL

 **Question debrief**

The following trial balance relates to Pricewell at 31 March 20X9:

	$000	$000
Leasehold property – at valuation 31 March 20X8 (note (i))	25,200	
Plant and equipment (owned) – at cost (note (i))	46,800	
Right-of-use assets – at cost (note (i))	20,000	
Accumulated depreciation at 31 March 20X8:		
Owned plant and equipment		12,800
Right-of-use plant		5,000
Lease payment (paid on 31 March 20X9) (note (i))	6,000	
Lease liability at 1 April 20X8 (note (i))		15,600
Contract with customer (note (ii))	14,300	
Inventory at 31 March 20X9	28,200	
Trade receivables	33,100	
Bank	5,500	
Trade payables		33,400
Revenue (note (iii))		310,000
Cost of sales (note (iii))	234,500	
Distribution costs	19,500	
Administrative expenses	27,500	
Equity dividend paid	8,000	
Equity shares of 50 cents each		40,000
Retained earnings at 31 March 20X8		44,100
Current tax (note (iv))	700	
Deferred tax (note (iv))		8,400
	469,300	469,300

The following notes are relevant:

(i) **Non-current assets:**

The 15 year leasehold property was acquired on 1 April 20X7 at a cost of $30 million. The accounting policy is to revalue the property at fair value at each year end. The valuation in the trial balance of $25.2 million as at 31 March 20X8 led to an impairment charge of $2.8 million which was reported in the statement of profit or loss and other comprehensive income in the year ended 31 March 20X8. At 31 March 20X9 the property was valued at $24.9 million.

Owned plant is depreciated at 25% per annum using the reducing balance method.

The right-of-use plant was acquired on 1 April 20X7. The rentals are $6 million per annum for four years payable in arrears on 31 March each year. The interest rate implicit in the lease is 8% per annum. Right-of-use plant is depreciated over the lease period.

No depreciation has yet been charged on any non-current assets for the year ended 31 March 20X9. All depreciation is charged to cost of sales.

(ii)   On 1 October 20X8 Pricewell entered into a contract to construct a bridge over a river. The performance obligation will be satisfied over time. The agreed price of the bridge is $50 million and construction was expected to be completed on 30 September 20Y0. The $14.3 million in the trial balance is:

	$000
Materials, labour and overheads	12,000
Specialist plant acquired 1 October 20X8	8,000
Payment from customer	(5,700)
	14,300

The sales value of the work done at 31 March 20X9 has been agreed at $22 million and the estimated cost to complete (excluding plant depreciation) is $10 million. The specialist plant will have no residual value at the end of the contract and should be depreciated on a monthly basis. Pricewell recognises progress towards satisfaction of the performance obligation on the outputs basis as determined by the agreed work to date compared to the total contract price.

(iii)   Pricewell's revenue includes $8 million for goods it sold acting as an agent for Trilby. Pricewell earned a commission of 20% on these sales and remitted the difference of $6.4 million (included in cost of sales) to Trilby.

(iv)   The directors have estimated the provision for income tax for the year ended 31 March 20X9 at $4.5 million. The required deferred tax provision at 31 March 20X9 is $5.6 million. All adjustments to deferred tax should be taken to the statement of profit or loss. The balance of current tax in the trial balance represents the under/over provision of the income tax liability for the year ended 31 March 20X8.

Required:

(a)   Prepare the statement of profit or loss and other comprehensive income for the year ended 31 March 20X9.   **(10 marks)**

(b)   Prepare the statement of financial position as at 31 March 20X9.   **(10 marks)**

Note: A statement of changes in equity and notes to the financial statements are not required.

(Total: 20 marks) ⊞

 Calculate your allowed time, allocate the time to the separate parts

353 HIGHWOOD

The following trial balance relates to Highwood at 31 March 20X1:

	$000	$000
Equity shares of 50 cents each		6,000
Retained earnings at 1 April 20X0		1,400
8% convertible loan note (note (i))		30,000
Property – at cost (land element $25m (note (ii)))	75,000	
Accumulated depreciation – 1 April 20X0 – building		10,000
Current tax (note (iii))		800
Deferred tax (note (iii))		2,600
Inventory at 31 March 20X1	36,000	
Trade receivables (note (iv))	47,100	
Bank		11,500
Trade payables		24,500
Revenue		339,650
Cost of sales	207,750	
Distribution costs	27,500	
Administrative expenses (note (iv))	30,700	
Loan interest paid (note (i))	2,400	
	426,450	426,450

The following notes are relevant:

(i)   The 8% $30 million convertible loan note was issued on 1 April 20X0 at par. Interest is payable in arrears on 31 March each year. The loan note is redeemable at par on 31 March 20X3 or convertible into equity shares at the option of the loan note holders on the basis of 30 equity shares for each $100 of loan note. Highwood's finance director has calculated that to issue an equivalent loan note without the conversion rights it would have to pay an interest rate of 10% per annum to attract investors.

Applicable discount rates are:

	8%	10%
End of year 1	0.93	0.91
End of year 2	0.86	0.83
End of year 3	0.79	0.75

(ii)   On 1 April 20X0 Highwood decided to revalue its property. The market value of the property on this date was $80 million, of which $30 million related to the land. At this date the remaining estimated life of the property was 20 years. Highwood does not make a transfer to retained earnings in respect of excess depreciation on the revaluation of its assets. All depreciation is charged to cost of sales.

(iii) Current tax represents the under/over provision of the tax liability for the year ended 31 March 20X0. The required provision for income tax for the year ended 31 March 20X1 is $19.4 million. The difference between the carrying amounts of the assets of Highwood (including the property revaluation in note (ii) above) and their (lower) tax base at 31 March 20X1 is $27 million. Highwood's rate of income tax is 25%.

(iv) On 31 March 20X1 Highwood factored (sold) trade receivables with a book value of $10 million to Easyfinance. Highwood received an immediate payment of $8.7 million and will pay Easyfinance 2% per month on any uncollected balances. Any of the factored receivables outstanding after six months will be refunded to Easyfinance. Highwood has derecognised the receivables in full and charged $1.3 million to administrative expenses. If Highwood had not factored these receivables it would have made an allowance of $600,000 against them.

Required:

(a) **Prepare the statement of profit or loss and other comprehensive income for Highwood for the year ended 31 March 20X1.** **(8 marks)**

(b) **Prepare the statement of financial position as at 31 March 20X1.** **(12 marks)**

Note: **your answers and workings should be presented to the nearest $000.**

(Total: 20 marks) ⊞

354 KEYSTONE

The following trial balance relates to Keystone at 30 September 20X1:

	$000	$000
Revenue		377,600
Material purchases (note (i))	64,000	
Production labour (note (i))	124,000	
Factory overheads (note (i))	80,000	
Distribution costs	14,200	
Administrative expenses (note (ii))	46,400	
Finance costs	350	
Investment income		800
Property – at cost (note (i))	50,000	
Plant and equipment – at cost (note (i))	44,500	
Accumulated amortisation/depreciation at 1 October 20X0		
– property		10,000
– plant and equipment		14,500
Inventory at 1 October 20X0	46,700	
Trade receivables	31,150	
Trade payables		27,800
Bank		2,300
Equity shares of 20 cents each		50,000
Retained earnings at 1 October 20X0		15,600
Deferred tax (note (iv))		2,700
	———	———
	501,300	501,300
	———	———

The following notes are relevant:

(i)   During the year Keystone manufactured an item of plant for its own use. The direct materials and labour were $3 million and $4 million respectively. Production overheads are 75% of direct labour cost and Keystone determines the final selling price for goods by adding a mark-up on total cost of 40%. These manufacturing costs are included in the relevant expense items in the trial balance. The plant was completed and put into immediate use on 1 April 20X1.

All plant and equipment is depreciated at 20% per annum using the reducing balance method with time apportionment in the year of acquisition.

The directors decided to revalue the property in line with recent increases in market values. On 1 October 20X0 an independent surveyor valued the property at $48 million, which the directors have accepted. The property was being amortised over an original life of 20 years which has not changed. Keystone does not make a transfer to retained earnings in respect of excess amortisation. The revaluation gain will create a deferred tax liability (see note (iv)).

All depreciation and amortisation is charged to cost of sales. No depreciation or amortisation has yet been charged on any non-current asset for the year ended 30 September 20X1.

(ii)   On 15 August 20X1, Keystone's share price stood at $2.40 per share. On this date Keystone paid a dividend (included in administrative expenses) that was calculated to give a dividend yield of 4%.

(iii) The inventory at 30 September 20X1 was valued at $56.6 million.

(iv)   A provision for income tax for the year ended 30 September 20X1 of $24.3 million is required. At 30 September 20X1, the tax base of Keystone's net assets was $15 million less than their carrying amounts. This excludes the effects of the revaluation of the leased property. The income tax rate of Keystone is 30%.

Required:

(a) Prepare the statement of profit or loss and other comprehensive income for Keystone for the year ended 30 September 20X1.   **(12 marks)**

(b) Prepare the statement of financial position for Keystone as at 30 September 20X1.
                                                                                    (8 marks)

A statement of changes in equity is not required.

                                                                       (Total: 20 marks) ▦

355 FRESCO

The following trial balance **extract** relates to Fresco at 31 March 20X2:

	$000	$000
Equity shares of 50 cents each (note (i))		45,000
Share premium (note (i))		5,000
Retained earnings at 1 April 20X1		5,100
Equity financial asset investments (note (v))	6,000	
Leased property (12 years) – at cost (note (ii))	48,000	
Plant and equipment – at cost (note (ii))	47,500	
Accumulated amortisation of leased property at 1 April 20X1		16,000
Accumulated depreciation of plant and equipment at 1 April 20X1		33,500
Deferred tax (note (iv))		3,200
Revenue		350,000
Cost of sales	298,700	
Lease payments (note (ii))	8,000	
Distribution costs	16,100	
Administrative expenses	26,900	
Bank interest	300	
Current tax (note (iv))	800	
Suspense account (note (i))		13,500

The following notes are relevant:

(i) The suspense account represents the corresponding credit for cash received for a fully subscribed rights issue of equity shares made on 1 January 20X2. The terms of the share issue were one new share for every five held at a price of 75 cents each.

(ii) Non-current assets:

To reflect a marked increase in property prices, Fresco decided to revalue its leased property on 1 April 20X1. The directors accepted the report of an independent surveyor who valued the leased property at $36 million on that date. Fresco has not yet recorded the revaluation. The remaining life of the leased property is eight years at the date of the revaluation. Fresco makes an annual transfer to retained profits to reflect the realisation of the revaluation surplus. In Fresco's tax jurisdiction the revaluation does not give rise to a deferred tax liability.

On 1 April 20X1, Fresco acquired an item of plant under a lease agreement that had an implicit finance cost of 10% per annum. The lease payments in the trial balance represent an initial deposit of $2 million paid on 1 April 20X1 and the first annual rental of $6 million paid on 31 March 20X2. The lease agreement requires further annual payments of $6 million on 31 March each year for the next four years. The present value of the lease payments, excluding the initial deposit, was $23 million.

Plant and equipment (other than the leased plant) is depreciated at 20% per annum using the reducing balance method.

No depreciation or amortisation has yet been charged on any non-current asset for the year ended 31 March 20X2. Depreciation and amortisation are charged to cost of sales.

(iii)   In March 20X2, Fresco's internal audit department discovered a fraud committed by the credit controller who did not return from a foreign business trip. The outcome of the fraud is that $4 million of the trade receivables have been stolen by the credit controller and are not recoverable. Of this amount, $1 million relates to the year ended 31 March 20X1 and the remainder to the current year. Fresco is not insured against this fraud.

(iv)   Fresco's income tax calculation for the year ended 31 March 20X2 shows a tax refund of $2.4 million. The balance on current tax in the trial balance represents the under/over provision of the tax liability for the year ended 31 March 20X1. At 31 March 20X2, Fresco had taxable temporary differences of $12 million requiring a deferred tax liability. The income tax rate of Fresco is 25%.

(v)   The investments had a fair value of $7.2 million as at 31 March 20X2. There were no acquisitions or disposals of these investments during the year ended 31 March 20X2.

Required:

(a)   **Prepare the statement of profit or loss and other comprehensive income for Fresco for the year ended 31 March 20X2.**   **(13 marks)**

(b)   **Prepare the statement of changes in equity for Fresco for the year ended 31 March 20X2.**   **(7 marks)**

(Total: 20 marks) ▦

356   QUINCY

The following trial balance relates to Quincy as at 30 September 20X2:

	$000	$000
Revenue (note (i))		213,500
Cost of sales	136,800	
Distribution costs	12,500	
Administrative expenses (note (ii))	19,000	
Loan note interest (note (ii))	1,500	
Dividend paid	19,200	
Investment income		400
Equity shares of 25 cents each		60,000
6% loan note (note (ii))		25,000
Retained earnings at 1 October 20X1		6,500
Plant and equipment at cost (note (iii))	83,700	
Accumulated depreciation at 1 October 20X1: plant and equipment		33,700
Equity financial asset investments (note (iv))	17,000	
Inventory at 30 September 20X2	24,800	
Trade receivables	28,500	
Bank	2,900	
Current tax (note (v))	1,100	
Deferred tax (note (v))		1,200
Trade payables		6,700
	———	———
	347,000	347,000
	———	———

The following notes are relevant:

(i)   On 1 October 20X1, Quincy sold one of its products for $10 million (included in revenue in the trial balance). As part of the sale agreement, Quincy is committed to the ongoing servicing of this product until 30 September 20X4 (i.e. three years from the date of sale). The value of this service has been included in the selling price of $10 million. The estimated cost to Quincy of the servicing is $600,000 per annum and Quincy's normal gross profit margin on this type of servicing is 25%. The service performance obligation will be satisfied over time. Ignore discounting.

(ii)   Quincy issued a $25 million 6% loan note on 1 October 20X1. Issue costs were $1 million and these have been charged to administrative expenses. The loan will be redeemed on 30 September 20X4 at a premium which gives an effective interest rate on the loan of 8%.

(iii)   Plant and equipment is depreciated at 15% per annum using the reducing balance method.

No depreciation has yet been charged for the year ended 30 September 20X2. All depreciation is charged to cost of sales.

(iv)   The investments had a fair value of $15.7 million as at 30 September 20X2. There were no acquisitions or disposals of these investments during the year ended 30 September 20X2.

(v)   The balance on current tax represents the under/over provision of the tax liability for the year ended 30 September 20X1. A provision for income tax for the year ended 30 September 20X2 of $7.4 million is required. At 30 September 20X2, Quincy had taxable temporary differences of $5 million, requiring a provision for deferred tax. Any deferred tax adjustment should be reported in the statement of profit or loss. The income tax rate of Quincy is 20%.

Required:

(a)   **Prepare the statement of profit or loss and other comprehensive income for Quincy for the year ended 30 September 20X2.**   **(10 marks)**

(b)   **Prepare the statement of financial position for Quincy as at 30 September 20X2.**

(10 marks)

Notes to the financial statements are not required.

(Total: 20 marks) ⊞

357 ATLAS

The following trial balance relates to Atlas at 31 March 20X3:

	$000	$000
Equity shares of 50 cents each		50,000
Retained earnings at 1 April 20X2		11,200
Land and buildings – at cost (land $10 million) (note (ii))	60,000	
Plant and equipment – at cost (note (ii))	94,500	
Accumulated depreciation at 1 April 20X2: – buildings		20,000
– plant and equipment		24,500
Inventory at 31 March 20X3	43,700	
Trade receivables	42,200	
Bank		6,800
Deferred tax (note (iv))		6,200
Trade payables		35,100
Revenue (note (i))		550,000
Cost of sales	411,500	
Distribution costs	21,500	
Administrative expenses	30,900	
Bank interest	700	
Current tax (note (iv))		1,200
	————	————
	705,000	705,000
	————	————

The following notes are relevant:

(i)   Revenue includes the sale of $10 million of maturing inventory made to Xpede on 1 October 20X2. The cost of the goods at the date of sale was $7 million and Atlas has an option to repurchase these goods at any time within three years of the sale at a price of $10 million plus accrued interest from the date of sale at 10% per annum. At 31 March 20X3 the option had not been exercised, but it is highly likely that it will be before the date it lapses.

(ii)   Non-current assets:

On 1 October 20X2, Atlas terminated the production of one of its product lines. From this date, the plant used to manufacture the product has been actively marketed at an advertised price of $4.2 million which is considered realistic. It is included in the trial balance at a cost of $9 million with accumulated depreciation (at 1 April 20X2) of $5 million.

On 1 April 20X2, the directors of Atlas decided that the financial statements would show an improved position if the land and buildings were revalued to market value. At that date, an independent valuer valued the land at $12 million and the buildings at $35 million and these valuations were accepted by the directors. The remaining life of the buildings at that date was 14 years. Atlas does not make a transfer to retained earnings for excess depreciation. Ignore deferred tax on the revaluation surplus.

Plant and equipment is depreciated at 20% per annum using the reducing balance method and time apportioned as appropriate.

All depreciation is charged to cost of sales, but none has yet been charged on any non-current asset for the year ended 31 March 20X3.

(iii) At 31 March 20X3, a provision is required for directors' bonuses equal to 1% of revenue for the year.

(iv) Atlas estimates that an income tax provision of $27.2 million is required for the year ended 31 March 20X3 and at that date the liability to deferred tax is $9.4 million. The movement on deferred tax should be taken to profit or loss. The balance on current tax in the trial balance represents the under/over provision of the tax liability for the year ended 31 March 20X2.

Required:

(i)   Prepare the statement of profit or loss and other comprehensive income for Atlas for the year ended 31 March 20X3.   (9 marks)

(ii) Prepare the statement of financial position of Atlas as at 31 March 20X3.

(11 marks)

Notes to the financial statements and a statement of changes in equity are not required.

(Total: 20 marks) ▦

358 MOBY

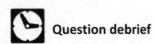 **Question debrief**

After preparing a draft statement of profit or loss for the year ended 30 September 20X4 and adding the year's profit (before any adjustments required by notes (i) to (v) below) to retained earnings, the summarised trial balance of Moby as 30 September 20X3 is:

	$000	$000
Contract to construct asset (note (i))	4,000	
Lease rental paid on 30 September 20X3 (note (ii))	9,200	
Land ($12 million) and building ($48 million) at cost (note (ii))	60,000	
Leased plant at initial carrying amount (note (ii))	35,000	
Accumulated depreciation at 1 October 20X2:		
building		10,000
leased plant		7,000
Inventory at 30 September 20X3	56,600	
Trade receivables	38,500	
Bank		7,300
Insurance provision (note (iii))		150
Deferred tax (note (iv))		8,000
Lease liability at 1 October 20X2 (note (ii))		29,300
Trade payables		21,300
Equity shares of $1 each		27,000
Loan note (note (v))		40,000
Retained earnings at 30 September 20X3		53,250
	———	———
	203,300	203,300
	———	———

The following notes are relevant:

(i)   During the year, Moby entered into a contract to construct an asset for a customer. The performance obligation is satisfied over time. The balance in the trial balance represents:

Cost incurred to date	$14 million
Value of contract billed (work certified) and cash received	$10 million

The contract commenced on 1 October 20X2 and is for a fixed price of $25 million. The costs to complete the contract at 30 September 20X3 are estimated at $6 million. Moby's policy is to measure progress based on the work certified as a percentage of the contract price.

(ii)   Non-current assets:

Moby decided to revalue its land and building, for the first time, on 1 October 20X2. A qualified valuer determined the relevant revalued amounts to be $16 million for the land and $38.4 million for the building. The building's remaining life at the date of the revaluation was 16 years. This revaluation has not yet been reflected in the trial balance figures. Moby does not make a transfer from the revaluation surplus to retained earnings in respect of the realisation of the revaluation surplus. Deferred tax is applicable to the revaluation surplus at 25%.

The leased plant was acquired on 1 October 20X1 under a five-year lease which has an implicit interest rate of 10% per annum. The rentals are $9.2 million per annum payable on 30 September each year.

No depreciation has yet been charged on any non-current asset for the year ended 30 September 20X3. All depreciation is charged to cost of sales.

(iii)   On 1 October 20X2, Moby received a renewal quote of $400,000 from their property insurer. The directors were surprised at how much it had increased and believed it would be less expensive to 'self-insure'. Accordingly, they charged $400,000 to operating expenses and credited the same amount to the insurance provision. During the year expenses of $250,000 were incurred, relating to previously insured property damage which Moby has debited to the provision.

(iv)   A provision for income tax for the year ended 30 September 20X3 of $3.4 million is required. At 30 September 20X3, the tax base of Moby's net assets was $24 million less than their carrying amounts. This does not include the effect of the revaluation in note (ii) above. The income tax rate of Moby is 25%.

(v)   The $40 million loan note was issued at par on 1 October 20X2. No interest will be paid on the loan. However, it will be redeemed on 30 September 20X5 for $53,240,000 which gives an effective finance cost of 10% per annum.

Required:

(a)   Prepare a schedule of adjustments required to the retained earnings of Moby as at 30 September 20X3 as a result of the information in notes (i) to (v) above.

(8 marks)

(b)   Prepare the statement of financial position for Moby as at 30 September 20X3.

(12 marks)

Note: A statement of changes in equity and notes to the financial statements are not required.

(Total: 20 marks) ▦

359 XTOL

The following trial balance relates to Xtol at 31 March 20X4:

	$000	$000
Revenue		490,000
Cost of sales	290,600	
Operating costs	70,300	
Loan note interest (note (ii))	2,500	
Bank interest	900	
Plant and equipment at cost (note (i))	155,500	
Accumulated depreciation at 1 April 20X3:		
plant and equipment		43,500
Inventory at 31 March 20X4	96,000	
Trade receivables	103,000	
Trade payables		32,200
Bank		5,500
Equity shares of $1 each (note (iv))		66,000
Share premium (note (iv))		15,000
Retained earnings at 1 April 20X3		15,200
5% convertible loan note (note (ii))		50,000
Current tax (note (iii))	3,200	
Deferred tax (note (iii))		4,600
	722,000	722,000

The following notes are relevant:

(i)   Plant and equipment is depreciated at 12½% per annum on the reducing balance basis. All amortisation/depreciation of non-current assets is charged to cost of sales.

(ii)   On 1 April 20X3, Xtol issued a 5% $50 million convertible loan note at par. Interest is payable annually in arrears on 31 March each year. The loan note is redeemable at par or convertible into equity shares at the option of the loan note holders on 31 March 20X6. The interest on an equivalent loan note without the conversion rights would be 8% per annum.

The present values of $1 receivable at the end of each year, based on discount rates of 5% and 8%, are:

	5%	8%
End of year 1	0.95	0.93
2	0.91	0.86
3	0.86	0.79

(iii)   The balance on current tax represents the under/over provision of the tax liability for the year ended 31 March 20X3. A provision of $28 million is required for current tax for the year ended 31 March 20X4 and at this date the deferred tax liability was assessed at $8.3 million.

(iv)   The equity shares and share premium balances in the trial balance above include a fully subscribed 1 for 5 rights issue at $1.60 per share which was made by Xtol on 1 October 20X3. The market value of Xtol's shares was $2.50 on 1 October 20X3.

Required:

(a)   **Prepare Xtol's statement of profit or loss for the year ended 31 March 20X4.**

(b)   **Prepare the statement of financial position for Xtol as at 31 March 20X4.**

(c)   **Calculate the basic earnings per share of Xtol for the year ended 31 March 20X4.**

Note: Answers and workings (for parts (a) to (b)) should be presented to the nearest $1,000. A statement of changes in equity is not required.

The following mark allocation is provided as guidance for this question:

(a)   **6 marks**

(b)   **9 marks**

(c)   **5 marks**

(Total: 20 marks) ⊞

360   DUNE

The following trial balance relates to Dune at 31 March 20X4:

	$000	$000
Equity shares of $1 each		40,000
Other components of equity		20,000
5% loan note (note (i))		20,000
Retained earnings at 1 April 20X3		38,400
Leasehold (15 years) property – at cost (note (ii))	45,000	
Plant and equipment – at cost (note (ii))	67,500	
Accumulated depreciation – 1 April 20X3 – leasehold property		6,000
– plant and equipment		23,500
Investments at fair value through profit or loss (note (iii))	26,500	
Inventory at 31 March 20X4	48,000	
Trade receivables	40,700	
Bank	15,500	
Deferred tax (note (iv))		6,000
Trade payables		52,000
Revenue		400,000
Cost of sales	294,000	
Distribution costs	26,400	
Administrative expenses (note (i))	34,200	
Dividend paid	10,000	
Loan note interest paid (six months)	500	
Bank interest	200	
Investment income		1,200
Current tax (note (iv))		1,400
	———	———
	608,500	608,500
	———	———

The following notes are relevant:

(i) The 5% loan note was issued on 1 April 20X3 at its nominal (face) value of $20 million. The direct costs of the issue were $500,000 and these have been charged to administrative expenses. The loan note will be redeemed on 31 March 20X6 at a substantial premium. The effective finance cost of the loan note is 10% per annum.

(ii) Non-current assets:

In order to fund a new project, on 1 October 20X3 Dune decided to sell its leasehold property. From that date it commenced a short-term rental of an equivalent property. The leasehold property is being marketed by a property agent at a price of $40 million, which was considered a reasonably achievable price at that date. The expected costs to sell have been agreed at $500,000. Recent market transactions suggest that actual selling prices achieved for this type of property in the current market conditions are 15% less than the value at which they are marketed. At 31 March 20X4 the property had not been sold.

Plant and equipment is depreciated at 15% per annum using the reducing balance method.

No depreciation/amortisation has yet been charged on any non-current asset for the year ended 31 March 20X4. Depreciation, amortisation and impairment charges are all charged to cost of sales.

(iii) The investments at fair value through profit or loss had a fair value of $28 million on 31 March 20X4. There were no purchases or disposals of any of these investments during the year.

(iv) A provision for income tax for the year ended 31 March 20X4 of $12 million is required. The balance on current tax represents the under/over provision of the tax liability for the year ended 31 March 20X3. At 31 March 20X4 the tax base of Dune's net assets was $14 million less than their carrying amounts. The income tax rate of Dune is 30%.

(v) Dune has accounted for a fully subscribed rights issue of equity shares made on 1 January 20X4 of one new share for every four in issue at 42 cents each, when the market value of a Dune share was 82 cents.

Required:

(a) **Prepare the statement of profit or loss for Dune for the year ended 31 March 20X4, and the statement of financial position for Dune as at 31 March 20X4.**

Notes to the financial statements and a statement of changes in equity are not required. **(15 marks)**

(b) **Using the information in note (v), calculate earnings per share for Dune for the year ended 31 March 20X4. Also, calculate the re-stated figure for 20X3 if the EPS figure in the original 20X3 financial statements was 68¢ per share.** **(5 marks)**

(Total: 20 marks) ⊞

361 KANDY

After preparing a draft statement of profit or loss for the year ended 30 September 20X4 and adding the year's profit (before any adjustments required by notes (i) to (iii) below) to retained earnings, the summarised trial balance of Kandy as at 30 September 20X4 is:

	$000	$000
Equity shares of $1 each		40,000
Retained earnings as at 30 September 20X4		19,500
Proceeds of 6% loan (note (i))		30,000
Land ($5 million) and buildings – at cost (note (ii))	55,000	
Plant and equipment – at cost (note (ii))	58,500	
Accumulated depreciation at 1 October 20X3: buildings		20,000
plant and equipment		34,500
Current assets	68,700	
Current liabilities		38,400
Deferred tax (note (iii))		2,500
Interest payment (note (i))	1,800	
Investments (note (iv))	2,000	
Current tax (note (iii))		1,100
	———	———
	184,000	184,000
	———	———

The following notes are relevant:

(i)   The loan note was issued on 1 October 20X3 and incurred issue costs of $1 million which were charged to profit or loss. Interest of $1.8 million ($30 million at 6%) was paid on 30 September 20X4. The loan is redeemable on 30 September 20X8 at a substantial premium which gives an effective interest rate of 9% per annum. No other repayments are due until 30 September 20X8.

(ii)   Non-current assets:

The price of property has increased significantly in recent years and on 1 October 20X3, the directors decided to revalue the land and buildings. The directors accepted the report of an independent surveyor who valued the land at $8 million and the buildings at $39 million on that date. The remaining life of the buildings at 1 October 20X3 was 15 years. Kandy does not make an annual transfer to retained earnings to reflect the realisation of the revaluation gain. However the revaluation will give rise to a deferred tax liability. The income tax rate of Kandy is 20%.

Plant and equipment is depreciated at 12½% per annum using the reducing balance method.

No depreciation has been charged for the year ended 30 September 20X4.

(iii)   A provision of $2.4 million is required for current income tax on the profit of the year to 30 September 20X4. The balance on current tax in the trial balance is the under/over provision of tax for the previous year. In addition to the temporary differences relating to the information in note (ii), Kandy has further taxable temporary differences of $10 million as at 30 September 20X4.

(iv)   The investments in the trial balance are held at their fair value at 1 October 20X3. At 30 September 20X4 the value had risen to $2.6 million.

Required:

(a) Prepare a schedule of adjustments required to the retained earnings of Kandy as at 30 September 20X4 as a result of the information in notes (i) to (iv) above.

(9 marks)

(b) Prepare the statement of financial position of Kandy as at 30 September 20X4.

(11 marks)

Note: The notes to the statement of financial position are not required.

(Total: 20 marks) ▦

362 CLARION

After preparing a draft statement of profit or loss for the year ended 30 September 20X4 and adding the year's profit (before any adjustments required by notes (i) to (v) below) to retained earnings, the summarised trial balance of Clarion as at 31 March 20X5 is:

	$000	$000
Equity shares of $1 each		35,000
Retained earnings – 31 March 20X5		33,100
8% loan notes (note (i))		20,000
Plant and equipment at cost (note (ii))	77,000	
Right-of-use plant (note (iii))	8,000	
Accumulated depreciation plant and equipment – 1 April 20X4		19,000
Investments through profit or loss – value at 1 April 20X4 (note (iv))	6,000	
Inventory at 31 March 20X5	11,700	
Trade receivables	20,500	
Bank		1,900
Deferred tax (note (v))		2,700
Trade payables		9,400
Environmental provision (note (ii))		4,000
Lease liability (note (iii))		4,200
Loan note interest paid (note (i))	800	
Suspense account (note (i))	5,800	
Investment income (note (iv))		500
	———	———
	129,800	129,800
	———	———

The following notes are also relevant.

(i)   On 31 March 20X5, one quarter of the 8% loan notes were redeemed at par and six months' outstanding loan interest was paid. The suspense account represents the debit entry corresponding to the cash payment for the capital redemption and the outstanding interest.

(ii)   Property, plant and equipment

Included in property, plant and equipment is an item of plant with a cost of $14 million purchased on 1 April 20X4. However, the plant will cause environmental damage which will have to be rectified when it is dismantled at the end of its five year life. The present value (discounting at 8%) on 1 April 20X4 of the rectification is $4 million. The environmental provision has been correctly accounted for, however, no finance cost has yet been charged on the provision.

No depreciation has yet been charged on plant and equipment which should be charged to cost of sales on a straight-line basis over a five-year life. No plant is more than four years old.

(iii)   The right-of-use plant was acquired on 1 April 20X4 under a five-year lease with an initial deposit of $2.3 million and annual payments of $1.5 million on 31 March each year. The present value of the annual payments under the lease (**excluding the initial deposit**) at 1 April 20X4 was $5.7 million, the lease has an implicit rate of interest of 10%, and the right-of-use plant has been correctly capitalised. The lease liability in the trial balance above represents the initial liability less the first annual payment.

(iv)   The investments through profit or loss are those held at 31 March 20X5 (after the sale below). They are carried at their fair value as at 1 April 20X4, however, they had a fair value of $6.5 million on 31 March 20X5. During the year an investment which had a carrying amount of $1.4 million was sold for $1.6 million. Investment income in the trial balance above includes the profit on the sale of the investment and dividends received during the year.

(v)   A provision for current tax for the year ended 31 March 20X5 of $3.5 million is required. At 31 March 20X5, the tax base of Clarion's net assets was $12 million less than their carrying amounts. The income tax rate of Clarion is 25%.

Required:

(a)   Prepare Clarion's statement of financial position as at 31 March 20X5.   (15 marks)

(b)   Prepare extracts from the statement of cash flows for Clarion for the year ended 31 March 20X5 in respect of cash flows from investing and financing activities.

(5 marks)

Notes to the financial statements are not required.

(Total: 20 marks) ⊞

363 MOSTON *Walk in the footsteps of a top tutor*

The following trial balance **extracts** (i.e. it is not a complete trial balance) relate to Moston as at 30 June 20X5:

	$000	$000
Revenue		113,500
Cost of sales	88,500	
Research and development costs (note (i))	7,800	
Distribution costs	2,800	
Administrative expenses (note (iii))	6,800	
Loan note interest and dividends paid (notes (iii) and (v))	5,000	
Investment income		300
Equity shares of $1 each (note (v))		30,000
5% loan note (note (iii))		20,000
Retained earnings as at 1 July 20X4		6,200
Revaluation surplus as at 1 July 20X4		3,000
Other components of equity		9,300
Property at valuation 1 July 20X4 (note (ii))	28,500	
Plant and equipment at cost (note (ii))	27,100	
Accumulated depreciation plant and equipment 1 July 20X4		9,100

The following notes are relevant:

(i)   Moston commenced a research and development project on 1 January 20X5. It spent $1 million per month on research until 31 March 20X5, at which date the project passed into the development stage. From this date it spent $1.6 million per month until the year end (30 June 20X5), at which date development was completed. However, it was not until 1 May 20X5 that the directors of Moston were confident that the new product would be a commercial success.

Expensed research and development costs should be charged to cost of sales.

(ii)   Non-current assets:

Moston's property is carried at fair value which at 30 June 20X5 was $29 million. The remaining life of the property at the beginning of the year (1 July 20X4) was 15 years. Moston does not make an annual transfer to retained earnings in respect of the revaluation surplus. Ignore deferred tax on the revaluation.

Plant and equipment is depreciated at 15% per annum using the reducing balance method.

No depreciation has yet been charged on any non-current asset for the year ended 30 June 20X5. All depreciation is charged to cost of sales.

(iii)   The 5% loan note was issued on 1 July 20X4 at its nominal value of $20 million incurring direct issue costs of $500,000 which have been charged to administrative expenses. The loan note will be redeemed after three years at a premium which gives the loan note an effective finance cost of 8% per annum. Annual interest was paid on 30 June 20X5.

(iv)   A provision for current tax for the year ended 30 June 20X5 of $1.2 million is required, together with an increase to the deferred tax provision to be charged to profit or loss of $800,000.

(v)   Moston paid a dividend of 20 cents per share on 30 March 20X5, which was followed the day after by an issue of 10 million equity shares at their full market value of $1.70. The share premium on the issue was recorded in other components of equity.

Required:

(a)   Prepare the statement of profit or loss and other comprehensive income for Moston for the year ended 30 June 20X5.   **(10 marks)**

(b)   Prepare the statement of changes in equity for Moston for the year ended 30 June 20X5.   **(5 marks)**

(c)   Prepare extracts from the statement of cash flows for Moston for the year ended 30 June 20X5 in respect of cash flows from investing and financing activities.
                                                                          (5 marks)

Note: The statement of financial position and notes to the financial statements are NOT required.

                                                                 (Total: 20 marks) ⊞

364   TRIAGE

After preparing a draft statement of profit or loss (before interest and tax) for the year ended 31 March 20X6 (before any adjustments which may be required by notes (i) to (iv) below), the summarised trial balance of Triage Co as at 31 March 20X6 is:

	$000	$000
Equity shares of $1 each		50,000
Retained earnings as at 1 April 20X5		3,500
Draft profit before interest and tax for year ended 31 March 20X6		30,000
6% convertible loan notes (note (i))		40,000
Property (original life 25 years) – at cost (note (ii))	75,000	
Plant and equipment – at cost (note (ii))	72,100	
Accumulated amortisation/depreciation at 1 April 20X5:		
leased property		15,000
plant and equipment		28,100
Trade receivables (note (iii))	28,000	
Other current assets	9,300	
Current liabilities		17,700
Deferred tax (note (iv))		3,200
Interest payment (note (i))	2,400	
Current tax (note (iv)	700	
	———	———
	187,500	187,500
	———	———

The following notes are relevant:

(i) Triage Co issued 400,000 $100 6% convertible loan notes on 1 April 20X5. Interest is payable annually in arrears on 31 March each year. The loans can be converted to equity shares on the basis of 20 shares for each $100 loan note on 31 March 20X8 or redeemed at par for cash on the same date. An equivalent loan without the conversion rights would have required an interest rate of 8%.

The present value of $1 receivable at the end of each year, based on discount rates of 6% and 8%, are:

		6%	8%
End of year	1	0.94	0.93
	2	0.89	0.86
	3	0.84	0.79

(ii) Non-current assets:

The directors decided to revalue the property at $66.3m on 1 October 20X5. Triage Co does not make an annual transfer from the revaluation surplus to retained earnings to reflect the realisation of the revaluation gain; however, the revaluation will give rise to a deferred tax liability at a tax rate of 20%.

The property is depreciated on a straight-line basis and plant and equipment at 15% per annum using the reducing balance method.

No depreciation has yet been charged on any non-current assets for the year ended 31 March 20X6.

(iii) In September 20X5, the directors of Triage Co discovered a fraud. In total, $700,000 which had been included as receivables in the above trial balance had been stolen by an employee. $450,000 of this related to the year ended 31 March 20X5, the rest to the current year. The directors are hopeful that 50% of the losses can be recovered from their insurers.

(iv) A provision of $2.7m is required for current income tax on the profit of the year to 31 March 20X6. The balance on current tax in the trial balance is the under/over provision of tax for the previous year. In addition to the temporary differences relating to the information in note (ii), at 31 March 20X6 the carrying amounts of Triage Co's net assets are $12m more than their tax base.

Required:

(a) **Prepare a schedule of adjustments required to the draft profit before interest and tax (in the above trial balance) to give the profit or loss of Triage Co for the year ended 31 March 20X6 as a result of the information in notes (i) to (iv) above.**
(5 marks)

(b) **Prepare the statement of financial position of Triage Co as at 31 March 20X6.**
(12 marks)

(c) The issue of convertible loan notes can potentially dilute the basic earnings per share (EPS).

Calculate the diluted earnings per share for Triage Co for the year ended 31 March 20X6 (there is no need to calculate the basic EPS). (3 marks)

Note: **A statement of changes in equity and the notes to the statement of financial position are not required.**

(Total: 20 marks)

365 HAVERFORD CO

Below is the trial balance for Haverford Co at 31 December 20X7:

	$000	$000
Property – carrying amount 1 January 20X7 (note (iv))	18,000	
Ordinary shares $1 at 1 January 20X7 (note (iii))		20,000
Other components of equity (Share premium) at 1 January 20X7 (note (iii))		3,000
Revaluation surplus at 1 January 20X7 (note (iv))		800
Retained earnings at 1 January 20X7		6,270
Draft profit for the year ended 31 December 20X7		2,250
4% Convertible loan notes (note (i))		8,000
Dividends paid	3,620	
Cash received from contract customer (note (ii))		1,400
Cost incurred on contract to date (note (ii))	1,900	
Inventories (note (v))	4,310	
Trade receivables	5,510	
Cash	10,320	
Current liabilities		1,940
	43,660	43,660

The following notes are relevant:

(i) On 1 January 20X7, Haverford Co issued 80,000 $100 4% convertible loan notes. The loan notes can be converted to equity shares on 31 December 20X9 or redeemed at par on the same date. An equivalent loan without the conversion rights would have required interest of 6%. Interest is payable annually in arrears on 31 December each year. The annual payment has been included in finance costs for the year. The present value of $1 receivable at the end of each year, based on discount rates of 4% and 6%, are:

	4%	6%
End of year 1	0.962	0.943
End of year 2	0.925	0.890
End of year 3	0.889	0.840

(ii) During the year, Haverford Co entered into a contract to construct an asset for a customer, satisfying the performance obligation over time. The contract had a total price of $14m. The costs to date of $1.9m are included in the above trial balance. Costs to complete the contract are estimated at $7.1m.

At 31 December 20X7, the contract is estimated to be 40% complete. To date, Haverford Co has received $1.4m from the customer and this is shown in the above trial balance.

(iii) Haverford Co made a 1 for 5 bonus issue on 31 December 20X7, which has not yet been recorded in the above trial balance. Haverford Co intends to utilise the share premium as far as possible in recording the bonus issue.

(iv) Haverford Co's property had previously been revalued upwards, leading to the balance on the revaluation surplus at 1 January 20X7. The property had a remaining life of 25 years at 1 January 20X7.

At 31 December 20X7, the property was valued at $16m.

No entries have yet been made to account for the current year's depreciation charge or the property valuation at 31 December 20X7. Haverford Co does not make an annual transfer from the revaluation surplus in respect of excess depreciation.

(v) It has been discovered that inventory totalling $0.39m had been omitted from the final inventory count in the above trial balance.

Required:

(a) **Calculate the adjusted profit for Haverford Co for the year ended 31 December 20X7.**   **(6 marks)**

(b) **Prepare the statement of changes in equity for Haverford Co for the year ended 31 December 20X7.**   **(6 marks)**

(c) **Prepare the statement of financial position for Haverford Co as at 31 December 20X7.**   **(8 marks)**

(Total: 20 marks) ▦

366 DUGGAN CO

The following **extracts** from the trial balance have been taken from the accounting records of Duggan Co as at 30 June 20X8:

	$000	$000
Convertible loan notes (note (iv))		5,000
Cost of sales	21,700	
Finance costs (note (iv))	1,240	
Investment income		120
Operating expenses (notes (ii) and (v))	13,520	
Retained earnings at 1 July 20X7		35,400
Revenue (note (i))		43,200
Equity share capital ($1 shares) at 1 July 20X7		12,200
Tax (note (iii))		130

The following notes are relevant:

(i) Duggan Co entered into a contract where the performance obligation is satisfied over time. The total price on the contract is $9m, with total expected costs of $5m.

Progress towards completion was measured at 50% at 30 June 20X7 and 80% on 30 June 20X8.

The correct entries were made in the year ended 30 June 20X7, but no entries have been made for the year ended 30 June 20X8.

(ii) On 1 January 20X8, Duggan Co was notified that an ex-employee had started court proceedings against them for unfair dismissal. Legal advice was that there was an 80% chance that Duggan Co would lose the case and would need to pay an estimated $1.012m on 1 January 20X9.

Based on this advice, Duggan Co recorded a provision of $800k on 1 January 20X8, and has made no further adjustments. The provision was recorded in operating expenses.

Duggan Co has a cost of capital of 10% per annum and the discount factor at 10% for one year is 0.9091.

(iii)   The balance relating to tax in the trial balance relates to the under/over provision from the prior period. The tax estimate for the year ended 30 June 20X8 is $2.1m.

In addition to this, there has been a decrease in taxable temporary differences of $2m in the year. Duggan Co pays tax at 25% and movements in deferred tax are to be taken to the statement of profit or loss.

(iv)   Duggan Co issued $5m 6% convertible loan notes on 1 July 20X7. Interest is payable annually in arrears. These bonds can be converted into one share for every $2 on 30 June 20X9. Similar loan notes, without conversion rights, incur interest at 8%. Duggan Co recorded the full amount in liabilities and has recorded the annual payment made on 30 June 20X8 of $0.3m in finance costs.

Relevant discount rates are as follows:

Present value of $1 in:	6%	8%
1 year	0.943	0.926
2 years	0.890	0.857

(v)   Duggan Co began the construction of an item of property on 1 July 20X7 which was completed on 31 March 20X8. A cost of $32m was capitalised. This included $2.56m, being a full 12 months' interest on a $25.6m 10% loan taken out specifically for this construction. On completion, the property has a useful life of 20 years.

Duggan Co also recorded $0.4m in operating expenses, representing depreciation on the asset for the period from 31 March 20X8 to 30 June 20X8.

(vi)   It has been discovered that the previous financial controller of Duggan Co engaged in fraudulent financial reporting. Currently, $2.5m of trade receivables has been deemed to not exist and requires to be written off. Of this, $0.9m relates to the year ended 30 June 20X8, with $1.6m relating to earlier periods.

(vii)   On 1 November 20X7, Duggan Co issued 1.5 million shares at their full market price of $2.20. The proceeds were credited to a suspense account.

Required:

(a)   Prepare a statement of profit or loss for Duggan Co for the year ended 30 June 20X8.   **(12 marks)**

(b)   Prepare a statement of changes in equity for Duggan Co for the year ended 30 June 20X8.   **(5 marks)**

(c)   Calculate the basic earnings per share for Duggan Co for the year ended 30 June 20X8.   **(3 marks)**

Note: All workings should be done to the nearest $000.

(Total: 20 marks) ▦

STATEMENT OF CASH FLOWS

These questions include the preparation of a full statement of cashflows (SCF). This skill is tested in FA and, as such, FR is unlikely to test the preparation of a full SCF. FR is more likely to test the elements not covered in FA (for example leases and loan notes), an SCF extract or the analysis of an SCF. In order to answer the above type of questions, candidates need to know how to prepare a full SCF, and the questions below are therefore included for revision purposes only.

367 COALTOWN *Walk in the footsteps of a top tutor*

 Question debrief

Coaltown is a wholesaler and retailer of office furniture. Extracts from their financial statements are set out below.

Statement of profit or loss and other comprehensive income for the year ended:

		31 March 20X9	
		$000	$000
Revenue	– cash	12,800	
	– credit	53,000	65,800
Cost of sales			(43,800)
Gross profit			22,000
Operating expenses			(11,200)
Finance costs	– loan notes	(380)	
	– overdraft	(220)	(600)
Profit before tax			10,200
Income tax expense			(3,200)
Profit for period			7,000
Other comprehensive income			
Gain on property revaluation			5,000
Total comprehensive income for the year			12,000

Statements of financial position as at 31 March:

	20X9		20X8	
	$000	$000	$000	$000
Assets				
Non-current assets (notes (i), (ii))				
Cost		93,500		80,000
Accumulated depreciation		(43,000)		(48,000)
		50,500		32,000
Current assets				
Inventory	5,200		4,400	
Trade receivables	7,800		2,800	
Bank	nil	13,000	700	7,900
Total assets		63,500		39,900
Equity and liabilities				
Equity shares of $1 each		16,600		6,000
Other components of equity		4,800		500
Revaluation surplus (note (ii))		6,500		2,500
Retained earnings (note (ii))		19,800		15,800
		47,700		24,800
Non-current liabilities				
10% loan notes	4,000		3,000	
Convertible loan (note (v))	Nil		2,000	
		4,000		5,000
Current liabilities				
Bank overdraft	3,600		Nil	
Trade payables	4,200		4,500	
Taxation	3,000		5,300	
Negligence claim (note (iii))	Nil		120	
Warranty provision	1,000	11,800	180	10,100
Total equity and liabilities		63,500		39,900

(i)   During the year Coaltown redesigned its display areas in all of its outlets. The previous displays had cost $10 million and had been written down by $9 million. There was an unexpected cost of $500,000 for the removal and disposal of the old display areas.

(ii)   Also during the year Coaltown revalued the carrying amount of its property upwards by $5 million, the accumulated depreciation on these properties of $2 million was reset to zero. All depreciation is charged to operating expenses. Coaltown makes annual reserves transfer from the revaluation surplus in respect of excess depreciation.

(iii) In June 20X9 Coaltown made an out of court settlement of a negligence claim brought about by a former employee. The dispute had been in progress for two years and Coaltown had made provisions for the potential liability in each of the two previous years. The unprovided amount of the claim at the time of settlement was $30,000 and this was charged to operating expenses.

(iv) The warranty provision relates to the future repair of goods and is charged to operating expenses.

(v) During the year 20% of the convertible loan holders exercised their right to convert to ordinary shares. The terms of conversion were 25 ordinary shares of $1 each for each $100 of convertible loan. The remainder were repaid in cash. Ignore any transfer from other components of equity to retained earnings in respect of the redemption of the loan notes.

Required:

Prepare a statement of cash flows for Coaltown for the year ended 31 March 20X9 in accordance with IAS 7 *Statement of Cash Flows* by the indirect method.

(Total: 20 marks)

 Calculate your allowed time, allocate the time to the separate parts

368 MONTY

Monty is a publicly listed entity. Its financial statements for the year ended 31 March 20X3 including comparatives are shown below:

Statement of profit or loss and other comprehensive income for the year ended 31 March 20X3

	$000
Revenue	31,000
Cost of sales	(21,800)
	————
Gross profit	9,200
Distribution costs	(3,450)
Administrative expenses	(2,200)
Finance costs – loan interest	(400)
– lease interest	(150)
	————
Profit before tax	3,000
Income tax expense	(1,000)
	————
Profit for the year	2,000
Other comprehensive income (note (i))	1,350
	————
	3,350
	————

Statements of financial position as at:

	31 March 20X3		31 March 20X2	
	$000	$000	$000	$000
Assets				
Non-current assets				
Property, plant and equipment		14,000		10,700
Deferred development expenditure		1,000		nil
		15,000		10,700
Current assets				
Inventory	3,300		3,800	
Trade receivables	2,950		2,200	
Bank	1,980	8,230	1,300	7,300
Total assets		23,230		18,000
Equity and liabilities				
Equity				
Equity shares of $1 each		7,000		7,000
Revaluation surplus		1,350		nil
Retained earnings		3,200		1,750
		11,550		8,750
Non-current liabilities				
8% loan notes (note(iii))	4,080		4,000	
Deferred tax	1,500		800	
Lease liability	1,200		900	
Government grant	200		100	
		6,980		5,800
Current liabilities				
Lease liability	750		600	
Trade payables	2,650		2,100	
Current tax payable	1,250		725	
Government grant	50	4,700	25	3,450
Total equity and liabilities		23,230		18,000

Notes:

(i)   On 1 July 20X2, Monty acquired additional plant under a lease with an initial value of $1.5 million. The right-of-use asset is included within property, plant and equipment. On this date it also revalued its property upwards by $2 million and transferred $650,000 of the resulting revaluation surplus this created to deferred tax. There were no disposals of non-current assets during the period.

(ii)   Depreciation of property, plant and equipment was $900,000 and amortisation of the deferred development expenditure was $200,000 for the year ended 31 March 20X3.

(iii) The 8% loan notes are repayable at a premium, giving them an effective rate of 10%. No loan notes were issued or redeemed during the year.

(iv) $25,000 was credited to administrative expenses in respect of government grants during the year.

Required:

Prepare a statement of cash flows for Monty for the year ended 31 March 20X3, in accordance with IAS 7 *Statement of Cash Flows*, using the indirect method.

(Total: 20 marks)

369   KINGDOM

 Question debrief

Kingdom is a publicly listed manufacturing entity. Its draft summarised financial statements for the year ended 30 September 20X3 (and 20X2 comparatives) are:

Statements of profit or loss and other comprehensive income for the year ended 30 September:

	20X3	20X2
	$000	$000
Revenue	44,900	44,000
Cost of sales	(31,300)	(29,000)
Gross profit	13,600	15,000
Distribution costs	(2,400)	(2,100)
Administrative expenses	(7,850)	(5,900)
Investment properties – rentals received	350	400
– fair value changes	(700)	500
Finance costs	(600)	(600)
Profit before taxation	2,400	7,300
Income tax	(600)	(1,700)
Profit for the year	1,800	5,600
Other comprehensive income	(1,300)	1,000
Total comprehensive income	500	6,600

Statements of financial position as at 30 September:

	20X3		20X2	
	$000	$000	$000	$000
Assets				
Non-current assets				
Property, plant and equipment		26,700		25,200
Investment properties		4,100		5,000
		———		———
		30,800		30,200
Current assets				
Inventory	2,300		3,100	
Trade receivables	3,000		3,400	
Bank	nil	5,300	300	6,800
	———	———	———	———
Total assets		36,100		37,000
		———		———
Equity and liabilities				
Equity				
Equity shares of $1 each		17,200		15,000
Revaluation surplus		1,200		2,500
Retained earnings		7,700		8,700
		———		———
		26,100		26,200
Non-current liabilities				
12% loan notes		5,000		5,000
Current liabilities				
Trade payables	4,200		3,900	
Accrued finance costs	100		50	
Bank	200		nil	
Current tax payable	500	5,000	1,850	5,800
	———	———	———	———
Total equity and liabilities		36,100		37,000
		———		———

On 1 July 20X3, Kingdom acquired a new investment property at a cost of $1.4 million. On this date, it also transferred one of its other investment properties to property, plant and equipment at its fair value of $1.6 million as it became owner-occupied on that date. Kingdom adopts the fair value model for its investment properties.

Kingdom also has a policy of revaluing its other properties (included as property, plant and equipment) to market value at the end of each year. Other comprehensive income and the revaluation surplus both relate to these properties.

Depreciation of property, plant and equipment during the year was $1.5 million. An item of plant with a carrying amount of $2.3 million was sold for $1.8 million during September 20X3.

Required:

(a) Prepare the statement of cash flows for Kingdom for the year ended 30 September 20X3 in accordance with IAS 7 *Statement of Cash Flows* using the indirect method.

(15 marks)

(b) At a board meeting to consider the results shown by the draft financial statements, concern was expressed that, although there had been a slight increase in revenue during the current year, the profit before tax had fallen dramatically. The purchasing director commented that he was concerned about the impact of rising prices. During the year to 30 September 20X3, most of Kingdom's manufacturing and operating costs have risen by an estimated 8% per annum.

Required:

Explain the causes of the fall in Kingdom's profit before tax. (5 marks)

(Total: 20 marks)

 Calculate your allowed time, allocate the time to the separate parts

---

BUSINESS COMBINATIONS

370 PREMIER *Walk in the footsteps of a top tutor*

On 1 June 20X0, Premier acquired 80% of the equity share capital of Sanford. The consideration consisted of two elements: a share exchange of three shares in Premier for every five acquired shares in Sanford and $800,000 cash. The share issue has not yet been recorded by Premier. At the date of acquisition shares in Premier had a market value of $5 each. Below are the summarised draft financial statements of both entities.

Statements of financial position as at 30 September 20X0	Premier	Sanford
Assets		
Non-current assets		
Property, plant and equipment	25,500	13,900
Investments	1,800	nil
	27,300	13,900
Current assets		
Inventory	5,300	500
Receivables	4,200	1,100
Bank	3,000	800
	12,500	2,400
Total assets	39,800	16,300

Equity and liabilities		
Equity		
Equity shares of $1 each	12,000	5,000
Other equity reserve – 30 September 20W9 (note (iv))	500	nil
Retained earnings	12,300	4,500
	24,800	9,500
Liabilities		
Current liabilities	15,000	6,800
Total equity and liabilities	39,800	16,300

The following information is relevant:

(i) At the date of acquisition, the fair values of Sanford's assets were equal to their carrying amounts with the exception of its property. This had a fair value of $1.2 million **below** its carrying amount, and had a remaining useful life of 8 years at the date of acquisition. Sanford has not incorporated this in its financial statements.

(ii) Premier had $2 million (at cost to Premier) of inventory that had been supplied in the post-acquisition period by Sanford as at 30 September 20X0. Sanford made a mark-up on cost of 25% on these sales.

(iii) Premier had a trade payable balance owing to Sanford of $350,000 as at 30 September 20X0. This did not agree with the corresponding receivable in Sanford's books due to a $130,000 payment made to Sanford, which Sanford has not yet recorded.

(iv) Premier's investments include investments in shares which at the date of acquisition were classified as fair value through other comprehensive income (FVTOCI). The investments have increased in value by $300,000 during the year. The other equity reserve relates to these investments and is based on their value as at 30 September 20W9. There were no acquisitions or disposals of any of these investments during the year ended 30 September 20X0.

(v) Premier's policy is to value the non-controlling interest at fair value at the date of acquisition, deemed to be $3.5 million.

(vi) Consolidated goodwill was impaired by $1.5 million at 30 September 20X0.

Required:

Prepare the consolidated statement of financial position for Premier as at 30 September 20X0. **(20 marks)** ⊞

371 PATRONIC *Walk in the footsteps of a top tutor*

On 1 August 20X7 Patronic purchased 18 million of a total of 24 million equity shares in Sardonic. The acquisition was through a share exchange of two shares in Patronic for every three shares in Sardonic. Both entities have shares with a par value of $1 each.

The market price of Patronic's shares at 1 August 20X7 was $5.75 per share.

Patronic will also pay in cash on 31 July 20X9 (two years after acquisition) $2.42 per acquired share of Sardonic. Patronic's cost of capital is 10% per annum.

The reserves of Sardonic on 1 April 20X7 were $69 million.

Patronic has held an investment of 30% of the equity shares in Acerbic for many years. Acerbic made a profit of $6 million in the year.

The summarised statement of profit or loss for the two entities for the year ended 31 March 20X8 are:

	Patronic $000	Sardonic $000
Revenue	150,000	78,000
Cost of sales	(94,000)	(51,000)
Gross profit	56,000	27,000
Distribution costs	(7,400)	(3,000)
Administrative expenses	(12,500)	(6,000)
Finance costs (note (ii))	(2,000)	(900)
Profit before tax	34,100	17,100
Income tax expense	(10,400)	(3,600)
Profit for the period	23,700	13,500

The following information is relevant:

(i) The fair values of the net assets of Sardonic at the date of acquisition were equal to their carrying amounts with the exception of property and plant. Property and plant had fair values of $4.1 million and $2.4 million respectively in excess of their carrying amounts. The increase in the fair value of the property would create additional depreciation of $200,000 in the consolidated financial statements in the post-acquisition period to 31 March 20X8 and the plant had a remaining life of four years (straight-line depreciation) at the date of acquisition of Sardonic. All depreciation is treated as part of cost of sales.

The fair values have not been reflected in Sardonic's financial statements.

No fair value adjustments were required on the acquisition of Acerbic.

(ii) The finance costs of Patronic do not include the finance cost on the deferred consideration.

(iii) Prior to its acquisition, Sardonic had been a good customer of Patronic. In the year to 31 March 20X8, Patronic sold goods at a selling price of $1.25 million per month to Sardonic both before and after its acquisition. Patronic made a profit of 20% on the cost of these sales. At 31 March 20X8 Sardonic still held inventory of $3 million (at cost to Sardonic) of goods purchased in the post-acquisition period from Patronic.

(iv) Patronic has a policy of valuing non-controlling interests using fair value. An impairment test on the goodwill of Sardonic conducted on 31 March 20X8 concluded that it should be written down by $2 million. The value of the investment in Acerbic was not impaired.

(v) All items are deemed to accrue evenly over the year.

Required:

(a) **Calculate the consideration paid on the acquisition of Sardonic at 1 August 20X7.**

(3 marks)

(b) **Prepare the consolidated statement of profit or loss for the Patronic Group for the year ended 31 March 20X8.** (17 marks)

(Total: 20 marks) ▦

372 PEDANTIC

On 1 April 20X8, Pedantic acquired 60% of the 4 million $1 equity shares of Sophistic in a share exchange of two shares in Pedantic for three shares in Sophistic. At the date of acquisition shares in Pedantic had a market value of $6 each. Below are the statements of profit or loss of both entities.

Statement of profit or loss for the year ended 30 September 20X8

	Pedantic $000	Sophistic $000
Revenue	85,000	42,000
Cost of sales	(63,000)	(32,000)
Gross profit	22,000	10,000
Distribution costs	(3,100)	(3,600)
Administration expenses	(5,200)	(2,000)
Profit before tax	13,700	4,400
Income tax expense	(4,700)	(1,400)
Profit for the year	9,000	3,000

The following information is relevant:

(i) At the date of acquisition, the fair values of Sophistic's assets were equal to their carrying amounts with the exception of an item of plant, which had a fair value of $2 million in excess of its carrying amount. It had a remaining life of five years at that date (straight-line depreciation is used). Sophistic has not adjusted the carrying amount of its plant as a result of the fair value exercise.

(ii) Sales from Sophistic to Pedantic in the post-acquisition period were $8 million. Sophistic made a mark-up on cost of 40% on these sales. Pedantic had sold $5.2 million (at cost to Pedantic) of these goods by 30 September 20X8.

(iii)   Other than where indicated, statement of profit or loss items are deemed to accrue evenly over time.

(iv)   At 30 September 20X8 the balance on Sophistic's retained earnings was $6.5 million.

(v)   Pedantic has a policy of accounting for any non-controlling interest at fair value. The fair value of the non-controlling interest at the acquisition date was $5.9 million.

(vi)   Consolidated goodwill was impaired by $1 million at 30 September 20X8.

Required:

(a)   **Prepare the consolidated statement of profit or loss for Pedantic for the year ended 30 September 20X8.**   **(12 marks)**

(b)   **Calculate the following values for inclusion on the consolidated statement of financial position as at 30 September 20X8:**

(i)   **Goodwill**   **(5 marks)**

(ii)   **Non-controlling interest**   **(3 marks)**

(Total: 20 marks) ▦

373   PANDAR   *Walk in the footsteps of a top tutor*

On 1 April 20X9 Pandar purchased 80% of the equity shares in Salva. On the same date Pandar acquired 40% of the 40 million equity shares in Ambra paying $2 per share.

The statement of profit or loss for the year ended 30 September 20X9 are:

	Pandar	Salva	Ambra
	$000	$000	$000
Revenue	210,000	150,000	50,000
Cost of sales	(126,000)	(100,000)	(40,000)
Gross profit	84,000	50,000	10,000
Distribution costs	(11,200)	(7,000)	(5,000)
Administrative expenses	(18,300)	(9,000)	(11,000)
Investment income (interest and dividends)	9,500		
Finance costs	(1,800)	(3,000)	Nil
Profit (loss) before tax	62,200	31,000	(6,000)
Income tax (expense) relief	(15,000)	(10,000)	1,000
Profit (loss) for the year	47,200	21,000	(5,000)

The following information is relevant:

(i)   The fair values of the net assets of Salva at the date of acquisition were equal to their carrying amounts with the exception of an item of plant which had a carrying amount of $12 million and a fair value of $17 million. This plant had a remaining life of five years (straight-line depreciation) at the date of acquisition of Salva. All depreciation is charged to cost of sales.

The fair value of the plant has not been reflected in Salva's financial statements.

No fair value adjustments were required on the acquisition of the investment in Ambra.

(ii)   Immediately after its acquisition of Salva, Pandar invested $50 million in an 8% loan note from Salva. All interest accruing to 30 September 20X9 has been accounted for by both entities. Salva also has other loans in issue at 30 September 20X9.

(iii)   Salva paid a dividend of $8 million during the year.

(iv)   After the acquisition, Pandar sold goods to Salva for $15 million on which Pandar made a gross profit of 20%. Salva had one third of these goods still in its inventory at 30 September 20X9. Pandar also sold goods to Ambra for $6 million, making the same margin. Ambra had half of these goods still in inventory at 30 September 20X9.

(v)   The non-controlling interest in Salva is to be valued at its (full) fair value at the date of acquisition.

(vi)   The goodwill of Salva has been impaired by $2 million at 30 September 20X9. Due to its losses, the value of Pandar's investment in Ambra has been impaired by $3 million at 30 September 20X9.

(vii)   All items in the above statement of profit or loss are deemed to accrue evenly over the year unless otherwise indicated.

Required:

(a)   **Calculate the carrying amount of the investment in Ambra to be included within the consolidated statement of financial position as at 30 September 20X9.**

(4 marks)

(b)   **Prepare the consolidated statement of profit or loss for the Pandar Group for the year ended 30 September 20X9.**   **(16 marks)**

(Total: 20 marks) ⊞

374   PICANT

On 1 April 20X3 Picant acquired 75% of Sander's equity shares in a share exchange of three shares in Picant for every two shares in Sander. The market prices of Picant's and Sander's shares at the date of acquisition were $3.20 and $4.50 respectively.

In addition to this Picant agreed to pay a further amount on 1 April 20X4 that was contingent upon the post-acquisition performance of Sander. At the date of acquisition Picant assessed the fair value of this contingent consideration at $4.2 million, but by 31 March 20X4 it was clear that the actual amount to be paid would be only $2.7 million (ignore discounting). Picant has recorded the share exchange and provided for the initial estimate of $4.2 million for the contingent consideration.

On 1 October 20X3 Picant also acquired 40% of the equity shares of Adler paying $4 in cash per acquired share and issuing at par one $100 7% loan note for every 50 shares acquired in Adler. This consideration has also been recorded by Picant.

Picant has no other investments.

The summarised statements of financial position of the three entities at 31 March 20X4 are:

	Picant $000	Sander $000	Adler $000
Assets			
Non-current assets			
Property, plant and equipment	37,500	24,500	21,000
Investments	45,000	nil	nil
	82,500	24,500	21,000
Current assets			
Inventory	10,000	9,000	5,000
Trade receivables	6,500	1,500	3,000
Total assets	99,000	35,000	29,000
Equity			
Equity shares of $1 each	25,000	8,000	5,000
Share premium	19,800	nil	nil
Retained earnings – at 1 April 20X3	16,200	16,500	15,000
– for the year ended 31 March 20X4	11,000	1,000	6,000
	72,000	25,500	26,000
Non-current liabilities			
7% loan notes	14,500	2,000	nil
Current liabilities			
Contingent consideration	4,200	nil	nil
Other current liabilities	8,300	7,500	3,000
Total equity and liabilities	99,000	35,000	29,000

The following information is relevant:

(i)   At the date of acquisition the fair values of Sander's property, plant and equipment was equal to its carrying amount with the exception of Sander's factory which had a fair value of $2 million above its carrying amount. Sander has not adjusted the carrying amount of the factory as a result of the fair value exercise. This requires additional annual depreciation of $100,000 in the consolidated financial statements in the post-acquisition period.

Also at the date of acquisition, Sander had an intangible asset of $500,000 for software in its statement of financial position. Picant's directors believed the software to have no recoverable value at the date of acquisition and Sander wrote it off shortly after its acquisition.

(ii)   At 31 March 20X4 Picant's current account with Sander was $3.4 million (debit). This did not agree with the equivalent balance in Sander's books due to some goods-in-transit invoiced at $1.8 million that were sent by Picant on 28 March 20X4, but had not been received by Sander until after the year end. Picant sold all these goods at cost plus 50%.

(iii)   Picant's policy is to value the non-controlling interest at fair value at the date of acquisition. For this purpose Sander's share price at that date can be deemed to be representative of the fair value of the shares held by the non-controlling interest.

(iv)   Impairment tests were carried out on 31 March 20X4 which concluded that the value of the investment in Adler was not impaired but, due to poor trading performance, consolidated goodwill was impaired by $3.8 million.

(v)   Assume all profits accrue evenly through the year.

Required:

(a)   Prepare the consolidated statement of financial position for Picant as at 31 March 20X4.   (15 marks)

(b)   At 31 March 20X4 the other equity shares (60%) in Adler were owned by many separate investors. Shortly after this date Spekulate (an entity unrelated to Picant) accumulated a 60% interest in Adler by buying shares from the other shareholders. In May 20X4 a meeting of the board of directors of Adler was held at which Picant lost its seat on Adler's board.

Required:

Explain, with reasons, the accounting treatment Picant should adopt for its investment in Adler when it prepares its financial statements for the year ending 31 March 20X5.   (5 marks)

(Total: 20 marks) ⊞

375   PRODIGAL

On 1 October 20X0 Prodigal purchased 75% of the equity shares in Sentinel. The summarised statements of profit or loss and other comprehensive income for the two entities for the year ended 31 March 20X1 are:

	Prodigal $000	Sentinel $000
Revenue	450,000	240,000
Cost of sales	(260,000)	(110,000)
Gross profit	190,000	130,000
Distribution costs	(23,600)	(12,000)
Administrative expenses	(27,000)	(23,000)
Finance costs	(1,500)	(1,200)
Profit before tax	137,900	93,800
Income tax expense	(48,000)	(27,800)
Profit for the year	89,900	66,000
Other comprehensive income		
Gain on revaluation of land (note (i))	2,500	1,000
Total comprehensive income	92,400	67,000

The following extracts for the equity of the entities at 1 April 20X0 (before acquisition) is available:

	$000	$000
Revaluation surplus (land)	8,400	nil
Retained earnings	90,000	125,000

The following information is relevant:

(i) Prodigal's policy is to revalue the group's land to market value at the end of each accounting period. Prior to its acquisition by Prodigal, Sentinel's land had been valued at historical cost. During the post-acquisition period Sentinel's land had increased in value over its value at the date of acquisition by $1 million. Sentinel has recognised the revaluation within its own financial statements.

(ii) Immediately after the acquisition of Sentinel on 1 October 20X0, Prodigal transferred an item of plant with a carrying amount of $4 million to Sentinel at an agreed value of $5 million. At this date the plant had a remaining life of two and half years. Prodigal had included the profit on this transfer as a reduction in its depreciation costs. All depreciation is charged to cost of sales.

(iii) After the acquisition Sentinel sold goods to Prodigal for $40 million. These goods had cost Sentinel $30 million. $12 million of the goods sold remained in Prodigal's closing inventory.

(iv) Prodigal's policy is to value the non-controlling interest of Sentinel at the date of acquisition at its fair value which the directors determined to be $100 million.

(v) The goodwill of Sentinel has not suffered any impairment.

(vi) All items in the above statements of comprehensive income are deemed to accrue evenly over the year unless otherwise indicated.

Required:

(a) **Prepare the consolidated statement of profit or loss and other comprehensive income of Prodigal for the year ended 31 March 20X1.** **(15 marks)**

(b) **Prepare extracts of the equity section (including the non-controlling interest) of the consolidated statement of financial position of Prodigal as at 31 March 20X1.** **(5 marks)**

Note: you are NOT required to calculate consolidated goodwill or produce the statement of changes in equity.

(Total: 20 marks) ▦

376 PALADIN

On 1 October 20X0, Paladin secured a majority equity shareholding in Saracen on the following terms:

– an immediate payment of $4 per share on 1 October 20X0.

– and a further amount deferred until 1 October 20X1 of $5.4 million.

The immediate payment has been recorded in Paladin's financial statements, but the deferred payment has not been recorded. Paladin's cost of capital is 8% per annum.

On 1 February 20X1, Paladin also acquired 25% of the equity shares of Augusta paying $10 million in cash. Augusta made a profit of $1.2 million for the year ended 30 September 20X1.

The summarised statements of financial position of the three entities at 30 September 20X1 are:

	Paladin	Saracen
Assets	$000	$000
Non-current assets		
Property, plant and equipment	40,000	31,000
Intangible assets	7,500	
Investments – Saracen (8 million shares at $4 each)	32,000	
– Augusta	10,000	nil
	89,500	31,000
Current assets	22,000	13,700
Total assets	111,500	44,700
Equity and liabilities		
Equity		
Equity shares of $1 each	50,000	10,000
Retained earnings – at 1 October 20X0	25,700	12,000
– for year ended 30 September 20X1	9,200	6,000
	84,900	28,000
Non-current liabilities		
Deferred tax	15,000	8,000
Current liabilities	11,600	8,700
Total equity and liabilities	111,500	44,700

The following information is relevant:

(i) Paladin's policy is to value the non-controlling interest at fair value at the date of acquisition. For this purpose the directors of Paladin considered a share price for Saracen of $3.50 per share to be appropriate.

(ii) At the date of acquisition, the fair values of Saracen's property, plant and equipment was equal to its carrying amount with the exception of Saracen's plant which had a fair value of $4 million above its carrying amount. At that date the plant had a remaining life of four years. Saracen uses straight-line depreciation for plant assuming a nil residual value.

Also at the date of acquisition, Paladin valued Saracen's customer relationships as an intangible asset at fair value of $3 million. Saracen has not accounted for this asset. Trading relationships with Saracen's customers last on average for six years.

(iii) At 30 September 20X1, Saracen's inventory included goods bought from Paladin (at cost to Saracen) of $2.6 million. Paladin had marked up these goods by 30% on cost.

(iv) Impairment tests were carried out on 30 September 20X1 which concluded that consolidated goodwill was not impaired, but, due to disappointing earnings, the value of the investment in Augusta was impaired by $2.5 million.

(v) Assume all profits accrue evenly through the year.

Required:

Prepare the consolidated statement of financial position for Paladin as at 30 September 20X1.

(Total: 20 marks) ⊞

377 PYRAMID

On 1 April 20X1, Pyramid acquired 80% of Square's equity shares by means of an immediate share exchange and a cash payment of 88 cents per acquired share, deferred until 1 April 20X2. Pyramid has recorded the share exchange, but not the cash consideration. Pyramid's cost of capital is 10% per annum.

The summarised statements of financial position of the two entities as at 31 March 20X2 are:

	Pyramid	Square
Assets	$000	$000
Non-current assets		
Property, plant and equipment	38,100	28,500
Investments – Square	24,000	
– Other equity (note (iii))	2,000	nil
	64,100	28,500
Current assets		
Inventory (note (ii))	13,900	10,400
Trade receivables (note (ii))	11,400	5,500
Bank (note (ii))	9,400	600
Total assets	98,800	45,000

Equity shares of $1 each	25,000	10,000
Share premium	17,600	nil
Retained earnings – at 1 April 20X1	16,200	18,000
– for year ended 31 March 20X2	14,000	8,000
	72,800	36,000
Non-current liabilities (note (i))	16,500	4,000
Current liabilities (note (ii))	9,500	5,000
Total equity and liabilities	98,800	45,000

The following information is relevant:

(i) At the date of acquisition, Pyramid conducted a fair value exercise on Square's net assets which were equal to their carrying amounts with the following exceptions:

- An item of plant had a fair value of $3 million above its carrying amount. At the date of acquisition it had a remaining life of five years. Ignore deferred tax relating to this fair value.

- Square had an unrecorded deferred tax liability of $1 million, which was unchanged as at 31 March 20X2.

Pyramid's policy is to value the non-controlling interest at fair value at the date of acquisition. For this purpose a share price for Square of $3.50 each is representative of the fair value of the shares held by the non-controlling interest.

(ii) Pyramid sells goods to Square at cost plus 50%. Below is a summary of the recorded activities for the year ended 31 March 20X2 and balances as at 31 March 20X2:

	Pyramid $000	Square $000
Sales to Square	16,000	
Purchases from Pyramid		14,500
Included in Pyramid's receivables	4,400	
Included in Square's payables		1,700

On 26 March 20X2, Pyramid sold and despatched goods to Square, which Square did not record until they were received on 2 April 20X2. Square's inventory was counted on 31 March 20X2 and does not include any goods purchased from Pyramid.

On 27 March 20X2, Square remitted to Pyramid a cash payment which was not received by Pyramid until 4 April 20X2. This payment accounted for the remaining difference on the current accounts.

(iii) The other equity investments of Pyramid are carried at their fair values on 1 April 20X1. At 31 March 20X2, these had increased to $2.8 million.

Required:

Prepare the consolidated statement of financial position for Pyramid as at 31 March 20X2.

(Total: 20 marks) ⊞

378 VIAGEM

 Question debrief

On 1 January 20X2, Viagem acquired 90% of the equity share capital of Greca in a share exchange in which Viagem issued two new shares for every three shares it acquired in Greca. Additionally, on 31 December 20X2, Viagem will pay the shareholders of Greca $1.76 per share acquired. Viagem's cost of capital is 10% per annum. The deferred consideration has not yet been recorded by Viagem.

At the date of acquisition, shares in Viagem and Greca had a stock market value of $6.50 and $2.50 each, respectively.

Statements of profit or loss for the year ended 30 September 20X2

	Viagem	Greca
	$000	$000
Revenue	64,600	38,000
Cost of sales	(51,200)	(26,000)
Gross profit	13,400	12,000
Distribution costs	(1,600)	(1,800)
Administrative expenses	(3,800)	(2,400)
Investment income	500	nil
Finance costs	(420)	nil
Profit before tax	8,080	7,800
Income tax expense	(2,800)	(1,600)
Profit for the year	5,280	6,200
Equity as at 1 October 20X1		
Equity shares of $1 each	30,000	10,000
Retained earnings	54,000	35,000

The following information is relevant:

(i)   At the date of acquisition, the fair values of Greca's assets were equal to their carrying amounts with the exception of two items:

- An item of plant had a fair value of $1.8 million above its carrying amount. The remaining life of the plant at the date of acquisition was three years. Depreciation is charged to cost of sales.

- Greca had a contingent liability which Viagem estimated to have a fair value of $450,000. This has not changed as at 30 September 20X2.

Greca has not incorporated these fair value changes into its financial statements.

(ii)   Viagem's policy is to value the non-controlling interest at fair value at the date of acquisition. For this purpose, Greca's share price at that date can be deemed to be representative of the fair value of the shares held by the non-controlling interest.

(iii)   Sales from Viagem to Greca throughout the year ended 30 September 20X2 had consistently been $800,000 per month. Viagem made a mark-up on cost of 25% on these sales. Greca had $1.5 million of these goods in inventory as at 30 September 20X2.

(iv)   Viagem's investment income is a dividend received from its investment in a 40% owned associate which it has held for several years. The underlying earnings for the associate for the year ended 30 September 20X2 were $2 million.

(v)   Although Greca has been profitable since its acquisition by Viagem, the market for Greca's products has been badly hit in recent months and Viagem has calculated that the goodwill has been impaired by $2 million as at 30 September 20X2.

Required:

(a)   Calculate the consolidated goodwill at the date of acquisition of Greca.   (7 marks)

(b)   Prepare the consolidated statement of profit or loss for Viagem for the year ended 30 September 20X2.   (13 marks)

(Total: 20 marks)

   Calculate your allowed time, allocate the time to the separate parts

---

379   PARADIGM

On 1 October 20X2, Paradigm acquired 75% of Strata's equity shares by means of a share exchange of two new shares in Paradigm for every five acquired shares in Strata. In addition, Paradigm issued to the shareholders of Strata a $100 10% loan note for every 1,000 shares it acquired in Strata. Paradigm has not recorded any of the purchase consideration, although it does have other 10% loan notes already in issue.

The market value of Paradigm's shares at 1 October 20X2 was $2 each.

The summarised statements of financial position of the two entities as at 31 March 20X3 are:

	Paradigm	Strata
Assets	$000	$000
Non-current assets		
Property, plant and equipment	47,400	25,500
Financial asset: equity investments (notes (i) and (iii))	7,500	3,200
	———	———
	54,900	28,700
Current assets		
Inventory (note (ii))	20,400	8,400
Trade receivables	14,800	9,000
Bank	2,100	nil
	———	———
Total assets	92,200	46,100
	———	———

Equity and liabilities

Equity

Equity shares of $1 each	40,000	20,000
Retained earnings/(losses) – at 1 April 20X2	19,200	(4,000)
– for year ended 31 March 20X3	7,400	8,000
	66,600	24,000
Non-current liabilities		
10% loan notes	8,000	nil
Current liabilities		
Trade payables	17,600	13,000
Bank overdraft	nil	9,100
Total equity and liabilities	92,200	46,100

The following information is relevant:

(i)   At the date of acquisition, Strata produced a draft statement of profit or loss which showed it had made a net loss after tax of $2 million at that date. Paradigm accepted this figure as the basis for calculating the pre- and post-acquisition split of Strata's profit for the year ended 31 March 20X3.

Also at the date of acquisition, Paradigm conducted a fair value exercise on Strata's net assets which were equal to their carrying amounts (including Strata's financial asset equity investments) with the exception of an item of plant which had a fair value of $3 million **below** its carrying amount. The plant had a remaining useful life of three years at 1 October 20X2.

Paradigm's policy is to value the non-controlling interest at fair value at the date of acquisition. For this purpose, a share price for Strata of $1.20 each is representative of the fair value of the shares held by the non-controlling interest.

(ii)   Each month since acquisition, Paradigm's sales to Strata were consistently $4.6 million. Paradigm had marked these up by 15% on cost. Strata had one month's supply ($4.6 million) of these goods in inventory at 31 March 20X3. Paradigm's normal mark-up (to third party customers) is 40%.

(iii) The financial asset equity investments of Paradigm and Strata are carried at their fair values as at 1 April 20X2. As at 31 March 20X3, these had fair values of $7.1 million and $3.9 million respectively.

(iv)   There were no impairment losses within the group during the year ended 31 March 20X3.

Required:

(a) **Prepare the consolidated statement of financial position for Paradigm as at 31 March 20X3.** **(15 marks)**

(b) A financial assistant has observed that the fair value exercise means that a subsidiary's net assets are included at acquisition at their fair (current) values in the consolidated statement of financial position. The assistant believes that it is inconsistent to aggregate the subsidiary's net assets with those of the parent because most of the parent's assets are carried at historical cost.

Required:

Comment on the assistant's observation and explain why the net assets of acquired subsidiaries are consolidated at acquisition at their fair values. **(5 marks)**

(Total: 20 marks) ▦

380 POLESTAR

On 1 April 20X3, Polestar acquired 75% of Southstar. Southstar had been experiencing difficult trading conditions and making significant losses. In allowing for Southstar's difficulties, Polestar made an immediate cash payment of only $1.50 per share. In addition, Polestar will pay a further amount in cash on 30 September 20X4 if Southstar returns to profitability by that date. The fair value of this contingent consideration at the date of acquisition was estimated to be $1.8 million, but at 30 September 20X3 in the light of continuing losses, its value was estimated at only $1.5 million. The contingent consideration has not been recorded by Polestar. Overall, the directors of Polestar expect the acquisition to be a bargain purchase leading to negative goodwill.

Below are the summarised draft financial statements of both entities.

Statements of profit or loss for the year ended 30 September 20X3

	Polestar	Southstar
	$000	$000
Revenue	110,000	66,000
Cost of sales	(88,000)	(67,200)
Gross profit (loss)	22,000	(1,200)
Operating expenses	(8,500)	(4,400)
Profit (loss) before tax	13,500	(5,600)
Income tax (expense)/relief	(3,500)	1,000
Profit (loss) for the year	10,000	(4,600)

Statements of financial position as at 30 September 20X3

	Polestar	Southstar
Assets	$000	$000
Non-current assets		
Property, plant and equipment	41,000	21,000
Investments	13,500	
Current assets	19,000	4,800
Total assets	73,500	25,800
Equity and liabilities		
Equity shares of 50 cents each	30,000	6,000
Retained earnings	28,500	12,000
	58,500	18,000
Current liabilities	15,000	7,800
Total equity and liabilities	73,500	25,800

The following information is relevant:

(i)   At the date of acquisition, the fair values of Southstar's assets were equal to their carrying amounts with the exception of a property. This had a fair value of $2 million above its carrying amount and a remaining useful life of 10 years at that date. All depreciation is included in cost of sales.

(ii)   Polestar transferred raw materials at their cost of $4 million to Southstar in June 20X3. Southstar processed all of these materials incurring additional direct costs of $1.4 million and sold them back to Polestar in August 20X3 for $9 million. At 30 September 20X3 Polestar had $1.5 million of these goods still in inventory. There were no other intra-group sales.

(iii)   Polestar's policy is to value the non-controlling interest at fair value at the date of acquisition. This was deemed to be $3.6 million.

(iv)   All items in the above statements of profit or loss are deemed to accrue evenly over the year unless otherwise indicated.

Required:

(a)   **Prepare the consolidated statement of profit or loss for Polestar for the year ended 30 September 20X3.**   **(11 marks)**

(b)   **Prepare the consolidated statement of financial position for Polestar as at 30 September 20X3.**   **(9 marks)**

(Total: 20 marks) ▦

381 PENKETH

On 1 October 20X3, Penketh acquired 90 million of Sphere's 150 million $0.50 equity shares. Penketh will pay $1.54 cash on 30 September 20X4 for each share acquired. Penketh's finance cost is 10% per annum. Sphere's share price as at 1 October 20X3 was $1.25. The statements of profit or loss and other comprehensive income for the year ended 31 March 20X4 are:

	Penketh	Sphere
	$000	$000
Revenue	620,000	310,000
Cost of sales	(400,000)	(150,000)
Gross profit	220,000	160,000
Distribution costs	(40,000)	(20,000)
Administrative expenses	(36,000)	(25,000)
Investment income	5,000	1,600
Finance costs	(2,000)	(5,600)
Profit before tax	147,000	111,000
Income tax expense	(45,000)	(31,000)
Profit for the year	102,000	80,000
Other comprehensive income		
Gain/(loss) on revaluation of land (note (ii))	(2,200)	1,000
Total comprehensive income for the year	99,800	81,000

The following information is relevant:

(i)   A fair value exercise on 1 October 20X3 concluded that the carrying amounts of Sphere's net assets were equal to their fair values with the following exceptions:

- Plant with a remaining life of two years had a fair value of $6 million in excess of its carrying amount. Plant depreciation is charged to cost of sales.

- Penketh placed a value of $5 million on Sphere's good relationships with its customers. Penketh expected, on average, a customer relationship to last for a further five years. Amortisation is charged to administrative expenses.

(ii)   Sphere's land, valued using the revaluation model, increased by $1 million since the acquisition.

(iii) After the acquisition Penketh sold goods to Sphere for $20 million at a 25% mark-up. Sphere had one fifth of these goods still in inventory at 31 March 20X4.

(iv)   All items accrue evenly over the year unless otherwise indicated. Sphere had retained earnings of $70 million at 1 April 20X3. There were no other components of equity at this date.

(v)   Penketh measures the non-controlling interest at fair value at the date of acquisition. To calculate fair value, the share price of Sphere should be used.

Required:

(a)   **Calculate goodwill arising on the acquisition of Sphere as at 1 October 20X3.**
(5 marks)

(b)   **Prepare the consolidated statement of profit or loss and other comprehensive income of Penketh for the year ended 31 March 20X4.**   **(15 marks)**

(Total: 20 marks)

382   PLASTIK

 Question debrief

On 1 January 20X4, Plastik acquired 80% of the equity share capital of Subtrak. The consideration was satisfied by a share exchange of two shares in Plastik for every three acquired shares in Subtrak. At the date of acquisition, shares in Plastik and Subtrak had a market value of $3 and $2.50 each respectively. Plastik will also pay cash consideration of 27.5 cents on 1 January 20X5 for each acquired share in Subtrak. Plastik has a cost of capital of 10% per annum. None of the consideration has been recorded by Plastik.

Below are the extracts from the draft financial statements of both entities.

Extracts from the statements of profit or loss and other comprehensive income for the year ended 30 September 20X4

	Plastik	Subtrak
	$000	$000
Revenue	62,600	30,000
Cost of sales	(45,800)	(24,000)
Finance costs	(200)	(nil)

Statements of financial position as at 30 September 20X4

Assets	Plastik	Subtrak
Non-current assets	$000	$000
Property, plant and equipment	18,700	13,900
Investments: 10% loan note from Subtrak (note (ii))	1,000	nil
	19,700	13,900
Current assets	9,000	4,000
Total assets	28,700	17,900

	Plastik $000	Subtrak $000
Equity and liabilities		
Equity		
Equity shares of $1 each	10,000	9,000
Revaluation surplus (note (i))	2,000	nil
Retained earnings	6,300	3,500
	18,300	12,500
Non-current liabilities		
10% loan notes (note (ii))	2,500	1,000
Current liabilities		
Trade payables (note (iv))	7,900	4,400
Total equity and liabilities	28,700	17,900

The following information is relevant:

(i) At the date of acquisition, the fair values of Subtrak's assets and liabilities were equal to their carrying amounts with the exception of Subtrak's property which had a fair value of $4 million above its carrying amount. For consolidation purposes, this led to an increase in depreciation charges (in cost of sales) of $100,000 in the post-acquisition period to 30 September 20X4. Subtrak has not incorporated the fair value property increase into its entity financial statements.

The policy of the Plastik group is to revalue all properties to fair value at each year end. On 30 September 20X4, the increase in Plastik's property has already been recorded, however, a further increase of $600,000 in the value of Subtrak's property since its value at acquisition and 30 September 20X4 has not been recorded.

(ii) On 30 September 20X4, Plastik accepted a $1 million 10% loan note from Subtrak.

(iii) Sales from Plastik to Subtrak throughout the year ended 30 September 20X4 had consistently been $300,000 per month. Plastik made a mark-up on cost of 25% on all these sales. $600,000 (at cost to Subtrak) of Subtrak's inventory at 30 September 20X4 had been supplied by Plastik in the post-acquisition period.

(iv) Plastik had a trade receivable balance owing from Subtrak of $1.2 million as at 30 September 20X4. This differed to the equivalent trade payable of Subtrak due to a payment by Subtrak of $400,000 made in September 20X4 which did not clear Plastik's bank account until 4 October 20X4. Both entities have overdrafts rather than positive cash balances.

(v) Plastik's policy is to value the non-controlling interest at fair value at the date of acquisition. For this purpose Subtrak's share price at that date can be deemed to be representative of the fair value of the shares held by the non-controlling interest.

(vi) Assume, except where indicated otherwise, that all items of income and expenditure accrue evenly throughout the year. Subtrak's profit for the year ended 30 September 20X4 was $2 million.

Required:

(a) Prepare extracts from Plastik's consolidated statement of profit or loss for the year ended 30 September 20X4 for:

  (i) revenue

  (ii) cost of sales

  (iii) finance costs. **(5 marks)**

(b) Prepare the consolidated statement of financial position for Plastik as at 30 September 20X4. **(15 marks)**

(Total: 20 marks) ▦

 Calculate your allowed time, allocate the time to the separate parts

---

383 BYCOMB

On 1 July 20X4 Bycomb acquired 80% of Cyclip's equity shares on the following terms:

- a share exchange of two shares in Bycomb for every three shares acquired in Cyclip; and

- a cash payment due on 30 June 20X5 of $1.54 per share acquired (Bycomb's cost of capital is 10% per annum).

At the date of acquisition, shares in Bycomb and Cyclip had a stock market value of $3.00 and $2.50 each respectively.

Statements of profit or loss for the year ended 31 March 20X5:

	Bycomb	Cyclip
	$000	$000
Revenue	24,200	10,800
Cost of sales	(17,800)	(6,800)
Gross profit	6,400	4,000
Distribution costs	(500)	(340)
Administrative expenses	(800)	(360)
Finance costs	(400)	(300)
Profit before tax	4,700	3,000
Income tax expense	(1,700)	(600)
Profit for the year	3,000	2,400

Equity in the separate financial statements of Cyclip as at 1 April 20X4:

	$000
Equity	
Equity shares of $1 each	12,000
Retained earnings	13,500

The following information is also relevant:

(i)   At the date of acquisition, the fair values of Cyclip's assets were equal to their carrying amounts with the exception of an item of plant which had a fair value of $720,000 above its carrying amount. The remaining life of the plant at the date of acquisition was 18 months. Depreciation is charged to cost of sales.

(ii)   On 1 April 20X4, Cyclip commenced the construction of a new production facility, financing this by a bank loan. Cyclip has followed the local GAAP in the country where it operates which prohibits the capitalisation of interest. Bycomb has calculated that, in accordance with IAS 23 *Borrowing Costs*, interest of $100,000 (which accrued evenly throughout the year) would have been capitalised at 31 March 20X5. The production facility is still under construction as at 31 March 20X5.

(iii)   Sales from Bycomb to Cyclip in the post-acquisition period were $3 million at a mark-up on cost of 20%. Cyclip had $420,000 of these goods in inventory as at 31 March 20X5.

(iv)   Bycomb's policy is to value the non-controlling interest at fair value at the date of acquisition. For this purpose Cyclip's share price at that date can be deemed to be representative of the fair value of the shares held by the non-controlling interest.

(v)   On 31 March 20X5, Bycomb carried out an impairment review which identified that the goodwill on the acquisition of Cyclip was impaired by $500,000. Impaired goodwill is charged to cost of sales.

Required:

(a)   **Calculate the consolidated goodwill at the date of acquisition of Cyclip.**   **(6 marks)**

(b)   **Prepare extracts from Bycomb's consolidated statement of profit or loss for the year ended 31 March 20X5, for:**

  (i)   **revenue**   **(1 mark)**

  (ii)   **cost of sales**   **(3 marks)**

  (iii)   **finance costs**   **(2½ marks)**

  (iv)   **profit or loss attributable to the non-controlling interest**   **(2½ marks)**

(Total for (b) 9 marks)

(c)   IFRS 3 *Business combinations* permits a non-controlling interest at the date of acquisition to be valued by one of two methods:

  (i)   at its proportionate share of the subsidiary's identifiable net assets; or

  (ii)   at its fair value (usually determined by the directors of the parent).

  Required: Explain the difference that the accounting treatment of these alternative methods could have on the consolidated financial statements, including where consolidated goodwill may be impaired.   **(5 marks)**

(Total: 20 marks)

384 PALISTAR

On 1 January 20X5, Palistar acquired 75% of Stretcher's equity shares by means of an immediate share exchange of two shares in Palistar for five shares in Stretcher. The fair value of Palistar and Stretcher's shares on 1 January 20X5 were $4 and $3 respectively. In addition to the share exchange, Palistar will make a cash payment of $1.32 per acquired share, deferred until 1 January 20X6. Palistar has not recorded any of the consideration for Stretcher in its financial statements. Palistar's cost of capital is 10% per annum.

The summarised statements of financial position of the two entities as at 30 June 20X5 are:

	Palistar $000	Stretcher $000
Assets		
Non-current assets (note (ii))		
Property, plant and equipment	55,000	28,600
Financial asset equity investments (note (v))	11,500	6,000
	66,500	34,600
Current assets		
Inventory (note (iv))	17,000	15,400
Trade receivables (note (iv))	14,300	10,500
Bank	2,200	1,600
	33,500	27,500
Total assets	100,000	62,100
Equity and liabilities		
Equity		
Equity shares of $1 each	20,000	20,000
Other component of equity	4,000	nil
Retained earnings – at 1 July 20X4	26,200	14,000
– for year ended 30 June 20X5	24,000	10,000
	74,200	44,000
Current liabilities (note (iv))	25,800	18,100
Total equity and liabilities	100,000	62,100

The following information is relevant:

(i)   Stretcher's business is seasonal and 60% of its annual profit is made in the period 1 January to 30 June each year.

(ii)   At the date of acquisition, the fair value of Stretcher's net assets was equal to their carrying amounts with the following exceptions:

The fair value of Stretcher's financial asset equity investments, carried at a value of $6 million, was $7 million (see also note (v)).

Stretcher owned the rights to a popular mobile (cell) phone game. At the date of acquisition, a specialist valuer estimated that the rights were worth $12 million and had an estimated remaining life of five years.

(iii)   Following an impairment review, consolidated goodwill is to be written down by $3 million as at 30 June 20X5.

(iv)   Palistar sells goods to Stretcher at cost plus 30%. Stretcher had $1.8 million of goods in its inventory at 30 June 20X5 which had been supplied by Palistar. In addition, on 28 June 20X5, Palistar processed the sale of $800,000 of goods to Stretcher, which Stretcher did not account for until their receipt on 2 July 20X5. The in-transit reconciliation should be achieved by assuming the transaction had been recorded in the books of Stretcher before the year end. At 30 June 20X5, Palistar had a trade receivable balance of $2.4 million due from Stretcher which differed to the equivalent balance in Stretcher's books due to the sale made on 28 June 20X5.

(v)   At 30 June 20X5, the fair values of the financial asset equity investments of Palistar and Stretcher were $13.2 million and $7.9 million respectively.

(vi)   Palistar's policy is to value the non-controlling interest at fair value at the date of acquisition. For this purpose the value given for Stretcher's shares may be used.

Required:

Prepare the consolidated statement of financial position for Palistar as at 30 June 20X5.

(Total: 20 marks) ▦

385 LAUREL

On 1 January 20X6, Laurel acquired 60% of the equity share capital of Rakewood in a share exchange in which Laurel issued three new shares for every five shares it acquired in Rakewood. The share issue has not yet been recorded by Laurel. Additionally, on 31 December 20X6, Laurel will pay to the shareholders of Rakewood $1.62 per share acquired. Laurel's cost of capital is 8% per annum.

At the date of acquisition, shares in Laurel and Rakewood had a market value of $7 and $2 each respectively.

Statements of profit or loss for the year ended 30 September 20X6

	Laurel	Rakewood
	$000	$000
Revenue	84,500	52,000
Cost of sales	(58,200)	(34,000)
Gross profit	26,300	18,000
Distribution costs	(2,000)	(1,600)
Administrative expenses	(4,100)	(2,800)
Investment income (note (iv))	500	400
Finance costs	(300)	nil
Profit before tax	20,400	14,000
Income tax expense	(4,800)	(3,600)
Profit for the year	15,600	10,400

Equity as at 1 October 20X5

	$000	$000
Equity shares of $1 each	20,000	15,000
Retained earnings	72,000	25,000

The following information is relevant:

(i) At the date of acquisition, Laurel conducted a fair value exercise on Rakewood's net assets which were equal to their carrying amounts with the following exceptions:

– an item of plant had a fair value of $4m above its carrying amount. At the date of acquisition it had a remaining life of two years.

– inventory of $800,000 had a fair value of $1m. All of this inventory had been sold by 30 September 20X6.

(ii) Laurel's policy is to value the non-controlling interest at fair value at the date of acquisition. For this purpose Rakewood's share price at 1 January 20X6 can be deemed to be representative of the fair value of the shares held by the non-controlling interest.

(iii) Laurel had traded with Rakewood for many years before the acquisition. Sales from Rakewood to Laurel throughout the year ended 30 September 20X6 were consistently $1.2m per month. Rakewood made a mark-up on cost of 20% on these sales. Laurel had $1.8m of these goods in inventory as at 30 September 20X6.

(iv) Laurel's investment income consists of:

– its share of a dividend of $500,000 paid by Rakewood in August 20X6.

– a dividend of $200,000 received from Artic, a 25% owned associate which it has held for several years. The profit after tax of Artic for the year ended 30 September 20X6 was $2.4m.

(v) Assume, except where indicated otherwise, that all items of income and expense accrue evenly throughout the year.

(vi) There were no impairment losses within the group during the year ended 30 September 20X6.

e the consolidated goodwill at the date of acquisition of Rakewood Co.

(7 marks)

the consolidated statement of profit or loss for Laurel Co for the year
0 September 20X6. (13 marks)

(Total: 20 marks)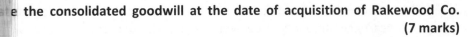

)

1 20X6 Dargent Co acquired 75% of Latree Co's equity shares by means of a
ge of two shares in Dargent Co for every three Latree Co shares acquired. On
ther consideration was also issued to the shareholders of Latree Co in the
00 8% loan note for every 100 shares acquired in Latree Co. None of the
sideration, nor the outstanding interest on the loan notes at 31 March 20X6,
recorded by Dargent Co. At the date of acquisition, the share prices of
nd Latree Co are $3.20 and $1.80 respectively.

sed statements of financial position of the two companies as at 31 March 20X6

	Dargent Co $000	Latree Co $000
assets		
nt and equipment (note (i))	75,200	31,500
n Amery Co at 1 April 20X5 (note (iv))	4,500	nil
	79,700	31,500
ts		
ote (iii))	19,400	18,800
ables (note (iii))	14,700	12,500
	1,200	600
	35,300	31,900
Total assets	115,000	63,400
Equity and liabilities		
Equity shares of $1 each	50,000	20,000
Retained earnings – at 1 April 20X5	20,000	19,000
– for year ended 31 March 20X6	16,000	8,000
	86,000	47,000
Non-current liabilities		
8% loan notes	5,000	nil
Current liabilities (note (iii))	24,000	16,400
Total equity and liabilities	115,000	63,400

The following information is relevant:

(i)   At the date of acquisition, the fair values of Latree Co's assets were equal to their carrying amounts. However, Latree Co operates a mine which requires to be decommissioned in five years' time. No provision has been made for these decommissioning costs by Latree Co. The present value (discounted at 8%) of the decommissioning is estimated at $4m and will be paid five years from the date of acquisition (the end of the mine's life).

(ii)   Dargent Co's policy is to value the non-controlling interest at fair value at the date of acquisition. Latree Co's share price at that date can be deemed to be representative of the fair value of the shares held by the non-controlling interest.

(iii)   The inventory of Latree Co includes goods bought from Dargent Co for $2.1m. Dargent Co applies a consistent mark-up on cost of 40% when arriving at its selling prices.

On 28 March 20X6, Dargent Co despatched goods to Latree Co with a selling price of $700,000. These were not received by Latree Co until after the year-end, and so have not been included in the above inventory at 31 March 20X6.

At 31 March 20X6, Dargent Co's records showed a receivable due from Latree Co of $3m. This differed to the equivalent payable in Latree Co's records due to the goods in transit.

The intra-group reconciliation should be achieved by assuming that Latree Co had received the goods in transit before the year-end.

(iv)   The investment in Amery Co represents 30% of its voting share capital and Dargent Co uses equity accounting to account for this investment. Amery Co's profit for the year ended 31 March 20X6 was $6m and Amery Co paid total dividends during the year ended 31 March 20X6 of $2m. Dargent Co has recorded its share of the dividend received from Amery Co in investment income (and cash).

(v)   All profits and losses accrued evenly throughout the year.

(vi)   There were no impairment losses within the group for the year ended 31 March 20X6.

Required:

Prepare the consolidated statement of financial position for Dargent Co as at 31 March 20X6.

(Total: 20 marks) ⊞

387 PARTY CO

The following are the draft statements of financial position of Party Co and St[reamer Co]
at 30 September 20X5:

	Party Co $000	Streamer $000
ASSETS		
Non-current assets		
Property, plant and equipment	392,000	84,000
Investments	120,000	Nil
	512,000	84,000
Current assets	94,700	44,650
Total assets	606,700	128,650
EQUITY AND LIABILITIES		
Equity		
Equity shares	190,000	60,000
Retained earnings	210,000	36,500
Revaluation surplus	41,400	4,000
	441,400	100,500
Non-current liabilities		
Deferred consideration	28,000	Nil
Current liabilities	137,300	28,150
Total equity and liabilities	606,700	128,650

Temple of S[...]

HIEROGLYPHIC AL[...]

Made In Egypt

The following information is relevant:

(i) On 1 October 20X4, Party Co acquired 80% of the share capital of Streamer Co. At this date the retained earnings of Streamer Co were $34m and the revaluation surplus stood at $4m. Party Co paid an initial cash amount of $92m and agreed to pay the owners of Streamer Co a further $28m on 1 October 20X6. The accountant has recorded the full amounts of both elements of the consideration in investments. Party Co has a cost of capital of 8%. The appropriate discount rate is 0·857.

(ii) On 1 October 20X4, the fair values of Streamer Co's net assets were equal to their carrying amounts with the exception of some inventory which had cost $3m but had a fair value of $3·6m. On 30 September 20X5, 10% of these goods remained in the inventories of Streamer Co.

(iii) During the year, Party Co sold goods totalling $8m to Streamer Co at a gross profit margin of 25%. At 30 September 20X5, Streamer Co still held $1m of these goods in inventory. Party Co's normal margin (to third party customers) is 45%.

(iv) The Party group uses the fair value method to value the non-controlling interest. At acquisition the non-controlling interest was valued at $15m.

Required:

(a) Prepare the consolidated statement of financial position of the Party group as at 30 September 20X5. **(15 marks)**

(b) Party Co has a strategy of buying struggling businesses, reversing their decline and then selling them on at a profit within a short period of time. Party Co is hoping to do this with Streamer Co.

As an adviser to a prospective purchaser of Streamer Co, explain any concerns you would raise about making an investment decision based on the information available in the Party Group's consolidated financial statements in comparison to that available in the individual financial statements of Streamer Co. **(5 marks)**

(Total: 20 marks) ⊞

ANALYSING FINANCIAL STATEMENTS

388 HARDY *Walk in the footsteps of a top tutor*

Hardy is a public listed manufacturing entity. Its summarised financial statements are shown below.

Statements of profit or loss for the year ended 30 September:

	20X6	20X5
	$000	$000
Revenue	29,500	36,000
Cost of sales	(25,500)	(26,000)
Gross profit	4,000	10,000
Distribution costs	(1,050)	(800)
Administrative expenses	(4,900)	(3,900)
Investment income	50	200
Finance costs	(600)	(500)
Profit (loss) before taxation	(2,500)	5,000
Income tax (expense) relief	400	(1,500)
Profit (loss) for the year	(2,100)	3,500

Statements of financial position as at 30 September:

	$000	20X6 $000	$000	20X5 $000
Assets				
Non-current assets				
Property, plant and equipment		17,600		24,500
Investments at fair value through profit or loss		2,400		4,000
		20,000		28,500
Current assets				
Inventory and work-in-progress	2,200		1,900	
Trade receivables	2,200		2,800	
Tax asset	600		nil	
Bank	1,200		100	
		6,200		4,800
Total assets		26,200		33,300
Equity and liabilities				
Equity				
Equity shares of $1 each		13,000		12,000
Share premium		1,000		nil
Revaluation surplus		nil		4,500
Retained earnings		3,600		6,500
		17,600		23,000
Non-current liabilities				
Bank loan		4,000		5,000
Deferred tax		1,200		700
Current liabilities				
Trade payables	3,400		2,800	
Current tax payable	nil		1,800	
		3,400		4,600
Total equity and liabilities		26,200		33,300

The following information has been obtained from the Chairman's Statement and the notes to the financial statements:

'Market conditions during the year ended 30 September 20X6 proved very challenging due largely to difficulties in the global economy as a result of a sharp recession which has led to steep falls in share prices and property values. Hardy has not been immune from these effects and our properties have suffered impairment losses of $6 million in the year.'

The excess of these losses over previous surpluses has led to a charge to cost of sales of $1.5 million in addition to the normal depreciation charge.

'Our portfolio of investments at fair value through profit or loss has been 'marked to market' (fair valued) resulting in a loss of $1.6 million (included in administrative expenses).'

There were no additions to or disposals of non-current assets during the year.

'In response to the downturn we have unfortunately had to make a number of employees redundant incurring severance costs of $1.3 million (included in cost of sales) and undertaken cost savings in advertising and other administrative expenses.'

'The difficulty in the credit markets has meant that the finance cost of our variable rate bank loan has increased from 4.5% to 8%. In order to help cash flows, we made a rights issue during the year and reduced the dividend per share by 50%.'

'Despite the above events and associated costs, the Board believes our underlying performance has been quite resilient in these difficult times.'

Required:

Analyse and discuss the financial performance and position of Hardy as portrayed by the above financial statements and the additional information provided.

Your analysis should be supported by any SEVEN profitability, liquidity and gearing and other appropriate ratios (up to 7 marks available).

(Total: 20 marks) 💻

389 PINTO

Pinto is a publicly listed entity. The statement of cash flows of Pinto is available:

Statement of cash flows of Pinto for the year to 31 March 20X8:

	$000	$000
Cash flows from operating activities		
Profit before tax		440
Depreciation		280
Loss on disposal of plant and machinery		90
Increase in warranty provision		100
Investment income		(60)
Finance costs		50
Redemption penalty costs included in administrative expenses		20
		────
		920
Increase in inventories	(400)	
Decrease in trade receivables	60	
Increase in trade payables	360	
	────	
		20
		────
Cash generated from operations		940
Interest paid		(50)
Tax refund received		60
		────
Net cash from operating activities		950

Cash flows from investing activities		
Purchase of property, plant and equipment	(1,440)	
Sale of property, plant and equipment	150	
Rental income received from investment property	40	
Net cash used in investing activities		(1,250)
Cash flows from financing activities		
Proceeds from issue of shares	1,000	
Repayment of loan notes	(420)	
Dividends paid	(150)	
Net cash from financing activities		430
Net increase in cash and cash equivalents		130
Cash and cash equivalents at beginning of period		(120)
Cash and cash equivalents at end of period		10

The following supporting information is available:

(i) An item of plant with a carrying amount of $240,000 was sold at a loss of $90,000 during the year. Depreciation of $280,000 was charged (to cost of sales) for property, plant and equipment in the year ended 31 March 20X8.

Pinto uses the fair value model in IAS 40 *Investment Property*. There were no purchases or sales of investment property during the year.

(ii) The 6% loan notes were redeemed early incurring a penalty payment of $20,000 which has been charged as an administrative expense in the statement of profit or loss and other comprehensive income.

(iii) There was an issue of shares for cash on 1 October 20X7.

(iv) Pinto gives a 12 month warranty on some of the products it sells. The amounts shown in current liabilities as warranty provision are an accurate assessment, based on past experience, of the amount of claims likely to be made in respect of warranties outstanding at each year end. Warranty costs are included in cost of sales.

Required:

(a) **Comment on the cash flow management of Pinto as revealed by the statement of cash flows and the information provided by the above financial statements.**

Note: **Ratio analysis is not required, and will not be awarded any marks.** **(15 marks)**

(b) In recent years many analysts have commented on a growing disillusionment with the usefulness and reliability of the information contained in some entities' statements of profit or loss and other comprehensive income.

Required:

Discuss the extent to which an entity's statement of cash flows may be more useful and reliable than its statement of profit or loss. **(5 marks)**

(Total: 20 marks) 🖩

390 HARBIN *Walk in the footsteps of a top tutor*

Shown below are the recently issued summarised financial statements of Harbin, a listed entity, for the year ended 30 September 20X7, together with comparatives for 20X6 and extracts from the Chief Executive's report that accompanied their issue.

Consolidated statements of profit or loss

	20X7	20X6
	$000	$000
Revenue	250,000	180,000
Cost of sales	(200,000)	(150,000)
Gross profit	50,000	30,000
Operating expenses	(26,000)	(22,000)
Finance costs	(8,000)	(Nil)
Profit before tax	16,000	8,000
Income tax expense (at 25%)	(4,000)	(2,000)
Profit for the period	12,000	6,000

Consolidated statement of financial position

	20X7	20X6
	$000	$000
Non-current assets		
Property, plant and equipment	210,000	90,000
Goodwill	10,000	Nil
	220,000	90,000
Current assets		
Inventory	25,000	15,000
Trade receivables	13,000	8,000
Bank	nil	14,000
	38,000	37,000
Total assets	258,000	127,000

Equity and liabilities		
Equity shares of $1 each	100,000	100,000
Retained earnings	14,000	12,000
	114,000	112,000
Non-current liabilities		
8% loan notes	100,000	Nil
Current liabilities		
Bank overdraft	17,000	Nil
Trade payables	23,000	13,000
Current tax payable	4,000	2,000
	44,000	15,000
Total equity and liabilities	258,000	127,000

Extracts from the Chief Executive's report:

'Highlights of Harbin's performance for the year ended 30 September 20X7:

- an increase in sales revenue of 39%

- gross profit margin up from 16.7% to 20%

- a doubling of the profit for the period.

In response to the improved position the Board paid a dividend of 10 cents per share in September 20X7 an increase of 25% on the previous year.'

You have also been provided with the following further information.

On 1 October 20X6 Harbin purchased the whole of the net assets of Fatima (previously a privately owned entity) for $100 million. The contribution of the purchase to Harbin's results for the year ended 30 September 20X7 was:

	$000
Revenue	70,000
Cost of sales	(40,000)
Gross profit	30,000
Operating expenses	(8,000)
Profit before tax	22,000

There were no disposals of non-current assets during the year.

The following ratios have been calculated for the year ended 30 September 20X6 and 20X7:

	20X7	20X6
Return on year-end capital employed		7.1%
(profit before interest and tax over total assets less current liabilities)		
Net asset (equal to capital employed) turnover	1.2	1.6
Net profit (before tax) margin	6.4%	4.4%
Current ratio		2.5
Closing inventory holding period (in days)		37
Trade receivables' collection period (in days)		16
Trade payables' payment period (based on cost of sales) (in days)	42	32
Gearing (debt over debt plus equity)		Nil

Required:

(a) **Calculate the missing ratios for 20X7.** **(5 marks)**

(b) **Assess the financial performance and position of Harbin for the year ended 30 September 20X7 compared to the previous year. Your answer should refer to the information in the Chief Executive's report and the impact of the purchase of the net assets of Fatima.** **(15 marks)**

(Total: 20 marks)

391 VICTULAR *Walk in the footsteps of a top tutor*

Victular would like to acquire 100% of a suitable private entity. It has obtained the following draft financial statements for two entities, Grappa and Merlot. They operate in the same industry and their managements have indicated that they would be receptive to a takeover.

Statements of profit or loss for the year ended 30 September 20X8

	Grappa	Merlot
	$000	$000
Revenue	12,000	20,500
Cost of sales	(10,500)	(18,000)
Gross profit	1,500	2,500
Operating expenses	(240)	(500)
Finance costs – loan	(210)	(300)
– overdraft	Nil	(10)
– lease	Nil	(290)
Profit before tax	1,050	1,400
Income tax expense	(150)	(400)
Profit for the year	900	1,000
Note: Dividends paid during the year	250	700

Statements of financial position as at 30 September 20X8

Assets

Non-current assets

Freehold factory (note (i))		4,400		Nil
Owned plant (note (ii))		5,000		2,200
Right-of-use asset (note (ii))		Nil		5,300
		9,400		7,500
Current assets				
Inventory	2,000		3,600	
Trade receivables	2,400		3,700	
Bank	600	5,000	Nil	7,300
Total assets		14,400		14,800
Equity and liabilities				
Equity shares of $1 each		2,000		2,000
Property revaluation surplus	900		Nil	
Retained earnings	2,600		800	
		3,500		800
		5,500		2,800
Non-current liabilities				
Lease liabilities (note (iii))	Nil		3,200	
7% loan notes	3,000		Nil	
10% loan notes	Nil		3,000	
Deferred tax	600		100	
Government grants	1,200		Nil	
		4,800		6,300
Current liabilities				
Bank overdraft	Nil		1,200	
Trade payables	3,100		3,800	
Government grants	400		Nil	
Lease liabilities (note (iii))	Nil		500	
Taxation	600		200	
		4,100		5,700
Total equity and liabilities		14,400		14,800

Notes

(i)   Both entities operate from similar premises.

(ii)   Additional details of the two entities' plant are:

	Grappa	Merlot
	$000	$000
Owned plant – cost	8,000	10,000
Right-of-use plant – initial value	Nil	7,500

There were no disposals of plant during the year by either entity.

(iii) The interest rate implicit within Merlot's leases is 7.5% per annum. For the purpose of calculating ROCE and gearing, **all** lease obligations are treated as long-term interest bearing borrowings.

(iv) The following ratios have been calculated for Grappa and can be taken to be correct:

Return on year end capital employed (ROCE) (capital employed taken as shareholders' funds plus long-term interest bearing borrowings – see note (iii) above)	14.8%
Gross profit margin	12.5%
Operating profit margin	10.5%
Current ratio	1.2:1
Closing inventory holding period	70 days
Trade receivables' collection period	73 days
Trade payables' payment period (using cost of sales)	108 days
Gearing (see note (iii) above)	35.3%

Required:

(a) Calculate for Merlot the ratios equivalent to all those given for Grappa above.

(4 marks)

(b) Assess the relative performance and financial position of Grappa and Merlot for the year ended 30 September 20X8 to inform the directors of Victular in their acquisition decision.

(11 marks)

(c) Outline the problems in using ratios for comparison purposes between entities, and suggest what additional information would be useful for Victular in reaching its decision.

(5 marks)

(Total: 20 marks) 🖳

392 QUARTILE

Quartile sells jewellery through stores in retail shopping centres throughout the country. Over the last two years it has experienced declining profitability and is wondering if this is related to the sector as whole. It has recently subscribed to an agency that produces average ratios across many businesses. Below are the ratios that have been provided by the agency for Quartile's business sector based on a year end of 30 June 20X2.

	Sector
Return on year-end capital employed (ROCE)	16.8%
Net asset (total assets less current liabilities) turnover	1.4 times
Gross profit margin	35%
Operating profit margin	12%
Current ratio	1.25:1
Average inventory turnover	3 times
Trade payables payment period	64 days
Debt to equity	38%

The financial statements of Quartile for the year ended 30 September 20X2 are shown below.

Statement of profit or loss

	$000	$000
Revenue		56,000
Opening inventory	8,300	
Purchases	43,900	
	52,200	
Closing inventory	(10,200)	
		(42,000)
Gross profit		14,000
Operating costs		(9,800)
Finance costs		(800)
Profit before tax		3,400
Income tax expense		(1,000)
Profit for the year		2,400

Statement of financial position

	$000	$000
Assets		
Non-current assets		
Property and shop fittings		25,600
Deferred development expenditure		5,000
		30,600
Current assets		
Inventory	10,200	
Bank	1,000	
		11,200
Total assets		41,800

Equity and liabilities

Equity

Equity shares of $1 each	15,000
Property revaluation surplus	3,000
Retained earnings	8,600
	──────
	26,600

Non-current liabilities

10% loan notes		8,000
Current liabilities		
Trade payables	5,400	
Current tax payable	1,800	7,200
	──────	──────
Total equity and liabilities		41,800
		──────

Note: The deferred development expenditure relates to an investment in a process to manufacture artificial precious gems for future sale by Quartile in the retail jewellery market.

Required:

(a) **Prepare the ratios for Quartile equivalent to those of the sector.** **(7 marks)**

(b) **Assess the financial and operating performance of Quartile in comparison to its sector averages.** **(13 marks)**

(Total: 20 marks) 🖳

393 BENGAL

Bengal is a public entity. Its most recent financial statements are shown below:

Statements of profit or loss for the year ended 31 March

	20X1	20X0
	$000	$000
Revenue	25,500	17,250
Cost of sales	(14,800)	(10,350)
	──────	──────
Gross profit	10,700	6,900
Distribution costs	(4,800)	(3,300)
Finance costs	(650)	(100)
	──────	──────
Profit before taxation	5,250	3,500
Income tax expense	(2,250)	(1,000)
	──────	──────
Profit for the year	3,000	2,500
	──────	──────

Statement of cash flows for the year ended 31 March 20X1:

	$000	$000
Cash flows from operating activities:		
Profit from operations		5,900
Adjustments for:		
depreciation of non-current assets		640
increase in inventories		(1,800)
increase in receivables		(1,000)
increase in payables		650
		_____
Cash generated from operations		4,390
Finance costs paid		(650)
Income tax paid		(1,250)
		_____
Net cash from operating activities		2,490
Cash flows from investing activities:		
Purchase of property, plant and equipment	(6,740)	
Purchase of intangibles	(6,200)	
	_____	
Net cash used in investing activities		(12,940)
Cash flows from financing activities:		
Issue of 8% loan note	7,000	
Equity dividends paid	(750)	
	_____	
Net cash from financing activities		6,250
		_____
Net decrease in cash and cash equivalents		(4,200)
Cash and cash equivalents at beginning of period		4,000
		_____
Cash and cash equivalents at end of period		(200)
		_____

Notes

(i)   There were no disposals of non-current assets during the period; however Bengal does have some non-current assets classified as 'held for sale' at 31 March 20X1.

(ii)   Depreciation of property, plant and equipment for the year ended 31 March 20X1 was $640,000.

A disappointed shareholder has observed that although revenue during the year has increased by 48% (8,250/17,250 × 100), profit for the year has only increased by 20% (500/2,500 × 100).

Required:

Comment on the performance (including addressing the shareholder's observation) and cash flow of Bengal for the year ended 31 March 20X1.

Note: up to 5 marks are available for the calculation of appropriate ratios.

(Total: 20 marks) 🖥

394   WOODBANK

Shown below are the financial statements of Woodbank for its most recent two years.

Consolidated statements of profit or loss for the year ended 31 March:

	20X4	20X3
	$000	$000
Revenue	150,000	110,000
Cost of sales	(117,000)	(85,800)
Gross profit	33,000	24,200
Distribution costs	(6,000)	(5,000)
Administrative expenses	(9,000)	(9,200)
Finance costs – loan note interest	(1,750)	(500)
Profit before tax	16,250	9,500
Income tax expense	(5,750)	(3,000)
Profit for the year	10,500	6,500

Statements of financial position as at 31 March:

	20X4	20X3
	$000	$000
Assets		
Non-current assets		
Property, plant and equipment	118,000	85,000
Goodwill	30,000	nil
	148,000	85,000
Current assets		
Inventory	15,500	12,000
Trade receivables	11,000	8,000
Bank	500	5,000
	27,000	25,000
Total assets	175,000	110,000

Equity and liabilities

Equity

Equity shares of $1 each	80,000	80,000
Retained earnings	15,000	10,000
	95,000	90,000

Non-current liabilities		
10% loan notes	55,000	5,000

Current liabilities		
Trade payables	21,000	13,000
Current tax payable	4,000	2,000
	25,000	15,000
Total equity and liabilities	175,000	110,000

The following information is available:

(i) On 1 January 20X4, Woodbank purchased the trading assets and operations of Shaw for $50 million and, on the same date, issued additional 10% loan notes to finance the purchase. Shaw was an unincorporated entity and its results (for three months from 1 January 20X4 to 31 March 20X4) and net assets (including goodwill not subject to any impairment) are included in Woodbank's financial statements for the year ended 31 March 20X4. There were no other purchases or sales of non-current assets during the year ended 31 March 20X4.

(ii) Extracts of the results (for three months) of the previously separate business of Shaw, which are included in Woodbank's statement of profit or loss for the year ended 31 March 20X4, are:

	$000
Revenue	30,000
Cost of sales	(21,000)
Gross profit	9,000
Distribution costs	(2,000)
Administrative expenses	(2,000)

(iii) The following six ratios have been correctly calculated for Woodbank for the year ended 31 March:

	20X3	20X4
Return on capital employed (ROCE)	10.5%	12.0%
(profit before interest and tax/year-end total assets less current liabilities)		
Net asset (equal to capital employed) turnover	1.16 times	1.0 times
Gross profit margin	22.0%	22.0%
Profit before interest and tax margin	9.1%	12.0%
Current ratio	1.7:1	1.08:1
Gearing (debt/(debt + equity))	5.3%	36.7%

Required:

(a) Calculate for the year ended 31 March 20X4 equivalent ratios to the first FOUR only for Woodbank excluding the effects of the purchase of Shaw.

Note: Assume the capital employed for Shaw is equal to its purchase price of $50 million. **(4 marks)**

(b) Assess the comparative financial performance and position of Woodbank for the year ended 31 March 20X4. Your answer should refer to the effects of the purchase of Shaw. **(12 marks)**

(c) Discuss what further information specific to the acquisition of Shaw that would allow you to make a more informed assessment of Woodbank's performance and position. **(4 marks)**

(Total: 20 marks) 💻

395 HYDAN

 Question debrief

Xpand is a publicly listed entity which has experienced rapid growth in recent years through the acquisition and integration of other entities. Xpand is interested in acquiring Hydan, a retailing business, which is one of several entities owned and managed by the same family, of which Lodan is the ultimate parent.

The summarised financial statements of Hydan for the year ended 30 September 20X4 are:

Statement of profit or loss

	$000
Revenue	70,000
Cost of sales	(45,000)
Gross profit	25,000
Operating costs	(7,000)
Directors' salaries	(1,000)
Profit before tax	17,000
Income tax expense	(3,000)
Profit for the year	14,000

Statement of financial position

	$000	$000
Assets		
Non-current assets		
Property, plant and equipment		32,400
Current assets		
Inventory	7,500	
Bank	100	
	———	7,600
Total assets		40,000
Equity and liabilities		
Equity		
Equity shares of $1 each		1,000
Retained earnings		18,700
		19,700
Non-current liabilities		
Directors' loan accounts (interest free)		10,000
Current liabilities		
Trade payables	7,500	
Current tax payable	2,800	
	———	10,300
Total equity and liabilities		40,000

From the above financial statements, Xpand has calculated for Hydan the ratios below for the year ended 30 September 20X4. It has also obtained the equivalent ratios for the retail sector average which can be taken to represent Hydan's sector.

	Hydan	Sector average
Return on equity (ROE) (including directors' loan accounts)	47.1%	22.0%
Net asset turnover	2.36 times	1.67 times
Gross profit margin	35.7%	30.0%
Net profit margin	20.0%	12.0%

From enquiries made, Xpand has learned the following information:

(i) Hydan buys all of its trading inventory from another of the family entities at a price which is 10% less than the market price for such goods.

(ii) After the acquisition, Xpand would replace the existing board of directors and need to pay remuneration of $2.5 million per annum.

(iii) The directors' loan accounts would be repaid by obtaining a loan of the same amount with interest at 10% per annum.

(iv) Xpand expects the purchase price of Hydan to be $30 million.

Required:

(a) Recalculate the ratios for Hydan after making appropriate adjustments to the financial statements for notes (i) to (iv) above. For this purpose, the expected purchase price of $30 million should be taken as Hydan's equity and net assets are equal to this equity plus the loan. You may assume the changes will have no effect on taxation. **(6 marks)**

(b) In relation to the ratios calculated in (a) above, and the ratios for Hydan given in the question, comment on the performance of Hydan compared to its retail sector average. **(9 marks)**

(c) One of Xpand's directors has suggested that it would be wise to look at the Lodan group's consolidated financial statements rather than Hydan's individual financial statements.

As an adviser to Xpand, explain any concerns you would raise about basing an investment decision on the information available in Lodan's consolidated financial statements and Hydan's entity financial statements. **(5 marks)**

(Total: 20 marks) 🖥

 Calculate your allowed time, allocate the time to the separate parts

396 YOGI

Yogi is a public entity and extracts from its most recent financial statements are provided below:

Statements of profit or loss for the year ended 31 March

	20X5	20X4
	$000	$000
Revenue	36,000	50,000
Cost of sales	(24,000)	(30,000)
Gross profit	12,000	20,000
Profit from sale of division (see note (i))	1,000	nil
Distribution costs	(3,500)	(5,300)
Administrative expenses	(4,800)	(2,900)
Finance costs	(400)	(800)
Profit before taxation	4,300	11,000
Income tax expense	(1,300)	(3,300)
Profit for the year	3,000	7,700

Statements of financial position as at 31 March

	20X5			20X4	
	$000	$000		$000	$000
Non-current assets					
Property, plant and equipment		16,300			19,000
Intangible – goodwill		nil			2,000
		16,300			21,000
Current assets					
Inventory	3,400			5,800	
Trade receivables	1,300			2,400	
Bank	1,500	6,200		nil	8,200
Total assets		22,500			29,200
Equity and liabilities					
Equity					
Equity shares of $1 each		10,000			10,000
Retained earnings		3,000			4,000
		13,000			14,000
Non-current liabilities					
10% loan notes		4,000			8,000
Current liabilities					
Bank overdraft	nil			1,400	
Trade payables	4,300			3,100	
Current tax payable	1,200	5,500		2,700	7,200
Total equity and liabilities		22,500			29,200

Notes

(i) On 1 April 20X4, Yogi sold the net assets (including goodwill) of a separately operated division of its business for $8 million cash on which it made a profit of $1 million. This transaction required shareholder approval and, in order to secure this, the management of Yogi offered shareholders a dividend of 40 cents for each share in issue out of the proceeds of the sale. The trading results of the division which are included in the statement of profit or loss for the year ended 31 March 20X4 above are:

	$000
Revenue	18,000
Cost of sales	(10,000)
Gross profit	8,000
Distribution costs	(1,000)
Administrative expenses	(1,200)
Profit before interest and tax	5,800

(ii)   The following selected ratios for Yogi have been calculated for the year ended 31 March 20X4 (as reported above):

Gross profit margin	40.0%
Operating profit margin	23.6%
Return on capital employed (profit before interest and tax/(total assets – current liabilities))	53.6%
Net asset turnover	2.27 times

Required:

(a)   Calculate the equivalent ratios for Yogi:

(i)   for the year ended 31 March 20X4, after excluding the contribution made by the division that has been sold;   and

(ii)   for the year ended 31 March 20X5, excluding the profit on the sale of the division.   (5 marks)

(b)   Comment on the comparative financial performance and position of Yogi for the year ended 31 March 20X5.   (10 marks)

(c)   On a separate matter, you have been asked to advise on an application for a loan to build an extension to a sports club which is a not-for-profit organisation. You have been provided with the audited financial statements of the sports club for the last four years.

Required:

Identify and explain the ratios that you would calculate to assist in determining whether you would advise that the loan should be granted.   (5 marks)

(Total: 20 marks) 🖳

397   XPAND

Xpand is a public entity which has grown in recent years by acquiring established businesses. The following financial statements for two potential target entities are shown below. They operate in the same industry sector and Xpand believes their shareholders would be receptive to a takeover. An indicative price for 100% acquisition of the entities is $12 million each.

Statements of profit or loss for the year ended 30 September 20X5

	Kandid $000	Kovert $000
Revenue	25,000	40,000
Cost of sales	(19,000)	(32,800)
Gross profit	6,000	7,200
Distribution and administrative expenses	(1,250)	(2,300)
Finance costs	(250)	(900)
Profit before tax	4,500	4,000
Income tax expense	(900)	(1,000)
Profit for the year	3,600	3,000

Statements of financial position as at 30 September 20X5

	$000	$000
Non-current assets		
Property	nil	3,000
Owned plant	4,800	2,000
Right-of-use asset	nil	5,300
	4,800	10,300
Current assets		
Inventory	1,600	3,400
Trade receivables	2,100	5,100
Bank	1,100	200
	4,800	8,700
Total assets	9,600	19,000
Equity and liabilities		
Equity		
Equity shares of $1 each	1,000	2,000
Property revaluation surplus	nil	900
Retained earnings	1,600	2,700
	2,600	5,600
Non-current liabilities		
Lease liability	nil	4,200
5% loan notes (31 December 20X6)	5,000	nil
10% loan notes (31 December 20X6)	nil	5,000
	5,000	9,200
Current liabilities		
Trade payables	1,250	2,100
Lease liability	nil	1,000
Taxation	750	1,100
	2,000	4,200
Total equity and liabilities	9,600	19,000

Notes

(i)   Carrying amount of plant:

	Kandid	Kovert
	$000	$000
Owned plant – cost	8,000	10,000
Less government grant	(2,000)	
	———	
	6,000	
Accumulated depreciation	(1,200)	(8,000)
	———	———
	4,800	2,000
Right-of-use asset – initial value	nil	8,000

(ii)   The following ratios have been calculated:

	Kandid	Kovert
Return on year-end capital employed (ROCE)	62.5%	
Net asset (taken as same figure as capital employed) turnover	3.3 times	2.5 times
Gross profit margin	24.0%	18.0%
Profit margin (before interest and tax)	19.0%	
Current ratio	2.4:1	2.1:1
Closing inventory holding period	31 days	38 days
Trade receivables collection period	31 days	47 days
Trade payables payment period (using cost of sales)	24 days	
Gearing (debt/(debt + equity))	65.8%	

Required:

(a)   Calculate the missing ratios for Kovert. All lease liabilities are treated as debt, and profit before interest and tax should be used for the calculation of return on capital employed. **(4 marks)**

(b)   Using the above information, assess the relative performance and financial position of Kandid and Kovert for the year ended 30 September 20X5 in order to assist the directors of Xpand to make an acquisition decision. **(12 marks)**

(c)   Describe what further information may be useful to Xpand when making an acquisition decision. **(4 marks)**

(Total: 20 marks) 💻

398 SCHRUTE

Schrute is a group in the farming industry and owns a number of 100% owned farming subsidiaries. Its financial statements for the last two years are shown below.

Consolidated statement of profit or loss for the year ended 30 September:

	20X3	20X2
	$000	$000
Revenue	94,000	68,500
Cost of sales	(46,000)	(28,000)
Gross profit	48,000	40,500
Distribution costs	(21,200)	(19,300)
Administrative expenses	(25,600)	(15,400)
Profit from operations	1,200	5,800
Investment income	0	600
Finance costs	(120)	0
Profit before tax	1,080	6,400
Taxation	(300)	(1,920)
Profit for the year	780	4,480
Attributable to:		
Shareholders of Schrute	1,580	4,480
Non-controlling interest	(800)	–
	780	4,480

Extracts from the consolidated statement of financial position as at 30 September:

	20X3	20X2
	$000	$000
Inventories	6,500	4,570
Trade receivables	17,000	15,600
Bank	610	6,000
Equity:		
Equity shares of $1 each	25,000	6,000
Retained earnings	73,500	72,500
Non-controlling interest	510	–
Non-current liabilities:		
Loan	20,000	–
Current liabilities	9,100	5,690

The following information is relevant:

(i)   Schrute has become increasingly worried about two major areas in its business environment. Firstly, there are concerns that reliance on large supermarkets is putting pressure on cash flow, as the supermarkets demand long payment terms. Secondly, the consistent increases in fuel prices mean that delivering the produce nationally is becoming extremely expensive.

(ii)   To manage this, Schrute acquired 80% of Howard on 1 October 20X2, which operates a small number of hotels. It was hoped that this would improve cash flow, as customers pay up front, and reduce the impact of further fuel price rises.

(iii)   To fund this, Schrute disposed of $11 million held in investments, making a $4.5 million profit on disposal. This profit is included within administrative expenses.

(iv)   Howard opened a new hotel in March 20X3. After poor reviews, Schrute Farms recruited a new marketing director in May. Following an extensive marketing campaign, online feedback improved.

(v)   The following ratios have been calculated for the year ended 30 September 20X2:

Gross profit margin	59.1%
Operating profit margin	8.5%
Return on Capital Employed	7.4%
Current ratio	4.6:1
Inventory turnover period	60 days
Receivables collection period	83 days

Required:

(a)   **For the ratios provided above, prepare the equivalent figures for the year ended 30 September 20X3.**   **(5 marks)**

(b)   **Analyse the performance and position of Schrute for the year ended 30 September 20X3, making specific reference to any concerns or expectations regarding future periods.**   **(15 marks)**

(Total: 20 marks) 🖥

399   PITCARN

The Pitcarn group owns a number of subsidiaries. On 31 March 20X6, the Pitcarn group sold its entire holding in Sitor. The consolidated statement of profit or loss of the Pitcarn group for 20X6 has been produced **without** the results of Sitor due to its disposal. No profit or loss on disposal has been included in the 20X6 consolidated statement of profit or loss.

Extracts from the consolidated statements of profit or loss for the Pitcarn group are below:

Statements of profit or loss (extracts) for the year ended 31 March

	20X6	20X5
	$000	$000
Revenue	86,000	99,000
Cost of sales (note (ii))	(63,400)	(67,200)
Gross profit	22,600	31,800
Other income (notes (i) and (iii))	3,400	1,500
Operating expenses	(21,300)	(23,200)
Profit from operations	4,700	10,100
Finance costs	(1,500)	(1,900)

The following notes are relevant:

(i)   Sitor was based in the Pitcarn head offices, for which it pays annual rent to Pitcarn of $300,000, significantly below the cost of equivalent office space in Sitor's local area. As Sitor is no longer in the group, Pitcarn has included this income within other income. Sitor expenses rent payments in operating expenses.

(ii)   Sitor sold goods totalling $8 million to Pitcarn (included in Pitcarn's cost of sales above) during the year. Pitcarn held none of these goods in inventory at 31 March 20X6. Sitor made a margin of 40% on all goods sold to Pitcarn.

(iii)   Pitcarn received a dividend of $1 million from Sitor during the year, as well as recording interest of $500,000 on a loan given to Sitor in 20X3. Both of these amounts are included within Pitcarn's other income.

The following selected ratios for the Pitcarn group have been calculated for the years ended 31 March 20X5 and 31 March 20X6 from the information above.

	20X6	20X5
Gross profit margin	26.3%	32.1%
Operating margin	5.5%	10.2%
Interest cover	3.1 times	5.3 times

(iv)   Sitor's individual statement of profit or loss for the year ended shows the following:

	$000
Revenue	16,000
Cost of sales	(10,400)
Gross profit	5,600
Operating expenses	(3,200)
Profit from operations	2,400
Finance costs	(900)

Required:

(a) Calculate the equivalent ratios for the consolidated statement of profit or loss for the year ended 31 March 20X6 if Sitor had been consolidated. **(7 marks)**

(b) Analyse the performance of the Pitcarn group for the year ended 31 March 20X6. This should also include a discussion of Sitor. **(8 marks)**

(c) Pitcarn acquired 80% of Sitor's 10 million $1 shares on 1 April 20X1 for $17 million when Sitor had retained earnings of $3 million. Pitcarn uses the fair value method for valuing the non-controlling interest. At acquisition the fair value of the non-controlling interest was $3 million.

On 31 March 20X6, Pitcarn sold its entire shareholding in Sitor for $25 million when Sitor had retained earnings of $7 million. Goodwill had suffered no impairment since acquisition.

Calculate the gain/loss on disposal to be shown in the consolidated statement of profit or loss for the year ended 31 March 20X6. **(5 marks)**

(Total: 20 marks) ⊞

400 GREGORY

Gregory is a listed entity and, until 1 October 20X5, it had no subsidiaries. On that date, it acquired 75% of Tamsin's equity shares by means of a share exchange of two new shares in Gregory for every five acquired shares in Tamsin. These shares were recorded at the market price on the day of the acquisition and were the only shares issued by Gregory during the year ended 31 March 20X6.

The summarised financial statements of Gregory as a group at 31 March 20X6 and as a single entity at 31 March 20X5 are:

Statements of profit or loss for the year ended	Gregory group 31 March 20X6	Gregory single entity 31 March 20X5
	$000	$000
Revenue	46,500	28,000
Cost of sales	(37,200)	(20,800)
Gross profit	9,300	7,200
Operating expenses	(1,800)	(1,200)
Profit before tax (operating profit)	7,500	6,000
Income tax expense	(1,500)	(1,000)
Profit for the year	6,000	5,000
Profit for year attributable to:		
Equity holders of the parent	5,700	
Non-controlling interest	300	
	6,000	

Statements of financial position as at	31 March 20X6	31 March 20X5
Assets	$000	$000
Non-current assets		
Property, plant and equipment	54,600	41,500
Goodwill	3,000	nil
	57,600	41,500
Current assets	44,000	36,000
Total assets	101,600	77,500

	31 March 20X6	31 March 20X5
Equity and liabilities	$000	$000
Equity		
Equity shares of $1 each	46,000	40,000
Other component of equity (share premium)	6,000	nil
Retained earnings	18,700	13,000
Equity attributable to owners of the parent	70,700	53,000
Non-controlling interest	3,600	nil
	74,300	53,000
Current liabilities	27,300	24,500
Total equity and liabilities	101,600	77,500

Other information:

(i) Each month since the acquisition, Gregory's sales to Tamsin were consistently $2m. Gregory had chosen to only make a gross profit margin of 10% on these sales as Tamsin is part of the group.

(ii) The values of property, plant and equipment held by both entities have been rising for several years.

(iii) On reviewing the above financial statements, Gregory's chief executive officer (CEO) made the following observations:

(1) I see the profit for the year has increased by $1m which is up 20% on last year, but I thought it would be more as Tamsin was supposed to be very profitable.

(2) I have calculated the earnings per share (EPS) for 20X6 at 13 cents (6,000/46,000 × 100) and for 20X5 at 12.5 cents (5,000/40,000 × 100) and, although the profit has increased 20%, our EPS has barely changed.

(3) I am worried that the low price at which we are selling goods to Tamsin is undermining our group's overall profitability.

(4) I note that our share price is now $2.30, how does this compare with our share price immediately before we bought Tamsin?

Required:

(a) Reply to the four observations of the CEO. **(8 marks)**

(b) Using the above financial statements, calculate the following ratios for Gregory for the years ended 31 March 20X6 and 20X5 and comment on the comparative performance:

(i) Return on capital employed (ROCE)

(ii) Net asset turnover

(iii) Gross profit margin

(iv) Operating profit margin.

Note: Four marks are available for the ratio calculations. **(12 marks)**

Note: Your answers to (a) and (b) should reflect the impact of the consolidation of Tamsin during the year ended 31 March 20X6.

(Total: 20 marks) 💻

401 LANDING

Landing is considering the acquisition of Archway, a retail entity. The summarised financial statements of Archway for the year ended 30 September 20X6 are:

Statement of profit or loss

	$000
Revenue	94,000
Cost of sales	(73,000)
Gross profit	21,000
Distribution costs	(4,000)
Administrative expenses	(6,000)
Finance costs	(400)
Profit before tax	10,600
Income tax expense (at 20%)	(2,120)
Profit for the year	8,480

Statement of financial position

	$000	$000
Non-current assets		
Property, plant and equipment		29,400
Current assets		
Inventory	10,500	
Bank	100	10,600
Total assets		40,000

Equity and liabilities

Equity shares of $1 each		10,000
Retained earnings		8,800
		18,800
Current liabilities		
4% loan notes (redeemable 1 November 20X6)	10,000	
Trade payables	9,200	
Current tax payable	2,000	21,200
Total equity and liabilities		40,000

From enquiries made, Landing has obtained the following information:

(i)   Archway pays an annual licence fee of $1m to Cardol (included in cost of sales) for the right to package and sell some goods under a well-known brand name owned by Cardol. If Archway is acquired, this arrangement would be discontinued. Landing estimates that this would not affect Archway's volume of sales, but without the use of the brand name packaging, overall sales revenue would be 5% lower than currently.

(ii)   Archway buys 50% of its purchases for resale from Cardol, one of Landing's rivals, and receives a bulk buying discount of 10% off normal prices (this discount does not apply to the annual licence fee referred to in note (i) above). This discount would not be available if Archway is acquired by Landing.

(iii) The 4% loan notes have been classified as a current liability due to their imminent redemption. As such, they should not be treated as long-term funding. However, they will be replaced immediately after redemption by 8% loan notes with the same nominal value, repayable in ten years' time.

(iv)   Landing has obtained some of Archway's retail sector average ratios for the year ended 30 September 20X6. It has then calculated the equivalent ratios for Archway as shown below:

	Sector average	Archway
Annual sales per square metre of floor space	$8,000	$7,833
Return on capital employed (ROCE)	18.0%	58.5%
Net asset (total assets less current liabilities) turnover	2.7 times	5.0 times
Gross profit margin	22.0%	22.3%
Operating profit (profit before interest and tax) margin	6.7%	11.7%
Gearing (debt/equity)	30.0%	nil

A note accompanying the sector average ratios explains that it is the practice of the sector to carry retail property at market value. The market value of Archway's retail property is $3m more than its carrying amount (ignore the effect of any consequent additional depreciation) and gives 12,000 square metres of floor space.

Required:

(a) After making adjustments to the financial statements of Archway which you think may be appropriate for comparability purposes, restate:

    (i)   Revenue

    (ii)   Cost of sales

    (iii) Finance costs

    (iv) Equity (assume that your adjustments to profit or loss result in retained earnings of $2.3 million at 30 September 20X6) and

    (v)   Non-current liabilities.   **(5 marks)**

(b) Recalculate comparable sector average ratios for Archway based on your restated figures in (a) above.   **(6 marks)**

(c) Comment on the performance and gearing of Archway compared to the retail sector average as a basis for advising Landing regarding the possible acquisition of Archway.   **(9 marks)**

        (Total: 20 marks) ▦

402 FUNJECT CO

Funject Co has identified Aspect Co as a possible acquisition within the same industry. Aspect Co is currently owned by the Gamilton Group and the following are extracts from the financial statements of Aspect Co:

Extract from the statement of profit or loss for the year ended 31 December 20X4

	$000
Revenue	54,200
Cost of sales	(21,500)
Gross profit	32,700
Operating expenses	(11,700)
Operating profit	21,000

Statement of financial position as at 31 December 20X4

	$000	$000
Non-current assets		24,400
Current assets		
Inventory	4,900	
Receivables	5,700	
Cash at bank	2,300	
		12,900
Total assets		37,300

Equity and liabilities

Equity shares		1,000
Retained earnings		8,000
		9,000
Non-current liabilities: Loan		16,700
Current liabilities		
Trade payables	5,400	
Current tax payable	6,200	
		11,600
Total equity and liabilities		37,300

Additional information:

(i) On 1 April 20X4, Aspect Co decided to focus on its core business, and so disposed of a non-core division. The disposal generated a loss of $1.5m which is included within operating expenses for the year. The following extracts show the results of the non-core division for the period prior to disposal which were included in Aspect Co's results for 20X4:

	$000
Revenue	2,100
Cost of sales	(1,200)
Gross profit	900
Operating expenses	(700)
Operating profit	200

(ii) At present Aspect Co pays a management charge of 1% of revenue to the Gamilton Group, which is included in operating expenses. Funject Co imposes a management charge of 10% of gross profit on all of its subsidiaries.

(iii) Aspect Co's administration offices are currently located within a building owned by the Gamilton Group. If Aspect Co were acquired, the company would need to seek alternative premises. Aspect Co paid rent of $46,000 in 20X4. Commercial rents for equivalent office space would cost $120,000.

(iv) The following is a list of comparable industry average key performance indicators (KPIs) for 20X4:

KPI	
Gross profit margin	45%
Operating profit margin	28%
Receivables collection period	41 days
Current ratio	1.6:1
Acid test (quick) ratio	1.4:1
Gearing (debt/equity)	240%

Required:

(a)   Redraft Aspect Co's statement of profit or loss for 20X4 to adjust for the disposal of the non-core division in note (i) and the management and rent charges which would be imposed per notes (ii) and (iii) if Aspect Co was acquired by Funject Co.

(5 marks)

(b)   Calculate the 20X4 ratios for Aspect Co equivalent to those shown in note (iv) based on the restated financial information calculated in part (a).

Note: You should assume that any increase or decrease in profit as a result of your adjustments in part (a) will also increase or decrease cash.   **(5 marks)**

(c)   Using the ratios calculated in part (b), comment on Aspect Co's 20X4 performance and financial position compared to the industry average KPIs provided in note (iv).

(10 marks)

(Total: 20 marks) ⊞

403   FLASH CO

Flash Co sells electrical products both directly to the public and also to business trade customers. Flash Co operates from several properties which it owns. During 20X4, one of Flash Co's competitors ceased trading and Flash Co acquired a number of its properties and opened new stores in those properties in February 20X4.

Extracts from the statements of profit or loss for the years ended 31 March 20X3 and 20X4 are shown below, in addition to the statement of cash flows for the year ended 31 March 20X4.

Statement of profit or loss for the years ended 31 March

	20X4 $000	20X3 $000
Revenue	92,600	81,700
Cost of sales	(55,600)	(52,300)
Gross profit	37,000	29,400
Operating expenses	(14,400)	(12,300)
Profit from operations	22,600	17,100
Finance costs	(5,100)	(4,200)
Profit before tax	17,500	12,900

Statement of cash flows for the year ended 31 March 20X4

	$000	$000
Cash flows from operating activities:		
Cash generated from operations (note (i))		29,900
Interest paid		(4,300)
Tax paid		(3,100)
Net cash flows from operating activities		22,500
Cash flows from investing activities:		
Purchase of property, plant and equipment		(31,600)
Cash flows from financing activities:		
8% loan notes issued	10,000	
Dividends paid	(4,000)	
		6,000
Net decrease in cash and cash equivalents		(3,100)
Cash and cash equivalents 31 March 20X3		4,700
Cash and cash equivalents 31 March 20X4		1,600

The following notes are relevant:

(i)   Cash generated from operations for the year ended 31 March 20X4 is calculated as follows:

	$000
Profit before tax	17,500
Finance costs	5,100
Depreciation	6,800
Decrease in inventories	3,100
Increase in trade receivables	(6,200)
Increase in trade payables	3,600
Cash generated from operations	29,900

Note: The cash generated from operations for the year ended 31 March 20X3 was $18m.

(ii)   During the year ended 31 March 20X4, the sale of solar panels was one of Flash Co's key areas of business. During that year, demand has often been greater than supply.

(iii)   During the year ended 31 March 20X4, Flash Co expanded into new geographical regions in which it was previously unrepresented.

(iv)   The geographical expansion has allowed Flash Co to negotiate improved terms with some of its major suppliers.

(v)   Flash Co's sales director has expressed confusion at the latest financial statements, not understanding the deterioration in cash position despite increased levels of profit.

Required:

(a) Calculate the following ratios for the years ended 31 March 20X3 and 20X4:

– Gross profit margin %

– Operating profit margin %

– Interest cover

– Cash generated from operations/profit from operations %.   (4 marks)

(b) Comment on the performance and cash flows of Flash Co for 20X4.

Note: Your answer should specifically address the sales director's confusion.

(16 marks)

(Total: 20 marks) ⌨

404 MOWAIR CO

Mowair Co is an international airline which flies to destinations all over the world. Mowair Co experienced strong initial growth but in recent periods the company has been criticised for under-investing in its non-current assets.

Extracts from Mowair Co's financial statements are provided below.

Statements of financial position as at 30 June:

	20X7	20X6
	$000	$000
Assets		
Non-current assets		
Property, plant and equipment	317,000	174,000
Intangible assets (note ii)	20,000	16,000
	337,000	190,000
Current assets		
Inventories	580	490
Trade and other receivables	6,100	6,300
Cash and cash equivalents	9,300	22,100
Total current assets	15,980	28,890
Total assets	352,980	218,890

Equity and liabilities

Equity

Equity shares	3,000	3,000
Retained earnings	44,100	41,800
Revaluation surplus	145,000	Nil
Total equity	192,100	44,800

Liabilities

Non-current liabilities

6% loan notes	130,960	150,400

Current liabilities

Trade and other payables	10,480	4,250
6% loan notes	19,440	19,440
Total current liabilities	29,920	23,690
Total equity and liabilities	352,980	218,890

Other EXTRACTS from Mowair Co's financial statements for the years ended 30 June:

	20X7	20X6
	$000	$000
Revenue	154,000	159,000
Profit from operations	12,300	18,600
Finance costs	(9,200)	(10,200)
Cash generated from operations	18,480	24,310

The following information is also relevant:

(i) Mowair Co had exactly the same flight schedule in 20X7 as in 20X6, with the overall number of flights and destinations being the same in both years.

(ii) In April 20X7, Mowair Co had to renegotiate its licences with five major airports, which led to an increase in the prices Mowair Co had to pay for the right to operate flights there. The licences with ten more major airports are due to expire in December 20X7, and Mowair Co is currently in negotiation with these airports.

Required:

(a) Calculate the following ratios for the years ended 30 June 20X6 and 20X7:

    (i) Operating profit margin

    (ii) Return on capital employed

    (iii) Net asset turnover

    (iv) Current ratio

    (v) Interest cover

    (vi) Gearing (Debt/Equity).

    Note: For calculation purposes, all loan notes should be treated as debt.　(6 marks)

(b) Comment on the performance and position of Mowair Co for the year ended 30 June 20X7.

Note: Your answer should highlight any issues which Mowair Co should be considering in the near future. **(14 marks)**

(Total: 20 marks) 💻

405 PERKINS

Below are extracts from the statements of profit or loss for the Perkins group and Perkins Co for the years ending 31 December 20X7 and 20X6 respectively.

	20X7 (Consolidated)	20X6 (Perkins Co individual)
	$000	$000
Revenue	46,220	35,714
Cost of sales	(23,980)	(19,714)
Gross profit	22,240	16,000
Operating expenses	(3,300)	(10,000)
Profit from operations	18,940	6,000
Finance costs	(960)	(1,700)
Profit before tax	17,980	4,300

The following information is relevant:

On 1 September 20X7, Perkins Co sold all of its shares in Swanson Co, its only subsidiary, for $28.64m. At this date, Swanson Co had net assets of $26.1m. Perkins Co originally acquired 80% of Swanson Co for $19.2m, when Swanson Co had net assets of $19.8m. Perkins Co uses the fair value method for valuing the non-controlling interest, which was measured at $4.9m at the date of acquisition. Goodwill in Swanson Co has not been impaired since acquisition.

In order to compare Perkin Co's results for the years ended 20X6 and 20X7, the results of Swanson Co need to be eliminated from the above consolidated statements of profit or loss for 20X7. Although Swanson Co was correctly accounted for in the group financial statements for the year ended 31 December 20X7, a gain on disposal of Swanson Co of $9.44m is currently included in operating expenses. This reflects the gain which should have been shown in Perkins Co's individual financial statements.

In the year ended 31 December 20X7, Swanson Co had the following results:

	$m
Revenue	13.50
Cost of sales	6.60
Operating expenses	2.51
Finance costs	1.20

During the period from 1 January 20X7 to 1 September 20X7, Perkins Co sold $1m of goods to Swanson Co at a margin of 30%. Swanson Co had sold all of these goods on to third parties by 1 September 20X7.

Swanson Co previously used space in Perkins Co's properties, which Perkins Co did not charge Swanson Co for. Since the disposal of Swanson Co, Perkins Co has rented that space to a new tenant, recording the rental income in operating expenses.

The following ratios have been correctly calculated based on the above financial statements:

	20X7 (Consolidated)	20X6 (Perkins Co individual)
Gross profit margin	48.1%	44.8%
Operating margin	41%	16.8%
Interest cover	19.7 times	3.5 times

Required:

(a) Calculate the gain on disposal which should have been shown in the consolidated statement of profit or loss for the Perkins group for the year ended 31 December 20X7. **(5 marks)**

(b) Remove the results of Swanson Co and the gain on disposal of the subsidiary to prepare a revised statement of profit or loss for the year ended 31 December 20X7 for Perkins Co only. **(4 marks)**

(c) Calculate the equivalent ratios to those given for Perkins Co for 20X7 based on the revised figures in part (b) of your answer. **(2 marks)**

(d) Using the ratios calculated in part (c) and those provided in the question, comment on the performance of Perkins Co for the years ended 31 December 20X6 and 20X7.

(9 marks)

(Total: 20 marks) ▦

406 DUKE CO

Duke Co is a retailer with stores in numerous city centres. On 1 January 20X8, Duke Co acquired 80% of the equity share capital of Smooth Co, a service company specialising in training and recruitment. This was the first time Duke Co had acquired a subsidiary.

The consideration for Smooth Co consisted of a cash element and the issue of some shares in Duke Co to the previous owners of Smooth Co.

Duke Co has begun to consolidate Smooth Co into its financial statements, but has yet to calculate the non-controlling interest and retained earnings. Details of the relevant information is provided in notes (i) and (ii).

Extracts from the financial statements for the Duke group for the year ended 30 June 20X8 and Duke Co for the year ended 30 June 20X7 are provided below:

	Duke Group 30 June 20X8 $000	Duke Co 30 June 20X7 $000
Profit from operations	14,500	12,700
Current assets	30,400	28,750
Share capital	11,000	8,000
Share premium	6,000	2,000
Retained earnings	Note (i) and (ii)	9,400
Non-controlling interest	Note (i) and (ii)	Nil
Long-term loans	11,500	7,000
Current liabilities	21,300	15,600

The following notes are relevant:

(i)   The fair value of the non-controlling interest in Smooth Co at 1 January 20X8 was deemed to be $3.4m. The retained earnings of Duke Co in its individual financial statements at 30 June 20X8 are $13.2m.

Smooth Co made a profit for the year ended 30 June 20X8 of $7m. Duke Co incurred professional fees of $0.5m during the acquisition, which have been capitalised as an asset in the consolidated financial statements.

(ii)   The following issues are also relevant to the calculation of non-controlling interest and retained earnings:

–   At acquisition, Smooth Co's net assets were equal to their carrying amount with the exception of a brand name which had a fair value of $3m but was not recognised in Smooth Co's individual financial statements. It is estimated that the brand had a five-year life at 1 January 20X8.

–   On 30 June 20X8, Smooth Co sold land to Duke Co for $4m when it had a carrying amount of $2.5m.

(iii)   Smooth Co is based in the service industry and a significant part of its business comes from three large, profitable contracts with entities which are both well-established and financially stable.

(iv)   Duke Co did not borrow additional funds during the current year and has never used a bank overdraft facility.

(v)   The following ratios have been correctly calculated based on the above financial statements:

	20X8	20X7
Receivables collection period	52 days	34 days
Inventory holding period	41 days	67 days

Other than the recognition of the non-controlling interest and retained earnings, no adjustment is required to any of the other figures in the draft financial statements. All items are deemed to accrue evenly across the year.

Required:

(a) Calculate the non-controlling interest and retained earnings to be included in the consolidated financial statements at 30 June 20X8. **(6 marks)**

(b) Based on your answer to part (a) and the financial statements provided, calculate the following ratios for the years ending 30 June 20X7 and 30 June 20X8:

Current ratio:

Return on capital employed

Gearing (debt/equity). **(4 marks)**

(c) Using the information provided and the ratios calculated above, comment on the comparative performance and position for the two years ended 30 June 20X7 and 20X8.

Note: Your answer should specifically comment on the impact of the acquisition of Smooth Co on your analysis. **(10 marks)**

(Total: 20 marks) 🖥

Section 4

ANSWERS TO OBJECTIVE TEST QUESTIONS – SECTION A

CONCEPTUAL FRAMEWORK/INTERNATIONAL FINANCIAL REPORTING STANDARDS

1

	Capitalise	Expense
Clearance of the site prior to commencement of construction	✓	
Professional surveyor fees for managing the construction work	✓	
EW's own staff wages for time spent working on construction	✓	
A proportion of EW's administration costs, based on staff time spent		✓

The allocation of EW's administration costs would not be included as these costs are not directly incurred as a result of carrying out the construction. All of the others are costs which would not have been incurred without the related asset being built.

2   B

The cost of the decommissioning is assumed to be an obligation for the entity. An amount should be included in the cost of the asset when it is first recognised (1 July 20X4).

The amount to include in the cost of the asset for decommissioning costs is the present value of the expected future decommissioning costs. The present value is calculated by multiplying the expected future cost by a discount factor, which in this case is the discount factor for Year 5 (20X9) at 12%. $4 million × 0.567 = $2.268 million.

Therefore:

Debit:	Cost of asset	$2.268 million
Credit:	Provision for decommissioning costs	$2.268 million

The asset is depreciated on a straight-line basis over five years.

In addition, the decommissioning cost should be increased to $4 million by the end of Year 5. This is done by charging a finance cost each year. This is charged at the cost of capital (12%) and applied to the balance on the provision account. The finance charge for the year to 30 June 20X5 is 12% × $2.268 million = $272,160.

Debit:	Finance cost	$272,160
Credit:	Provision for decommissioning costs	$272,160

	$
Depreciation charge ($2.268 million/5 years)	453,600
Finance charge	272,160
Total charge	725,760

If you selected A, you have included the depreciation without the finance cost. If you selected C, you have just spread the present value of the dismantling over 5 years. If you selected D, you have expensed the whole asset value.

3   A

	Land	Buildings	Total
	$ million	$ million	$ million
Cost 1 July 20X3	1.00	5.00	6.00
Building depreciation			
= $5 million/50 years = $0.1m per year × 2		(0.2)	(0.2)
Carrying amount 30 June 20X5	1.00	4.80	5.80
Revaluation gain	0.24	1.96	1.20
Revalued amount	1.24	5.76	7.00
Building depreciation			
= $5.76 million/48 years = $0.12m per year × 2		(0.24)	(0.24)
Carrying amount 30 June 20X7	1.24	5.52	6.76
Disposal proceeds			6.80
Gain on disposal			0.04

The gain on disposal is $40,000. The $1.2 million balance on the revaluation reserve is transferred from the revaluation reserve to another reserve account (probably retained earnings) but is not reported through the statement of profit or loss for the year.

If you selected answer B, you have forgotten to record depreciation between 30 June 20X5 and 30 June 20X7. If you selected answer C, you have based the profit on the original depreciation. If you selected D, you have incorrectly transferred the remaining revaluation reserve into the statement of profit or loss.

4 $900,000

The grant should be released over the useful life, not based on the possibility of the item being repaid. Therefore the $1m should be released over 5 years, being a release of $200,000 a year. At 30 June 20X1, 6 months should be released, meaning $100,000 has been released ($^6/_{12}$ × $200,000). This leaves $900,000 in deferred income.

5   B

This is a revenue grant, and would therefore be released to the statement of profit or loss over the 4 year life. By the end of year one, $250,000 would have been credited to the statement of profit or loss, leaving $750,000 held in deferred income. At this point the amount is repaid, meaning that the deferred income is removed, as well as the $250,000 income previously recorded.

If you selected A, you have not removed the income that was released in the prior year. If you selected C, you have missed that $250,000 would have been released in the previous year. If you have chosen D, you have made errors over the deferring of the grant and that the repayment would be treated as an expense.

6   B

Asset A would be classed as a non-current asset held for sale under IFRS 5 *Non-current Assets Held for Sale and Discontinued Operations*. Assets C and D would both be classified as property, plant and equipment per IAS 16 *Property, Plant and Equipment*.

7 $32,000

The weighted average cost of borrowing is 8% (($1m × 6%) + ($2m × 9%))/$3m.

Therefore the amount to be capitalised = 8% × $600,000 × $^{8}/_{12}$ = $32,000.

8

	Statement 1	Statement 2
True	✓	
False		✓

IAS 16 (para 31) states that when the revaluation model is used, revaluations should be made with sufficient regularity to ensure that the carrying value of the assets remains close to fair value. IAS 16 also states (para 36) that, if one item in a class of assets is revalued, all the assets in that class must be revalued.

9   A, B

The maintenance and training costs should be expensed as incurred. The residual value should be taken into account for the purposes of calculating depreciation, but not for the amount to be capitalised.

10   A

Six months' depreciation is required on the building structure and air conditioning system.

	$000
Land (not depreciated)	2,000
Building structure $(10,000 - (10,000/25 \times {}^6/_{12}))$	9,800
Air conditioning system $(4,000 - (3,500/10 \times {}^6/_{12}))$	3,825
	15,625

11 $700,000

Six months' depreciation to the date of the revaluation will be $300,000 (12,000/20 years $\times {}^6/_{12}$). Six months' depreciation from the date of revaluation to 31 March 20X5 would be $400,000 (10,800/13.5 years remaining life $\times {}^6/_{12}$). Total depreciation is $700,000.

12   B, C

Item A is incorrect as the deferred income method can be used. Item D is incorrect as any repayment is corrected in the current period, not retrospectively.

13   A

Six months' depreciation should be accounted for up to 30 June 20X5, which is $100,000 expense ($10 million/50 years $\times {}^6/_{12}$).

When the asset is transferred to investment property it should be revalued to the fair value of $11 million. At the date that the asset's use is changed, this gain should be recorded in other comprehensive income and in a revaluation surplus, not in the statement of profit or loss.

From this date, the fair value model is used. No depreciation is accounted for, but the asset will be revalued to fair value with gains or losses going through the statement of profit or loss. As there is a gain of $500,000 from June 20X5 to December 20X5, this would be included in the statement of profit or loss.

Therefore the total net income will be **$400,000**, being the $500,000 fair value gain less the depreciation expense of $100,000 for the first 6 months of the year.

14 $602,500

The interest can only be capitalised during the period of construction, which is from 1 February 20X6. Therefore the interest can be capitalised for 10 months, being from 1 February to 30 November 20X6. This gives $625,000 ($7.5 million $\times 10\% \times {}^{10}/_{12}$).

Any temporary investment income earned during this period should be netted off the amount capitalised. The amount earned from 1 February to 1 May 20X6 is $22,500 ($2 million $\times 4.5\% \times {}^3/_{12}$).

Therefore the amount to be capitalised is $625,000 − $22,500 = **$602,500**.

Note that all interest incurred and earned in January 20X6 is before the construction period and therefore is recorded in the statement of profit or loss.

15 $1,000,000

The fair value gain of $1 million ($9m – $8m) should be taken to the statement of profit or loss. Costs to sell are ignored and, since Croft uses the fair value model, no depreciation will be charged on the building.

16   A

The finance was only available after the year end. Therefore the criteria of recognising an asset were not met, as the resources were not available to complete the project.

Even though the brand is internally generated in the subsidiary's accounts, it can be recognised at fair value for the group. Item C can be recognised as a purchased intangible and item D meets the criteria for being capitalised as development costs.

17   D

Item A cannot be capitalised because it does not meet all the criteria as it is not viable.

Item B is research and cannot be capitalised.

Item C cannot be capitalised because it does not meet all the criteria as it is making a loss.

18   B, C

Key staff cannot be capitalised as firstly they are not controlled by an entity. Secondly, the value that one member of key staff contributes to an entity cannot be measured reliably.

19   A

The costs of $750,000 relate to ten months of the year (up to April 20X5). Therefore the costs per month were $75,000. As the project was confirmed as feasible on 1 January 20X5, the costs can be capitalised from this date. So four months of these costs can be capitalised = $75,000 × 4 = $300,000.

The asset should be amortised from when the products go on sale, so one month's amortisation should be charged to 30 June 20X5. Amortisation is ($300,000/5) × $^1/_{12}$ = $5,000. The carrying amount of the asset at 30 June 20X5 is $300,000 – $5,000 = $295,000.

If you chose C you have forgotten to amortise the development costs. If you chose B or D you have either capitalised the full amount or capitalised none of the costs.

20   B

The brand can be measured reliably, so this should be accounted for as a separate intangible asset on consolidation. The customer list cannot be valued reliably, and so will form part of the overall goodwill calculation. It will be subsumed within the goodwill value.

21   D

Write off to 1 January 20X4 to 28 February 20X4 (2 × $40,000)	$80,000
Capitalise March to June = 4 × 40,000 = $160,000	
Amortisation 160,000/5 years × $^3/_{12}$ (July to September)	8,000
	———
	88,000
	———

22

	True	False
All intangible assets must be carried at amortised cost or at an impaired amount, they cannot be revalued upwards.		✓
The development of a new process which is not expected to increase sales revenues may still be recognised as an intangible asset.	✓	

Intangible assets may be revalued upwards using the revaluation model if an active market exists for the asset, although this is unusual.

A new process may produce benefits other than increased revenues (e.g. it may reduce costs) and therefore be recognised as an asset.

23   A

In a cash generating unit, no asset should be impaired below its recoverable amount. The valuation of $2.5 million is an indication that the property is not impaired and should therefore be left at $2.3 million.

$2.5 million cannot be chosen as the entity uses the cost model. If you chose item C or D then you have impaired the asset.

24 $689,000

The cash generating unit is impaired by $1,180,000, being the difference between the recoverable amount of $4 million and the total carrying values of the assets of $5,180,000. In a cash generating unit, no asset should be impaired below its recoverable amount, meaning that the property and other net assets are not impaired. The impairment is allocated to goodwill first, resulting in the entire $700,000 being written off. This leaves a remaining impairment of $480,000 to be allocated across plant and intangible assets.

This should be allocated on a pro-rata basis according to their carrying value. The plant and intangible assets have a total carrying value of $1,750,000 ($950,000 plant and $800,000 intangible assets). Therefore the impairment should be allocated to plant as follows:

$950,000/$1,750,000 × $480,000 = $261,000.

The carrying value of plant is therefore $950,000 – $261,000 = $689,000

25 $6,500

The recoverable amount of an asset is the higher of its value in use (being the present value of future cash flows) and fair value less costs to sell. Therefore the recoverable amount is $6,500.

26   A

Goodwill should be written off in full and the remaining loss is allocated pro rata to property plant and equipment and the product patent.

	Carrying amount $	Impairment $	Recoverable amount $
Property, plant and equipment	200,000	(45,455)	154,545
Goodwill	50,000	(50,000)	nil
Product patent	20,000	(4,545)	15,455
Net current assets (at NRV)	30,000	nil	30,000
	300,000	(100,000)	200,000

27   D

Although the estimated net realisable value is lower than it was (due to fire damage), the entity will still make a profit on the inventory and thus it is not an indicator of impairment.

28 $17,785

	$
Cost 1 October 20X9	100,000
Depreciation 1 October 20X9 to 30 September 20Y4 ($100,000 \times {}^{5}/_{10}$)	(50,000)
Carrying amount	50,000

The recoverable amount is the higher of fair value less costs to sell ($30,000) and the value in use ($8,500 \times 3.79 = $32,215$). Recoverable amount is therefore $32,215.

	$
Carrying amount	50,000
Recoverable amount	(32,215)
Impairment to statement of profit or loss	17,785

29 $214,600

Is the lower of its carrying amount ($217,000) and recoverable amount ($214,600) at 31 March 20X4.

Recoverable amount is the higher of value in use ($214,600) and fair value less costs to ($200,000).

Carrying amount = $217,000 (248,000 – (248,000 \times 12.5%))

Value in use is based on present values = $214,600

30   C

Asset held for sale will be measured at lower of carrying amount and fair value less cost to sell. Once reclassified, the asset held for sale is not depreciated.

	$m
Cost	45.0
Depreciation to 30 September 20X3	(6.0)
Depreciation to 1 April 20X4 ($45 \times {}^{1}/_{15} \times {}^{6}/_{12}$)	(1.5)
Carrying amount 1 April 20X4	37.5

Fair value less cost to sell = $36.8 million (($42,000 \times 90\%$) – 1,000).

Therefore the asset is reported at $36.8 million.

31   A

Assets held for sale should be held at the lower of carrying value and fair value less costs to sell. Therefore the asset should be held at $750.

Item B is just the fair value. Item C is the fair value plus the costs to sell, which is incorrect. Item D is the carrying value.

32   C

A sale has to be expected within 12 months, not one month. The others are all criteria which must be met to classify an asset as held for sale.

33

	Shown on the face of the statement of profit or loss	Not shown
Revenue		✓
Gross profit		✓
Profit after tax	✓	

One line should be shown regarding profit from discontinued operations. This line is the profit after tax from the discontinued operation, with a full breakdown of the amount in the notes to the accounts.

34

	Discontinued operation Yes/No
Sector X	No
Sector Y	Yes

Although Sector X is the only operation of Rural in Country A, it is not a separate major line of geographical operations, as it only contributes 0.5% of total revenue. Therefore Rural would not report this as a discontinued operation.

Sector Y is a separate major line of business operations, as it contributes a significant amount of Rural revenue, and produces a different item from the other parts of Rural. Therefore Rural would report Sector Y as a discontinued operation.

35   B

Although disclosing discontinued operations separately may help with business valuation, and understanding the business, the primary reason discontinued operations are separately presented is to enhance the predictive nature of the financial statements. Financial statements are historic, and this is a major limitation of them. Separating information about discontinued operations means that the users of the financial statements can use information about just the continuing operations when predicting the future performance of an entity.

36   A

The property would be depreciated by $25,000 (800,000/16 × $^{6}/_{12}$) for six months giving a carrying amount of $775,000 (800,000 – 25,000) before being classified as held-for-sale. This would also be the value at 31 March 20X5 as the property is no longer depreciated and is lower than its fair value less cost to sell.

37   D

The objectives of financial statements are set out in the IASB Framework. Note that providing information about changes in the financial position, as well as information about financial position and financial performance, is included within these objectives.

38   B

You should learn the IASB definitions of both assets and liabilities.

39

	Faithful representation	Relevance
Completeness	✓	
Predictive value		✓
Neutrality	✓	

Information that is relevant has predictive or confirmatory value. For information to have faithful representation, it must be complete, neutral and free from error.

40   B, D

It is important to learn that the two fundamental characteristics are relevance and faithful representation.

41

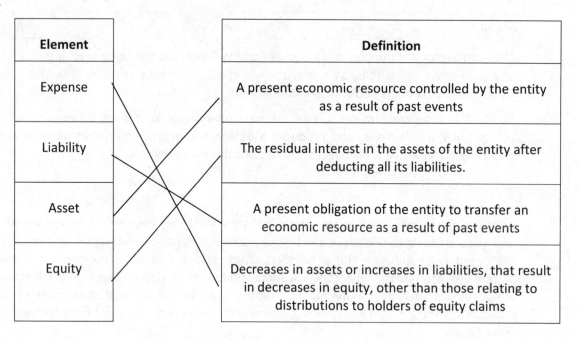

Element	Definition
Expense	A present economic resource controlled by the entity as a result of past events
Liability	The residual interest in the assets of the entity after deducting all its liabilities.
Asset	A present obligation of the entity to transfer an economic resource as a result of past events
Equity	Decreases in assets or increases in liabilities, that result in decreases in equity, other than those relating to distributions to holders of equity claims

42   C

Relevant information contains information which has both predictive and confirmatory value.

43   D

Faithful representation means presenting transactions according to their economic substance rather than their legal form. Items A to C all represent incorrect accounting treatments, and item D reflects that a sale and repurchase agreement with a bank is likely to represent a secured loan rather than a sale.

44   B

You should learn the IASB definitions of both assets and liabilities. .

45   A

Elements are recognised if recognition provides users with useful financial information. In other words recognition must provide relevant information and a faithful representation.

46   D

Information is relevant if it influences the economic decisions of the users. The other definitions describe good treatment but are not explaining the concept of relevance.

47

	True	False
It is a principles-based framework	✓	
It is a legal obligation		✓

IFRS Standards are based on a principles-based framework, as they are based on the IASB's Conceptual Framework for Financial Reporting. It does not represent a legal obligation.

48

	Advantage	Not advantage
Greater comparability between different firms	✓	
Greater compatibility with legal systems		✓
Easier for large international accounting firms	✓	

Harmonisation would not provide greater compatibility with legal systems, as legal systems differ worldwide. Greater compatibility would arise when a country develops its own accounting standards within the context of their specific legal framework.

49   A, B, C

A principles-based framework recognises that is not possible to draw up a set of rules to cover every eventuality and therefore does not attempt to do so. It is also harder to prove compliance as there are fewer prescriptive rules in place.

50   D

Where there is conflict between the conceptual framework and an IFRS Standard, the IFRS Standard will prevail. An example of this is IAS 20 *Government* grants, where deferred grant income is held as a liability, despite not satisfying the definition of a liability.

51   C

Receivables sold with recourse do not represent a transfer of control to the purchaser, as the purchaser does not carry the risk of irrecoverable debts. Thus the substance of the transaction is that the receivables have not been transferred and should not be derecognised.

52   D

The substance is that there is no free finance. Its cost is built into the selling price and this will represent a significant financing component.

53   B

By definition irredeemable preference shares do not have a contractual obligation to be repaid and thus do not meet the definition of a liability. They are therefore classed as equity.

54

Historical cost	✓	Current cost	✓
$300,000		$384,000	✓
$320,000	✓	$600,000	

Historical cost annual depreciation = $90,000 ((500,000 × 90%)/5 years).

After two years carrying amount would be $320,000 (500,000 – (2 × 90,000)).

Current cost annual depreciation = $108,000 ((600,000 × 90%)/5 years).

After two years carrying amount would be $384,000 (600,000 – (2 × 108,000)).

55

	Liability	Not a liability
The signing of a non-cancellable contract in September 20X4 to supply goods in the following year on which, due to a pricing error, a loss will be made.	✓	
The cost of a reorganisation which was approved by the board in August 20X4 but has not yet been implemented, communicated to interested parties or announced publicly.		✓
An amount of deferred tax relating to the gain on the revaluation of a property during the current year. Tynan has no intention of selling the property in the foreseeable future.	✓	
The balance on the warranty provision which relates to products for which there are no outstanding claims and whose warranties had expired by 30 September 20X4.		✓

The non-cancellable contract is an onerous contract. The deferred tax provision is required even if there is no intention to sell the property.

56   D

As the receivable is 'sold' with recourse it must remain as an asset on the statement of financial position and is not derecognised.

57   D

As it is a new type of transaction, comparability with existing treatments is not relevant.

58   B

Historical cost is the easiest to verify as the cost can be proved back to the original transaction. Fair value is often more difficult to verify as it may involve elements of estimation.

59   C

The prior period error is corrected by restating the comparative amounts for the previous period at their correct value. A note to the accounts should disclose the nature of the error, together with other details.

60   B

Level 3 inputs do include the best information available, but this is not regarded as the most reliable evidence of fair value, as level 1 inputs are likely to provide the most reliable evidence.

61   B

A change in the method of inventory valuation would be classed as a change in accounting policy under IAS 8. The allowance for receivables, useful life and depreciation method are all accounting estimates.

62   A, D

A change in accounting policy may be made firstly if this is required by an IFRS Standard. If there is no requirement, an entity can choose to change their accounting policy if they believe a new accounting policy would result in a more reliable and relevant presentation of events and transactions.

Entities cannot change their accounting policies simply to make financial reporting easier, or to try and show a more favourable picture of results.

63

	Can be used	Cannot be used
Historical cost	✓	
Present value	✓	
Realisable value	✓	

64   A

In times of rising prices, asset values will be understated, as historical cost will not be a true representation of the asset values. Additionally, the real purchase cost of replacement items will not be incorporated, meaning that profits are overstated.

B and D relate to asset values being overstated, which is incorrect. Unrecognised gains is irrelevant.

65 D

The capital maintenance concept aims to ensure that excess dividends are not paid in times of rising prices, by considering the effects of both inflation and specific price rises.

A, B and C are all key concepts regarding financial statements, but do not cover rising prices.

66

	Change in accounting policy	Change in accounting estimate
Classifying commission earned as revenue in the statement of profit or loss, having previously classified it as other operating income	✓	
Revising the remaining useful life of a depreciable asset		✓

A change of classification in presentation in financial statements is a change of accounting policy under IAS 8.

67 B

Item A is an adjustment when preparing consolidated financial statements. Item C is an accounting estimate, and item D is applying the same policy as previously, with a correction to the figure used.

68 A

IAS 10 defines adjusting events as those providing '**evidence of conditions existing at the end of the reporting period**' (IAS 10, para 3(a)). In the case of inventories, it may be sales of inventory in this period indicate that the net realisable value of some items of inventory have fallen below their cost and require writing down to their net realisable value as at 30 September 20X4.

69 B

The logs will be classed as inventory. The land will be classed as property, plant and equipment. The development costs will be treated as an intangible asset.

70 B, D, E

IAS 2 *Inventories* states that:

(a)   selling costs cannot be included in inventory cost, therefore item A cannot be included

(b)   general overheads cannot be included (item C)

(c)   overhead costs should be added to inventory cost on the basis of '**normal capacity of the production facilities**' (IAS 2, para 13), therefore item F cannot be included in cost

(d)   the cost of **factory** management and administration can be included, so that item D can be included in inventory values.

71 $55,800

	Cost	Net Realisable Value (NRV)	Lower of cost and NRV
Item 1	$24,000	(note 1)	$24,000
Item 2	$33,600	$31,800 (note 2)	$31,800
			$55,800

Notes:

(1)   The recoverable amount is not known, but it must be above cost because the contract is 'expected to produce a high profit margin'. The subsequent fall in the cost price to $20,000 is irrelevant for the inventory valuation.

(2)   The recoverable amount is $36,000 minus 50% of $8,400.

72   B

The costs of inventory should include all costs of bringing inventory to its present location and condition, so Mario should include the raw material cost, import duties, direct labour, subcontracted labour and production overheads in its inventory.

Sales tax would not be included as it is recoverable.

Storage costs are specifically excluded from the value of inventory, as they are incurred once the inventory is ready to be sold.

Abnormal wastage costs are excluded from the valuation of inventory per IAS 2 *Inventories*.

73 $970,000

The normal selling price of the damaged inventory is $300,000 ($210,000/70%). This will now sell for $240,000 ($300,000 × 80%), less commission of $60,000 ($240,000 × 25%) to give a NRV of $180,000. The expected loss on the damaged inventory is $30,000 ($210,000 cost – $180,000 NRV) and therefore the total inventory should be valued at $970,000 ($1,000,000 – $30,000).

74

	Accounted for under IAS 41 *Agriculture*	Outside the scope of IAS 41 *Agriculture*
Dairy cattle	✓	
Milk	✓	
Cheese		✓

The cheese will be a product which is the result of processing after harvest, so will be outside the scope of IAS 41 *Agriculture*.

75 D

Biological assets should be revalued to fair value less point of sale costs at the year end, with the gain or loss being taken to the statement of profit or loss.

If you chose A, you have used the cost model. If you chose B or C, you have not deducted the point of sale costs.

76 C

Depreciation of leased plant $68,000 ($340,000/5 years)

Finance cost $25,000 (($340,000 – $90,000) × 10%)

Rental of equipment $13,500 ($18,000 × $^9/_{12}$)

Total $106,500.

77 B

Year end	B/f $	Interest 7% $	Payment $	c/f $
31 October 20X3	45,000	3,150	(10,975)	37,175
31 October 20X4	37,175	2,602	(10,975)	28,802

The figure to the right of the payment in the next year is the non-current liability. Once 20X4's payment has been made, $28,802 will still be owed, making this the non-current liability. The current liability will be the difference between the total liability of $37,175 and the non-current liability of $28,802, which is $8,373.

If you selected C, you chose the total year-end liability rather than the non-current liability. If you selected A, you deducted the payment of $10,975 from the total. If you selected D you recorded the payment in advance and chose the year end liability rather than the non-current liability.

78 D

Assets permitted to be exempted from recognition are low-value assets and those with a lease term of 12 months or less. The use of the asset is irrelevant, and, although IFRS 16 *Leases* does not define low-value, it is the cost when new that is considered rather than current fair value.

79   A

Initial value of lease liability is the present value of lease payments, $86,240.

	Balance b/f	Payment	Subtotal	Interest @ 8%	Balance c/f
20X3	86,240	(20,000)	66,240	5,299	71,539
20X4	71,539	(20,000)	51,539	4,123*	55,662
20X5	55,662	(20,000)*	35,662*		

The non-current liability at 20X4 is the figure to the right of the payment in 20X5, $35,662. The current liability is the total liability of $55,662 less the non-current liability of $35,662, which is $20,000.

The finance cost is the figure in the interest column for 20X4, $4,123.

If you chose B you have done the entries for year one. If you chose C or D, you have recorded the payments in arrears, not in advance.

80   C

The transfer of ownership at the end of the lease indicates that Pigeon will have use of the asset for its entire life, and therefore 7 years is the appropriate depreciation period. Potential transactions at market rate would be ignored as they do not confer any benefit on Pigeon, and Pigeon's depreciation policy for purchased assets is irrelevant.

81   A

Reverse incorrect treatment of rental:

Dr Liability $210,000, Cr Retained Earnings $210,000

Charge asset depreciation ($635,000/5):

Dr Retained earnings $127,000, Cr Property, plant and equipment $127,000

Charge finance cost ($635,000 × 12.2%):

Dr Retained Earnings $77,470, Cr Liability $77,470

This gives a net adjustment of $5,530 to be credited to opening retained earnings.

If you selected B, you have missed the depreciation. If you selected C you have simply reversed the rental payment. If you selected D you assumed that the entries were correct.

82 $58,000

The asset would initially be capitalised at $87,000. This is then depreciated over six years, being the shorter of the useful life and the lease term (including any secondary period).

This would give a depreciation expense of $14,500 a year. After two years, accumulated depreciation would be $29,000 and therefore the carrying amount would be $58,000.

83   A

Sideshow is only leasing the asset for 5 years out of its remaining life of 20 years, so control of the asset has been passed to the purchaser.

The initial liability recognised will be the present value of lease rentals, $599,000, giving a finance cost for the year of $47,920 ($599,000 × 8%).

The proportion of the right-of-use asset retained by Sideshow will be equal to the initial liability as a proportion of the proceeds. So the initial value of the right-of-use asset will be

(599,000/2,000,000) × 1,600,000 = $479,200

Depreciation over 5 years would give an expense of $95,840.

The profit to be recognised on disposal can be calculated in one of two ways.

Create the initial recognition journal and calculate a balancing figure:

	Dr $	Cr $
Bank	2,000,000	
Property, plant & equipment	479,200	
Property plant & equipment		1,600,000
Lease liability		599,000
Profit on disposal (SPL) – balancing figure		280,200

Alternatively the profit to be recognised could be calculated by taking the proportion of the asset not retained by Sideshow (i.e. difference between sale proceeds and lease liability):

$$\frac{(\$2,000,000 - \$599,000)}{\$2,000,000} \times (\$2,000,000 - \$1,600,000) = \$280,200$$

If you chose B you have not capitalised the leased asset. If you chose C you recognised the full profit. If you chose D you capitalised the asset at the present value of the lease payments.

84   B

	b/f $000	Interest @ 10% $000	Payment $000	c/f $000
Year end				
30 September 20X4	23,000	2,300	(6,000)	19,300
30 September 20X5	19,300	1,930	(6,000)	15,230

Current liability at 30 September 20X4 = 19,300,000 – 15,230,000 = $4,070,000

85   D

The value recognised in respect of the lease payments will be the present value of future lease payments rather than the total value.

86 $1,090

As Stark has retained control of the asset, the asset cannot be treated as sold, and will be retained at its carrying amount, depreciated over the remaining life of 10 years. The sale proceeds will effectively be treated as a loan of $7 million, on which interest will be charged at 7%. Therefore the following items will be included in the statement of profit or loss, all figures in $000:

Depreciation: $6,000/10 years = $600

Finance cost: $7,000 × 7% = $490

Total expense = $600 + $490 = $1,090

87   B

The loan notes should initially be recorded at their net proceeds, being the $100,000 raised less the $3,000 issue costs, giving $97,000. This should then be held at amortised cost, taking the effective rate of interest to the statement of profit or loss. The annual payment will be the coupon rate, which will be 5% × $100,000 = $5,000 a year.

Applying this to an amortised cost table gives $7,981, as shown below.

	B/f	Interest 8%	Payment	c/f
	$	$	$	$
20X4	97,000	7,760	(5,000)	99,760
20X5	99,760	**7,981**		

If you chose C, you have done the calculation for 20X4. If you chose D, you have used 8% of the full $100,000 and done the calculation for 20X4. If you chose A, you have used 8% of the full $100,000.

88   B

The amount payable each year is based on the coupon rate of 7%, giving an amount of $210,000 payable each year ($3 million × 7%). This should be discounted at the market rate of interest of 9%, together with the capital repayment to find the value of the liability.

Year 1 ($210,000 × 0.914)	191,940
Year 2 ($210,000 × 0.837)	175,770
Year 3 ($3,210,000 × 0.766)	2,458,860
Total present value of debt	**2,826,570**
Equity element (balance)	**173,430**
Total bond value	3,000,000

If you chose A, you used the incorrect discount rate. If you chose C you forgot to calculate the repayment of $3 million. If you chose D you have not used split accounting.

89   A

The business model test must also be passed, which means that the objective is to hold the instrument to collect the cash flows rather than to sell the asset. The others are irrelevant.

90   A

The default position for equity investments is fair value through profit or loss, meaning the investment is revalued each year end, with the gain or loss being taken to the statement of profit or loss.

Fair value through other comprehensive income is the alternative position.

Amortised cost is an alternative treatment for debt instruments.

Net proceeds relates to financial liabilities.

91 $9,500

The investment should be classified as fair value through other comprehensive income.

As such, they will initially be valued inclusive of transaction costs.

Therefore, the initial value is 10,000 × $3.50 = $35,000 + $500 = $35,500.

At year-end, these will be revalued to fair value of $4.50 each, therefore 10,000 × $4.50 = $45,000.

The gain is therefore $45,000 – $35,500 = $9,500.

92

Gain		Where recorded
18,750		Statement of profit or loss

Financial assets held for trading will be valued at fair value through profit or loss. These are therefore valued excluding any transaction costs, which will be expensed to profit or loss.

The initial value of the investment is therefore 15,000 × $6.50 = $97,500

The shares will be revalued to fair value as at year-end, and the gain will be taken to profit or loss. The year-end value of the shares is 15,000 × $7.75 = $116,250, giving a gain of $18,750. This is recognised within profit or loss.

93   B

Transaction costs are included when measuring all financial assets and liabilities at amortised cost, and when valuing financial assets valued at fair value through other comprehensive income.

Transaction costs for financial assets valued at fair value through profit or loss are expensed through the statement of profit or loss and not included in the initial value of the asset.

94   **$810,000**

Year ended 30 September	Cash flow	Discount rate	Discounted cash flows
	$000	at 8%	$000
20X4	500	0.93	465
20X5	500	0.86	430
20X6	10,500	0.79	8,295
			———
Value of debt component			9,190
Equity (balance)			**810**
			———
Proceeds			10,000
			———

95   **$768,000**

The initial liability should be recorded at the net proceeds of $9.6 million. The finance cost should then be accounted for using the effective rate of interest of 8%. Therefore the finance cost for the year is **$768,000** ($9.6 million × 8%).

96

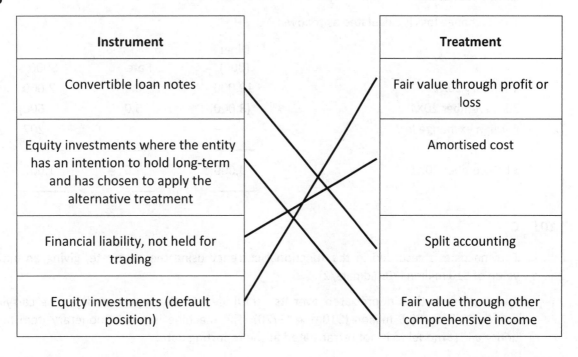

Instrument	Treatment
Convertible loan notes	Fair value through profit or loss
Equity investments where the entity has an intention to hold long-term and has chosen to apply the alternative treatment	Amortised cost
Financial liability, not held for trading	Split accounting
Equity investments (default position)	Fair value through other comprehensive income

97   **D**

Functional currency is defined as the currency of the primary economic environment in which an entity operates.

Answer A is the definition of presentation currency. Answer C is one of the primary methods of determining an entity's functional currency.

98   A

Overseas transactions are recorded in the functional currency using the spot rate of exchange. Therefore, the land is initially recorded at $10 million (30m dinars/3). Land is a non-monetary asset and so is not retranslated, meaning that its carrying amount remains at $10 million.

If you selected answer B then you retranslated the land at the closing rate of exchange. If you selected answer C then you translated the land at the average rate of exchange. If you selected answer D then you measured the land at its fair value, despite the fact that it is held using the cost model.

99   B

Statement (i) is false. Exchange gains and losses arising on the retranslation of monetary items are recognised in profit or loss in the period.

100 $207,000

The loan should initially be translated into dollars using the spot rate of 6.0.

The repayment of the loan should be translated using the spot rate of 5.0.

The outstanding loan at the reporting date is a monetary item so is retranslated using the closing rate of 5.6.

The exchange loss is calculated as follows:

	Dinar (000)	Rate	$000
1 January 20X1	12,000	6.0	2,000
30 November 20X1	(3,000)	5.0	(600)
Foreign exchange loss	–		207
31 December 20X1	9,000	5.6	1,607

101   C

The machine is recorded in the functional currency using the spot rate, giving an initial value of $10 million (20m dinars/2).

The machine is then depreciated over its useful life. By the reporting date, the carrying amount will be $9.5 million ($10m × 19/20). The machine is a non-monetary item held under a cost model so is not retranslated at the reporting date.

If you selected answer A then you have translated the depreciation at the closing rate of exchange. If you selected answer B then you have translated depreciation at the average rate of exchange. If you selected answer D then you have retranslated the machine at the closing rate of exchange.

102 D

The sale should be treated as a loan secured against the inventory. The inventory would remain with Mango, and a $500,000 loan would be recorded. This loan would incur interest at 10% a year. In year one $50,000 would therefore be recorded as a finance cost.

Answers A and B treat this as a sale, which is incorrect. Deferred income is not taken to the statement of profit or loss, so item C is incorrect.

103 C

Although the invoiced amount is $180,000, $30,000 of this has not yet been earned and must be deferred until the servicing work has been completed.

104

Step 1 – Overall		$m
Price		5.0
Total cost	– incurred to date	(1.6)
	– estimated future	(2.4)
Overall profit		1.0

Step 2 – Progress

Progress = work certified 1.8/total price 5 = 36%

Step 3 – Profit
Profit to recognise = $1m × 36% = $0.36m

Step 4 – Statement of financial position	$m
Costs to date	1.60
Profit to date	0.36
Less: Amount billed	(1.80)
Contract asset	0.16

105

Revenue	Cost of sales
$63 million	$83 million

Step 1 – Overall		$m
Price		90
Total cost	– incurred to date	(77)
	– estimated future	(33)
		‾‾‾‾
Overall **loss**		(20)
		‾‾‾‾

Step 2 – Progress

Progress = work certified 63/total price 90 = 70%

Step 3 – SPL	$m
Revenue (70% of 90)	63
Cost of sales (balancing figure to recognise full loss)	(83)
	‾‾‾‾
FULL loss to be recognised immediately	(20)
	‾‾‾‾

106 $90

The discount should be allocated to each part of the bundled sale. Applying the discount across each part gives revenue as follows:

Goods	$50	($75 × $100/$150)
Installation	$20	($30 × $100/$150)
Service	$30	($45 × $100/$150)

The revenue in relation to the goods and installation should be recognised on 1 May 20X1. As 8 months of the service has been performed (from 1 May to 31 December 20X1), then $20 should be recognised ($30 × $8/12$).

This gives a total revenue for the year of 50 + 20 + 20 = $90.

107

Step	Correct order
Identify the separate performance obligations within a contract	Identify the contract
Identify the contract	Identify the separate performance obligations within a contract
Determine the transaction price	Determine the transaction price
Recognise revenue when (or as) a performance obligation is satisfied	Allocate the transaction price to the performance obligations in the contract
Allocate the transaction price to the performance obligations in the contract	Recognise revenue when (or as) a performance obligation is satisfied

108 D

		$m
Price		40
Total cost	– incurred to date	(16)
	– estimated future	(18)
		——
Overall profit		6
		——

Progress = 45%

	$m
Revenue (45% of 40)	18.0
Cost of sales (45% of total costs of 34)	(15.3)
	——
Gross profit	2.7
	——

Items A and B incorrectly include the full revenue. Item C includes the actual costs to date incorrectly.

109 $30,000

	$
Contract price	200,000
Total contract cost (130,000 + 20,000)	(150,000)
	————
Estimated total profit	50,000
	————

Progress 180,000/200,000 = 90%

	$
Profit earned = 50,000 × 90% =	45,000
Recognised in previous year	(15,000)
	————
Current year profit	30,000
	————

110 B

For item B the sale of the goods has fulfilled a contractual obligation so the revenue in relation to this can be recognised. The service will be recognised over time, so the revenue should be deferred and recognised as the obligation is fulfilled.

For item A Hatton acts as an agent, so only the commission should be included in revenue.

For item C any profit or loss on disposal should be taken to the statement of profit or loss. The proceeds should not be included within revenue.

For item D the $1 million should be initially discounted to present value as there is a significant financing component within the transaction. The revenue would initially be recognised at $826,000, with an equivalent receivable. This receivable would then be held at amortised cost with finance income of 10% being earned each year.

111 $500,000

	$000
Costs to date	4,500
Loss	(2,000)
Less: Amount billed	(3,000)
	———
Contract liability	(500)
	———

As the contract is loss-making, Sugar should record the full loss immediately.

112 A

Using the work certified basis, the progress of this contract is 1,050/1,500= 70%.

Therefore 70% of the total contract costs should be recognised, giving 800 × 70% = $560,000.

As $240,000 of costs were recognised in the prior year, costs of $320,000 ($560,000 – $240,000) should be recognised in the current year statement of profit or loss.

113 A

Contract price	1,000,000
Total contract cost (530,000 + 170,000)	(700,000)
	———
Estimated total profit	300,000
	———

Progress 600,000/1,000,000 = 60%

Revenue (60% × 1,000,000)	600,000
Cost of sales (60% × 700,000)	(420,000)
	———
Profit	180,000
	———
Costs to date	530,000
Profit to date	180,000
Less: amount billed	(600,000)
	———
Contract asset	110,000
	———

114 D

At 31 March 20X5, the deferred consideration of $12,650 would need to be discounted by 10% for one year to $11,500 (effectively deferring a finance cost of $1,150). The total amount credited to profit or loss would be $24,150 (12,650 + 11,500).

115 D

The tax expense in the statement of profit or loss is made up of the current year estimate, the prior year overprovision and the movement in deferred tax. The prior year overprovision must be deducted from the current year expense, and the movement in deferred tax must be added to the current year expense, as the deferred tax liability has increased.

Tax expense = $60,000 – $4,500 + $600 = $56,100

If you chose A, you have deducted the movement in deferred tax, even though the liability has increased. If you chose C you have added the overprovision. If you chose B you have added the overprovision and the closing deferred tax liability.

116

Statement of profit or loss	Statement of financial position
$88,000	$83,000

The tax expense in the statement of profit or loss is made up of the current year estimate and the prior year underprovision. The year-end liability in the statement of financial position is made up of the current year estimate only.

Tax expense = $83,000 + $5,000 underprovision from previous year = $88,000

Tax liability = $83,000 year end estimate only.

117 C

Deferred tax provision required	9,000 (30,000 × 30%)
Opening balance per trial balance	12,000
	———
Reduction in provision	(3,000)
	———

Tax expense:

Current year estimate	15,000
Prior year overprovision	(4,000)
Deferred tax, as above	(3,000)
	———
Charge for year	8,000
	———

If you chose A, you have added in the full deferred tax liability. If you chose B you have added the full liability and the overprovision. If you chose D, you have not dealt with the overprovision.

118 A

Deferred taxation increase	7,000 (23,000 – 16,000)
Less tax on revaluation gain	(3,000) recognised as OCI (10,000 × 30%)
	———
Charge to SPL	4,000
	———

Tax expense:

Current year estimate	12,000
Prior year overprovision	(7,000)
Deferred tax, as above	4,000
	———
Charge for year	9,000
	———

If you chose B, you have used the full deferred tax increase. If you chose C you have added the overprovision. If you chose D you have deducted the deferred tax movement.

119 89.1¢

EPS = $3,000,000/3,366,667 (W1) = 89.1¢

(W1) Weighted average number of shares

Step 1 – Theoretical ex-rights price (TERP)

2 shares @ $2 =	$4.00
1 share @ $1.40 =	$1.40
3 shares	$5.40

TERP = $5.40/3 = $1.80

Step 2 – Rights fraction = 2/1.8

Step 3 – Weighted average number of shares (WANS)

Date	Number	Fraction of year	Rights fraction	Weighted average
1 January	2,400,000	3/12	2/1.8	666,667
1 April	3,600,000	9/12		2,700,000
				3,366,667

120 A

EPS = $2,000,000/4,250,000 (W1) = 47.1¢

(W1) Weighted average number of shares

Date	Number	Fraction of year	Bonus fraction	Weighted average
1 January	3,000,000	5/12	4/3	1,666,667
1 June	4,000,000	4/12		1,333,333
30 September	5,000,000	3/12		1,250,000
				4,250,000

If you chose C or D, you have failed to apply the bonus fraction correctly. If you chose B you have ignored the bonus fraction.

121 75¢

The prior year earnings per share figure must be restated by the inverse of the rights fraction that relates to the current year earnings per share calculation.

The current year rights fraction is calculated below.

Step 1 – Theoretical ex-rights price (TERP)

3 shares @ $2.20 =	$6.60
1 share @ $1.40 =	$1.60
4 shares	$8.20

TERP = $8.20/4 = $2.05

Step 2 – Rights fraction

$$\frac{2.20}{2.05}$$

Therefore the restated earnings per share figure is 81c × 2.05/2.20 = 75¢.

122 D

Diluted EPS is calculated as 10,644,000/7,250,000 = 146.8¢

The earnings adjustment is:	$
Earnings for basic EPS	10,500,000
Plus interest saved (2.5m × 8%)	200,000
Less tax (200,000 × 28%)	(56,000)
Earnings for Diluted EPS	10,644,000

Shares for basic EPS	6,000,000	
Shares issued on conversion	1,250,000	(2,500,000/100) × 50
Shares for diluted EPS	7,250,000	

123 C

To calculate diluted earnings per share with an option, you need to work out the number of 'free' shares that will be issued if the options are exercised, and add that to the weighted average number of shares.

If the options are exercised, $3 million will be received ($3 × 1 million options).

At the market value of $5, $3 million would buy 600,000 shares ($3m/$5).

Therefore the cash received is the equivalent of 600,000 shares. As there are 1 million options, this means that 400,000 shares are being issued for free.

Diluted EPS = $2m/(4 million + 400,000) = **45.5¢**

124 $2,250,000

The Earnings figure for the EPS calculation is the profit attributable to the parent shareholders.

125 A, E

Redeemable preference dividends will already have been removed from net profit when arriving at this figure in a statement of profit or loss. Therefore this adjustment is not necessary. Dividends are simply the cash paid out of the earnings, and are often compared to the earnings per share. All the other items will need to be removed from the overall net profit figure in the statement of profit or loss.

126

Considered within DEPS	Considered within Basic EPS
The issue during the year of a convertible (to equity shares) loan note	A 1 for 5 rights issue of equity shares during the year at $1.20 when the market price of the equity shares was $2.00
The granting during the year of directors' share options exercisable in three years' time	Equity shares issued during the year as the purchase consideration for the acquisition of a new subsidiary

127 B

A and D will give the same impression as overall profit for the year. C is incorrect as diluted EPS is not an indication of future profit.

128 A

(1,550/((2,500 × 2) + 1,200 see below))

2 million shares at $1.20 = $2.4 million which would buy 800,000 shares at full price of $3. Therefore, dilution element (free shares) is 1,200,000 (2,000 – 800).

129

Legal action against AP	Legal action by AP
Provision	Contingent asset

The legal action against AP has a probable outflow, so AP should make a provision. The legal action taken by AP is a contingent asset. As it is probable, it should be disclosed in a note. Assets should only be recognised when there is a virtually certain inflow.

130 C

A provision is only required when there is a present obligation arising as a result of a past event, it is probable that an outflow of resources embodying economic benefits will be required to settle the obligation, and a reliable estimate can be made of the amount. Only answer C meets all these criteria. Answer A is incorrect because the obligation does not exist at the reporting date and also cannot be reliably measured at present. Answer B is an example of an adjusting event after the reporting date as it provides evidence of conditions existing at the reporting. Answer D is a contingent liability. However, as its likelihood is remote no provision is necessary.

131 C

The warehouse fire is an adjusting event as it occurred before the reporting date. Settlement of the insurance claim should therefore be included in the financial statements.

The other events are non-adjusting as they occurred after the reporting date and do not provide evidence of conditions existing at the reporting date. Issue B is a brand new event, and therefore should not be adjusted. As it is clearly material the event should be disclosed in the notes to the accounts.

132 $3,500,000

Per IAS 37 *Provisions, Contingent Liabilities and Contingent Assets*, the amount payable relates to a past event (the sale of faulty products) and the likelihood of payout is probable (i.e. more likely than not). Hence, the full amount of the payout should be provided for.

133 B

The costs associated with ongoing activities (relocation and retraining of employees) should not be provided for.

134 B

Extraction provision at 30 September 20X4 is $2.5 million ($250 \times 10$).

Dismantling provision at 1 October 20X3 is $20.4 million ($30,000 \times 0.68$).

This will increase by an 8% finance cost by 30 September 20X4 = $22,032,000.

Total provision is $24,532,000.

135 B, C

The change in tax rate and the fire will be non-adjusting events as the conditions did not exist at the reporting date.

136

	Adjusting	Non-adjusting
A public announcement in April 20X5 of a formal plan to discontinue an operation which had been approved by the board in February 20X5.		✓
The settlement of an insurance claim for a loss sustained in December 20X4.	✓	

A board decision to discontinue an operation does not create a liability. A provision can only be made on the announcement of a formal plan (as it then raises a valid expectation that the action will be carried out). As this announcement occurs during the year ended 31 March 20X6, this a non-adjusting event for the year ended 31 March 20X5.

The insurance claim was in existence at the year end, so this will be an adjusting event as it provides further evidence of conditions in existence.

137 D

Deferred tax relating to the revaluation of an asset must be provided for even if there is no intention to sell the asset in accordance with IAS 12 *Income Taxes*.

138

	True	False
IAS 10 *Events After the Reporting Period* covers the period from the reporting date to the annual general meeting		✓
According to IAS 10 *Events After the Reporting Period*, any non-adjusting event should be disclosed as a note in the financial statements		✓

Both are false. IAS 10 *Events After the Reporting Period* covers the period from the reporting date up to the date the financial statements are authorised for issue. Only material non-adjusting events need to be disclosed as notes in the financial statements.

139

There is a present obligation from a past event	No
A reliable estimate can be made	Yes
There is a probable outflow of economic benefits	Yes

Whilst there is an estimate of $500,000 and it is probable that Faubourg will make the changes, there is no present obligation at 31 December 20X4.

If Faubourg changes its mind and sells the building prior to June 20X5, no obligation would arise. Future obligations are not accounted for as provisions.

140 A, D

Changes in provisions are regarded as changes in accounting estimates so should be accounted for prospectively rather than retrospectively.

Provisions should be recorded at the best estimate, reflecting the amount most likely to be paid out, rather than the highest possible liability.

CONSOLIDATED FINANCIAL STATEMENTS

141

	Consolidated	Not to be consolidated
Beta is a bank and its activity is so different from the engineering activities of the rest of the group that it would be meaningless to consolidate it.	✓	
Delta is located in a country where local accounting standards are compulsory and these are not compatible with IFRS Standards used by the rest of the group.	✓	
Gamma is located in a country where a military coup has taken place and Petre has lost control of the investment for the foreseeable future.		✓

The investment in Gamma no longer meets the definition of a subsidiary (ability to control) and therefore would not be consolidated.

142 A

Is the correct treatment for a bargain purchase (negative goodwill).

143 C

While having the majority of shares may be a situation which leads to control, it does not feature in the definition of control per IFRS 10 *Consolidated Financial Statements*.

144 D

At 31 December 20X2 the deferred consideration needs to be discounted to present value by one year.

$200,000/1.1 = $181,818

If you chose C, you have not discounted the consideration. If you chose A, you have not unwound the discount. If you chose B, you have only done the first year calculation.

145 $371,000

To work out the net assets at acquisition, the retained earnings at acquisition must be calculated.

The retained earnings at the end of the year are given as $180,000, and there has been a profit of $36,000 for the year.

As Philip has owned Stanley for 3 months, then 3 months of this profit is regarded as post-acquisition. Therefore $9,000 has been made since acquisition.

Once this has been worked out, the retained earnings at acquisition can be calculated by deducting the post-acquisition retained earnings of $9,000 from the closing retained earnings of $180,000 to give $171,000.

Net assets at acquisition = $200,000 share capital + $171,000 retained earnings = $371,000.

146 $2,780,000

The cost of investment is worked out as follows:

Shares: 800,000 × ¾ × $3.80 = $2,280,000

Deferred cash = $550,000 × $^1/_{1.1}$ = $500,000

The professional fees cannot be capitalised as part of the cost of investment. Therefore the total cost of investment is $2,280,000 + $500,000 = **$2,780,000**

147 B

The profit on the $800,000 sale is $160,000 ($800,000 × $^{25}/_{125}$).

As 75% of the goods have been sold on to third parties, 25% remain in inventory at the year end. Unrealised profits only arise on goods remaining in inventory at the year end, so the unrealised profit is $40,000 ($160,000 × 25%).

148 $352,000

The unrealised profit on the non-current asset transfer needs to be removed.

The carrying amount at the year-end after the transfer is $32,000 ($40,000 less 1 year's depreciation).

The carrying amount of the asset if it had not been transferred would have been $24,000 ($30,000 less 1 year's depreciation).

Therefore the unrealised profit on the non-current asset is $8,000 ($32,000 – $24,000)

The total property, plant and equipment is $300,000 + $60,000 – $8,000 = **$352,000**.

149 B, E

The fact that unanimous consent is required would suggest that there is no control over the investee. Preference shares carry no voting rights and therefore are excluded when considering the control held over an investee.

150

	Include in cost of investment	Do not include in the cost of investment
An agreement to pay a further $30,000 if the subsidiary achieves an operating profit of over $100,000 in the first 3 years after acquisition	✓	
Professional fees of $10,000 in connection with the investment		✓

Any incidental costs associated with the acquisition should be expensed as incurred. Contingent consideration can all be included as part of the cost of an investment in a subsidiary.

151 D

All of Paul's revenue and expenses will be time-apportioned from the date of acquisition to the date of consolidation to reflect the period for which these were controlled by Peter.

152 A

The asset has not been sold outside of the group and therefore there is an unrealised profit to adjust for on consolidation.

153

	True	False
It will always be deducted in full from the parent retained earnings		✓
It will be apportioned between the parent and the non-controlling interest (NCI) when the NCI is valued at fair value	✓	

Where the NCI is valued at fair value, the goodwill impairment will be split between the parent and the NCI in accordance with their shareholdings.

154 A

The activities of the subsidiary are irrelevant when making the decision as to whether to produce consolidated financial statements or not.

155 $160m

	$000	
Consideration – shares	100,000	(see below)
Consideration – cash	60,000	

Branch purchased 75% of Leaf's 80 million shares, giving them 60 million shares. Branch issued 2 shares for every 3 purchased, meaning 40 million shares have been issued (60m × 2/3). At a market value of $2.50 each, 40 million shares have a value of $100 million.

156 $108,000

NCI % × S's PAT = 20% × $600k = $120k

NCI% × PUP (S selling to P) = 20% × 60k = ($12k)

Total NCI = $120k – $12k = **$108k**

157 D

Cost of sales = $14.7m + $8.7m ($^9/_{12}$ × $11.6m) – $4.3m (intra-group sale) + $0.2m (PUP) = **$19.3m**

The PUP is $2.2m × $^{10}/_{110}$ = $0.2m.

If you chose B, you have not time-apportioned the results. If you chose A you have deducted the PUP rather than adding it. If you chose C, you have missed the PUP.

158 $970,000

Operating expenses = $600,000 + $350,000 + $20,000 (FV depreciation) = $970,000

The only adjustments to the statement of profit or loss should be the current year income or expenses. Therefore the prior year fair value depreciation and goodwill impairment are ignored.

159 B

The finance costs for the subsidiary must be time apportioned for six months, as A has only owned them for that period of time. Also, the intra-group interest must be split out. The intra-group interest would not have existed in the first half of the year, as the loan was only given to B in July.

The intra-group interest for the second 6 months would have been $20,000 ($500,000 × 8% × $^{6}/_{12}$). Without this, B's finance costs would have been $50,000 for the year. Splitting this evenly across the year would mean that $25,000 was incurred in each six month period.

Therefore the total finance costs would be $200,000 + $25,000 = **$225,000**.

160 A

	Impacts the NCI share of profit	Does not impact the NCI share
Goodwill impairment	✓	
The parent transferring an item of inventory to the subsidiary for $10,000 greater than its carrying amount, all of which remains in the group at the year end		✓
The subsidiary having an item of plant with a fair value of $500,000 above its carrying amount, and a remaining life of 10 years	✓	

The parent transferring inventory at a profit would mean that the parent's profits are overstated. This would have no impact on the non-controlling interest.

161 $6,600,000

Consolidated revenue: AB $5.5m + CD $2.1m – $1m intra-group= $6.6 million

All intra-group sales and cost of sales are removed from the group accounts.

162 B

The dividend would not have been in Allen's statement of profit or loss, so no adjustment to this would be made. The adjustment to remove the dividend would be made in investment income, where Burridge will have recorded the income in its individual financial statements.

The profit needs to be time-apportioned for the six months of ownership, with the $10,000 impairment then deducted.

Share of profit of associate = 30% × $200,000 ($400,000 × 6/12) – $10,000 = **$50,000**

If you chose D, you have not time-apportioned the associate. If you chose C, you have not deducted the impairment. If you chose A, you have only recognised 30% of the impairment.

163 B

Beasant own 30% of Arnie's shares, which is 30,000 shares (30% of Arnie's 100,000 shares).

As Beasant issued 1 share for every 3 purchased, Beasant issued 10,000 shares. These had a market value of $4.50 and were therefore worth $45,000.

In valuing an associate Beasant must include 30% of Arnie's post-acquisition movement in net assets. Arnie has made a post-acquisition loss of $40,000 (net assets at acquisition were $500,000 and net assets at 31 December were $460,000). Therefore Beasant's share of this is a $12,000 loss (30%).

Cost of investment	$45,000
Share of post-acquisition loss	($12,000)
	————
Investment in associate	$33,000
	————

If you chose D, you based the consideration on 30,000 shares rather than 10,000. If you chose C, you have ignored share capital from the net assets movement. If you chose A, you have used the wrong share price for consideration.

164

	Single entity concept	Going concern concept
Removing unrealised profits on group sales	✓	
Removing intra-group balances	✓	

165

30% of the share capital of Hansen Co. The other 70% is owned by Lawro, another listed entity, whose directors make up Hansen's board.	Subsidiary
80% of the share capital of Kennedy Co, whose activities are significantly different from the rest of the Nicol group.	Associate
30% of the share capital of Bruce Co. The Nicol group have appointed 2 of the 5 board members of Bruce Co, with the other board members coming from three other entities.	Investment

Normally 30% would suggest that Nicol have significant influence, making Hansen an associate. However, Lawro having 70% and controlling the entire board would mean that it is unlikely that Nicol have influence and therefore treat it as a trade investment.

166 A

	$
Cost of Investment	5,500,000
Badger % of post-acquisition profits	46,875
$30\% \times (625,000 \times {}^{3}/_{12})$	
Total	**5,546,875**

167 $325,000

	$
Share of Net Profit: $30\% \times 1,500,000$	450,000
Share of PUP: $30\% \times ((2m \times 50\%) \times 30\%)$	(90,000)
Current year impairment	(35,000)
Total	**325,000**

168 A

IFRS 10 *Consolidated Financial Statements* states that where the reporting date for a parent is different from that of a subsidiary, the subsidiary should prepare additional financial information as of the same date as the financial statements of the parent unless it is impracticable to do so.

If it is impracticable to do so, IFRS 10 allows use of subsidiary financial statements made up to a date of not more than three months earlier or later than the parent's reporting date, with due adjustment for significant transactions or other events between the dates.

The companies do not have to have the same policies in their individual financial statements, but adjustments will be made to prepare the consolidated financial statements using the group policies.

Only the profit relating to goods remaining in the group at year end needs to be adjusted.

169 A, B

Items C and D would signify control.

170 C, D

While the same accounting policies must be used in the consolidated financial statements, the subsidiaries do not have to operate the same policies as the parent. Having different activities is not an acceptable reason for non-consolidation.

171 B

	$000
Cost (240,000 × $6)	1,440
Share of associate's profit (400 × $^6/_{12}$ × 240/800)	60
	———
	1,500
	———

172 $63,800,000

	$000
Viagem	51,200
Greca (26,000 × $^9/_{12}$)	19,500
Intra-group purchases (800 × 9 months)	(7,200)
URP in inventory (1,500 × $^{25}/_{125}$)	300
	———
	63,800
	———

173 C

Market price of Sact's shares at acquisition was $2.50 ($3 × $^{100}/_{120}$), therefore non-controlling interest (NCI) at acquisition was $50,000 (100,000 × 20% × $2.50). NCI share of the post-acquisition profit is $6,000 (40,000 × $^9/_{12}$ × 20%). Therefore non-controlling interest as at 31 March 20X5 is $56,000.

174 C

Germaine only owns 40% of Foll's voting shares so is unlikely to exercise control.

175 $546,000

	$
Wilmslow	450,000
Post-acquisition Zeta ((340 − 200) × 80%)	112,000
Inventory PUP (320,000 × ¼ × $^{25}/_{125}$)	(16,000)
	———
	546,000
	———

176 C, D

The fair value of deferred consideration is its present value. Fair values are applied to the subsidiary's assets, liabilities and contingent liabilities.

While the use of fair value seems to not comply with the historical cost principle, this will effectively form part of the cost of the subsidiary to the parent, so the principle is still applied. Depreciation will not increase if the fair value of assets is lower than the current carrying amount. Patents can be recorded as intangible assets as they are separable.

177

	True	False
The profit made by a parent on the sale of goods to a subsidiary is only realised when the subsidiary sells the goods to a third party	✓	
Eliminating intra-group unrealised profits never affects non-controlling interests		✓
The profit element of goods supplied by the parent to an associate and held in year-end inventory must be eliminated in full		✓

178 $1,335,000

	$000	
Investment at cost	1,200	
Share of post-acq profit	150	$(750 \times {}^{8}/_{12} \times 30\%)$
Inventory PUP	(15)	$(300 \times {}^{20}/_{120} \times 30\%)$
	———	
	1,335	
	———	

179 $98,600,000

The $1 million cash in transit should be treated as if received (Dr Cash $1 million, Cr Receivables $1 million). After this, an intra-group balance of $3 million will remain. This is then removed (Dr Payables $3 million, Cr Receivables $3 million).

Therefore consolidated receivables = 64.6 + 38 − 1.0 − 3.0 = **$98.6m**

180

	True	False
If a subsidiary is disposed of on the last day of the reporting period then its assets and liabilities must still be included in the consolidated statement of financial position		✓
The gain or loss arising on the disposal of a subsidiary in the financial statements is recorded in other comprehensive income		✓

181

> Cash consideration of $4.8 million

> Deferred cash consideration of $8.3 million

The professional fees cannot be capitalised. The deferred cash should be discounted to present value at the date of acquisition, $10 million/$1.1^2$ = $8.3 million.

182 B

The profit or loss on the disposal is calculated as follows:

Proceeds	10m
Goodwill at disposal	(2m)
Net assets at disposal	(9m)
Non-controlling interest at disposal	3m
Profit on disposal	2m

If you selected answer A you have incorrectly identified it as a loss. If you selected answer C you have added the goodwill instead of deducting it. If you selected answer D you have added the non-controlling interest onto the carrying amount of the subsidiary (rather than deducting it) when calculating the profit or loss on disposal.

183 $6,000,000

The profit arising in the individual financial statements of Wind will be the difference between the proceeds received of $10 million and the purchase price of $4 million.

184 $2,500,000

	$m
Proceeds	9.0
Goodwill at disposal	(4.6)
Net assets at disposal	(5.0)
Non-controlling interest at disposal	3.1
Profit on disposal	2.5

185   A

	$m	$m
Proceeds		15
Goodwill at disposal		Nil
Net assets at disposal		(8)
Non-controlling interest:		
At acquisition	2.2	
NCI % of post-acquisition net assets	1.2	
40% × ($8m – $5m)		
NCI % of goodwill impairment (40% × $1m)	(0.4)	
Non-controlling interest at disposal		3
Profit on disposal		10

If you selected answer B you have used the non-controlling interest at acquisition when calculating the profit or loss on disposal, instead of the non-controlling interest at disposal. If you selected answer C you have not reduced the non-controlling interest by its share of the goodwill impairment. If you selected answer D you have valued the non-controlling interest at its share of the disposal date net assets.

INTERPRETATION OF FINANCIAL STATEMENTS

186   A

A not-for-profit entity is not likely to have shareholders or 'earnings'.

187   B

A, C and D are all ratios associated with profit. A charity is more likely to be concerned with liquidity rather than the profits made by the entity.

188

	Limitation	Not a limitation
Different ways of calculating certain ratios exist	✓	
Accounting policy choices can limit comparability between different companies	✓	

189   35

Inventory turnover is six times, so inventory days must be 365/6 = 61 days.

The cash collection period is inventory days plus receivables days less payables days.

Therefore the trade payables period is 61 + 42 – 68 = 35 days.

190 C, E

A new website selling direct to the public is unlikely to be on credit terms, as payment will be taken on the order.

This should therefore reduce the receivables collection period, as will the new retail units to the public, which will be cash based.

191 C

Return on capital employed is calculated as profit from operations/capital employed. Capital employed consists of debt and equity.

The deferred tax and payables are not included. Therefore the return on capital employed = $240,000/$900,000 = **26.7%**.

192 0.87:1

The quick ratio is made up of the current assets excluding inventory divided by the current liabilities = ($80,000 + $10,000)/($70,000 + $34,000) = **0.87:1**.

193 A

While the website is new in the year, the additional delivery costs are likely to be incurred every year in the future, meaning it is not a 'one-off' item.

194 C

Delivery costs to customers are not part of cost of sales, so increased prices will have no impact on the gross profit margin.

195

	Available to KRL to use	Not available to KRL to use
Details of the overseas country in which the target entity operates	✓	
Recent financial statements of the entity	✓	
Internal business plans of the takeover target		✓

Internal business plans would be internal information for an entity so KRL would not be able to use this information.

196 A

P/E ratio is seen as a marker of risk, and a high P/E ratio is indicative of a lower perceived risk than an entity with a lower P/E ratio. Therefore Marcel is seen as less risky than the sector average.

P/E ratio is also indicative of market confidence, and a high P/E ratio means that high future growth is expected. Therefore, there is more confidence about the future prospects of Marcel than the sector average.

197

	True	False
It acts as a prediction of the future Earnings Per Share figure		✓
It discloses that Earnings Per Share could have been higher		✓

Diluted EPS is not a prediction of the future EPS figure as firstly there is no forecast made of the earnings figure.

Secondly, if there were a range of conversion terms for a convertible, the terms giving the maximum number of issued shares would always be used in the diluted EPS calculation, rather than the most likely conversion terms.

Diluted EPS is a warning to shareholders that the EPS calculation could have been lower if the commitments to issue ordinary shares had been issued as shares in the current period.

198 B

The finance cost in the profit or loss account will be based on the effective interest rate, so the charge will be $2.5m × 8% = $200,000.

If the interest cover to be maintained is 9, then the minimum operating profit to be maintained must be $200 × 9 = $1.8m.

Option A used the coupon rate of 6% to calculate the finance cost, giving $150k.

Option C used the difference between the effective and coupon rate which is $50k.

Option D includes the transaction costs in the initial value of the loan, when calculating effective interest, giving $220k.

199 5.6

Price-earnings (P/E) ratio is current market price per share/earnings per share.

The earnings per share (EPS) for Rogers is net profit/number of ordinary shares in issue. The share capital is $1 million, and as the share capital is divided into 50¢ shares there must be 2 million shares in issue.

Therefore, EPS is 1,250/2,000 = $0.625, or 62.5¢

P/E ratio is therefore 3.50/0.625 = 5.6

200 21.4%

The dividend yield is calculated as the dividend per share/current share price × 100%

Dividend per share is total dividend/total number of shares

Dividend per share is therefore $1.5m/2m = $0.75, or 75¢

The current share price is $3.50

Therefore the dividend yield is 0.75/3.5 × 100% = 21.4%

201 B

ROCE can be sub-divided into net profit × asset turnover.

Alco has a higher net profit, and therefore must be a high end retailer. Its asset turnover is 0.4 times, so it does not use assets intensively to generate a profit.

This would be expected of a high end retailer, as they are not volume driven.

Saleco has a low net profit, and therefore must be a lower end retailer. Its asset turnover is 5 times, so it uses assets intensively to generate a profit.

This would be expected of a lower end retailer, as they are volume driven.

202

	Limitation	Not a limitation
Financial statements often use historic cost, meaning that inflation is not taken into account	✓	
Complex items may not fit into any accounting standards and therefore may be omitted from the financial statements		✓

While complex items may exist which don't fit easily into an accounting standard, these cannot simply be omitted from the financial statements. The IFRS Conceptual Framework for Financial Reporting is a principles-based framework, so these would be accounted for using the principles contained within it.

203 A

Lepchem have not yet made any sales, so any ratio involving profit or revenue is irrelevant. The current ratio will be relevant, as Lepchem may have cash flow problems as they spend cash to develop new pharmaceuticals without any cash receipt until they are successful. This could threaten Lepchem's ability to continue as a going concern.

204 C

	Could be used to assess	Will not be used
The return given to investors		✓
The success in achieving the organisation's stated aims	✓	
How well costs are being managed	✓	

Not-for-profit entities do not exist to make profits, therefore the return given to investors is irrelevant.

205 D

With a property management business, the value of that business is linked to the properties and the income which they can generate. Therefore the revenue and profits generated will be relevant.

However, there is unlikely to be any inventory so inventory turnover will not be a key measure that is used.

206 B, C

Rising costs are likely to affect the whole industry and would still mean that Quartile could be compared to the sector. As the error has been corrected, there will be no issues over comparability this year.

207 51

Year-end inventory of six times is 61 days (365/6).

Trade payables period is 42 days (230,000 × 365/2,000,000).

Therefore receivables collection period is 51 days (70 – 61 + 42).

208 B, D

Factoring with recourse means Trent still has the risk of an irrecoverable receivable and therefore could not derecognise the receivable. The cash sales are irrelevant as Trent does not include them within the calculation.

209 D

Acquisition of an asset under a lease agreement will increase debt and so increase gearing. The other options either increase equity or have no impact.

210 C

Use of average cost gives a higher cost of sales (and in turn lower operating profit) than FIFO during rising prices.

STATEMENT OF CASH FLOWS

211 A

	PPE		
b/f	14,400	Disposal (CA)	3,000
Revaluation	2,000	Depreciation	2,500
Provision	4,000		
Additions (balance)	**8,500**	b/f	23,400
	28,900		28,900

212 B

	$
Accrued interest b/f	12,000
Interest per statement of profit or loss	41,000
Less unwinding (this is not cash, $150,000 × 6%)	(9,000)
Accrued interest c/f	(15,000)
Paid	29,000

If you chose A, you have ignored the unwinding of the discount. If you chose C you have made an error between the opening and closing liability. If you chose D you have simply taken the expense for the year.

213 $98,000

Tax liabilities

		b/f (27 + 106)	133
Paid (balance)	98	Statement of profit or loss	122
c/f (38 + 119)	157		
	255		255

214 A

Cash paid to employees is shown when using the direct method, not the indirect method.

215 A, C

Purchase of investments and purchase of equipment would both be shown within cash flows from investing activities.

216 D

	$
Profit	37,500
Depreciation	2,500
Increase in receivables	(2,000)
Decrease in inventory	3,600
Increase in payables	700
Cash generated from operations	42,300
Purchase of non-current assets	(16,000)
Net increase in cash and cash equivalents	26,300

If you chose A, you have deducted depreciation. If you chose C you have deducted the payables movement. If you chose B, you have added the movement in receivables.

217 D

	Add to profit before tax	Deduct from profit before tax
Decrease in trade receivables	✓	
Increase in inventories		✓
Profit on sale of non-current assets		✓
Depreciation	✓	

Profit on disposal of non-current assets will be deducted from profit, as it relates to non-cash income. Increases in inventories would be deducted as they have a negative impact on cash flow. Decreases in receivables would have a positive impact on cash flow. Depreciation should be added to profit as it relates to a non-cash expense.

218 $10,000

There will be an inflow of $30,000 relating to a share issue (being the total movement in share capital and share premium), and a $20,000 outflow on repayment of the debentures. Therefore the overall movement will be a net $10,000 inflow.

219 A

	PPE		
b/f	180	Disposal	60
Revaluation	25	Depreciation	20
Paid (balance)	**125**	c/f	250
	———		———
	330		330
	———		———

The amounts to be shown in investing activities will be:

Purchase of PPE: ($125,000) (See working above)

Sale of PPE: $50,000 (Given in question)

This gives a **net outflow of $75,000**

If you chose B or D, you have only accounted for one of the cash flows. If you chose C, you have missed the disposal from your PPE working.

220

Amortisation of government grant	Receipt of grant
	Cash received from grant $300,000 in investing activities
Decrease of 100,000 to cash generated from operations	

The release of government grant should be deducted within the reconciliation of cash generated from operations, as this represents non-cash income. The grant received of $300,000 can be calculated using a working, as shown below.

Grant liability

		b/f	900,000
Release to SPL	100,000	**Receipt of grant (balance)**	**300,000**
c/f	1,100,000		
	————		————
	1,200,000		1,200,000
	————		————

Section 5

ANSWERS TO OBJECTIVE CASE QUESTIONS – SECTION B

CONCEPTUAL FRAMEWORK/INTERNATIONAL FINANCIAL REPORTING STANDARDS

221 $300,000

The engine will be depreciated over the life of 36,000 flight hours. As the aircraft has flown for 1,200 hours in the first 6 months, the depreciation for the engine will be $9 million × 1,200/36,000 = $300,000.

222 D

Replacement components of complex assets can be capitalised. As the new engine has a life of 36,000 hours, the engine will be depreciated over this life rather than the based on the remaining life of the damaged engine.

223

	Capitalise	Expense
$3 million repair of the wing		✓
$2 million repainting of the exterior		✓

Both costs will be regarded as repairs and must be expensed.

224 B

Cabin fittings – at 1 October 20X8 the carrying amount of the cabin fittings is $7.5 million $(25,000 - (25,000 \times {}^{3.5}/_5))$. The cost of improving the cabin facilities of $4.5 million should be capitalised as it led to enhanced future economic benefits in the form of substantially higher fares.

The cabin fittings would then have a carrying amount of $12 million (7,500 + 4,500) and an unchanged remaining life of 18 months. Thus depreciation for the six months to 31 March 20X9 is $4 million $(12,000 \times {}^6/_{18})$, giving a carrying amount of $8 million.

If you selected A, you have depreciated the upgrade over 5 years rather than the remaining life. If you selected C, you have not capitalised the upgrade. If you selected D, you have done a full year's depreciation on the upgrade.

225 Carrying amount

Recoverable amount is calculated by comparing value in use and fair value less costs to sell, so neither of those would be correct, and replacement cost is not relevant to an impairment calculation.

226 A

As Speculate uses the fair value model for investment properties, the asset should be revalued to fair value before being classed as an investment property. The gain on revaluation should be taken to other comprehensive income, as the asset is being revalued while held as property, plant and equipment.

At 1 October, the carrying amount of the asset is $1,950, being $2 million less 6 months' depreciation. As the fair value at 1 October is $2.3 million, this leads to a $350,000 gain which will be recorded in other comprehensive income.

227 B

Investment properties can be accounted for under the cost or fair value model but not the revaluation model, which applies to property, plant and equipment.

228 $190,000

		$000
Gain on investment properties:	A (2,340 – 2,300)	40
	B (1,650 – 1,500)	150

229

Individual	✓	Consolidated	✓
Investment property	✓	Investment property	
Property, plant & equipment		Property, plant & equipment	✓
Within goodwill		Cancelled as an intra-group item	

In the individual financial statements Speculate would treat property B as an investment, but in Speculate's consolidated financial statements property B would be accounted for under IAS 16 *Property, Plant and Equipment* and be classified as owner-occupied. The group is regarded as a single entity, and the group use the building.

230 B

If Speculate uses the cost model, the asset would be transferred to investment properties at its carrying amount and then depreciated over its remaining life. This would mean that the asset would have a year's depreciation applied to it, 6 months while held as property, plant and equipment, 6 months while held as an investment property. Fair values would be irrelevant.

The depreciation would therefore be $2 million/20 years = $100,000, giving a carrying amount of $1.9 million.

If you selected A, you have only accounted for depreciation for 6 months. If you selected C or D, you have applied depreciation to the fair value of the asset.

231 D

Loans are regarded as financial liabilities and should be held at amortised cost.

232 A, B

Borrowing costs must be capitalised if they are directly attributable to qualifying assets, which are assets that take a substantial time to complete. Capitalisation should cease once substantially all the activities to prepare the asset are complete. Capitalisation commences when expenditure is incurred on the asset, borrowing costs are being incurred **and** preparation activities have commenced.

233 $125,000

The finance cost of the loan must be calculated using the effective rate of 7.5%, so the total finance cost for the year ended 31 March 20X8 is $750,000 ($10 million × 7.5%). As the loan relates to a qualifying asset, the finance cost (or part of it in this case) can be capitalised in accordance with IAS 23 *Borrowing Costs*.

Capitalisation commences from when expenditure is being incurred (1 May 20X7) and must cease when the asset is ready for its intended use (28 February 20X8), in this case a 10 month period.

The finance cost to be capitalised = $625,000 ($750,000 × $^{10}/_{12}$). The remaining two months finance costs of $125,000 must be expensed.

234 $625,000

The finance cost to be capitalised = $625,000 ($750,000 × $^{10}/_{12}$).

235 B

Temporary investment income earned during the construction period should be netted off the amount capitalised. However, the interest was earned **prior to the period of construction**. Therefore the investment income earned should be taken to the statement of profit or loss as investment income.

236 $320,000

The dismantling costs should be capitalised at the present value of $4 million, with an equivalent liability created. Each year the discount is unwound at 8%, charged to finance cost and increasing the liability.

Finance cost is therefore $4 million × 8% = $320,000

237 A

The $1.2 million government grant should be released over the 5 year life of the asset, meaning that $240,000 will be released to the statement of profit or loss each year. As Shawler only received the grant on 1 October 20X3, only $120,000 ($^6/_{12}$) should be released to the statement of profit or loss in the year.

Therefore there is a remaining balance of $1,080,000 at the year-end. Of this, $240,000 will be released in the next year, so $840,000 will be shown as a non-current liability.

If you selected B, you have not split the year-end liability into current and non-current. If you selected C, you have released a full year of the grant and then not split the year-end liability. If you selected D, you have split the year-end liability but have released a full year of the grant rather than 6 months.

238 $3,000,000

The land is initially translated using the spot rate of exchange and so is recognised at $3 million (12m dinar/4).

Land is a non-monetary asset and so is **not** retranslated at the reporting date.

239 B

Training costs cannot be capitalised as it is not possible to restrict the access of others to the economic benefit as staff could leave and take their skills elsewhere.

240 A, B

The deferred income should be removed, with an expense recorded in the statement of profit or loss. No prior year adjustment should be made. The plant cost would only be increased if the grant was accounted for using the netting off method.

241 B, D

Whilst items A and C are necessary for an item to be capitalised as an asset, they are not linked to the characteristic of them being identifiable.

242

	Capitalise	Expense
Training courses for staff		✓
Expenditure on processor chip		✓

Training courses for staff cannot be capitalised as Darby will not be able to restrict the access of others to the economic benefit. The expenditure on the chip would be classed as research expenditure.

243 $320,000

The amounts incurred from 1 February to 30 April should be expensed, meaning that $300,000 (3 × $100,000) should be expensed. Following this, the costs from 1 May to 30 October should be capitalised, meaning that $600,000 should be capitalised.

The development asset should then be amortised over the 5-year remaining life, giving $120,000 amortisation each year. This should be amortised from 1 November, meaning that 2 months' amortisation should be expensed in the year, so $120,000 × $^2/_{12}$ = $20,000.

Therefore the total expense = $300,000 + $20,000 = **$320,000**.

244 C

The development costs will not be subject to an annual impairment review, but will be amortised over the 5 year useful life. The development costs will be held at the carrying value, and will not be revalued each year.

Plant used solely on the development project will result in the depreciation being a directly attributable cost of the project. Therefore any depreciation on the asset will be included in the costs to be capitalised and will be taken to the statement of profit or loss as the project is amortised over the 5 year life.

245 D

At the date of the impairment review, the asset had a carrying amount of $450,000 ($^9/_{10}$ × $500,000).

The recoverable amount of the asset is the **higher** of the fair value less costs to sell of $380,000 ($400,000 – $20,000) and the value in use of $480,000. The recoverable amount is therefore $480,000.

The carrying amount of the asset is **lower** than the recoverable amount, so no impairment is charged.

246   D

Depreciation 1 January to 30 June 20X4 (80,000/10 × $^6/_{12}$) = 4,000

Depreciation 1 July to 31 December 20X4 (81,000/9 × $^6/_{12}$) = 4,500

Total depreciation = 8,500

247 A, D

A fall in the cost of capital would increase the value in use of an asset and would therefore not indicate potential impairment.

The entity's market capitalisation would not be reflected within the values on the statement of financial position.

248 B

Value in use of $38,685 is lower than fair value less costs to sell of $43,000, so recoverable amount is $43,000 and impairment is $60,750 – $43,000 = $17,750.

249 D, E

There is no requirement to test cash generating units (CGUs) more often than other assets. A CGU could be a subsidiary, but not necessarily, and the CGU needs to be consistently identified.

250 $262,500

The impairment loss of $220,000 ($1,170 – $950) is allocated: $35,000 to damaged plant and $85,000 to goodwill, the remaining $100,000 allocated proportionally to the building and the undamaged plant. The impairment to be allocated to the plant will be $37,500 ($100,000 × ($300/$(300+500))), leaving an amended carrying amount of the plant of $262,500 ($300,000 – $37,500).

251 A, D, E

Assets held for sale must be available for immediate sale, being actively marketed under a committed plan which is unlikely to be withdrawn, and expected to sell within 12 months. Whether the asset is in use or not is irrelevant, and it is not necessary for the sale to have been agreed.

252 A

The disposal of outlets in country A represents a separate geographical location and should be treated as a discontinued operation. The change in focus in Country B is not regarded as a separate major line of business, as it is just targeting different customers.

253 D

Depreciation should cease on the date that the asset is classified as held for sale. In this case, this will be 1 January 20X3. Therefore depreciation would be $150,000 ($4 million/ 20 years × $^9/_{12}$), giving a carrying amount of $3,850,000.

As the asset is expected to sell for $4 million, the asset should be held at $3,850,000 as the asset should be held at the lower of carrying amount and fair value less costs to sell.

254 A

Costs relating to the ongoing activities of the entity cannot be provided for according to IAS 37 *Provisions, Contingent Liabilities and Contingent Assets*. Therefore only the redundancy costs of $300,000 can be provided.

255

	Adjusting event	Non-adjusting event
Disposal of plant	✓	
Redundancy settlement	✓	

Both events relate to conditions in existence at the reporting date, so both events should be regarded as adjusting events.

256 B, C

Accounting policies should only be changed if required by a new IFRS Standards or if doing so results in the production of more reliable and relevant information.

257

The change in useful life of the plant will be a change in accounting **estimate** and should be applied **prospectively**.

258 A

A change in accounting policy must be accounted for as if the new policy had always been in place, retrospectively. In this case, for the year ended 30 September 20X9, both the opening and closing inventories would need to be measured at AVCO which would reduce reported profit by the movement in the values of the opening and closing inventories of $400,000 (($20 million – $18 million) – ($15 million – $13.4 million).

The other effect of the change will be on the retained earnings brought forward at 1 October 20X8. These will be restated (reduced) by the effect of the reduced inventory value at 30 September 20X8 i.e. $1.6 million ($15 million – $13.4 million). This adjustment would be shown in the statement of changes in equity.

259 $88,000

The inventories should be valued at the lower of cost and net realisable value (NRV). The items have a cost of $100,000 (20,000 at $5). The NRV is $88,000, being the 20,000 units at their net selling price of $44 ($55 less 20% commission).

260 B

The inventories should be held at the cost of $80,000 as the net realisable value of $150,000 less $20,000 to complete will be higher than the cost. The replacement cost of $50,000 is irrelevant.

261 C

The cattle will be classed as a biological asset and the milk will be classed as agricultural produce. The cheese is produced after processing so will be classed as inventory.

262 $19,000

The sheep will be held at fair value less point of sale costs. Initially the sheep would have been recognised at $95,000, being the $100,000 less 5% selling costs. At 31 March 20X6, they will be valued at $114,000, being $120,000 less 5% selling costs. Therefore a gain of $19,000 will be recorded in the statement of profit or loss.

263 B

Current cost accounting will apply the current cost of the asset less depreciation to date to reflect the age of the asset. As a new asset would cost $300,000, a 4 year old asset under current cost accounting will be valued at $180,000 ($300,000 – ($4/_{10} \times $300,000)).

264 B

This will be a level 2 input, as it is using the price of similar assets without adjustment.

265 A, C

The revaluation will increase equity, therefore affecting the gearing and return on capital employed. The depreciation will also increase. As Schrute charges depreciation to operating expenses, this will affect the net profit margin.

266 C

The lease grants the lessee the beneficial rights of asset use, meaning that a right-of-use asset and lease liability are recorded.

A is incorrect as it treats the rental as an expense, which is not permitted under IFRS 16 *Leases*.

B outlines incorrect treatment for interest, which should decrease over the life of the lease as the lease liability decreases.

D is incorrect as the payments reduce the lease liability rather than being treated as prepayments.

267 A

Leased assets are exempt from capitalisation where the lease period is for 12 months or less, or the assets are low-value assets. IFRS 16 *Leases* does not give a value for what is meant by low-value assets, but gives examples, including telephones. In this case the lease rentals would be charged as an expense within the statement of profit or loss.

268 $306,250

The plant would be capitalised at $350,000, equal to the lease liability plus the initial payment. This would then be depreciated over the four year lease term, giving depreciation of $87,500 a year.

As Fino only entered into the lease halfway through the year, this would give depreciation of $43,750. Therefore the carrying amount would be $350,000 less $43,750, which is $306,250.

269 A

	$
Present value of total lease payments	350,000
Less initial lease rental	(100,000)
Initial lease liability	250,000
Interest to 30 September 20X7 (6 months at 10%)	12,500

270

	Increase	Decrease
Return on Capital Employed		✓
Gearing	✓	
Interest cover		✓

Recognition of the lease liability would cause debt liabilities and finance costs to increase. This means that the capital employed would be higher, therefore decreasing return on capital employed. Gearing would increase due to the increased debt. Interest cover would decrease due to the higher level of finance costs.

271 $75,780

The initial lease liability will be $1,263,000, on which 12 months interest at 6% would be $75,780.

272 B

	b/f	Interest @ 6%	Payment	c/f
	$000	$000	$000	$000
20X6	1,263	76	(300)	1,039
20X7	1,039	62	(300)	801

At 31 December 20X6 the total lease liability is $1,039,000. This must be split into current and non-current liabilities. The non-current liability is $801,000, being the amount remaining after the payment in 20X7. Therefore the current liability is $238,000, being the difference between $1,039,000 and $801,000.

If you selected A, you have calculated the liability as if payments were made in advance rather than arrears.

If you selected C, you have chosen the total liability.

If you selected D, you have chosen the non-current liability.

273 C

A leased asset would normally be depreciated over the shorter of the lease term and useful life of the asset. However, as ownership transfers to Lotso at the end of the lease term, Lotso will be using the asset for the entire 6 year period. Therefore the asset is depreciated over 6 years, recognising $210,500 ($1,263,000/6) depreciation a year, and leaving a carrying amount as at 31 December 20X6 of $1,052,500.

274 B

This represents a sale and leaseback where the seller-lessee retains the full benefit of the asset over its remaining life. The asset is not derecognised and remains on the statement of financial position at its carrying amount of $10 million, to be depreciated over the remaining 20 years at a rate of $500,000 ($10m/20) per annum. The value after one year is therefore $9.5 million.

The sale proceeds of $11.5 million would be treated as a loan.

275

	True	False
Statement 1		✓
Statement 2		✓

In a sale and leaseback where the seller-lessee does not retain use of the asset over its remaining life then the seller-lessee is deemed to have disposed of part of the asset, and any profit or loss would be recognised on this element of the asset no longer retained.

Sale proceeds in a sale and leaseback transaction would only be treated as a loan where the seller-lessee retains use of the asset over its remaining life.

276 D

Laidlaw should not 'derecognise' the receivables, but instead treat the $1.8 million cash received from Finease as a current liability (a loan or financing arrangement secured on the receivables).

This is a 'with recourse' factoring arrangement, as Finease can return the receivables to Laidlaw, meaning that Laidlaw carries the risk of these.

277 $810,000

The payments should be discounted at the market rate to find the split of the liability and equity, shown in the working below.

Year ended 30 September	Cash flow	Discount rate at	Discounted cash flows
	$000	8%	$000
20X3	500	0.93	465
20X4	500	0.86	430
20X5	10,500	0.79	8,295
			———
Liability component			9,190
Equity (balance)			**810**
			———
Total proceeds			10,000
			———

278 A, D

The substance of this transaction is that the bank has granted a loan of $5 million to Laidlaw. Control of the inventory has not been transferred, so the 'sale' should not be recognised as revenue. Therefore the loan should be recognised, in addition to the interest expense.

279 D

5% will not be charged to the statement of profit or loss, as the liability element will be held at amortised cost with 8% on the outstanding balance being charged to the statement of profit or loss each year.

280 A

Applying split accounting is essential for faithful representation, otherwise the correct accounting treatment is not being applied. While the disclosures may assist relevance, applying the correct accounting treatment is ensuring the fundamental characteristic of faithful representation is met.

281 D

All three items fall under the description of financial instruments. A financial instrument is a contract that gives rise to a financial asset of one entity and a financial liability or equity instrument of another entity. The convertible loan notes will be split between a financial liability and equity. The loan notes will be a financial liability and the investments will be a financial asset.

282 C

The liability should be held at amortised cost using the effective rate of interest at 10%.

	B/f	Interest 10%	Payment	c/f
	$000	$000	$000	$000
20X5	28,508	2,851	(2,400)	28,959

283 $768,000

	$
Nominal value issued	10,000,000
Less: issue costs	(400,000)
	————
Initial value	9,600,000
	————
Interest at effective rate of 8%	$768,000
	————

284 B

Howard should record the dividend income of $100,000 (10 cents × 1 million shares) as well as the gain in value of $1 million.

285

	Capitalised	Not capitalised
Fair value through other comprehensive income investments	✓	
Fair value through profit or loss investments		✓
Amortised cost investments	✓	

Transaction costs relating to fair value through profit or loss investments should be expensed in the statement of profit or loss.

286 C

The payable should initially be translated at the spot rate of Kr10:$1, giving a payable of $1,000. As payables are a monetary liability, they should be retranslated at the closing rate of Kr8:$1. This gives a closing payable of $1,250. Therefore the foreign exchange loss is $250, as it will now cost $250 more to settle the liability. This will be charged to the statement of profit or loss.

287 B

The receivable should initially be translated at the spot rate of Kr10:$1, giving a receivable of $6,000. When the cash of Kr 30,000 is received, the foreign currency gain or loss should be recorded.

At the rate of Kr10.5:$1, this will give a value of $2,857. As the Kr 30,000 would have originally been included at $3,000, this gives a loss of $143.

Finally, the year-end balance must be retranslated at the closing rate of Kr8:$1. This gives a closing receivable of $3,750. As this would originally have been included at $3,000, this gives a gain of $750. Therefore the net gain is $750 – $143 = $607.

288

	True	False
Statement 1		✓
Statement 2		✓

Inventory should not be retranslated as it is not a monetary item. Foreign exchange gains will not be included in revenue.

289 $3,000

The tax expense in the statement of profit or loss consists of the current tax estimate and the movement on deferred tax in the year. The closing deferred tax liability is $90,000, being the temporary differences of $360,000 at the tax rate of 25%. This means that the deferred tax liability has decreased by $40,000 in the year. This decrease should be deducted from the current tax estimate of $43,000 to give a total expense of $3,000.

290 C

A debit balance represents an under-provision of tax from the prior year. This should be added to the current year's tax expense in the statement of profit or loss.

An under- or over-provision only arises when the prior year tax estimate is paid so there is no adjustment required to the current year liability.

291 $8,000,000

Revenue should be recorded by multiplying the contract price by the progress to date. Therefore the revenue to be recorded is $10 million × 80% = $8 million.

292 D

This is a loss making contract. In this situation, the loss should be recorded in full immediately. Revenue should be based on the progress to date.

	$000
Step 1 – Overall	
Price	8,000
Total cost – incurred to date	(4,000)
– estimated future	(6,000)
	———
Overall loss	(2,000)
	———

	$000
Step 2 – Progress	
60%	
Step 3 – SPL	$000
Revenue (60% of 8,000)	4,800
Cost of sales (balancing figure)	**(6,800)**
	———
FULL loss to be recognised immediately	(2,000)
	———

293 C

See the workings below

	$000
Step 1 – Overall	
Contract price	4,000
Total contract cost (500 + 2,000)	(2,500)
Estimated total profit	1,500

Step 2 – Progress = 25%

	$000
Step 3 – SPL	
Revenue (25% × 4,000)	1,000
Cost of sales (25% × 2,500)	(625)
Profit	375

	$000
Step 4 – SFP	
Costs to date	500
Profit to date	375
Less: Amount billed	(1,000)
Contract liability	(125)

294

	True	False
Statement 1		✓
Statement 2	✓	

There may be a contract asset based on the amount spent to date compared to the amount billed to the customer.

Where the progress and overall profit of a contract are uncertain, revenue is recognised to the level of recoverable costs.

295 As a change in accounting **estimate**, applied **prospectively**.

IFRS 15 *Revenue from Contracts with Customers* explains that a change in the method of measuring progress is a change in accounting estimate. Changes in accounting estimate are always applied prospectively.

296 D

The revenue in relation to the installation and the machine itself can be recognised, with the revenue on the service recognised over time as the service is performed. The service will be recognised over the 2 year period. By 31 December 20X7, 2 months of the service has been performed. Therefore $20,000 can be recognised ($240,000 × $^2/_{24}$).

Total revenue is therefore $580,000, being the $800,000 less the $220,000 relating to the service which has not yet been recognised.

297

Sales element	Discount applied	Discount not applied
Machine	✓	
Installation	✓	
Service	✓	

Discounts should be applied evenly across the components of a sale unless any one element is regularly sold separately at a discount. As Creg does not sell the service and installation separately, the discount must be applied evenly to each of the three elements.

298 B

Revenue as an agent is made by earning commission. Therefore the revenue on these sales should only be $600,000 (10% of $6 million). As Creg currently has $6 million in revenue, $5.4 million needs to be removed, with $5.4 million also removed from cost of sales.

299 $9,490,000

The fact that Creg has given the customer a year to pay on such a large amount suggests there is a significant financing component within the sale.

The $990,000 received can be recognised in revenue immediately. The remaining $9.01 million must be discounted to its present value of $8.5 million. This is then unwound over the year, with the interest recognised as finance income.

Therefore total initial revenue = $990,000 + $8,500,000 = $9,490,000.

300 D

This does not represent a real sale as control has not passed to the bank. Creg still maintains responsibility for the upkeep of the goods.

The bank cannot benefit from the price rise as Creg holds the option to repurchase the goods for a price below the expected fair value.

Therefore this will be treated as a $3 million loan. The additional $630,000 represents interest of 10% a year over two years on the $3 million.

301 D

EPS for the year ended 30 September 20X7
($15 million/43.25 million × 100)   34.7¢

Step 1 – Theoretical ex rights price (TERP)

4 shares at $3.80	15.2
1 share at $2.80	2.8
	___
5 shares at **$3.60** (TERP)	18
	___

Step 2 – Rights fraction

Market value before issue/TERP = $3.80/$3.60

Step 3 – Weighted average number of shares

36 million × $^3/_{12}$ × $^{\$3.80}/_{\$3.60}$	9.50 million
45 million × $^9/_{12}$	33.75 million
	43.25 million

If you selected A, you have simply divided the profit for the year by the number of shares at the start of the year. If you selected B, you have used the inverse of the rights fraction. If you selected C, you have applied the rights fraction for the whole year rather than for the period up to the rights issue.

302 A

Diluted EPS for the year ended 30 September 2009 ($15.6 million/45.75 million × 100)	34¢
Adjusted earnings	
15 million + (10 million × 8% × 75%)	$15.6 million
Adjusted number of shares	
43.25 million + (10 million × $^{25}/_{100}$)	45.75 million

If you selected B, you have ignored the additional tax that would be payable on the interest saved. If you selected C, you have ignored the additional shares that would be issued. If you selected D, you have ignored the impact to the profit and simply increased the number of shares.

303 C

EPS for the year ended 30 September 20X7 ($12 million/43.2 million × 100)		28¢
Weighted average number of shares		
1 Oct	34 million × $^4/_{12}$ × $^6/_5$	13.6 million
1 Feb	37 million × $^5/_{12}$ × $^6/_5$	18.5 million
1 July	44.4 million × $^3/_{12}$	11.1 million
		43.2 million

The bonus fraction should be applied from the start of the year up to the date of the bonus issue. If you selected A, you have added the bonus issue in July to the number of shares in addition to the bonus fraction, effectively double counting the bonus issue. If you selected B, you have missed out the bonus fraction completely. If you selected D you have just added the 3 million market issue without considering the bonus issue.

304

Company	Comparative restated	No restatement
Barstead	✓	
Cabott		✓
Dunstan	✓	

Prior year earnings per share figures must be restated when there is a bonus element to a share issue. Rights issues contain a bonus element so Barstead must restate the prior year figure. Dunstan performed a bonus issue so must restate the prior year figure.

305

	Correct	Incorrect
Statement 1		✓
Statement 2	✓	

Diluted EPS uses the current year's profit, adjusted for items currently in existence such as options or convertibles. It is not a predictor of future earnings.

306 C

To recognise a provision, it must be **probable** that an outflow of resources will be required.

307 C

A provision is recognised at the best estimate of the expenditure required. For a single obligation, this should be the most likely outcome.

If you selected answer B you have calculated an expected value. This is used when the provision being measured involves a large population of items.

308 $840,000

The provision being measured involves a large population of items, so an expected value must be calculated:

$(100,000 \times 6\% \times \$100) + (100,000 \times 8\% \times \$30) = \$840,000$

309 A

The employees affected have been told about the restructuring and therefore a constructive obligation exists. The provision must not include any costs related to the ongoing activities of the entity. This means that only the redundancy payments should be provided for.

310

	Provision	No provision
Situation 1		✓
Situation 2		✓

A provision should not be recognised for situation 1 because it does not give rise to an obligation. Hermione could change its operations in order to avoid the legal requirement to fit smoke filters.

A provision should not be recognised for situation 2. Future operating losses can be avoided, meaning that no obligation exists.

311 B

Provisions must be made if a legal or constructive obligation exists. The provision will be made at present value and added to the cost of the asset. Over the 10 year period, the asset will be depreciated and the discount on the provision will be unwound.

312 $7,452,000

The provision should be recorded at the present value of $6.9 million initially ($15 million × 0.46). After this, the discount on the provision must be unwound, meaning the provision will increase by 8% a year. Therefore the year-end provision is $6.9 million × 1.08 = $7,452,000.

313

	Adjusting	Non-adjusting
Fire in the warehouse		✓
Sale of inventory	✓	

The fire will be a non-adjusting event as the condition did not exist at the year end. The sale of inventory will be an adjusting event, as this shows that the net realisable value of the inventory is lower than its cost, meaning that inventory was incorrectly valued at the year end.

314 C

The date of the government announcement of the tax change is beyond the period of consideration in IAS 10 *Events After the Reporting Period*. Thus this would be neither an adjusting nor a non-adjusting event. The increase in the deferred tax liability will be provided for in the year to 30 September 20X9. Had the announcement been before 6 November 20X8, it would have been treated as a non-adjusting event requiring disclosure of the nature of the event and an estimate of its financial effect in the notes to the financial statements.

315 A

From Promoil's perspective, as a separate entity, the guarantee for Hamlet's loan is a contingent liability of $10 million. As Hamlet is a separate entity, Promoil has no liability for the secured amount of $15 million, not even for the potential shortfall for the security of $3 million. The $10 million contingent liability would be disclosed in the notes to Promoil's financial statements.

In Promoil's consolidated financial statements, the full liability of $25 million would be included in the statement of financial position as part of the group's non-current liabilities – there would be no contingent liability disclosed.

CONSOLIDATED FINANCIAL STATEMENTS

316 B

Share for share exchange: 15m × 80% = 12m shares acquired × $^2/_5$ = 4.8m Penfold shares issued @ $5.30 = $25,440,000 consideration given for Superted.

Penfold have issued 4.8m shares so 4.8m will be added to share capital with the remaining $20.64m added to other components of equity. As Penfold currently has $6m other components of equity, the total will be $26,640,000.

If you selected C, you have added Superted's other components of equity, and the subsidiary's equity is not included in the consolidated equity.

If you selected A, you have added the entire share consideration, and if you selected D, you have added the entire share consideration and Superted's other components of equity.

317 $62,400,000

The cash-in-transit must be treated as if received. To do this, $2 million will be added to cash and deducted from receivables. This will leave a $6 million intra-group receivable balance, which will then be removed along with the $6 million intra-group payable balance.

Total receivables = 32,400 + 38,000 – 2,000 – 6,000 = $62,400,000.

318 A

The non-controlling interest **at acquisition** will be $7.2 million.

Penfold has owned Superted for 6 months so 6 months' profit should be included in the consolidated financial statements for the year. Therefore the NCI's share of this will be $2.4 million ($24 million × $^6/_{12}$ × 20%).

The sale of plant from Penfold to Superted requires an adjustment to the depreciation charge recorded within the accounts of Superted. The increase in value of $5 million will result in an additional depreciation charge of $0.5 million ($5m × $^1/_5$ × $^6/_{12}$) to be reversed as part of the PUP adjustment. The NCI's share of this is $0.5m × 20% = $0.1 million.

Therefore NCI = $7.2 million + $2.4 million + $0.1 million = $9.7 million.

If you selected B, you deducted the PUP adjustment.

If you selected C, you have taken the NCI at acquisition.

If you selected D, you have ignored the PUP adjustment.

319 $481,500,000

The unrealised profit on the non-current asset transfer needs to be removed.

The carrying amount at the year-end after the transfer is $22.5 million ($25 million less 6 months depreciation).

The carrying amount of the asset if it had never been transferred would have been $18 million ($20 million less 6 months depreciation).

Therefore the unrealised profit on the non-current asset is $4.5 million.

The total PPE is therefore $345 million + $141 million − $4.5 million = $481.5 million.

320 C

There is no control or significant influence as Arnold is controlled by the other investor. Therefore the investment in Arnold will be held as an equity investment, which is a financial instrument.

321 $5,350,000

The deferred consideration should be discounted to the present value at acquisition. $6 million/$1.08^2$ = $5.144 million.

At 31 March 20X5, 6 months have elapsed, so the discount needs to be unwound for 6 months. $5.144 million × 8% × $^6/_{12}$ = $206,000. Therefore the liability at 31 March 20X5 = $5,144,000 + $206,000 = $5,350,000.

322 B

(Workings in $000)

Cost of sales = 319,200 + (176,400 × $^6/_{12}$) − 6,000 (intra-group) + 360 (PUP) = 401,760

PUP = $6,000 × 20% margin × 30% remaining = $360

If you selected A, you have adjusted for all the profit, rather than the 30% remaining in the group at the year-end. If you selected C you have taken out a full year's sales rather than 6 months. If you selected D you have taken out a full year's sales and adjusted for all the profit rather than the amount remaining in the group.

323 D

Operating expenses = 50,610 + (33,120 × $^6/_{12}$) + 100 FV depreciation* + 600 impairment = 67,870.

*Fair value depreciation = $4 million/20 years = $200,000 a year × $^6/_{12}$ = $100,000.

If you selected A, you have added a full year's fair value depreciation. If you selected B, you have deducted the fair value depreciation. If you selected C, you have either time apportioned the impairment or deducted a full year's fair value depreciation.

324 C

Unrealised profits from note (i) would only affect the non-controlling interest if the subsidiary sold goods to the parent, which is not the case. Fair value depreciation (note (ii)) always affects the NCI. Goodwill impairment (note (iii)) will affect the NCI if the NCI is measured at fair value, which it is here.

325

	Correct	Incorrect
Statement 1	✓	
Statement 2		✓

A subsidiary's assets, liabilities and contingent liabilities must be included at fair value in the consolidated financial statements. Professional fees associated with the acquisition of a subsidiary cannot be capitalised, regardless of which method is used to measure the non-controlling interest.

326 D

Consolidated retained earnings will consist of 100% of Prunier's retained earnings plus 80% of Sheringham's post acquisition loss ($3.5m – $4m), including the fair value depreciation on Sheringham's assets ($800 × $\frac{1}{20}$).

	$000
Prunier	11,000
Sheringham (500 + 40) × 80%	(432)
	————
	10,568
	————

327 $2,400,000

The other comprehensive income attributable to the parent will be 100% of Prunier's revaluation gain in the year and 80% of Sheringham's post acquisition revaluation gain. Prunier has made a gain of $2 million in the year and Sheringham has made $500,000. Therefore the other comprehensive income attributable to the parent is $2 million plus 80% × $500,000 = $2,400,000.

328

	Recognise	Not to be recognised
Sheringham's brand name, which was internally generated so not shown in Sheringham's financial statements but has a fair value of $3 million	✓	
A research project in progress, which was one of the main reasons Prunier purchased Sheringham and has a fair value of $2 million	✓	
An intangible asset related to an encryption process which has now been deemed illegal. This is included within intangibles at $1.5 million		✓

Internally generated assets and research projects can be recognised within consolidated financial statements if a fair value can be attached to them. The encryption process is now illegal so cannot be recognised as an asset.

329 B

Profit on all sales = 3,000 × 20/120 = $500,000. Anderson has a quarter left, so this is $125,000. As Anderson is an associate, only 30% of this needs to be removed, which is $37,500. If you selected A, you have used margin and not mark-up, and not adjusted for the associate. If you selected C, you have taken all of the unrealised profit, rather than 30%. If you selected D, you have used margin and not mark-up.

330 A

The profit or loss on the disposal is calculated as follows:

	$000
Proceeds	9,000
Goodwill at disposal	(1,000)
Net assets at disposal	(10,600)
Non-controlling interest at disposal	2,500
	———
Loss on disposal	(100)
	———

If you selected B, you have added the goodwill instead of deducting it. If you selected C, you have deducted the non-controlling interest at disposal. If you selected D, you have deducted 80% of the net assets, rather than all of them.

INTERPRETATION OF FINANCIAL STATEMENTS

331 B

B is correct, as follows:

	A		B
	$m		$m
Gross profit = 26% × $160m	41.6	Gross profit = 17% × $300m	51
Operating profit = 9% × $160m	14.4	Operating profit = 11% × $300m	33
Operating expenses	27.2		18

A is incorrect. A's revenue is significantly lower than B's and therefore B is more likely to be benefiting from economies of scale.

C is incorrect. A has higher gearing than B and would therefore be considered a higher risk by lenders. (The low interest rate may however explain why A are using debt finance in the first place.)

D is incorrect. LOP's gross profit margin is higher than both A's and B's and therefore acquisition of either entity is likely to reduce the overall margin of the combined business (unless cost savings can be achieved as a result of the acquisition).

332 A, D

B is incorrect. A has higher gearing than B and therefore reduced capacity for additional borrowings.

C is incorrect. LOP's P/E ratio is higher than B's suggesting that the market is more confident about the future performance of LOP.

E is incorrect. The share price may react positively or negatively, depending on the investor's view of the impact the acquisition will have on LOP.

333 B

A and B may target different customers, but that would not mean that their financial statements are incomparable. It may lead to different margins earned, but comparison could still be made, and would help LOP to assess which type of customer and market they made wish to target.

334 24.5%

	LOP		B
	$m		$m
Gross profit = 28% × $500m	140	Gross profit = 17% × $300m	51

Without the cost savings, LOP and B are making a gross profit of $191 million on revenue of $800 million. If the cost savings of $5 million are taken into account, the gross profit will increase to $196 million. This will give a gross profit margin of **24.5%** (196/800).

335

	Correct	Incorrect
Statement 1		✓
Statement 2	✓	

If B has treated the leases incorrectly, then B's liabilities will be understated, meaning that gearing would be understated. B would also not have included any finance costs in the statement of profit or loss, meaning the average interest rate expensed will not have included the interest on the lease.

336 7.5%

1,500/(15,000 + 3,000 + 2,000) = 1,500/20,000 = 7.5%

337 D

Combined profit from operations = $1,5m − $0.6m = $900,000.

Combined revenue = $9.4m + $1.2m = $10,600,000.

Operating margin = 900/10,600 = 8.5%.

If you selected C, you have just used Franck's profit. If you selected B, you have added the loss of 600 rather than deducting it. If you selected A, you have just used Franck's revenue rather than the combined revenue.

338

	Correct	Incorrect
Statement 1	✓	
Statement 2	✓	

Return on capital employed will clearly decrease, as Franck has made a loss. The capital employed will increase, but overall profit will decrease. Duik has a higher level of gearing (4,000/22,800 = 17.5%) compared to Franck (2,000/18,000 = 11%), which means gearing will increase when the two companies are combined.

339 C

Individual entity financial statements should not contain errors, and if they do, this is not a problem specific to being a subsidiary of another entity.

340 C

The upcoming projects are unlikely to be publicly available information, whereas A, B and D can all be assessed from looking at Duik's financial statements for the current or previous periods.

STATEMENT OF CASH FLOWS

341 C

Cooper has used the indirect method. The direct method is an alternative method of calculating cash generated from operations.

Classification by function and nature relate to the way that items are presented in the statement of profit or loss.

342

	$000
Profit from operations	3,500
Depreciation	4,600
Release of government grant	1,400
Profit on disposal of property	(3,700)
Increase in inventories	(400)
Decrease in trade and other receivables	(300)
Increase in trade and other payables	900

The release of government grant is non-cash income, so should be deducted from profit from operations.

The decrease in trade receivables is good for cash so would be added to profit rather than being deducted.

343 A

Property			
b/f	39,500	Depreciation	4,600
		Disposal (balance)	**5,900**
		c/f	29,000
	─────		─────
	39,500		39,500
	─────		─────

The carrying amount of the property disposed was $5.9 million. As Cooper made a profit of $3.7 million on disposal, the sale proceeds must have been **$9.6 million**.

If you selected B, you have deducted the profit on disposal rather than adding it.

If you selected C, you have used the profit on disposal.

If you selected D, you have selected the carrying amount disposed rather than the sale proceeds.

344 **$3,400,000**

Grant deferred income

		b/f	6,000
Released in year	1,400	**Received (balance)**	**3,400**
c/f	8,000		
	9,400		9,400

345 **B**

A rights issue will mean that cash has been raised, increasing the cash from financing activities. Intangible assets can affect the statement of cash flow if they are purchased as this will lead to an outflow of cash.

346 **A**

Retained earnings

		b/f	940
Dividend paid (balance)	**145**	Revaluation surplus	20
c/f	900	Profit for the year	85
	1,045		1,045

When the land is disposed, the remaining revaluation surplus will be taken to retained earnings. If you selected B, you have deducted the revaluation surplus. If you selected C, you have taken the movement in retained earnings. If you selected D, you have missed out the revaluation surplus transfer into retained earnings.

347 **C**

The loan notes should be held at amortised cost, with the effective rate of interest being taken to the statement of profit or loss. As these have an effective rate of 8%, $40,000 has been taken to the statement of profit or loss. However, it is only the coupon rate of 5% which has been paid in the year, so $500,000 × 5% = $25,000.

In addition Depay has paid interest on the lease. The total interest charge for the year is $60,000, comprising loan note and lease interest. The loan note interest charged is $40,000, which means that the lease interest, paid as part of the lease payment on 30 September 20X2, must be the balance, $20,000.

So the total interest paid in the year is $45,000.

348 $42,000

Tax liabilities ($000)

		b/f (40 + 125)	165
Tax paid (balance)	**42**	Tax expense	57
c/f (30 + 150)	180		
	222		222

349 B

Dividends received are shown within cash flows from investing activities.

350 $80,000

Lease liabilities ($000)

		b/f	310
Paid (balance)	**80**	New asset additions	70
c/f	300		
	380		380

As the interest has been both charged and paid during the year we may ignore it in our T-account calculation. The resulting calculation above uses the capital balances to identify the capital repaid.

Section 6

ANSWERS TO CONSTRUCTED RESPONSE QUESTIONS – SECTION C

PREPARATION OF SINGLE ENTITY FINANCIAL STATEMENTS

351 CANDEL *Walk in the footsteps of a top tutor*

(a) **Candel – Revised profit for the year**

	$000
Draft profit before tax	59,100
Depreciation (W3) – leasehold property	(2,500)
– plant and equipment	(9,600)
Removal of disposal proceeds	(2,500)
Loss on disposal of plant (4,000 – 2,500)	(1,500)
Amortisation of development costs (W3)	(4,000)
Research and development expenses (1,400 + 2,400 (W3))	(3,800)
Removal of legal provision (W1)	400
Inclusion of provision for legal costs (W1)	(100)
Finance costs (W2)	(1,200)
Income tax expense (11,400 + (6,000 – 5,800 deferred tax))	(11,600)
Profit for the year	22,700

(b)   Candel – Statement of financial position as at 30 September 20X8

Assets	$000	$000
Non-current assets (W3)		
Property, plant and equipment (43,000 + 38,400)		81,400
Development costs (W3)		14,800
		96,200
Current assets		
Inventory	20,000	
Trade receivables	43,100	63,100
Total assets		159,300
Equity and liabilities:		
Equity shares of 25 cents each		50,000
Revaluation surplus (10,000 – 4,500)	5,500	
Retained earnings (18,500 + 22,700)	41,200	46,700
		96,700
Non-current liabilities		
Deferred tax	6,000	
8% redeemable preference shares (20,000 + 400 (W2))	20,400	26,400
Current liabilities		
Trade payables (23,800 – 400 + 100 – re legal action (W2))	23,500	
Bank overdraft	1,300	
Current tax payable	11,400	36,200
Total equity and liabilities		159,300

Workings (figures in brackets in $000)

(W1)   Legal case

As it is considered that the outcome of the legal action against Candel is unlikely to succeed (only a 20% chance) it is inappropriate to provide for any damages. The potential damages are an example of a contingent liability which should be disclosed (at $2 million) as a note to the financial statements. Therefore the legal provision of $400,000 should be removed. The unrecoverable legal costs are a liability (the start of the legal action is a past event) and should be provided for in full at $100,000.

(W2) Preference shares

Tutorial note

This requires knowledge of accounting for financial instruments under IAS 32 Financial Instruments: Presentation and IFRS 9 Financial Instruments.

The finance cost of $1.2 million for the preference shares is based on the effective rate of 12% applied to $20 million issue proceeds of the shares for the six months they have been in issue (20m × 12% × 6/12). The dividend paid of $800,000 is based on the nominal rate of 8%. The additional $400,000 (accrual) is added to the carrying amount of the preference shares in the statement of financial position. As these shares are redeemable they are treated as debt and their dividend is treated as a finance cost.

(W3) Non-current assets:

Leasehold property

Valuation at 1 October 20X7	50,000
Depreciation for year (20 year life)	(2,500)
Carrying amount at date of revaluation	47,500
Valuation at 30 September 20X8	(43,000)
Revaluation deficit	4,500

Tutorial note

Remember to write off the disposed asset, both cost and b/fwd accumulated depreciation before calculating the current year depreciation charge.

	$000
Plant and equipment per trial balance (76,600 – 24,600)	52,000
Disposal (8,000 – 4,000)	(4,000)
	48,000
Depreciation for year (20%)	(9,600)
Carrying amount at 30 September 20X8	38,400

Tutorial note

Remember research costs are to be expensed and development costs are to be capitalised only when the recognition criteria in IAS38 Intangible Assets are met. In this question- the directors do not become confident that the project will be successful until 1 April – therefore development costs on the new project in January – March must be expensed.

Capitalised/deferred development costs

Carrying amount at 1 October 20X7 (20,000 – 6,000)	14,000
Amortised for year (20,000 × 20%)	(4,000)
Capitalised during year (800 × 6 months)	4,800
Carrying amount at 30 September 20X8	14,800

Note: Development costs can only be treated as an asset from the point where they meet the recognition criteria in IAS 38 *Intangible Assets*. Thus development costs from 1 April to 30 September 20X8 of $4.8 million (800 × 6 months) can be capitalised. These will not be amortised as the project is still in development. The research costs of $1.4 million plus three months' development costs of $2.4 million (800 × 3 months) (i.e. those incurred before the criteria were met) must be expensed.

352 PRICEWELL

(a) **Pricewell – Statement of profit or loss for the year ended 31 March 20X9**

	$000
Revenue (310,000 + 22,000 (W1) – 6,400 (W2))	325,600
Cost of sales (W3)	(255,100)
Gross profit	70,500
Distribution costs	(19,500)
Administrative expenses	(27,500)
Finance costs (W5)	(1,248)
Profit before tax	22,252
Income tax expense (700 + 4,500 – 2,800 (W7))	(2,400)
Profit for the year	19,852

(b) **Pricewell – Statement of financial position as at 31 March 20X9**

Assets	$000	$000
Non-current assets		
Property, plant and equipment (W4)		66,400
Current assets		
Inventory	28,200	
Trade receivables	33,100	
Contract asset (W1)	17,100	
Bank	5,500	83,900
Total assets		150,300
Equity and liabilities		
Equity shares of 50 cents each		40,000
Retained earnings (W6)		55,952
		95,952
Non-current liabilities		
Deferred tax (W7)	5,600	
Lease liability (W5)	5,716	
		11,316
Current liabilities		
Trade payables	33,400	
Lease liability (W5)	5,132	
Current tax payable	4,500	43,032
Total equity and liabilities		150,300

Workings

(W1) Contract with customer:

(i) **Overall**

	$000
Selling price	50,000
Estimated cost	
To date	(12,000)
To complete	(10,000)
Plant	(8,000)
Estimated profit	20,000

(ii) **Progress**

Work completed to date has been agreed at $22 million so the contract is 44% complete ($22m/$50m).

(iii) **Statement of profit or loss**

Revenue	22,000
Cost of sales (44% × $30m total costs)	(13,200)
	───────
Profit to date	8,800
	───────

(iv) **Statement of financial position**

Costs to date (12,000 + 2,000 depreciation (W4))	14,000
Profit to date	8,800
Payment from customer	(5,700)
	───────
Contract asset	17,100
	───────

(W2) Pricewell is acting as an agent (not the principal) for the sales on behalf of Trilby. Therefore the statement of comprehensive income should only include $1.6 million (20% of the sales of $8 million). Therefore $6.4 million ($8m − $1.6m) should be deducted from revenue and cost of sales. It would also be acceptable to show agency sales (of $1.6 million) separately as other income.

(W3) **Cost of sales**

	$000
Per question	234,500
Contract (W1)	13,200
Agency cost of sales (W2)	(6,400)
Depreciation (W4) − leasehold property	1,800
− owned plant	8,500
− right-of-use asset (20,000 × 25%)	5,000
Surplus on revaluation of leasehold property (W4)	(1,500)
	───────
	255,100
	───────

(W4) **Non-current assets**

Property, plant and equipment

	Leasehold property	Owned plant & equipment	Right-of-use plant	Specialist plant for contract	Total
	$000	$000		$000	$000
Valuation/cost 1 April 20X8	25,200	46,800	20,000		
Depreciation 1 April 20X8		(12,800)	(5,000)		
Acquisition				8,000	
		———			
		34,000			
Depreciation charge					
$25,200 \times {}^1/_{14}$	(1,800)				
$34,000 \times 25\%$		(8,500)			
$8,000 \times \frac{1}{2} \times {}^6/_{12}$				(2,000)	
$20,000 \times 25\%$			(5,000)		
	———				
	23,400				
Revaluation surplus	1,500				
	———	———	———	———	
Revaluation/carrying amount 31 March 20X9	24,900	25,500	10,000	6,000	66,400

The leasehold property has 14 years useful life remaining at the beginning of the year. The specialist plan was acquired on 1 October 20X8 and is therefore only depreciated for 6 months.

The $1.5 million revaluation surplus is credited to cost of sales (W3) in the statement of profit or loss because this represents the partial reversal of the $2.8 million impairment loss recognised in the statement of profit or loss in the previous year ended 31 March 20X8.

(W5) **Lease liability ($000)**

	Balance b/f	Interest 8%	Payment	Balance c/f
Year to 31 March 20X9	15,600	1,248	(6,000)	10,848
Year to 31 March 20Y0	10,848	868	(6,000)	5,716

Finance cost to profit or loss	1,248
Non-current liability	5,716
Current liability (10,848 – 5,716)	5,132

(W6) Retained earnings

	$000
Balance at 1 April 20X8	44,100
Profit for year per part (a)	19,852
Equity dividend paid per trial balance	(8,000)
Balance at 31 March 20X9	55,952

(W7) Deferred taxation

	$000
Provision required at 31 March 20X9	5,600
Balance b/f per trial balance	(8,400)
Credit to tax expense	(2,800)

Marking scheme		Marks
(a)	Statement of profit or loss	
	Revenue	2
	Cost of sales	4½
	Distribution costs	½
	Administrative expenses	½
	Finance costs	1
	Income tax expense	1½
	Maximum	10
(b)	Statement of financial position	
	Property, plant and equipment	1½
	Right-of-use asset	½
	Inventory	½
	Due on construction contract	2
	Trade receivables and bank	½
	Equity shares	½
	Retained earnings	1
	Deferred tax	1
	Lease – non-current liability	½
	Trade payables	½
	Lease – current liability	1
	Current tax payable	½
	Maximum	10
Total		**20**

353 HIGHWOOD

(a)   **Highwood – Statement of profit or loss and other comprehensive income for the year ended 31 March 20X1**

	$000
Revenue	339,650
Cost of sales (W1)	(210,250)
Gross profit	129,400
Distribution costs	(27,500)
Administrative expenses (30,700 – 1,300 + 600 allowance (W4))	(30,000)
Finance costs (W5)	(2,848)
Profit before tax	69,052
Income tax expense (19,400 – 800 + 400 (W6))	(19,000)
Profit for the year	50,052
Other comprehensive income:	
Gain on revaluation of property (W3)	11,250
Total comprehensive income	61,302

(b)   **Highwood – Statement of financial position as at 31 March 20X1**

Assets	$000	$000
Non-current assets		
Property, plant and equipment (W2)		77,500
Current assets		
Inventory	36,000	
Trade receivables (47,100 + 10,000 – 600 allowance (W4))	56,500	
		92,500
Total assets		170,000

Equity and liabilities

Equity

Equity shares of 50 cents each	6,000
Other component of equity – equity option	1,524
Revaluation surplus (W3)	11,250
Retained earnings (1,400 + 50,052)	51,452
	70,476

Non-current liabilities

Deferred tax (W6)	6,750	
8% convertible loan note (W5)	28,924	
		35,674

Current liabilities

Trade payables	24,500	
Factor loan (W4)	8,700	
Bank overdraft	11,500	
Current tax payable	19,400	
		64,100
Total equity and liabilities		170,000

Workings (figures in brackets in $000)

(W1) Cost of sales

	$000
Per trial balance	207,750
Depreciation – building (W2)	2,500
	210,250

(W2) Property, plant and equipment

	Land	Building	Total
	$000	$000	$000
Cost b/f	25,000	50,000	75,000
Depreciation b/f		(10,000)	(10,000)
Carrying amount b/f	25,000	40,000	65,000
Gain on revaluation (balance)	5,000	10,000	15,000
Revaluation 1 April 20X0	30,000	50,000	80,000
Depreciation (20 years)	-	(2,500)	(2,500)
Carrying amount on SFP	30,000	47,500	77,500

(W3) Revaluation surplus

	$000
Gain (W2)	15,000
Less: deferred tax at 25%	(3,750)
	11,250

(W4) Factored receivables

As Highwood still bears the risk of the non-payment of the receivables, the substance of this transaction is a loan. Thus the receivables must remain on Highwood's statement of financial position and the proceeds of the 'sale' treated as a current liability. The difference between the factored receivables ($10m) and the loan received ($8.7m) of $1.3 million, which has been charged to administrative expenses, should be reversed except for $600,000 which should be treated as an allowance for uncollectable receivables.

(W5) 8% convertible loan note

This is a compound financial instrument having a debt (liability) and an equity component. These must be quantified and accounted for separately:

Year ended 31 March	Outflow	10% factor	Present value
	$000		$000
20X1	2,400	0.91	2,184
20X2	2,400	0.83	1,992
20X3	32,400	0.75	24,300
Liability component			28,476
Equity component (balance)			1,524
Proceeds of issue			30,000

The equity component remains unremeasured on the statement of financial position. The debt component is carried at amortised cost.

b/f 1 April 20X0	Interest at 10%	Paid ($30m × 8%)	c/f 31 March 20X1
28,476	2,848	(2,400)	28,924
	(Finance cost)		(NCL on SFP)

(W6) Deferred tax

Credit balance required at 31 March 20X1 (27,000 × 25%)	6,750
Revaluation of property (W3)	(3,750)
Balance at 1 April 20X0	(2,600)
Charge to statement of profit or loss	400

Marking scheme		
		Marks
(a)	Statement of profit or loss	
	Revenue	½
	Cost of sales	1½
	Distribution costs	½
	Administrative expenses	1½
	Finance costs	1
	Income tax expense	1½
	Other comprehensive income	1½
		———
	Maximum	8
		———
(c)	Statement of financial position	
	Property, plant and equipment	1½
	Inventory	½
	Trade receivables	1½
	Share capital	½
	Equity option	1
	Revaluation surplus	1
	Retained earnings	1
	Deferred tax	1
	Issue of 8% loan note	1½
	Factor loan	1
	Bank overdraft	½
	Trade payables	½
	Current tax payable	½
		———
	Maximum	12
		———
Total		**20**
		———

354 KEYSTONE

(a) **Keystone – Statement of profit or loss and other comprehensive income for the year ended 30 September 20X1**

	$000	$000
Revenue		377,600
Cost of sales (W1)		(258,100)
Gross profit		119,500
Distribution costs		(14,200)
Administrative expenses		
(46,400 – 24,000 dividend (50,000 × 5 × $2.40 × 4%))		(22,400)
Profit from operations		82,900
Investment income		800
Finance costs		(350)
Profit before tax		83,350
Income tax expense (24,300 + 1,800 (W3))		(26,100)
Profit for the year		57,250
Other comprehensive income		
Revaluation of leased property	8,000	
Transfer to deferred tax (W3)	(2,400)	
		5,600
Total comprehensive income for the year		62,850

(b) **Keystone – Statement of financial position as at 30 September 20X1**

	$000	$000
Assets		
Non-current assets		
Property, plant and equipment (W2)		78,000
Current assets		
Inventory	56,600	
Trade receivables	31,150	
		87,750
Total assets		165,750

Equity and liabilities		
Equity shares of 20 cents each		50,000
Revaluation surplus (W2)	5,600	
Retained earnings (15,600 + 57,250 – 24,000 dividend paid)	48,850	
		54,450
		104,450
Non-current liabilities		
Deferred tax (W3)		6,900
Current liabilities		
Trade payables	27,800	
Bank overdraft	2,300	
Current tax payable	24,300	
		54,400
Total equity and liabilities		165,750

Workings (figures in brackets in $000)

(W1) Cost of sales

	$000
Opening inventory	46,700
Materials (64,000 – 3,000)	61,000
Production labour (124,000 – 4,000)	120,000
Factory overheads (80,000 – (4,000 × 75%))	77,000
Amortisation of leased property (W2)	3,000
Depreciation of plant (1,000 + 6,000 (W2))	7,000
Closing inventory	(56,600)
	258,100

The cost of the self-constructed plant is $10 million (3,000 + 4,000 + 3,000 for materials, labour and overheads respectively that have also been deducted from the above items in cost of sales). It is not permissible to add a profit margin to self-constructed assets.

(W2) Non-current assets

The leased property has been amortised at $2.5 million per annum (50,000/ 20 years). The accumulated amortisation of $10 million therefore represents four years, so the remaining life at the date of revaluation is 16 years.

	$000
Carrying amount at date of revaluation (50,000 – 10,000)	40,000
Revalued amount	48,000
Gross gain on revaluation	8,000
Transfer to deferred tax at 30%	(2,400)
Net gain to revaluation surplus	5,600

The revalued amount of $48 million will be amortised over its remaining life of 16 years at $3 million per annum.

The self-constructed plant will be depreciated for six months by $1 million ($10m × 20% × 6/12) and have a carrying amount at 30 September 20X1 of $9 million. The plant in the trial balance will be depreciated by $6 million ((44.5m − 14.5m) × 20%) for the year and have a carrying amount at 30 September 20X1 of $24 million.

In summary:

	$000
Leased property (48,000 – 3,000)	45,000
Plant (9,000 + 24,000)	33,000
	———
Property, plant and equipment	78,000
	———

(W3) Deferred tax

Provision required at 30 September 20X1 ((15,000 + 8,000) × 30%)	6,900
Provision at 1 October 20X0	(2,700)
	———
Increase required	4,200
Transferred from revaluation surplus (W2)	(2,400)
	———
Charge to statement of profit or loss	1,800
	———

Marking scheme		
		Marks
(a)	Statement of profit or loss	
	Revenue	½
	Cost of sales	5½
	Distribution costs	½
	Administrative expenses	1½
	Investment income	1
	Finance costs	½
	Income tax expense	1½
	Other comprehensive income	1
		———
	Maximum	12
(b)	Statement of financial position	
	Property, plant and equipment	1
	Inventory	½
	Trade receivables	½
	Equity shares	½
	Revaluation surplus	1½
	Retained earnings	1½
	Deferred tax	1
	Trade payables & overdraft	1
	Current tax payable	½
		———
	Maximum	8
Total		**20**
		———

355 FRESCO

(a) **Fresco – Statement of profit or loss and other comprehensive income for the year ended 31 March 20X2**

	$000
Revenue	350,000
Cost of sales (W1)	(311,000)
Gross profit	39,000
Distribution costs	(16,100)
Administrative expenses (26,900 + 3,000 re fraud)	(29,900)
Gain on investments (7,200 – 6,000)	1,200
Finance costs (300 + 2,300 (W3))	(2,600)
Loss before tax	(8,400)
Income tax relief (2,400 + 200 (W4) – 800)	1,800
Loss for the year	(6,600)
Other comprehensive income	
Revaluation of leased property (W2)	4,000
Total comprehensive losses	(2,600)

(b) **Fresco – Statement of changes in equity for the year ended 31 March 20X2**

	Share capital	Share premium	Revaluation surplus	Retained earnings	Total equity
	$000	$000	$000	$000	$000
Balances at 1 April 20X1	45,000	5,000	nil	5,100	55,100
Prior period adjustment (re fraud)				(1,000)	(1,000)
Restated balance				4,100	
Rights share issue (see below)	9,000	4,500			13,500
Total comprehensive losses (see (i) above)			4,000	(6,600)	(2,600)
Transfer to retained earnings (W2)			(500)	500	
Balances at 31 March 20X2	54,000	9,500	3,500	(2,000)	65,000

The rights issue was 18 million shares (45,000/50 cents each × $^1/_5$) at 75 cents = $13.5 million. This equates to the balance on the suspense account. This should be recorded as $9 million equity shares (18,000 × 50 cents) and $4.5 million share premium (18,000 × (75 cents – 50 cents)).

The discovery of the fraud represents an error part of which is a prior period adjustment ($1 million) in accordance with IAS 8 *Accounting Policies, Changes in Accounting Estimates and Errors*. The balance of $3m is charged to administrative expenses.

Workings (figures in brackets are in $000)

(W1) Cost of sales

	$000
Per question	298,700
Amortisation of leased property (W2)	4,500
Depreciation of right-of-use asset (W2)	5,000
Depreciation of other plant and equipment (W2)	2,800
	311,000

(W2) Property, plant and equipment

	Leasehold property	Plant & Equipment	Right-of-use plant	Total
	$000	$000	$000	$000
1 April 20X1 Cost b/f	48,000	47,500		
Depreciation b/f	(16,000)	(33,500)		
Addition (23,000 + 2,000 deposit)			25,000	
	32,000	14,000		
Revaluation gain *	4,000			
Revaluation	36,000			
Amortisation/depreciation				
$36,000 \times \frac{1}{8}$	(4,500)			
$14,000 \times 20\%$		(2,800)		
$25,000 \times \frac{1}{5}$			(5,000)	
	31,500	11,200	20,000	62,700

* $500,000 (4,000/8 years) of the revaluation surplus will be transferred to retained earnings (reported in the statement of changes in equity).

(W3) Lease liability

	Balance b/f	Interest @ 10%	Payment	Balance c/f
Year to 31 March 20X2	23,000	2,300	(6,000)	19,300
Finance cost:		$2,300		

(W4) Deferred tax

Provision required at 31 March 20X2 (12,000 × 25%)	3,000
Provision at 1 April 20X1	(3,200)
Credit (reduction in provision) to statement of profit or loss	(200)

Marking scheme		Marks
(a)	Statement of profit or loss and other comprehensive income	
	Revenue	½
	Cost of sales	4
	Distribution costs	1
	Administrative expenses	1½
	Gain on investment	1
	Finance costs	2
	Income tax expense	2
	Other comprehensive income	1
	Maximum	13
(b)	Statement of changes in equity	
	Balances brought forward ½ each	1½
	Prior period adjustment	1
	Rights issue	2
	Total comprehensive income	1
	Retained earnings transfer	1½
	Maximum	7
Total		20

356 QUINCY

(a) **Quincy – Statement of profit or loss and other comprehensive income for the year ended 30 September 20X2**

	$000
Revenue (213,500 – 1,600 (W1))	211,900
Cost of sales (W2)	(144,300)
Gross profit	67,600
Distribution costs	(12,500)
Administrative expenses (19,000 – 1,000 loan issue costs (W4))	(18,000)
Loss on fair value of equity investments (17,000 – 15,700)	(1,300)
Investment income	400
Finance costs (W4)	(1,920)
Profit before tax	34,280
Income tax expense (1,100 + 7,400 – 200 (W5))	(8,300)
Profit for the year	25,980

(b)   **Quincy – Statement of financial position as at 30 September 20X2**

Assets	$000	$000
Non-current assets		
Property, plant and equipment (W3)		42,500
Equity financial asset investments		15,700
		58,200
Current assets		
Inventory	24,800	
Trade receivables	28,500	
Bank	2,900	
		56,200
Total assets		114,400
Equity and liabilities		
Equity shares of 25 cents each		60,000
Retained earnings (6,500 + 25,980 – 19,200)		13,280
		73,280
Non-current liabilities		
Deferred tax (W5)	1,000	
Deferred revenue (W1)	800	
6% loan note (W4)	24,420	
		26,220
Current liabilities		
Trade payables	6,700	
Deferred revenue (W1)	800	
Current tax payable	7,400	
		14,900
Total equity and liabilities		114,400

Workings (figures in brackets in $000)

(W1) The revenue for the service must be deferred. The deferred revenue must include the normal profit margin (25%) for the deferred work. At 30 September 20X2, there are two more years of servicing work, thus $1.6 million ((600 × 2) × $^{100}/_{75}$) must be deferred, split equally between current and non-current liabilities.

(W2) Cost of sales

	$000
Per trial balance	136,800
Depreciation of plant (W3)	7,500
	144,300

(W3) Plant and equipment:

	$000
Carrying amount as at 1 October 20X1 (83,700 – 33,700)	50,000
Depreciation at 15% per annum	(7,500)
Carrying amount as at 30 September 20X2	42,500

(W4) Loan note

The finance cost of the loan note is charged at the effective rate of 8% applied to the carrying amount of the loan. The issue costs of the loan ($1 million) should be deducted from the proceeds of the loan ($25 million) and not treated as an administrative expense, to give an initial carrying amount of $24 million and a finance cost of $1,920,000 (24,000 × 8%). The interest actually paid is $1.5 million (25,000 × 6%) and the difference between these amounts, of $420,000 (1,920 – 1,500), is accrued and added to the carrying amount of the loan note. This gives $24.42 million (24,000 + 420) for inclusion as a non-current liability in the statement of financial position.

(W5) Deferred tax

	$000
Provision required as at 30 September 20X2 (5,000 × 20%)	1,000
Less provision b/f	(1,200)
Credit to statement of profit or loss	(200)

Marking scheme		Marks
(a)	Statement of profit or loss	
	Revenue	1½
	Cost of sales	1½
	Distribution costs	½
	Administrative expenses	1½
	Loss on investments	1
	Investment income	½
	Finance costs	1½
	Income tax expense	2
		___
	Maximum	10
		___
(b)	Statement of financial position	
	Property, plant and equipment	1
	Equity investments	1
	Inventory	½
	Trade receivables	½
	Bank	½
	Share capital	½
	Retained earnings	1½
	Deferred tax	1
	Deferred revenue	1
	6% loan note	1½
	Trade payables	½
	Current tax payable	½
		___
	Maximum	10
		___
		20
		___

357 ATLAS

(i) **Atlas – Statement of profit or loss and other comprehensive income for the year ended 31 March 20X3**

Monetary figures in brackets are in $000

	$000
Revenue (550,000 – 10,000 in substance loan (W3))	540,000
Cost of sales (W1)	(420,600)
	_____
Gross profit	119,400
Distribution costs	(21,500)
Administrative expenses (30,900 + 5,400 re directors' bonus of 1% of sales made)	(36,300)
Finance costs (700 + 500 (10,000 × 10% × $^6/_{12}$ re in substance loan))	(1,200)
	_____
Profit before tax	60,400
Income tax expense (27,200 – 1,200 + (9,400 – 6,200) deferred tax)	(29,200)
	_____
Profit for the year	31,200
Other comprehensive income	
Revaluation gain on land and buildings (W2)	7,000
	_____
Total comprehensive income for the year	38,200
	_____

(ii)   **Atlas – Statement of financial position as at 31 March 20X3**

Assets	$000	$000
Non-current assets		
Property, plant and equipment (44,500 + 52,800 (W2))		97,300
Current assets		
Inventory (43,700 + 7,000 re in substance loan (W3))	50,700	
Trade receivables	42,200	92,900
Plant held for sale (W2)		3,600
Total assets		193,800

Equity and liabilities		
Equity		
Equity shares of 50 cents each		50,000
Revaluation surplus		7,000
Retained earnings (11,200 + 31,200)		42,400
		99,400
Non-current liabilities		
In-substance loan from Xpede		
(10,000 + 500 accrued interest (W3))	10,500	
Deferred tax	9,400	
		19,900
Current liabilities		
Trade payables	35,100	
Income tax	27,200	
Accrued directors' bonus	5,400	
Bank overdraft	6,800	
		74,500
Total equity and liabilities		193,800

Workings (figures in brackets are in $000)

(W1) Cost of sales

	$000
Per question	411,500
Closing inventory re in substance loan (W3)	(7,000)
Depreciation of buildings (W2)	2,500
Depreciation of plant and equipment (W2)	13,600
	420,600

(W2) **Non-current assets**

Land and buildings

The gain on revaluation and carrying amount of the land and buildings will be:

	$000
Carrying amount at 1 April 20X2 (60,000 – 20,000)	40,000
Revaluation at that date (12,000 + 35,000)	47,000
Gain on revaluation	7,000
Buildings depreciation (35,000/14 years)	(2,500)
Carrying amount of land and buildings at 31 March 20X3 (47,000 – 2,500)	44,500

Plant

The plant held for sale should be shown separately and not be depreciated after 1 October 20X2.

Other plant	
Carrying amount at 1 April 20X2 (94,500 – 24,500)	70,000
Plant held for sale (9,000 – 5,000)	(4,000)
	66,000
Depreciation for year ended 31 March 20X3 (20% reducing balance)	(13,200)
Carrying amount at 31 March 20X3	52,800

Plant held for sale:	
At 1 April 20X2 (from above)	4,000
Depreciation to date of reclassification (4,000 × 20% × $^6/_{12}$)	(400)
Carrying amount at 1 October 20X2	3,600

Total depreciation of plant for year ended 31 March 20X3 (13,200 + 400)	13,600

As the fair value of the plant held for sale at 1 October 20X2 is $4.2 million, it should continue to be carried at its (lower) carrying amount, and no longer depreciated.

(W3) The transaction with Xpede will not be recognised as a sale. The presence of the option suggests that control of the goods has not passed to Xpede. Therefore this transaction will be recognised as a financial liability, with interest of 10% accruing each year.

As the transaction occurred partway through the year, 6 months interest ($500k) should be included within finance costs and added to the liability.

As this is not a sale, the goods should be transferred back into inventory at the cost of $7 million. This amount should also be deducted from cost of sales.

	Marking scheme		Marks
(i)	Statement of profit or loss and other comprehensive income		
	Revenue		1
	Cost of sales		3
	Distribution costs		½
	Administrative expenses		1
	Finance costs		1
	Income tax		1½
	Other comprehensive income		1
		Maximum	9
(ii)	Statement of financial position		
	Property, plant and equipment		2½
	Inventory		1
	Trade receivables		½
	Plant held for sale (at 3,600)		1
	Retained earnings		1
	Revaluation surplus		1
	In substance loan		1
	Deferred tax		1
	Trade payables		½
	Current tax		½
	Directors' bonus		½
	Bank overdraft		½
		Maximum	11
Total			20

358 MOBY

(a)   Moby – Statement of adjustments to retained earnings as at 30 September 20X3

	$000
Retained earnings balance per trial balance	53,250
Contract with customer (W1)	2,000
Depreciation: building (W2)	(2,400)
Depreciation: right-of-use asset (W2)	(7,000)
Lease interest (W3)	(2,930)
Current year taxation provision (note (iv))	(3,400)
Deferred tax reduction (W4)	2,000
Removal of provision (W5)	150
Loan note interest ($40m × 10% (note (v)))	(4,000)
Restated retained earnings per statement of financial position	37,670

(b) **Moby – Statement of financial position as at 30 September 20X3**

Assets	$000	$000
Non-current assets		
Property, plant and equipment (W2)		73,000
Current assets		
Inventory	56,600	
Trade receivables	38,500	
Contract asset (W1)	6,000	
	———	101,100
		———
Total assets		174,100
		———
Equity and liabilities		
Equity shares of $1 each		27,000
Revaluation surplus (4,400 (W2) – 1,100 (W4))	3,300	
Retained earnings (per (a))	37,670	
	———	40,970
		———
		67,970
Non-current liabilities		
Lease liability (W3)	16,133	
Deferred tax (W4)	7,100	
Loan note (40,000 + 4,000 interest)	44,000	
	———	67,233
Current liabilities		
Lease liability (W3)	6,897	
Trade payables	21,300	
Bank overdraft	7,300	
Current tax payable	3,400	
	———	38,897
		———
Total equity and liabilities		174,100
		———

Workings (monetary figures in brackets in $000)

(W1) Contract with customer

Step 1 – Overall

	$000	$000
Total contract revenue		25,000
Costs incurred to date	14,000	
Estimated costs to complete	6,000	
	————	(20,000)
Total contract profit		5,000

Step 2 – Progress

Percentage of completion is 40% (10,000/25,000)

Step 3 – Statement of profit or loss

Revenue	10,000
Cost of sales (40% × 20,000 total costs)	(8,000)
Profit for year	2,000

Step 4 – Statement of financial position

Costs to date	14,000
Profit to date	2,000
Billed to date	(10,000)
Contract asset	6,000

(W2) Property, plant & equipment

	Land	Building	Right-of-use plant	Total
	$000	$000	$000	$000
1 October 20X2 Cost	12,000	48,000	35,000	
Accumulated depreciation		(10,000)	(7,000)	
	12,000	38,000	28,000	
Revaluation gain	4,000	400		
Revalued amount	16,000	38,400		
Depreciation charge				
38,400 × $^1/_{16}$		(2,400)		
35,000 × $^1/_5$			(7,000)	
	16,000	36,000	21,000	73,000

(W3) Lease liability

	Balance b/f	Interest @ 10%	Payment	Balance c/f
Year to 30 September 20X3	29,300	2,930	(9,200)	23,030
Year to 30 September 20X4	23,030	2,303	(9,200)	16,133

Finance cost:	$2,930
Non-current liability:	$16,133
Current liability: (23,030 – 16,133)	$6,897

(W4) Deferred tax

	$000	$000
Provision b/f at 1 October 20X2		(8,000)
Provision c/f required at 30 September 20X3		
Temporary differences per question	24,000	
Revaluation of land and buildings (W2)	4,400	
	——	
	28,400	
	× 25%	7,100
		——
Net reduction in provision		(900)
Charged to other comprehensive income on revaluation gain (4,400 × 25%)		(1,100)
		——
Credit to profit or loss		2,000
		——

(W5) Insurance provision

The remaining provision balance of $150,000 does not meet the criteria to be recognised as a provision as there is no present obligation. The balance is therefore reversed, removing the provision and increasing the retained earnings.

Marking scheme		Marks
(a)	Statement of adjustments to retained earnings	
	Retained earnings balance	½
	Contract with customer	1
	Depreciation: building	1
	Depreciation: right-of-use asset	1
	Lease interest	1
	Current year tax	½
	Deferred tax	1
	Removal of provision	1
	Loan note interest	1
	Maximum	8
(b)	Statement of financial position	
	Property, plant and equipment	2
	Inventory	½
	Contract asset	1
	Trade receivables	½
	Equity shares	½
	Revaluation surplus	2
	Retained earnings	½
	Non-current lease obligation	1
	Deferred tax	1
	Loan note	1
	Current lease obligation	½
	Bank overdraft	½
	Trade payables	½
	Current tax payable	½
	Maximum	12
Total		**20**

359 XTOL

(a) Xtol – Statement of profit or loss for the year ended 31 March 20X4

	$000
Revenue	490,000
Cost of sales (W1)	(304,600)
Gross profit	185,400
Operating costs	(70,300)
Finance costs (900 bank + 3,676 (W2))	(4,576)
Profit before tax	110,524
Income tax expense (3,200 + 28,000 + 3,700 (W3))	(34,900)
Profit for the year	75,624

(b) **Xtol – Statement of financial position as at 31 March 20X4**

	$000	$000
Non-current assets		
Property, plant and equipment		98,000
(155,500 – 43,500 – 14,000 (W1))		
Current assets		
Inventory	96,000	
Trade receivables	103,000	
	———	199,000
		———
Total assets		297,000
		———

	$000	$000
Equity and liabilities		
Equity shares of $1 each		66,000
Share premium		15,000
Other component of equity – equity option (W2)		4,050
Retained earnings (15,200 + 75,624 profit for year)		90,824
		———
		175,874
Non-current liabilities		
Deferred tax	8,300	
5% convertible loan note (W2)	47,126	
	———	55,426
Current liabilities		
Trade payables	32,200	
Bank overdraft	5,500	
Current tax payable	28,000	
	———	65,700
		———
Total equity and liabilities		297,000
		———

(c) **Basic earnings per share for the year ended 31 March 20X4**

Profit per statement of profit or loss	$75.624 million
Weighted average number of shares (W4)	62.255 million
Earnings per share (75.624/62.255)	121.5¢

Workings (figures in brackets in $000)

(W1) Cost of sales

	$000
Cost of sales per question	290,600
Depreciation of plant and equipment ((155,500 – 43,500) × 12½%)	14,000
	———
	304,600
	———

(W2) 5% convertible loan note

The convertible loan note is a compound financial instrument having a debt and an equity component which must be accounted for separately:

Year ended 31 March	Outflow	8%	Present value
	$000		$000
20X4	2,500	0.93	2,325
20X5	2,500	0.86	2,150
20X6	52,500	0.79	41,475
			———
Debt component			45,950
Equity component (= balance)			4,050
			———
Proceeds of issue			50,000
			———

The finance cost for the year will be $3,676,000 (45,950 × 8%) and the carrying amount of the loan as at 31 March 20X4 will be $47,126,000 (45,950 + 3,676 interest – 2,500 paid).

(W3) Deferred tax

	$000
Provision at 31 March 20X4	8,300
Balance at 1 April 20X3	(4,600)
	———
Charge to statement of profit or loss	3,700
	———

(W4) Earnings per share

Step 1 – Theoretical ex-rights price (TERP)

5 shares @ $2.50 =	$12.50
1 share @ $1.60 =	$1.60
	———
6 shares	$14.10

TERP = $14.10/6 = $2.35

Step 2 – Rights fraction = $^{2.50}/_{2.35}$

Step 3 – Weighted average number of shares

Date	Number	Fraction of year	Rights fraction	Weighted average
1 April	55,000,000	$^{6}/_{12}$	$^{2.50}/_{2.35}$	29,255,319
1:5 rights	11,000,000			
	———			
1 October	66,000,000	$^{6}/_{12}$		33,000,000
	———			———
				62,255,319
				———

There are 66 million shares at 31 March 20X4, after the 1 for 5 rights issue. Therefore anyone who held 5 shares at the start of the year now has 6 shares, and the opening number of shares would be 55 million (66 million × $^{5}/_{6}$).

Marking scheme		
		Marks
(a)	Statement of profit or loss	
	Revenue	½
	Cost of sales	1½
	Operating costs	½
	Finance costs	1½
	Income tax expense	2
(b)	Statement of financial position	
	Property, plant and equipment	1
	Inventory	½
	Trade receivables	½
	Share capital	½
	Share premium	½
	Convertible option – Equity component	1
	Retained earnings	1
	5% loan note	1½
	Deferred tax	1
	Trade payables	½
	Bank overdraft	½
	Current tax	½
(c)	Calculation of opening shares	1
	Calculation of TERP	1
	Application of fraction to first 6 months only	1
	Time apportionment	1
	Use of own profit from SPL	1
		——
Total		20
		——

360 DUNE

Key answer tips

This question contained many of the usual adjustments that you would expect with a published accounts question such as depreciation and tax adjustments. You were also expected to demonstrate your knowledge of accounting for held for sale assets and financial assets and liabilities in this time-consuming question.

(a)   **Dune – Statement of profit or loss for the year ended 31 March 20X4**

	$000
Revenue (400,000	400,000
Cost of sales (W1)	(306,100)
Gross profit	93,900
Distribution costs	(26,400)
Administrative expenses (34,200 – 500 loan note issue costs)	(33,700)
Investment income	1,200
Gain on investments at fair value through profit or loss (28,000 – 26,500)	1,500
Finance costs (200 + 1,950 (W3)	(2,150)
Profit before tax	34,350
Income tax expense (12,000 – 1,400 – 1,800 (W4))	(8,800)
Profit for the year	25,550

Dune – Statement of financial position as at 31 March 20X4

	$000	$000
Assets		
Non-current assets		
Property, plant and equipment (W5)		37,400
Investments at fair value through profit or loss		28,000
		65,400
Current assets		
Inventory	48,000	
Trade receivables	40,700	
Bank	15,500	104,200
Non-current assets held for sale (W2)		33,500
Total assets		203,100

Equity and liabilities

Equity

Equity shares of $1 each	40,000
Other components of equity	20,000
Retained earnings (38,400 + 25,550 – 10,000 dividend)	53,950
	113,950

Non-current liabilities

Deferred tax (W4)	4,200	
5% loan notes (W3)	20,450	24,650

Current liabilities

Trade payables	52,000	
Accrued loan note interest (W3)	500	
Current tax payable	12,000	64,500

Total equity and liabilities	203,100

(b) **Earnings per share:**

EPS = $25,550,000/36,594,595 (W6)) = $0.70

Re-stated 20X3 EPS = 68c $\times$ $(^{0.74}/_{0.82})$ = $0.61

Workings (figures in brackets in $000)

(W1) Cost of sales

	$000
Per question	294,000
Depreciation of leasehold property (see below)	1,500
Impairment of leasehold property (see below)	4,000
Depreciation of plant and equipment ((67,500 – 23,500) × 15%)	6,600
	306,100

(W2) The leasehold property must be classed as a non-current asset held for sale from 1 October 20X3 at its fair value less costs to sell. It must be depreciated for six months up to this date (after which depreciation ceases). This is calculated at $1.5 million (45,000/15 years × $^6/_{12}$). Its carrying amount at 1 October 20X3 is therefore $37.5 million (45,000 – (6,000 + 1,500)).

Its fair value less cost to sell at this date is $33.5 million ((40,000 × 85%) – 500). It is therefore impaired by $4 million (37,500 – 33,500).

(W3) The finance cost of the loan note, at the effective rate of 10% applied to the correct carrying amount of the loan note of $19.5 million, is $1.95 million. The issue costs must be deducted from the proceeds of the loan note as they are not an administrative expense. The interest actually paid is $500,000 (20,000 × 5% × $^6/_{12}$) but a further $500,000 needs to be accrued as a current liability (as it will be paid soon). The difference between the total finance cost of $1.95 million and the $1 million interest payable is added to the carrying amount of the loan note to give $20.45 million (19,500 + 950) for inclusion as a non-current liability in the statement of financial position.

(W4) Deferred tax

Provision required at 31 March 20X4 (14,000 × 30%)	4,200
Less provision at 1 April 20X3	(6,000)
	———
Credit (reduction in provision) to statement of profit or loss	(1,800)
	———

(W5) Property, plant and equipment

Property, plant and equipment (67,500 – 23,500 – 6,600)	37,400

(W6) Weighted average number of shares

Step 1 – Theoretical ex-rights price (TERP)

4 shares @ $0.82 =	$3.28
1 share @ $0.42 =	$0.42
	———
5 shares	$3.70

TERP = $3.70/5 = $0.74

Step 2 – Rights fraction = $^{0.82}/_{0.74}$

Step 3 – Weighted average number of shares

Date	Number	Fraction of year	Rights fraction	Weighted average
1 April	32,000,000	$^9/_{12}$	$^{0.82}/_{0.74}$	26,594,595
1 January	40,000,000	$^3/_{12}$		10,000,000
				———————
				36,594,595
				———————

Based on 40 million shares in issue at 31 March 20X4, a rights issue of 1 for 4 on 1 January 20X4 would have resulted in the issue of 8 million new shares (40 million × $^1/_5$). Therefore there would have been 32 million shares at the start of the year.

	Marking scheme		
			Marks
(a)	**Statement of profit or loss**		
	Revenue		½
	Cost of sales		2
	Distribution costs		½
	Administrative expenses		1
	Investment income		½
	Gain on investments		½
	Finance costs		1½
	Income tax expense		2
		Maximum	7½
	Statement of financial position		
	Property, plant and equipment		½
	Investments		½
	Inventory		½
	Trade receivables		½
	Bank		½
	Non-current asset held for sale		1
	Equity shares		½
	Retained earnings (1 for dividend)		1
	Deferred tax		1
	5% loan note		1
	Trade payables		½
	Accrued loan note interest		½
	Current tax payable		½
		Maximum	7½
(b)	Number of shares at start of year		1
	TERP		1
	Application of rights fraction and time apportionment		1
	Use of own profit		1
	Restatement of prior year		1
Total			**20**

Examiner's comments

This was a question of preparing financial statements from a trial balance with various adjustments required. These involved the dealing with the use of the effective interest rate for a loan, a fair value investment, an impairment of a leasehold property (including presenting it as 'held for sale'), and accounting for taxation. The most common errors were:

- loan: the issue costs were often ignored and calculating the finance charge at the nominal rate of 5% instead of the effective rate of 10%. Omission of accrued interest from current liabilities or including it at the incorrect amount

- leasehold property: a failure to depreciate it up to the date it became 'held for sale', not calculating the subsequent impairment loss, and most candidates continuing to show it as a non-current, rather than a current, asset

- there were many errors in the treatment of the taxation, including debiting the over provision of the previous year's tax instead of crediting, treating the closing provision of deferred tax as the charge in the statement of profit or loss and confusion over SFP entries.

361 KANDY

(a)   **Kandy – Schedule of retained earnings of Kandy as at 30 September 20X4**

		$000
Retained earnings per trial balance		19,500
Adjustments re:		
Note (i)	Add back issue costs of loan note (W1)	1,000
	Loan finance costs (W1)	(2,610)
Note (ii)	Depreciation of buildings (W2)	(2,600)
	Depreciation of plant and equipment (W2)	(3,000)
Note (iii)	Income tax expense (W3)	(800)
Note (iv)	Gain on investments at fair value through profit or loss ($2.6m – $2m)	600
	Adjusted retained earnings	12,090

(b)   **Kandy – Statement of financial position as at 30 September 20X4**

Assets	$000	$000
Non-current assets		
Property, plant and equipment (W2)		65,400
Investments at fair value through profit or loss (per note (iv))		2,600
Current assets (per trial balance)		68,700
Total assets		136,700
Equity and liabilities		
Equity		
Equity shares of $1 each		40,000
Revaluation surplus (12,000 – 2,400 (W2 and W3))	9,600	
Retained earnings (from (a))	12,090	
		21,690
		61,690
Non-current liabilities		
Deferred tax (W3)	4,400	
6% loan note (W1)	29,810	
		34,210
Current liabilities (per trial balance)	38,400	
Current tax payable	2,400	40,800
Total equity and liabilities		136,700

Workings

(W1) Loan note

	$000
Proceeds	30,000
Less issue costs incorrectly charged as expense	(1,000)
Initial liability	29,000
Interest at 9% effective rate	2,610
Less interest paid per trial balance	(1,800)
	29,810

The loan note is carried at amortised cost, calculated as above. The initial value is calculated by deducting the issue costs from the proceeds of the loan note. Interest is always calculated using the effective rate.

(W2) Non-current assets

	Land	Buildings	Plant & equipment	Total
	$000	$000	$000	$000
Cost b/f	5,000	50,000	58,500	
Depreciation b/f	–	(20,000)	(34,500)	
	5,000	30,000	24,000	
Gain on revaluation	3,000	9,000		
Revaluation	8,000	39,000		
Depreciation charge				
$39,000 \times {}^{1}/_{15}$		(2,600)		
$24,000 \times 12{}^{1}/_{2}\%$			(3,000)	
	8,000	36,400	21,000	65,400

Total revaluation gain is $12 million ($3m + $9m).

(W3) Taxation

Income tax expense	$000
Provision for year ended 30 September 20X4	2,400
Less over-provision in previous year	(1,100)
Deferred tax (see below)	(500)
	800

Deferred tax	$000
Provision required at 30 September 20X4 (($10m temporary differences + $12m revaluation) × 20%)	4,400
Provision b/f at 1 October 20X3	(2,500)
	———
Movement in provision	1,900
Charge to revaluation of land and buildings ($12m × 20%)	(2,400)
	———
Balance – credit to profit or loss above	(500)
	———

	Marking scheme		
			Marks
(a)	Schedule of retained earnings as at 30 September 20X4		
	Retained earnings per trial balance		1
	Issue costs		1
	Loan finance costs		2
	Depreciation charges		2
	Income tax expense		2
	Investments		1
			—
		Maximum	9
			—
(b)	Statement of financial position		
	Property, plant and equipment		2
	Investments		1
	Current assets		1½
	Equity shares		½
	Revaluation surplus		2
	Deferred tax		1
	6% loan note		1½
	Current liabilities (per trial balance)		½
	Current tax payable		1
			—
		Maximum	11
			—
Total			**20**
			—

362 CLARION

(a) Clarion – Statement of financial position as at 31 March 20X5

	$000	$000
Assets		
Property, plant and equipment		49,000
(77,000 + 8,000 – 19,000 – 17,000 (W1))		
Investments through profit or loss		6,500
		———
		55,500
Current assets		
Inventory	11,700	
Trade receivables	20,500	
	———	
		32,200
		———
Total assets		87,700
		———
Equity		
Equity shares of $1 each		35,000
Retained earnings (W1)		10,810
		———
		45,810
Non-current liabilities		
8% loan notes (20,000 – 5,000 redeemed)	15,000	
Deferred tax (W3)	3,000	
Environmental provision (4,000 + 320 (W1))	4,320	
Lease liability (W4)	3,747	
	———	
		26,067
Current liabilities		
Trade payables	9,400	
Lease liability (W4)	1,023	
Bank overdraft	1,900	
Current tax payable	3,500	
	———	
		15,823
		———
Total equity and liabilities		87,700
		———

(b) Clarion – Extracts from the statement of cash flows for the year ended 31 March 20X5

	$000
Cash flows from investing activities	
Purchase of plant and equipment (note (ii))	(14,000)
Dividends received (W2)	300
Sale of investments (note (iv))	1,600
Cash flows from financing activities	
Redemption of loan notes (W5)	(5,000)
Repayment of lease liability (2,300 + (1,500 – 570)) (W5)	(3,230)

Workings (figures in brackets in $000)

(W1) Retained earnings

	$000
Per trial balance	33,100
Depreciation of plant and equipment ((77,000 + 8,000) × 20%)	(17,000)
Finance costs: 8% loan notes (800 TB + 800 suspense (W5))	(1,600)
Lease interest (W4)	(570)
Environmental provision (4,000 × 8%)	(320)
Investment income (W2)	1,000
Tax: current year	(3,500)
Deferred tax (W3)	(300)
	10,810

(W2) Investment income

Dividends received and profit on sale per TB *	500
Gains on fair value (6,500 – 6,000)	500
	1,000

*Profit on sale = 200 (1,600 – 1,400), dividends received = 300 (500 – 200)

(W3) Deferred tax

Provision required as at 31 March 20X5 (12,000 × 25%)	3,000
Balance at 1 April 20X4	(2,700)
Charge to retained earnings	300

(W4) Lease liability

	Balance b/f	Interest at 10%	Paid	Balance c/f
	$000	$000	$000	$000
Year to 31 March 20X5	5,700	570	(1,500)	4,770
Year to 31 March 20X6	4,770	477	(1,500)	3,747

Interest charge		$570
Non-current liability		$3,747
Current liability	(4,770 – 3747)	$1,023

(W5) Elimination of suspense account

	$000
Cash cost of loan note redemption (20,000 × 25%)	5,000
Six months' interest on loan note (20,000 × 8% × $^6/_{12}$)	800
	5,800

Marking scheme		
		Marks
(a)	Statement of financial position	
	Property, plant and equipment	1½
	Investments through profit or loss	½
	Inventory	½
	Receivables	½
	Share capital	½
	Retained earnings	5½
	8% loan notes	1
	Deferred tax	1
	Environmental provision	1
	Non-current lease obligation	1
	Trade payables	½
	Bank overdraft	½
	Current lease obligation	½
	Current tax payable	½
		15
(b)	Extract from statement of cash flows	
	Purchase of property, plant and equipment	½
	Sale of investments	½
	Dividends received	1
	Redemption of loan notes	1
	Payment of lease liability	2
		5
Total		**20**

363 MOSTON *Walk in the footsteps of a top tutor*

(a) **Moston – Statement of profit or loss and other comprehensive income for the year ended 30 June 20X5**

	$000
Revenue	113,500
Cost of sales (W1)	(97,700)
Gross profit	15,800
Distribution costs	(2,800)
Administrative expenses (6,800 – 500 loan note issue costs)	(6,300)
Investment income	300
Finance costs (W2)	(1,560)
Profit before tax	5,440
Income tax expense (1,200 + 800)	(2,000)
Profit for the year	3,440
Other comprehensive income	
Items that will not be reclassified to profit or loss	
Gain on revaluation of property (29,000 – (28,500 – 1,900) (W1))	2,400
Total comprehensive income for the year	5,840

(b) **Moston – Statement of changes in equity for the year ended 30 June 20X5**

	Share capital	Other components of equity	Revaluation surplus	Retained earnings	Total equity
	$000	$000	$000	$000	$000
Balance at 1 July 20X4	20,000	2,300	3,000	6,200	31,500
Share issue (W3)	10,000	7,000			17,000
Total comprehensive income for the year			2,400	3,440	5,840
Dividends paid (W3)				(4,000)	(4,000)
Balance at 30 June 20X5	30,000	9,300	5,400	5,640	50,340

(c) **Moston – Statement of cash flows for the year ended 30 June 20X5**

	$000
Cash flows from investing activities	
Capitalised development costs	(3,200)
Investment income	300
Cash flows from financing activities	
Shares issued	17,000
Dividends paid	(4,000)
Loan notes issued	19,500

Tutorial note

It is crucial that you know what each section of the statement of cash flows contains so that you are able to produce extracts if required. This is likely to contain a number of figures given to you in the question, such as the loan notes and shares issued so there is scope to pick up some simpler marks here.

Workings (monetary figures in brackets in $000)

(W1) Cost of sales

	$000
Per trial balance	88,500
Depreciation of property (28,500/15 years)	1,900
Depreciation of plant and equipment ((27,100 – 9,100) × 15%)	2,700
Research and development expenses (see below)	4,600
	97,700

Tutorial note

Development costs can only be capitalised from the date the directors became confident that the new product would be commercially successful, which is 1 May. Research of $3 million (3 months at $1 million per month) from January to March and April's costs of $1.6 million should be expensed, a total of $4.6m. This leaves $3.2 million (2 months at $1.6 million per month) to be capitalised at the year end.

(W2) Loan interest

	$000
5% loan note ((20,000 – 500) × 8% see below)	1,560

The 5% loan note issue costs should not be charged to administrative expenses, but deducted from the proceeds of the loan, leaving an initial value of $19.5m.

(W3) Dividend paid and share issue

Note that the dividend was paid prior to the share issue and is therefore calculated based on 20 million shares (30 million – 10 million).

	$000
Dividend paid 20 million × 20¢	4,000

Share issue: 10 million × $1.70 = $17m, split $10m capital, $7m premium.

Marking scheme

		Marks
(a)	Statement of profit or loss and other comprehensive income	
	Revenue	½
	Cost of sales	3½
	Distribution	½
	Administration	1½
	Investment income	½
	Finance costs	1½
	Income tax expense	1
	Gain on property	1
		———
		10
		———
(b)	Statement of changes in equity	
	Balances brought forward	1
	Share issue	2
	Comprehensive income	1
	Dividend	1
		———
		5
		———
(c)	Extract from statement of cash flows	
	Capitalised development costs	1
	Investment income	½
	Shares issued	1
	Dividends paid	1
	Loan notes issued	1½
		———
		5
		———
Total		**20**
		———

364 TRIAGE

(a) **Triage – schedule of adjustments to profit for the year ended 31 March 20X6**

	$000
Draft profit before interest and tax per trial balance	30,000
Adjustments re:	
Note (i)	
Convertible loan note finance costs (W1)	(3,023)
Note (ii)	
Depreciation of property (1,500 + 1,700 (W2)	(3,200)
Depreciation of plant and equipment (W2)	(6,600)
Note (iii)	
Current year loss on fraud (700 – 450 see below)	(250)
Note (iv)	
Income tax expense (2,700 + 700 – 800 (W3))	(2,600)
	———
Profit for the year	14,327
	———

(b) **Triage– Statement of financial position as at 31 March 20X6**

	$000	$000
Assets		
Non-current assets		
Property, plant and equipment (64,600 + 37,400 (W2))		102,000
Current assets		
Trade receivables (28,000 – 700 fraud)	27,300	
Other current assets per trial balance	9,300	36,600
Total assets		138,600
Equity and liabilities		
Equity		
Equity shares of $1 each		50,000
Other component of equity (W1)	2,208	
Revaluation surplus (7,800 – 1,560 (W2))	6,240	
Retained earnings (W4)	17,377	25,825
		75,825
Non-current liabilities		
Deferred tax (W3)	3,960	
6% convertible loan notes (W1)	38,415	42,375
Current liabilities		
Per trial balance	17,700	
Current tax payable	2,700	20,400
Total equity and liabilities		138,600

(c) **Diluted earnings per share (W5)   28.9 cents**

Workings (monetary figures in brackets in $000)

Note:

The $450,000 fraud loss in the previous year is a prior period adjustment (reported in the statement of changes in equity). The possible insurance claim is a contingent asset and should be ignored.

(W1) 6% convertible loan notes

The convertible loan notes are a compound financial instrument having a debt and an equity component which must both be quantified and accounted for separately:

Year ended 31 March	Outflow	8% factor	Present value
	$000		$000
20X6 Interest – $4m × 6%	2,400	0.93	2,232
20X7 Interest	2,400	0.86	2,064
20X8 Capital + interest	42,400	0.79	33,496
			————
Debt component			37,792
Equity component (= balance)			2,208
			————
Proceeds of issue			40,000
			————

The finance cost will be $3,023,000 (37,792 × 8%) and the carrying amount of the loan notes at 31 March 20X6 will be $38,415,000 (37,792 + 3,023 – 2,400).

(W2) Non-current assets

	$000
Property carrying amount at 1 April 20X5 (75,000 – 15,000)	60,000
Depreciation to date of revaluation (1 October 20X5)	
$(75,000 \times {}^{6}/_{12})$	(1,500)
	————
Carrying amount at revaluation	58,500
Gain on revaluation = balance	7,800
	————
Revaluation at 1 October 20X5	66,300
Depreciation to year ended 31 March 20X6 (66,300/19.5 years	
$\times {}^{6}/_{12})$	(1,700)
	————
Carrying amount at 31 March 20X6	64,600
	————

Prior to the revaluation annual depreciation is $3m (75,000/25 years). Therefore the accumulated depreciation at 1 April 20X5 of $15m represents five years' depreciation. At the date of revaluation (1 October 20X5), there will be a remaining life of 19.5 years.

Of the revaluation gain, $6.24m (80%) is credited to the revaluation surplus and $1.56m (20%) is credited to deferred tax.

Plant and equipment

	$000
Carrying amount at 1 April 20X5 (72,100 – 28,100)	44,000
Depreciation for year ended 31 March 20X6 (15% reducing	
balance)	(6,600)
	————
Carrying amount at 31 March 20X6	37,400
	————

(W3) Deferred tax

Provision required at 31 March 20X6:

Revalued property and other assets (7,800 + 12,000) × 20%)	3,960
Provision at 1 April 20X5	(3,200)
Increase in provision	760
Revaluation of land and buildings (7,800 × 20%)	(1,560)
Balance credited to profit or loss	800

(W4) Retained earnings

Balance at 1 April 20X5	3,500
Prior period adjustment (fraud)	(450)
Adjusted profit for year (from (a))	14,327
Balance at 31 March 20X6	17,377

(W5) The maximum additional shares on conversion is 8 million (40,000 × $^{20}/_{100}$), giving total shares of 58 million. The notional saving in loan interest is $2.418m (3,023 (from (W1) above × 80% (i.e. after tax)), giving adjusted earnings of $16.745m (14,327 + 2,418).

Therefore diluted EPS is $\dfrac{\$16,745,000 \times 100}{58 \text{ million shares}} = 28.9$ cents

Marking scheme		
		Marks
(a)	Schedule of adjustments to profit for year ended 31 March 20X6	
	Profit before interest and tax b/f	½
	Loan finance costs	1
	Depreciation charges	1½
	Fraud loss	½
	Income tax expense	1½
		5
(b)	Statement of financial position	
	Property, plant and equipment	2½
	Trade receivables	1
	Other current assets (per trial balance)	½
	Equity shares	½
	Equity option	1
	Revaluation surplus	1
	Retained earnings	1½
	Deferred tax	1
	6% loan note	1½
	Current liabilities (per trial balance)	½
	Current tax payable	1
		12
(c)	Diluted earnings per share	3
Total		**20**

Examiner's comments

The question was reasonably well answered with many candidates scoring at least half marks.

In part (a) a significant number of candidates prepared a series of workings but did not attempt to either summarise these or state their effect on the statement of profit or loss, which restricted the number of marks that could be awarded. The requirement for a schedule is an alternative approach to the preparation of a full statement of profit or loss, whilst still testing key principles of profit measurement. Future candidates should ensure that they avoid the common errors noted in this session:

- Some candidates did not attempt to calculate the debt component of the convertible loan note and a few calculated interest paid at the underlying rate rather than the "coupon" rate.

- A number of candidates did not correctly split the amortisation of the leased property between the two halves of the year and often used an incorrect remaining useful life to determine the amortisation charge for the second half of the year.

- Many candidates did not correctly split the fraud between the amount related to the current year and the remainder which related to the previous year and therefore was not relevant to profit or loss.

- Some candidates included the estimated amount the directors hoped could be recovered from insurers. This was a contingent asset and, as many candidates correctly noted, should be ignored.

- Candidates' understanding of current and deferred tax issues seems to have been a particular problem.

Part (b) required the preparation of the statement of financial position incorporating figures in the given trial balance and the adjustments from part (a). Common errors noted were:

- Some candidates did not include the equity component of the convertible loan note as an "other component of equity" and sometimes included it as a liability rather than equity.

- A number of candidates did not reduce the revaluation surplus by the deferred tax element or did not report the revaluation surplus at all.

- Candidates also incorrectly showed an incomplete (or omitted to show) deferred tax provision.

- Some candidates omitted the current tax liability or incorrectly adjusted it by the underprovision for the previous year.

Part (c) required a calculation of Triage's potential diluted earnings per share for the year. Many candidates either did not attempt this part of the question or made no adjustment for dilution. As the question did not ask for the basic earnings per share no marks were awarded for calculating it – the marks were specifically for the diluting adjustments.

365 HAVERFORD CO

(a) **Adjustments to Haverford Co's profit for the year ended 31 December 20X7**

	$000
Draft profit	2,250
Convertible loan notes (w1)	(135)
Contract revenue (w2)	5,600
Contract cost of sales (w2)	(3,600)
Depreciation (w4)	(720)
Property impairment (w4)	(480)
Closing inventories (w5)	390
Revised profit	3,305

(b) **Statement of changes in equity for the year ended 31 December 20X7**

	Share capital	OCE	Retained earnings	Revaluation surplus	Option
Balance as at 1 January 20X7	20,000	3,000	6,270	800	–
Profit – from (a)			3,305		
Revaluation loss (w4)				(800)	
Bonus issue (w3)	4,000	(3,000)	(1,000)		
Convertible loan notes issued (w1)					424
Dividend paid			(3,620)		
Balance as at 31 December 20X7	24,000	–	4,955	–	424

(c) **Statement of financial position for Haverford Co as at 31 December 20X7**

	$000
Assets	
Non-current assets:	
Property (w3)	16,000
Current assets:	
Inventory (w5)	4,700
Trade receivables	5,510
Contract asset (w2)	2,500
Cash	10,320
Total assets	39,030

Equity and liabilities

Equity:

Share capital	24,000
Retained earnings	4,955
Convertible option	424
Total equity	29,379

Non-current liabilities:

Convertible loan notes (w1)	7,711
Current liabilities:	1,940
Total equity and liabilities	39,030

Working 1 – Convertible loan notes

	Payment	Discount rate	Present value
	$000	$000	$000
20X7	320	0.943	302
20X8	320	0.890	285
20X9	8,320	0.840	6,989
			7,576

As the full amount of $8m has been taken to liabilities, adjustment required is:

Dr Liability	$424k
Cr Equity	$424k

The liability should then be held at amortised cost, using the effective interest rate.

Balance b/f $000	Interest 6% $000	Payment Payment $000	Balance c/f $000
7,576	455	(320)	7,711

As only $320k has been recorded in finance costs:

Dr Finance costs	$135k
Cr Liability	$135k

Working 2 – Contract with customer

Overall contract:

	$000
Price	14,000
Costs to date	(1,900)
Costs to complete	(7,100)
	5,000

Progress: 40%

Statement of profit or loss:

	$000
Revenue ($14,000 × 40%)	5,600
Cost of sales ($9,000 × 40%)	(3,600)
	2,000

Statement of financial position:

	$000
Costs to date	1,900
Profit to date	2,000
Amount billed to date	(1,400)
	2,500

$5.6m should be recorded in revenue, and $3.6m in cost of sales, giving an overall increase to the draft profit of $2m. $2.5m should then be recorded in the statement of financial position as a current asset.

Working 3 – Bonus issue

The 1 for 5 bonus issue will lead to an increase in share capital of $4m ($20m x 1/5). Of this, $3m will be debited to other components of equity to take it to zero. The remaining $1m will be deducted from retained earnings.

Adjustment:

Dr Share premium	$3m
Dr Retained earnings	$1m
Cr Share capital	$4m

Working 4 – Property

The asset should first be depreciated. $18m/25 = $720k. This should be deducted from the draft profit and the asset, giving a carrying amount of $17,280k.

Dr Draft profit	$720k
Cr Property	$720k

Then the asset should be revalued from $17,280k to $16,000k, giving a revaluation loss of $1,280k. As the revaluation surplus is only $800k, only $800k can be debited to this, with the remaining $480k being debited from the draft profit for the year.

Dr Revaluation surplus	$800k
Dr Draft profit	$480k
Cr Property	$1,280k

Working 5 – Inventories

Closing inventories should be adjusted from $4,310k to $4,700k.

Dr Inventories	$390k
Cr Draft profit	$390k

ACCA marking guide			
			Marks
(a)		Convertible loan notes	1
		Contract	2
		Depreciation/impairment	2
		Inventory	1
			6
(b)		Opening balances	1
		Convertible loan notes	1
		Bonus issue	2
		Profit/dividend/revaluation	2
			6
(c)		PPE	1
		Contract	2
		Other current assets	2
		Equity	½
		Convertible loan notes	2
		Current liabilities	½
			8
Total			**20**

366 DUGGAN CO

(a) **Duggan Co statement of profit or loss for the year ended 30 June 20X8**

	$000
Revenue (43,200 + 2,700 (W1))	45,900
Cost of sales (21,700 + 1,500 (W1))	(23,200)
Gross profit	22,700
Operating exp (13,520 + 120 (W2) – 8 (W5) + 900 (W6))	(14,532)
Profit from operations	8,168
Finance costs (1,240 + 46 (W2) + 86 (W4) + 640 (W5))	(2,012)
Investment income	120
Profit before tax	6,276
Income tax expense (2,100 – 500 – 130 (W3))	(1,470)
Profit for the year	4,806

(b) **Statement of changes in equity for the year ended 30 June 20X8**

	Share capital $000	Share premium $000	Retained earnings $000	Convertible option $000
Balance at 1 July 20X7	12,200		35,400	
Prior year error			(1,600)	
Restated balance			33,800	
Share issue	1,500	1,800		
Profit (from (a))			4,806	
Convertible issue				180
Balance at 30 June 20X8	13,700	1,800	38,606	180

(c) **Basic earnings per share:**

$$\frac{4,806}{13,200} \quad \begin{array}{l}\text{Profit from (a)}\\ \text{(W7)}\end{array}$$

= $0.36 per share

Working 1 – Contract

	$000	
Revenue	2,700	(80% × $9m = $7.2m. As $4.5m (50%) in X7, X8 = $2.7m)
COS	1,500	(80% × $5m = $4m. As $2.5m (50%) in X7, X8 = $1.5m)

Working 2 – Court case

As the most likely outcome is that $1.012m will be paid, this must be included in full. This is discounted to present value as the payment was not expected for 12 months. The initial entry on 1 January 20X8 in operating expenses should be $920,000 (rounded), being $1.012m × 1/1.1 (or $1.012m × 0.9091). As $800,000 has been included, an adjustment of $120,000 is required.

This discount should then be unwound for six months, resulting in an increase in finance costs of $46,000.

Working 3 – Tax

	$000	
Current estimate	2,100	Add to expense and current liabilities
Decrease in deferred tax	(500)	$2m decrease in temporary differences × 25%
Prior year overprovision	(130)	Credit balance in trial balance
	1,470	

Working 4 – Convertible

	Payment $000	Discount factor	Present value
Year ended 30 June 20X8	300	0.926	278
Year ended 30 June 20X9	5,300	0.857	4,542
Liability element			4,820

The equity element is therefore $180,000, to be shown in the statement of changes in equity.

Interest needs to be applied to the liability element. $4,820 × 8% = $386,000. As $300,000 has been recorded, an adjustment of $86,000 is required.

Working 5 – Capitalised interest

Of the $2.56m capitalised, 3/12 of this was after the construction was complete and so should be expensed. This will lead to an increase in finance costs of $640,000.

An adjustment must also be made to the depreciation, being $640,000/20 × 3/12 = $8,000 reduction in the depreciation charge for the year.

Working 6 – Fraud

The $1.6m must be taken to retained earnings as a prior year error. The remaining $0.9m will be taken to operating expenses.

Working 7 – Weighted average number of shares

Date	No. of shares	Fraction of year	Weighted average number of shares
	000		000
1 July 20X7	12,200	4/12	4,067
1 November 20X7	13,700	8/12	9,133
			13,200

ACCA marking guide			
			Marks
(a)	Revenue and COS		2½
	Operating costs		3½
	Finance costs		3½
	Investment income and tax		2½
			12
(b)	Opening balances (incl error)		2
	Share issue, profit, loan notes		3
			5
(c)	EPS calculation		3
Total			20

Examiner's Comments

Parts (a) and (b) to this question required candidates to prepare a statement of profit or loss and a statement of changes in equity for a single entity, from a trial balance. Overall the performance on this question was reasonably good. There were, however, some common errors and weaknesses:

A contract, where the performance obligation was satisfied over the time, was well attempted by most candidates. However, several candidates recorded the profit for the year as revenue instead of recognising the revenue and costs separately. Some marks were awarded for this, but candidates needed to record both the revenue and the costs to achieve the full marks available. Some candidates also failed to spot that this contract was in the second year and recorded the total revenue and costs to date.

There were several variations being noted by the marking team on the accounting for the unfair dismissal. Many candidates attempted to discount the $800,000 or to include the full $1.021 million. The question had included a provision of $800,000 to date, being 80% of the future expected payment. However, this treatment is incorrect. In accordance with IAS 37, the future liability should be recognised in full, but at present value (to take into account the liability being paid 12 months after recognition). Many candidates attempted discounting, but then failed to unwind the discount and recognise the subsequent finance cost.

Generally, the convertible loan was dealt with well. The most common mistake was where the market rate of interest was taken to finance costs in full and candidates did not deduct the interest already paid. Some candidates incorrectly split the convertible loan between the debt and equity components using the coupon rate of interest at 6%, this was then generally accounted for correctly thereafter earning 'own figure' marks. For those candidates who dealt with the convertible loan correctly, only a minority transferred the equity component into the statement of changes in equity. Many candidates failed to discount the liability to present value at all and made no attempt to split it. This is surprising as convertible loans have been tested on numerous occasions. Candidates are therefore encouraged to revise this topic area.

The borrowing cost treatment varied considerably with many candidates making no adjustment for borrowing costs at all. The interest on borrowing costs must be capitalised on a qualifying asset, but only for the period up to the date that the asset is complete. For Duggan, interest should have been capitalised between 1 July 20X7 and 31 March 20X8 (9 months). A full 12 months' interest had been capitalised and therefore three months' interest needed to be removed from property, plant and equipment and allocated to finance costs. This then had a knock-on-effect in the depreciation calculation which had been overstated by Duggan. A further adjustment was then required to eliminate this excess depreciation for the three-month period from the date the asset was completed.

It was pleasing to see that most candidates dealt with the fraud correctly identifying that $900,000 should be recorded as an expense in the statement of profit of loss and $1.6 million being recognised as a prior year error in the statement of changes in equity.

The share issue was also well done by the majority of candidates and recorded in the statement of changes in equity. Most candidates, however, did not deal with the share issue correctly in part (c) when asked to calculate the earnings per share for Duggan. The market issue of shares would require a weighted average of the share capital to be performed when calculating EPS and only a small minority of candidates remembered to do this.

Candidates should know that all of these issues have been assessed previously by the FR examiner and so they should attempt as many past exam questions as possible for practice and exposure to all possible learning outcomes.

STATEMENT OF CASH FLOWS

367 COALTOWN *Walk in the footsteps of a top tutor*

Coaltown – Statement of cash flows for the year ended 31 March 20X9:

Note: Figures in brackets in $000

		$000
Cash flows from operating activities		
Profit before tax		10,200
Adjustments for:		
depreciation of non-current assets (W1)	6,000	
loss on disposal of displays (W1)	1,500	
Interest expense		600
Increase in warranty provision (1,000 – 180)		820
increase in inventory (5,200 – 4,400)		(800)
increase in receivables (7,800 – 2,800)		(5,000)
Decrease in payables (4,500 – 4,200)		(300)
Negligence claim previously provided		(120)
Cash generated from operations		12,900
Interest paid		(600)
Income tax paid (W2)		(5,500)
Net cash from operating activities		6,800
Cash flows from investing activities (W1)		
Purchase of non-current assets	(20,500)	
Disposal cost of non-current assets	(500)	
Net cash used in investing activities		(21,000)
		(14,200)
Cash flows from financing activities		
Issue of equity shares (10,500 capital (W5) + 4,000 premium (W6))	14,500	
Issue of 10% loan notes	1,000	
Convertible loan repaid	(1,600)	
Equity dividends paid (W4)	(4,000)	
Net cash from financing activities		9,900
Net decrease in cash and cash equivalents		(4,300)
Cash and cash equivalents at beginning of period		700
Cash and cash equivalents at end of period		(3,600)

Key answer tips

This proved to be a relatively straightforward statement of cash flow. Watch out for the disposal, Coaltown has an unexpected COST associated with disposal that will represent a cash outflow rather than an inflow.

Workings (Columnar format)

(W1) Non-current assets

Cost	$000
Balance b/f	80,000
Revaluation (5,000 – 2,000 depreciation)	3,000
Disposal	(10,000)
Balance c/f	(93,500)
Cash flow for acquisitions	**20,500**

Depreciation	$000
Balance b/f	48,000
Revaluation	(2,000)
Disposal	(9,000)
Balance c/f	(43,000)
Difference – charge for year	**6,000**

Disposal of displays	$000
Cost	10,000
Depreciation	(9,000)
Cost of disposal	500
Loss on disposal	**1,500**

(W2) Income tax paid

	$000
Provision b/f	(5,300)
Statement of profit or loss tax charge	(3,200)
Provision c/f	3,000
Difference – cash paid	**(5,500)**

(W3) Revaluation surplus

	$000
Balance b/f	2,500
Gain on revaluation	5,000
Balance c/f	(6,500)
Difference – reserves transfer to retained earnings	**(1,000)**

(W4) Retained earnings

	$000
Balance b/f	15,800
Profit for year	7,000
Reserves transfer from revaluation surplus (W3)	1,000
Balance c/f	(19,800)
Difference – dividend paid	**(4,000)**

(W5) Share capital

	$000
Balance b/f	6,000
Loan note converted to shares (see below)	100
Balance c/f	(16,600)
Difference – shares issued	**10,500**

(W6) Other components of equity

	$000
Balance b/f	500
Loan note converted to shares (see below)	300
Balance c/f	4,800
Difference – premium on shares issued	**4,000**

Therefore the total cash from share issue = 10,500 + 4,000 = $14,500.

Note:

The $2 million convertible has 20% of it converted into shares. As each holder choosing conversion gets 25 shares for every $100 held, the entries for this will be:

Dr Convertible loan $400,000

Cr Share Capital $100,000 ($400,000 × 25/100)

Cr Other components of equity $300,000

The remaining 80% has been repaid, and the double entries for this would be:

Dr Convertible loan $1,600,000

Cr Cash $1,600,000

Workings (T-account format)

(W1) Non-current assets – Cost

b/f	80,000		
Revaluation	3,000	Disposals	10,000
Cash additions (balance)	**20,500**		
		c/f	93,500
	———		———
	103,500		103,500
	———		———

Non-current assets – Accumulated depreciation

Revaluation	2,000	b/f	48,000
Disposal	9,000	**Charge for year (balance)**	**6,000**
c/f	43,000		
	———		———
	54,000		54,000
	———		———

Note: The disposal had a carrying amount of $1m at disposal (cost $10m, accumulated depreciation $9m), and cost $500k to dispose, making a loss on disposal of $1,500k.

(W2) Tax Liabilities

		b/f	5,300
Tax paid (balance)	**5,500**	Charge from P/L	3,200
c/f	3,000		
	———		———
	8,500		8,500
	———		———

(W3) Revaluation surplus

		b/f	2,500
Retained earnings (balance)	**1,000**	PP&E	5,000
c/f	6,500		
	———		———
	7,500		7,500
	———		———

(W4) Retained earnings

		b/f	15,800
Dividend paid (balance)	**4,000**	Profit for the year	7,000
c/f	19,800	Revaluation surplus (W3)	1,000
	———		———
	23,800		23,800
	———		———

(W5) Share capital

		b/f	6,000
		Convertible loan (see note under (W6) in columnar format	100
c/f	16,600	**Shares issued (balance)**	**10,500**
	16,600		16,600

(W6) Other components of equity

		b/f	500
		Convertible (see note under (W6) in columnar format	300
c/f	4,800	**Shares issued (balance)**	**4,000**
	4,800		4,800

Marking scheme	
	Marks
Profit from operations (PBT + finance costs)	1
Depreciation charge	2
Loss on disposal	1
Warranty adjustment	1
Negligence claim	1
Working capital items	1½
Finance costs	1
Income tax paid	1
Purchase of non-current assets	2
Disposal cost of non-current assets	1
Issue of equity shares	2
Convertible repaid	1
Issue of 10% loan note	1
Dividend paid	2
Cash and cash equivalents b/f and c/f, movement	1½
Total	**20**

368 MONTY

Monty – Statement of cash flows for the year ended 31 March 20X3:

(Note: Figures in brackets are in $000)

	$000	$000
Cash flows from operating activities:		
Profit before tax		3,000
Adjustments for:		
depreciation of non-current assets		900
amortisation of non-current assets		200
release of government grant		(25)
finance costs (400 + 150)		550
decrease in inventories (3,800 – 3,300)		500
increase in receivables (2,950 – 2,200)		(750)
increase in payables (2,650 – 2,100)		550
		———
Cash generated from operations		4,925
Finance costs paid (320 (W6) + 150 lease)		(470)
Income tax paid (W1)		(425)
		———
Net cash from operating activities		4,030
Cash flows from investing activities:		
Purchase of property, plant and equipment (W2)	(700)	
Deferred development expenditure (1,000 + 200)	(1,200)	
Receipt of government grant (W5)	150	
	———	
Net cash used in investing activities		(1,750)
Cash flows from financing activities:		
Repayment of lease liabilities (W3)	(1,050)	
Equity dividend paid (W4)	(550)	
	———	
Net cash used in financing activities		(1,600)
		———
Net increase in cash and cash equivalents		680
Cash and cash equivalents at beginning of period		1,300
		———
Cash and cash equivalents at end of period		1,980
		———

Workings (columnar format)

(W1) Income tax paid

	$000
Provision b/f – current	(725)
– deferred	(800)
Tax charge	(1,000)
Transfer from revaluation surplus	(650)
Provision c/f – current	1,250
– deferred	1,500
Balance – cash paid	**(425)**

(W2) Property, plant and equipment

	$000
Balance b/f	10,700
Revaluation	2,000
New right-of-use asset	1,500
Depreciation	(900)
Balance c/f	(14,000)
Balance – cash purchases	**(700)**

(W3) Lease liabilities

	$000
Balances b/f – current	(600)
– non-current	(900)
New lease	(1,500)
Balances c/f – current	750
– non-current	1,200
Balance cash repayment	**(1,050)**

(W4) Equity dividend

	$000
Retained earnings b/f	1,750
Profit for the year	2,000
Retained earnings c/f	(3,200)
Balance – dividend paid	**(550)**

(W5) Government grant

	$000
Liabilities b/f (100 + 25)	125
Released to statement of profit or loss in the year	(25)
Liabilities c/f	(250)
Balance – receipt of government grant	**150**

(W6) Finance costs

As the loan notes are repayable at a premium, the effective rate of interest of 10% will be expensed to the statement of profit or loss each year. However, it is only the amount paid (the coupon rate of 8%) which will be taken to the statement of cash flows.

Loan notes	$000
Balance b/f	4,000
Statement of profit or loss expense	400
Liabilities c/f	(4,080)
Balance – interest paid	**(320)**

Workings (T-account format)

(W1) Tax Liabilities

		b/f (725 + 800)	1,525
Tax paid (balance)	**425**	Charge from SPL	1,000
c/f (1,250 + 1,500)	2,750	Transfer from revaluation surplus	650
	3,175		3,175

(W2) Property, plant and equipment

b/f	10,700		
Revaluation	2,000	Depreciation	900
Right-of-use additions (W3)	1,500		
Cash additions (balance)	**700**		
		c/f	14,000
	14,900		14,900

(W3) Lease liabilities

		b/f (600 + 900)	1,500
Liabilities repaid (balance)	**1,050**	New PP&E (W2)	1,500
c/f (750 + 1,200)	1,950		
	3,000		3,000

(W4) Retained earnings

		b/f	1,750
Dividend paid (balance)	550	Profit for year	2,000
c/f	3,200		
	———		———
	3,750		3,750
	———		———

(W5) Government grants

		b/f (100 + 25)	125
Release of grant	25	**Receipt of grant (balance)**	**150**
c/f (200 + 50)	250		
	———		———
	275		275
	———		———

(W6) Loan note

		b/f	4,000
Interest paid (balance)	320	Interest expensed	400
c/f	4,080		
	———		———
	4,400		4,400
	———		———

Marking scheme	Marks
Profit from operations (PBT + finance costs)	1
Depreciation	1
Amortisation	1
Release of grant	1
Working capital items	1½
Interest paid	2
Tax paid	2
Purchase of PPE	3
Development costs	1
Grant received	2
Lease payment	2
Dividends paid	1
Movement in cash	1½
	——
Total	**20**
	——

369 KINGDOM

(a) **Kingdom – Statement of cash flows for the year ended 30 September 20X3:**

	$000	$000
Cash flows from operating activities:		
Profit before tax		2,400
Adjustments for:		
depreciation of property, plant and equipment		1,500
loss on sale of property, plant and equipment (2,300 – 1,800)		500
finance costs		600
investment properties – rentals received		(350)
– fair value changes		700
		5,350
decrease in inventory (3,100 – 2,300)		800
decrease in receivables (3,400 – 3,000)		400
increase in payables (4,200 – 3,900)		300
Cash generated from operations		6,850
Interest paid (600 – 100 + 50)		(550)
Income tax paid (W1)		(1,950)
Net cash from operating activities		4,350
Cash flows from investing activities:		
Purchase of property, plant and equipment (W2)	(5,000)	
Sale of property, plant and equipment	1,800	
Purchase of investment property	(1,400)	
Investment property rentals received	350	
Net cash used in investing activities		(4,250)
Cash flows from financing activities:		
Issue of equity shares (17,200 – 15,000)	2,200	
Equity dividends paid (W3)	(2,800)	
Net cash used in financing activities		(600)
Net decrease in cash and cash equivalents		(500)
Cash and cash equivalents at beginning of period		300
Cash and cash equivalents at end of period		(200)

Workings – columnar format

(W1) Income tax

	$000
Provision b/f	(1,850)
Profit or loss charge	(600)
Provision c/f	500
Balance – tax paid	**(1,950)**

(W2) Property, plant and equipment

	$000
Balance b/f	(25,200)
Depreciation	1,500
Revaluation (downwards)	1,300
Disposal (at carrying amount)	2,300
Transfer from investment properties	(1,600)
Balance c/f	26,700
Balance – acquired during year	**(5,000)**

(W3) Equity dividends

	$000
Retained earnings b/f	8,700
Profit for the year	1,800
Retained earnings c/f	(7,700)
Balance – dividends paid	**2,800**

Note: For tutorial purposes the reconciliation of the investment properties is:

	$000
Balance b/f	5,000
Acquired during year (from question)	1,400
Loss in fair value	(700)
Transfer to property, plant and equipment	(1,600)
Balance c/f	4,100

Workings – T account format

(W1) Tax liabilities

		b/f	1,850
Tax paid (balance)	**1,950**	Charge from SPL	600
c/f	500		
	2,450		2,450

(W2) Property, plant and equipment

b/f	25,200	Revaluation	1,300
Transfer from investment properties	1,600	Depreciation	1,500
		Disposal	2,300
Cash additions (balance)	**5,000**		
		c/f	26,700
	31,800		31,800

(W3) Retained earnings

		b/f	8,700
Dividend paid (balance)	**2,800**	Profit for year	1,800
c/f	7,700		
	10,500		10,500

(W4) Investment properties

b/f	5,000	Transfer to PP&E	1,600
Additions	1,400	Loss in fair value	700
		c/f	4,100
	6,400		6,400

(b) The fall in the Kingdom's profit before tax can be analysed in three elements: changes at the gross profit level, the effect of overheads and the relative performance of the investment properties. The absolute effect on profit before tax of these elements are reductions of $1.4 million (15,000 – 13,600), $2.25 million (10,250 – 8,000) and $1.25 million (900 + 350) respectively, amounting to $4.9 million in total. Many businesses would consider returns on investment properties as not being part of operating activities, however these returns do impact on profit before tax.

Gross profit

Despite slightly higher revenue, gross profit fell by $1.4 million. This is attributable to a fall in the gross profit margin (down from 34.1% to 30.3%). Applying the stated 8% rise in the cost of sales, last year's cost of sales of $29 million would translate to an equivalent figure of $31.32 million in the current year which is almost the same as the actual figure ($31.3 million). This implies that the production activity/volume of sales has remained the same as last year. As the increase in revenue in the current year is only 2%, the decline in gross profitability has been caused by failing to pass on to customers the percentage increase in the cost of sales. This may be due to management's slow response to rising prices and/or to competitive pressures in the market.

Although there has been a purchase of new plant of $5 million (from the statement of cash flows), it would seem that this is a replacement of the $2.3 million of plant sold during the year. This is supported by the stagnation in the (apparent) volume of sales. The replacement of plant has probably led to slightly higher depreciation charges.

Operating costs/overheads

The administrative expenses and distribution costs are the main culprit of the fall in profit before tax as these are $2.25 million (or 28%) higher than last year. Even if they too have increased 8%, due to rising prices, they are still much higher than would have been expected, which implies a lack of cost control of these overheads.

Performance of investment properties

The final element of the fall in profit before tax is due to declining returns on the investment properties. This has two elements. First, a reduction in rentals received which may be due to the change in properties under rental (one transferred to owner-occupation and one newly let property) and/or a measure of falling rentals generally. The second element is clearer: there has been a decrease in the fair values of the properties in the current year compared to a rise in their fair values in the previous year. The fall in investment properties mirrors a fall in the value of Kingdom's other properties within property, plant and equipment (down $1.3 million), which suggests problems in the commercial property market.

	Marking scheme	
		Marks
(a)	Profit from operations (PBT + finance costs – investment income)	2
	Depreciation/loss on sale	1
	Working capital items	1½
	Interest paid	1
	Tax paid	1½
	Purchase of PPE	3
	Sale of PPE	½
	Purchase of investment property	1
	Investment property rentals	1
	Share issue	½
	Dividends paid	1
	Movement in cash	1
(b)	One per point made	5 max
Total		**20**

BUSINESS COMBINATIONS

370 PREMIER *Walk in the footsteps of a top tutor*

Consolidated statement of financial position as at 30 September 20X0

		$000
Non-current assets		
Property, plant and equipment		38,250
(25,500 + 13,900 – 1,200 (FV adj) + 50 (FV adj))		
Goodwill (W3)		7,800
Investments (1,800 – 800 (consideration) + 300 (gain on FVOCI))		1,300
		47,350
Current assets		
Inventory (5,300 + 500 – 400 (W2))	5,400	
Receivables	4,820	
(4,200 + 1,100 – 130 (cash in transit) – 350 (intra-group))		
Bank (3,000 + 800 +130 (cash in transit))	3,930	
		14,150
		61,500
Equity		
Equity shares of $1 each ((12,000 + 2,400 (W3))		14,400
Share premium (W3)		9,600
Other equity reserve (500 + 300 (gain on FVOCI))		800
Retained earnings (W5)		11,860
		36,660
Non-controlling interest (W4)		3,390
		40,050
Current liabilities		21,450
(15,000 + 6,800 – 350 intra group balance)		
		61,500

Workings in $000

(W1) Group structure

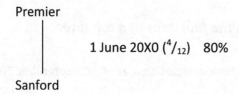

Premier

1 June 20X0 ($^4/_{12}$)   80%

Sanford

(W2) Net assets

	At acquisition	At reporting date	Post-acquisition
Share capital	5,000	5,000	–
Retained earnings (4,500 – (3900 × $^4/_{12}$))	3,200	4,500	1,300
Property fair value	(1,200)	(1,200)	–
Depreciation reduction (below)		50	50
PUP (below)		(400)	(400)
	7,000	7,950	950
	W3		W4/W5

The depreciation reduction is calculated as $1,200/8 years × $^4/_{12}$ = $50,000.

The unrealised profit in inventory is calculated as $2m × $^{25}/_{125}$ = $400,000.

Tutorial note

The fair value adjustment for property is a downwards fair value adjustment and therefore should be deducted from W2 and non-current assets. The reduction in depreciation should be added back in W2 and added back to non-current assets.

(W3) Goodwill

Parent holding (investment) at fair value:	
Shares ((5,000 × 80%) × $^3/_5$ × $5)	12,000
Cash	800
NCI value at acquisition	3,500
	16,300
Less: Fair value of net assets at acquisition (W2)	(7,000)
Goodwill on acquisition	9,300
Impairment	(1,500)
	7,800

Tutorial note

The 2.4 million shares (5,000 × 80% × $^3/_5$) issued by Premier at $5 each would be recorded as share capital of $2.4 million and share premium of $9.6 million.

(W4) Non-controlling interest (SFP)

NCI value at acquisition	3,500
NCI share of post-acquisition reserves (W2) (950 × 20%)	190
NCI share of impairment (W3) (1,500 × 20%)	(300)
	3,390

(W5) Consolidated retained earnings

Premier	12,300
Share of Sanford post-acquisition reserves (W2) (950 × 80%)	760
Share of impairment (W3) (1,500 × 80%)	(1,200)
	11,860

Marking scheme	
	Marks
Property, plant and equipment	2
Goodwill	4
Investments	1
Inventory	1½
Receivables	1½
Bank	1
Equity shares	1½
Share premium	1
Other equity reserve	1
Retained earnings	2½
Non-controlling interest	2
Current liabilities	1
Total	**20**

371 PATRONIC *Walk in the footsteps of a top tutor*

Key answer tip

Part (a) requires the calculation of the purchase consideration, testing the commonly examined areas of share exchanges and deferred cash payments. Part (b) requires the preparation of a consolidated statement of profit or loss – be careful to ensure that you pro-rate the subsidiary's results to take into account that they have only been a subsidiary for eight months.

(a) Cost of control in Sardonic:

	$000
Parent holding (investment) at fair value:	
Share exchange (18,000 × $^2/_3$ × $5.75)	69,000
Deferred payment ((18,000 × 2.42) × $1/1.1^2$)	36,000
	———
	105,000
	———

Tutorial note

The acquisition of 18 million out of a total of 24 million equity shares is a 75% interest.

(b) Patronic Group

Consolidated statement of profit or loss for the year ended 31 March 20X8

	$000
Revenue (150,000 + (78,000 × $^8/_{12}$) – (1,250 × 8 months intra group))	192,000
Cost of sales (W1)	(119,100)
	———
Gross profit	72,900
Distribution costs (7,400 + (3,000 × $^8/_{12}$))	(9,400)
Administrative expenses (12,500 + (6,000 × $^8/_{12}$))	(16,500)
Finance costs (W2)	(5,000)
Impairment of goodwill	(2,000)
Share of profit from associate (6,000 × 30%)	1,800
	———
Profit before tax	41,800
Income tax expense (10,400 + (3,600 × $^8/_{12}$))	(12,800)
	———
Profit for the year	29,000
	———

Attributable to:

Equity holders of the parent (balance)	27,400
Non-controlling interest (W3)	1,600
	29,000

Workings

(W1) Cost of sales

	$000	$000
Patronic		94,000
Sardonic (51,000 × $^{8}/_{12}$)		34,000
Intra group purchases (1,250 × 8 months)		(10,000)
Additional depreciation: plant (2,400/4 years × $^{8}/_{12}$)	400	
property (per question)	200	600
Unrealised profit in inventories (3,000 × $^{20}/_{120}$)		500
		119,100

Tutorial note

For both sales revenues and cost of sales, only the post-acquisition intra-group trading should be eliminated.

(W2) Finance costs

	$000
Patronic per question	2,000
Unwinding interest – deferred consideration (36,000 × 10% × $^{8}/_{12}$)	2,400
Sardonic (900 × $^{8}/_{12}$)	600
	5,000

(W3) Non-controlling interest

Sardonic post-acquisition profit (13,500 × $^{8}/_{12}$)	9,000
Fair value depreciation (W1)	(600)
Impairment	(2,000)
Sardonic adjusted profit	6,400
Non-controlling interest at 25%	1,600

Examiner's comments

The main areas where candidates went wrong were:

In **part (a)** – cost of investment

- most candidates correctly calculated the share exchange consideration, but failed to discount (for two years) the deferred cash consideration correctly.

Part (b) – consolidated statement of profit or loss

- a surprisingly common error was not time-apportioning (for 8 months) the subsidiary's results, instead a full year's results were often included. This is a fundamental error showing a lack of understanding of the principle that a subsidiary's results are only included the consolidated accounts from date it becomes a member of the group. A small minority of candidates proportionally consolidated, rather than equity accounted, the associate (some even proportionately consolidated the subsidiary), however this error is now becoming much less common.

- many candidates did not correctly eliminate the intra-group trading, with either no adjustment at all or eliminating pre-acquisition trading as well.

- the unrealised profit in inventory was often calculated as a gross profit percentage, whereas the question stated it was a mark-up was on cost. It was also common for this adjustment to be deducted from cost of sales rather than added.

- impairment/amortisation of goodwill was often omitted.

- the finance cost relating to the unwinding of the deferred consideration was omitted by most candidates.

- the calculation of the non-controlling interest (now called non-controlling interest) was sometimes ignored or did not take account the post-acquisition additional depreciation adjustment or time apportionment.

Marking scheme		Marks
(a) Goodwill of Sardonic:		
Consideration		3
(b) Statement of profit or loss:		
Revenue		2
Cost of sales		5
Distribution costs and administrative expenses		1
Finance costs		2
Impairment of goodwill		1
Share of associate's profit		2
Income tax		1
Parent's share		1
Non-controlling interest		2
	Maximum	17
Total		20

372 PEDANTIC

(a) **Consolidated statement of profit or loss for the year ended 30 September 20X8**

	$000
Revenue (85,000 + (42,000 × $^6/_{12}$) – 8,000 intra-group sales)	98,000
Cost of sales (W2)	(72,000)
Gross profit	26,000
Distribution costs (3,100 + (3,600 × $^6/_{12}$)	(4,900)
Administration expenses (5,200 + (2,000 × $^6/_{12}$) + 1,000 impairment))	(7,200)
Profit before tax	13,900
Income tax expense (4,700 + (1,400 × $^6/_{12}$))	(5,400)
Profit for the year	8,500
Attributable to:	
Equity holders of the parent (balance)	8,700
Non-controlling interest (W3)	(200)
	8,500

(b) (i) **Goodwill**

	$000
Parent holding (investment) at fair value:	
Share exchange ((4,000 × 60%) × $^2/_3$ × $6)	9,600
NCI value at acquisition (given)	5,900
Less: Fair value of net assets at acquisition (W4)	(11,000)
	4,500
Less impairment	(1,000)
Goodwill as at 30 September 20X8	3,500

(ii) **Non-controlling interest**

	$000
NCI value at acquisition, per goodwill calculation	5,900
NCI share of adjusted Sophistic loss (500 × 40%)	(200)
	5,700

Alternative calculation:

	$000
NCI value at acquisition, per goodwill calculation	5,900
NCI share of post-acquisition reserves (W4) (500 × 40%)	200
NCI share of impairment (1,000 × 40%)	(400)
	─────
	5,700
	─────

Workings

(W1) Group structure

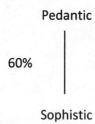

Pedantic

60%

Sophistic

Investment acquired on 1 April 20X8 so has been held for 6 months.

(W2) Cost of sales

	$000
Pedantic	63,000
Sophistic (32,000 × $^6/_{12}$)	16,000
Intra-group sales	(8,000)
PUP in inventory ($8 million − $5.2 million) × $^{40}/_{140}$	800
Additional depreciation ($2 million × $^1/_5$ × $^6/_{12}$)	200
	─────
	72,000
	─────

(W3) Non-controlling interest (SPL)

Sophistic's post acquisition profit (3,000 × $^6/_{12}$)	1,500
Fair value depreciation (W2)	(200)
PUP (W2)	(800)
Impairment	(1,000)
	─────
Sophistic adjusted loss	(500)
	─────
Non-controlling interest at 40%	(200)
	─────

(W4) Net assets of Sophistic

	Acquisition	Reporting date	Post-acquisition
	$000	$000	$000
Share capital	4,000	4,000	
Retained earnings $(6,500 – (3,000 \times {}^6/_{12}))$	5,000	6,500	1,500
Fair value adjustment:			
Plant	2,000	2,000	
Depreciation (W2)		(200)	(200)
PUP (W2)		(800)	(800)
	11,000	11,500	500

Tutorial note

Note that the calculation of the post-acquisition figure is not necessary unless using the alternative NCI calculation in part (ii).

Marking scheme		
		Marks
(a)	Statement of profit or loss:	
	Revenue	2
	Cost of sales	4
	Distribution costs	½
	Administrative expenses	1
	Income tax expense	1
	Parent's share	½
	Non-controlling interest	3
		12
(b)	(i) Goodwill	
	Share exchange	2
	NCI	½
	Net assets	2
	Impairment	½
		5
	(ii) Non-controlling interest	
	Value at acquisition	1
	Post-acquisition profit	1
	Impairment	1
		3
		20

373 PANDAR *Walk in the footsteps of a top tutor*

(a) **Carrying amount of investment in Ambra at 30 September 20X9**

	$000
Cost (40 million × 40% × $2)	32,000
Share of post-acquisition losses (5,000 × 40% × $^6/_{12}$)	(1,000)
Impairment charge	(3,000)
Unrealised profit (6,000 × 20% × ½ × 40%)	(240)
	27,760

(b) **Pandar Group**

Consolidated statement of profit or loss for the year ended 30 September 20X9

	$000	$000
Revenue (210,000 + (150,000 × $^6/_{12}$) – 15,000 intra-group sales)		270,000
Cost of sales (W1)		(162,500)
Gross profit		107,500
Distribution costs (11,200 + (7,000 × $^6/_{12}$))		(14,700)
Administrative expenses (18,300 + (9,000 × $^6/_{12}$) + 2,000 impairment)		(24,800)
Investment income (W2)		1,100
Finance costs (W3)		(2,300)
Share of loss from associate (5,000 × 40% × $^6/_{12}$)	(1,000)	
Impairment of investment in associate	(3,000)	
Unrealised profit in associate (see (a))	(240)	(4,240)
Profit before tax		62,560
Income tax expense (15,000 + (10,000 × $^6/_{12}$))		(20,000)
Profit for the year		42,560
Attributable to:		
Owners of the parent		41,160
Non-controlling interest (W4)		1,400
		42,560

Workings (figures in brackets in $000)

(W1) Cost of sales

		$000
Pandar		126,000
Salva (100,000 × $^6/_{12}$)		50,000
Intra-group purchases		(15,000)
Additional depreciation: plant (5,000/5 years × $^6/_{12}$)		500
Unrealised profit in inventories (15,000/3 × 20%)		1,000
		162,500

(W2) Investment income

		$000
Per statement of comprehensive income		9,500
Intra-group interest (50,000 × 8% × $^6/_{12}$)		(2,000)
Intra-group dividend (8,000 × 80%)		(6,400)
		1,100

(W3) Finance costs

		$000
Pandar		1,800
Salva post-acquisition (((3,000 – 2,000) × $^6/_{12}$) + 2,000)		2,500
Intra-group interest (W2)		(2,000)
		2,300

Tutorial note

The interest on the loan note is $2 million ($50 million × 8% × $^6/_{12}$). This is in Salva's profit in the post-acquisition period. Thus Salva's profit of $21 million has a split of $11.5 million pre-acquisition ((21 million + 2 million interest) × $^6/_{12}$) and $9.5 million post-acquisition.

(W4) Non-controlling interest

Salva's post-acquisition profit (see tutorial note above)	9,500
Fair value depreciation (W1)	(500)
Impairment (W1)	(2,000)
	7,000
Non-controlling interest share at 20%	1,400

Marking scheme			Marks
(a)	Carrying amount of Ambra		
	Cost		1
	Share of post-acquisition losses		1
	Unrealised profit		1
	Impairment charge		1
		Maximum	4
(b)	Statement of comprehensive income:		
	Revenue		1½
	Cost of sales		3
	Distribution costs and administrative expenses		½
	Administrative expenses		1½
	Investment income		2½
	Finance costs		1½
	Share of associate's losses and impairment charge		1½
	Income tax		1
	Non-controlling interests		3
		Maximum	16
Total			**20**

Examiner's comments

The main areas where candidates made errors were:

In **part (a)** calculation of associate:

- the calculation of the carrying amount of the associate was also very good, often gaining full marks. The main problems were not apportioning (by $^6/_{12}$) the losses in the year of acquisition and not applying the 40% group holding percentage. Some treated the losses as profits.

The consolidated statement of profit or loss (b). Again well-prepared candidates gained good marks with most understanding the general principles. The main errors were with the more complex adjustments:

- a full year's additional depreciation of the plant was charged, but it should have been only for the post-acquisition period of six months

- many candidates incorrectly amortised the domain name. Its registration was renewable indefinitely at negligible cost so it should not have been amortised

- surprisingly a number of candidates incorrectly calculated the PUP on inventory by treating the gross profit of 20% as if it were a mark-up on cost of 20%

- the elimination of intra-group dividend was often ignored or the full $8 million was eliminated instead

- often the trading and impairment losses of the associate were ignored in preparing the statement of comprehensive income

- the non-controlling interest was frequently ignored and where it was calculated, many forgot to adjust for the additional depreciation on the fair value of the plant.

Despite the above, this was the best answered question and many candidates gained good marks.

374 PICANT

Key answer tips

Part (a) required the preparation of a statement of financial position that is relatively straightforward. Ensure that you do not include the associate on a line-by-line basis and equity account instead. One of the complications in this question is the contingent consideration. The contingent consideration should be accounted for at the acquisition date regardless of its probability providing it can be reliably measured. The fair value of the consideration has then changed at the year end. Under IFRS 3 Business Combinations the change in the consideration is taken via group retained earnings and the goodwill calculation is not adjusted for.

(a) **Consolidated statement of financial position of Picant as at 31 March 20X4**

	$000	$000
Non-current assets:		
Property, plant and equipment (37,500 + 24,500 + 2,000 FV adj – 100 FV depn)		63,900
Goodwill (16,000 – 3,800 (W3))		12,200
Investment in associate (W6))		13,200
		–––––––
		89,300
Current assets		
Inventory (10,000 + 9,000 + 1,800 GIT – 600 PUP (W7)))	20,200	
Trade receivables (6,500 + 1,500 – 3,400 intra-group (W7))	4,600	24,800
	–––––	–––––––
Total assets		114,100
		–––––––

Equity and liabilities
Equity attributable to owners of the parent

Equity shares of $1 each		25,000
Share premium	19,800	
Retained earnings (W5))	27,500	47,300
		72,300
Non-controlling interest (W4))		8,400
		80,700
Total equity		
Non-current liabilities		
7% loan notes (14,500 + 2,000)		16,500
Current liabilities		
Contingent consideration	2,700	
Other current liabilities (8,300 + 7,500 – 1,600 intra-group (W7))	14,200	16,900
Total equity and liabilities		114,100

Workings (all figures in $ million)

(W1) Group structure

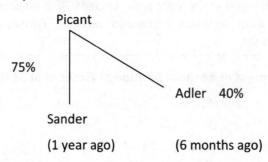

```
                    Picant
                   /      \
              75% /        \
                 /          \
                /         Adler   40%
            Sander
          (1 year ago)      (6 months ago)
```

(W2) Net assets

	Acquisition	Reporting date	Post-acq
	$000	$000	$000
Share capital	8,000	8,000	–
Retained earnings	16,500	17,500	1,000
Fair value adjustments:			
Factory	2,000	2,000	–
Fair value depreciation		(100)	(100)
Software written off	(500)		500
	26,000	27,400	1,400
	W3		W4/W5

(W3) Goodwill

Parent holding (investment) at fair value

	$000
– Share exchange (8,000 × 75% × $^3/_2$ × $3.20)	28,800
– Contingent consideration	4,200
	33,000
NCI value at acquisition (8,000 × 25% × $4.50)	9,000
	42,000
Less:	
Fair value of net assets at acquisition (W2)	(26,000)
Goodwill on acquisition	16,000
Impairment	(3,800)
	12,200

(W4) Non-controlling interest

	$000
NCI value at acquisition (W3)	9,000
NCI share of post-acquisition reserves (1,400 × 25% (W2))	350
NCI share of impairment (3,800 × 25%)	(950)
	8,400

(W5) Group retained earnings

	$000
Picant's retained earnings	27,200
Sanders post-acquisition profits (1,400 × 75% (W2))	1,050
Group share of impairment (3,800 × 75%)	(2,850)
Adler's post-acquisition profits (6,000 × $^6/_{12}$ × 40%)	1,200
PUP in inventories (1,800 × $^{50}/_{150}$)	(600)
Gain from reduction of contingent consideration (4,200 – 2,700)	1,500
	27,500

(W6) Investment in associate

	$000
Investment at cost:	
Cash consideration (5,000 × 40% × $4)	8,000
7% loan notes (5,000 × 40% × $100/$_{50}$)	4,000
	12,000
Adler's post-acquisition profits (6,000 × $^6/_{12}$ × 40%)	1,200
	13,200

(W7) Goods in transit and unrealised profit (PUP)

The intra-group current accounts differ by the goods-in-transit sales of $1.8 million on which Picant made a profit of $600,000 (1,800 × $^{50}/_{150}$). Thus inventory must be increased by $1.2 million (its cost), $600,000 is eliminated from Picant's profit, $3.4 million is deducted from trade receivables and $1.6 million (3,400 − 1,800) is deducted from trade payables (other current liabilities).

(b) An associate is defined by IAS 28 *Investments in Associates and Joint Ventures* as an investment over which an investor has significant influence. There are several indicators of significant influence, but the most important are usually considered to be a holding of 20% or more of the voting shares and board representation. Therefore it was reasonable to assume that the investment in Adler (at 31 March 20X4) represented an associate and was correctly accounted for under the equity accounting method.

The current position (from May 20X4) is that although Picant still owns 30% of Adler's shares, Adler has become a subsidiary of Spekulate as it has acquired 60% of Adler's shares. Adler is now under the control of Spekulate (part of the definition of being a subsidiary), therefore it is difficult to see how Picant can now exert significant influence over Adler. The fact that Picant has lost its seat on Adler's board seems to reinforce this point. In these circumstances the investment in Adler falls to be treated under IFRS 9 *Financial Instruments*. It will cease to be equity-accounted from the date of loss of significant influence. Its carrying amount at that date will be its initial recognition value under IFRS 9 (fair value) and thereafter it will be accounted for in accordance with IFRS 9.

375 PRODIGAL

(a) **Prodigal – Consolidated statement of profit or loss and other comprehensive income for the year ended 31 March 20X1**

	$000
Revenue (450,000 + (240,000 × $^6/_{12}$) – 40,000 intra-group sales)	530,000
Cost of sales (W1)	(278,800)
Gross profit	251,200
Distribution costs (23,600 + (12,000 × $^6/_{12}$))	(29,600)
Administrative expenses (27,000 + (23,000 × $^6/_{12}$))	(38,500)
Finance costs (1,500 + (1,200 × $^6/_{12}$))	(2,100)
Profit before tax	181,000
Income tax expense (48,000 + (27,800 × $^6/_{12}$))	(61,900)
Profit for the year	119,100
Other comprehensive income	
Gain on revaluation of land (2,500 + 1,000)	3,500
Total comprehensive income	122,600
Profit attributable to:	
Owners of the parent (balance)	111,550
Non-controlling interest (W2)	7,550
	119,100
Total comprehensive income attributable to:	
Owners of the parent (balance)	114,800
Non-controlling interest (W2)	7,800
	122,600

(b) **Prodigal – Equity section of the consolidated statement of financial position as at 31 March 20X1**

	$000
Equity attributable to owners of the parent	
Revaluation surplus (land) (W6)	11,650
Retained earnings (W5)	201,550
	———
	213,200
Non-controlling interest (W4)	107,800
	———
Total equity	321,000
	———

Workings

(W1) Cost of sales

	$000
Prodigal	260,000
Sentinel (110,000 × $^6/_{12}$)	55,000
Intra-group purchases	(40,000)
Unrealised profit on sale of plant	1,000
Depreciation adjustment on sale of plant (1,000/2½ years × $^6/_{12}$)	(200)
Unrealised profit in inventory (12,000 × 10,000/40,000)	3,000
	———
	278,800
	———

(W2) NCI (SPL)

	$000
Sentinel's post-acquisition profit (66,000 × $^6/_{12}$)	33,000
PUP – inventory (W1)	(3,000)
PUP – plant depreciation (W1)	200
	———
Sentinel's adjusted profit	30,200
	———
Non-controlling interest at 25%	7,550
	———
NCI (Total comprehensive income)	
As above	7,550
Other comprehensive income (1,000 × 25%)	250
	———
	7,800
	———

(W3) Net assets

	Acquisition	Reporting date	Post-acquisition	
	$000	$000	$000	
Retained earnings	158,000	191,000	33,000	
Revaluation surplus	–	1,000	1,000	(W6)
PUP – inventory	–	(3,000)	(3,000)	
PUP – plant depreciation	–	200	200	
	158,000	189,200	31,200	

Note: Only the post-acquisition impact on retained earnings should go to the group retained earnings. This will be the 33,000 post acquisition profits less the 3,000 PUP on inventory plus the PUP on plant depreciation. Therefore Prodigal's share of Sentinel's post-acquisition retained earnings = 75% × 30,200 = 22,650.

(W4) Non-controlling interest

	$000
NCI value at acquisition (note (iv))	100,000
NCI share of post-acquisition reserves (31,200 × 25% (W3))	7,800
	107,800

(W5) Group retained earnings

	$000
Prodigal's retained earnings (90,000 b/f + 89,900 profit for year)	179,900
Sentinel's post-acquisition profits (30,200 (W3) × 75%)	22,650
NCA PUP	(1,000)
	201,550

(W6) Revaluation surplus

	$000
Prodigal's revaluation surplus (8,400 + 2,500 gain in year)	10,900
Sentinel's post-acquisition surplus (1,000 (W3) × 75%)	750
	11,650

Alternative workings for the equity section:

Prodigal – Equity section

Equity attributable to owners of the parent	$000
Revaluation surplus (land) (8,400 + 2,500 + (1,000 × 75%))	11,650
Retained earnings (see below)	201,550
	―――――
	213,200
Non-controlling interest (see below)	107,800
	―――――
Total equity	321,000
	―――――

Retained earnings

	$000
Prodigal at 1 April 20X0	90,000
Per statement of profit or loss	111,550
	―――――
	201,550
	―――――

NCI

	$000
At acquisition	100,000
Per statement of profit or loss	7,800
	―――――
	107,800
	―――――

Marking scheme		
		Marks
(a)	**Statement of profit or loss and other comprehensive income**	
	Revenue	2
	Cost of sales	5
	Distribution costs and administrative expenses	1
	Finance costs	1
	Income tax expense	1
	Non-controlling interest in profit for year	2
	Other comprehensive income	1
	Non-controlling interest in other comprehensive income	2
		――
	Maximum	15
		――
(b)	**Consolidated equity**	
	Revaluation surplus	1½
	Retained earnings	2
	Non-controlling interest	1½
		――
	Maximum	5
		――
Total		**20**
		――

376   PALADIN

Consolidated statement of financial position of Paladin as at 30 September 20X1

	$000
Assets	
Non-current assets:	
Property, plant and equipment (40,000 + 31,000 + 4,000 FV – 1,000 FV depreciation)	74,000
Intangible assets	
– goodwill (W3)	15,000
– other intangibles (7,500 + 3,000 FV – 500 FV amortisation)	10,000
Investment in associate (W6)	7,700
	———
	106,700
Current assets (22,000 + 13,700 – 600 PUP (W7))	35,100
	———
Total assets	141,800
	———
Equity and liabilities	
Equity attributable to owners of the parent	
Equity shares of $1 each	50,000
Retained earnings (W5)	35,200
	———
	85,200
Non-controlling interest (W4)	7,900
	———
Total equity	93,100
Non-current liabilities	
Deferred tax (15,000 + 8,000)	23,000
Current liabilities (11,600 + 8,700 + 5,400 deferred consideration)	25,700
	———
Total equity and liabilities	141,800
	———

Workings

(W1) Group structure

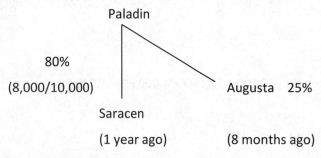

Paladin

80%
(8,000/10,000)

Augusta   25%

Saracen

(1 year ago)   (8 months ago)

(W2) Net assets

	Acquisition	Reporting date	Post-acquisition
	$000	$000	$000
Share capital	10,000	10,000	–
Retained earnings	12,000	18,000	6,000
Fair value adjustment to plant	4,000	4,000	–
Fair value depreciation (4,000/4 years)		(1,000)	(1,000)
Fair value adjustment to intangible	3,000	3,000	–
Fair value amortisation (3,000/6 years)		(500)	(500)
	29,000	33,500	4,500
	W3		W4/W5

(W3) Goodwill

	$000
Cash on acquisition	32,000
Deferred consideration (5,400 × $^{100}/_{108}$)	5,000
NCI at acquisition (2,000 shares owned × $3.50)	7,000
Less: Fair value of net assets at acquisition (W2)	(29,000)
Goodwill on acquisition	15,000

(W4) Non-controlling interest

	$000
Fair value on acquisition (W3)	7,000
Post-acquisition profits (4,500 (W2) × 20%)	900
	7,900

(W5) Group retained earnings

	$000
Paladin's retained earnings (25,700 + 9,200)	34,900
Saracen's post-acquisition profits (4,500 (W2) × 80%)	3,600
Augusta's post-acquisition profits (W6)	200
Augusta's impairment loss	(2,500)
PUP (W7)	(600)
Finance cost of deferred consideration (5,000 × 8%)	(400)
	35,200

(W6) Investment in associate

	$000
Cash consideration	10,000
Share of post-acquisition profits (1,200 × $^8/_{12}$ × 25%)	200
Impairment loss	(2,500)
	7,700

(W7) PUP

The PUP in Saracen's inventory is $600,000 (2,600 × $^{30}/_{130}$).

Marking scheme	
	Marks
Property, plant and equipment	2
Goodwill	5
Other intangibles	1½
Investment in associate	1½
Current assets	1½
Equity shares	½
Retained earnings	5
Non-controlling interest	1
Deferred tax	½
Current liabilities	1½
Total	**20**

377 PYRAMID

Pyramid – Consolidated statement of financial position as at 31 March 20X2

	$000	$000
Assets		
Non-current assets:		
Property, plant and equipment (38,100 + 28,500 + 3,000 fair value – 600 depreciation)		69,000
Goodwill (W3)		7,400
– fair value equity investments		2,800
		79,200
Current assets		
Inventory (13,900 + 10,400 + 1,500 GIT (W7) – 500 PUP (W6))	25,300	
Trade receivables (11,400 + 5,500 – 1,200 CIT – 3,200 intra group (W7))	12,500	
Bank (9,400 + 600 + 1,200 CIT (W7))	11,200	
		49,000
Total assets		128,200
Equity and liabilities		
Equity attributable to owners of the parent		
Equity shares of $1 each		25,000
Reserves:		
Share premium	17,600	
Retained earnings (W5)	35,780	
		53,380
		78,380
Non-controlling interest (W4)		8,480
Total equity		86,860
Non-current liabilities (16,500 + 4,000 + 1,000 deferred tax)		21,500
Current liabilities		
Deferred consideration (6,400 + 640 unwinding of discount (W5))	7,040	
Other current liabilities (9,500 + 5,000 + 1,500 GIT – 3,200 intra group (W7)	12,800	
		19,840
Total equity and liabilities		128,200

Workings

(W1) Group structure

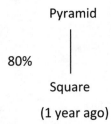

Pyramid

80%

Square

(1 year ago)

(W2) Net assets

	Acquisition	Reporting date	Post-acquisition
	$000	$000	$000
Share capital	10,000	10,000	–
Retained earnings	18,000	26,000	8,000
Fair value: plant	3,000	3,000	–
Fair value plant depreciation		(600)	(600)
Fair value: deferred tax	(1,000)	(1,000)	–
	30,000	37,400	7,400
	W3		W4/W5

(W3) Goodwill

	$000
Shares	24,000
Deferred consideration (8,000 × 88c × $^{1}/_{1.1}$)	6,400
	30,400
NCI at acquisition (2,000 shares owned × $3.50)	7,000
	37,400
Less:	
Fair value of net assets at acquisition (W2)	(30,000)
Goodwill on acquisition	7,400

(W4) Non-controlling interest

	$000
Fair value on acquisition (W3)	7,000
Post-acquisition profits (7,400 (W2) × 20%)	1,480
	8,480

(W5) Group retained earnings

	$000
Pyramid's retained earnings (16,200 + 14,000)	30,200
Square's post-acquisition profits (7,400 (W2) × 80%)	5,920
Gain on equity investments (2,800 – 2,000)	800
PUP (W7)	(500)
Finance cost of deferred consideration (6,400 × 10%)	(640)
	35,780

(W6) PUP

The PUP in inventory is $500,000 ($1.5m × $^{50}/_{150}$).

(W7) Intra-group current accounts

The goods-in-transit and cash-in-transit need to be dealt with first.

Goods in transit: Dr Inventory 1,500, Cr Payables 1,500

Cash in transit: Dr Cash 1,200, Cr Receivables 1,200

This leaves $3,200 in receivables/payables, which can now be cancelled down.

Marking scheme	
	Marks
Statement of financial position:	
Property, plant and equipment	2
Goodwill	4½
Other equity investments	1
Inventory	1½
Receivables	1½
Bank	1
Share capital and share premium	½
Retained earnings	3½
Non-controlling interest	1
Non-current liabilities	1
Deferred consideration	1
Other current liabilities	1½
Total	**20**

378 VIAGEM

(a) **Viagem consolidated goodwill on acquisition of Greca as at 1 January 20X2**

	$000	$000
Investment at cost		
Shares (10,000 × 90% × $^2/_3$ × $6.50)		39,000
Deferred consideration (9,000 × $1.76/1.1)		14,400
Non-controlling interest (10,000 × 10% × $2.50)		2,500
		_____
		55,900
Net assets (based on equity) of Greca as at 1 January 20X2		
Equity shares	10,000	
Retained earnings b/f at 1 October 20X1	35,000	
Earnings 1 October 20X1 to acquisition (6,200 × $^3/_{12}$)	1,550	
Fair value adjustments: plant	1,800	
contingent liability recognised	(450)	
	_____	
Net assets at date of acquisition		(47,900)
		_____
Consolidated goodwill		8,000
		_____

(b) **Viagem Consolidated statement of profit or loss for year ended 30 September 20X2**

	$000
Revenue (64,600 + (38,000 × $^9/_{12}$) – 7,200 intra-group sales)	85,900
Cost of sales (W1)	(64,250)
	_____
Gross profit	21,650
Distribution costs (1,600 + (1,800 × $^9/_{12}$))	(2,950)
Administrative expenses (3,800 + (2,400 × $^9/_{12}$) + 2,000 goodwill impairment)	(7,600)
Income from associate (2,000 × 40% based on underlying earnings)	800
Finance costs (420 + (14,400 × 10% × $^9/_{12}$ re deferred consideration))	(1,500)
	_____
Profit before tax	10,400
Income tax expense (2,800 + (1,600 × $^9/_{12}$))	(4,000)
	_____
Profit for the year	6,400
	_____
Profit for year attributable to:	
Equity holders of the parent (balance)	6,180
Non-controlling interest (W2)	220
	_____
	6,400
	_____

Workings

(W1) Cost of sales

	$000
Viagem	51,200
Greca (26,000 × $^9/_{12}$)	19,500
Intra-group purchases (800 × 9 months)	(7,200)
PUP in inventory (1,500 × $^{25}/_{125}$)	300
Additional depreciation (1,800/3 years × $^9/_{12}$)	450
	_____
	64,250
	_____

(W2) NCI

	$000
Greca post-acquisition profit (6,200 × $^9/_{12}$)	4,650
Fair value depreciation	(450)
Impairment	(2,000)
	_____
Greca adjusted profit	2,200
	_____
Non-controlling interest at 10%	220
	_____

Marking scheme			
			Marks
(a)	Consolidated goodwill:		
	Consideration	– share exchange	1½
		– deferred	1½
		– NCI	1
	Net assets	– equity	½
		– retained at acquisition	1
		– fair value adjustments	1½
			___
		Maximum	7
(b)	Consolidated statement of profit or loss		
	Revenue		1½
	Cost of sales		3½
	Distribution costs		½
	Administrative expenses		1½
	Income from associate		1½
	Finance costs		2
	Income tax		½
	NCI		2
			___
		Maximum	13
			___
Total			**20**
			___

379 PARADIGM

(a) **Paradigm – Consolidated statement of financial position as at 31 March 20X3**

	$000	$000
Assets		
Non-current assets:		
Property, plant and equipment (47,400 + 25,500 – 3,000 fair value + 500 depreciation)		70,400
Goodwill (W3)		8,500
Financial asset: equity investments (7,100 + 3,900)		11,000
		89,900
Current assets		
Inventory (20,400 + 8,400 – 600 PUP (W6))	28,200	
Trade receivables (14,800 + 9,000)	23,800	
Bank	2,100	
		54,100
Total assets		144,000
Equity and liabilities		
Equity attributable to owners of the parent		
Equity shares of $1 each (40,000 + 6,000 (W3))		46,000
Share premium (W3)		6,000
Retained earnings (W5)		33,925
Non-controlling interest (W4)		8,800
Total equity		94,725
10% loan notes (8,000 + 1,500 (W3))		9,500
Current liabilities		
Trade payables (17,600 + 13,000 + 75 interest (W7))	30,675	
Bank overdraft	9,100	
		39,775
Total equity and liabilities		144,000

Workings

(W1) Group structure

Paradigm

75%

Strata
(6 months)

(W2) Net assets

	At acquisition	At reporting date	Post-acquisition
	$000	$000	$000
Share capital	20,000	20,000	–
Retained earnings	(6,000)	4,000	10,000
Fair value adjustment	(3,000)	(3,000)	–
Fair value depreciation $(3,000 \times {}^6/_{36})$		500	500
Gain on equity investment		700	700
	11,000	22,200	11,200

(W3) Goodwill

	$000
Share exchange $((20,000 \times 75\%) \times {}^2/_5 \times \$2)$	12,000
10% loan notes $(15,000 \times {}^{\$100}/_{1,000})$	1,500
Non-controlling interest $(20,000 \times 25\% \times \$1.20)$	6,000
Less: Fair value of net assets at acquisition (W2)	(11,000)
Goodwill on acquisition	8,500

The market value of the shares issued of $12 million would be recorded as $6 million share capital and $6 million share premium as the shares have a nominal value of $1 each and an issue value of $2 each.

(W4) Non-controlling interest

	$000
Fair value on acquisition (W3)	6,000
Post-acquisition profits (11,200 (W2) × 25%)	2,800
	8,800

(W5) Group retained earnings

	$000
Paradigm's retained earnings (19,200 + 7,400)	26,600
Strata's post-acquisition profit (11,200 (W2) × 75%)	8,400
PUP in inventory (W6)	(600)
Loss on equity investments (7,500 – 7,100)	(400)
Interest on unrecorded loan notes (W7)	(75)
	33,925

(W6) PUP

Strata's inventory (from Paradigm) at 31 March 20X3 is $4.6 million (one month's supply). At a mark-up on cost of 15%, there would be $600,000 of profit $(4,600 \times {}^{15}/_{115})$ in the inventory.

(W7) Interest

Paradigm must accrue for the interest on the loan notes issued to Strata's previous owners. This is $1,500 \times 10\% \times {}^{6}/_{12} = 75$.

(b) IFRS 3 *Business Combinations* requires the purchase consideration for an acquired entity to be allocated to the fair value of the assets, liabilities and contingent liabilities acquired (henceforth referred to as net assets) with any residue being allocated to goodwill. This also means that those net assets will be recorded at fair value in the consolidated statement of financial position. This is entirely consistent with the way other net assets are recorded when first transacted (i.e. the initial cost of an asset is normally its fair value). This ensures that individual assets and liabilities are correctly valued in the consolidated statement of financial position. Whilst this may sound obvious, consider what would happen if say a property had a carrying amount of $5 million, but a fair value of $7 million at the date it was acquired. If the carrying amount rather than the fair value was used in the consolidation it would mean that tangible assets (property, plant and equipment) would be understated by $2 million and intangible assets (goodwill) would be overstated by the same amount.

There could also be a 'knock-on' effect with incorrect depreciation charges in the years following an acquisition and incorrect calculation of any goodwill impairment. Thus the use of carrying amounts rather than fair values would not give a 'faithful representation' as required by the Framework.

The assistant's comment regarding the inconsistency of value models in the consolidated statement of financial position is a fair point, but it is really a deficiency of the historical cost concept rather than a flawed consolidation technique. Indeed the fair value of the subsidiary's net assets represent the historical cost to the parent. To overcome much of the inconsistency, there would be nothing to prevent the parent from applying the revaluation model to its property, plant and equipment.

Marking scheme		
		Marks
(a)	Property, plant and equipment	1½
	Goodwill	3½
	Equity investments	1
	Inventory	½
	Receivables	½
	Bank	½
	Equity shares	1
	Share premium	½
	Retained earnings	2½
	Non-controlling interest	1½
	10% loan notes	1
	Trade payables	½
	Bank overdraft	½
(b)	One mark per point made	5
Total		**20**

380 POLESTAR

(a)   **Consolidated statement of profit or loss for the year ended 30 September 20X3**

	$000
Revenue (110,000 + (66,000 × $^6/_{12}$) – (4,000 + 9,000 intra-group sales))	130,000
Cost of sales (W6)	(109,300)
Gross profit	20,700
Operating expenses (8,500 + (4,400 × $^6/_{12}$) – 3,400 negative goodwill (W3)	(7,300)
Decrease in contingent consideration (1,800 – 1,500)	300
Profit before tax	13,700
Income tax expense (3,500 – (1,000 × $^6/_{12}$))	(3,000)
Profit for the year	10,700
Profit for year attributable to:	
Equity holders of the parent	11,450
Non-controlling interest losses (W7)	(750)
	10,700

(b)   **Consolidated statement of financial position as at 30 September 20X3**

	$000
Assets	
Non-current assets	
Property, plant and equipment (41,000 + 21,000 + 2,000 FV – 100 dep'n)	63,900
Investments (13,500 – (13,500 cash consideration))	–
	63,900
Current assets (19,000 + 4,800 – 600 PUP)	23,200
Total assets	87,100

Equity attributable to owners of the parent

Equity shares of 50 cents each	30,000
Retained earnings (W5)	29,950
	59,950
Non-controlling interest (W4)	2,850
Total equity	62,800
Current liabilities	
Contingent consideration	1,500
Other (15,000 + 7,800)	22,800
Total equity and liabilities	87,100

Workings

(W1) Group structure

Polestar

75%

Southstar

(6 months)

(W2) Net assets

	At acquisition	At reporting date	Post-acquisition
	$000	$000	$000
Share capital	6,000	6,000	–
Retained earnings	14,300	12,000	(2,300)
Fair value adjustment	2,000	2,000	–
Fair value depreciation (2,000/10 years × $^6/_{12}$)		(100)	(100)
PUP (W6)		(600)	(600)
	22,300	19,300	(3,000)
	W3		W4/W5

(W3) Goodwill

	$000
Cash consideration (6,000/0.5 × 75% × $1.50)	13,500
Contingent consideration	1,800
Non-controlling interest	3,600
	18,900
Fair value of net assets at acquisition (W2)	(22,300)
Gain on bargain purchase	(3,400)

(W4) Non-controlling interest

	$000
Fair value on acquisition (W3)	3,600
Post-acquisition losses ((3,000) (W2) × 25%)	(750)
	2,850

(W5) Group retained earnings

	$000
Polestar's retained earnings	28,500
Southstar's post-acquisition losses((3,000) (W2) × 75%)	(2,250)
Change in contingent consideration	300
Gain on bargain purchase (W3)	3,400
	29,950

(W6) Cost of sales

	$000
Polestar	88,000
Southstar (67,200 × 6/12)	33,600
Intra-group purchases (4,000 + 9,000)	(13,000)
PUP in inventory (see below)	600
Additional depreciation on leased property (W2)	100
	109,300

The profit on the sale of the goods back to Polestar is $3.6 million (9,000 − (4,000 + 1,400)). Therefore the unrealised profit in the inventory of $1.5 million at 30 September 20X3 is $600,000 (3,600 × $^{1,500}/_{9,000}$).

(W7) NCI (SPL)

	$000
Southstar post-acquisition loss $((4,600) \times {}^6/_{12})$	(2,300)
PUP (W6)	(600)
Fair value depreciation (W2)	(100)
Southstar adjusted profit	(3,000)
Non-controlling interest at 25%	(750)

Note: IFRS 3 *Business Combinations* says negative goodwill should be credited to the acquirer, thus none of it relates to the non-controlling interests.

Marking scheme		
		Marks
(a)	Consolidated statement of profit or loss	
	Revenue	1½
	Cost of sales	3
	Operating expenses – other than negative goodwill	½
	– negative goodwill finance costs	3½
	Decrease in contingent consideration	½
	Income tax expense	½
	Non-controlling interest	1½
	Maximum	11
(b)	Consolidated statement of financial position	
	Property, plant and equipment	1½
	Current assets	1½
	Equity shares	½
	Retained earnings	3
	Non-controlling interest	1
	Contingent consideration	1
	Other current liabilities	½
	Maximum	9
Total		**20**

381 PENKETH

(a) Goodwill

	$000
Deferred consideration $(1.54 \times 90,000 \times {}^1/_{1.1})$	126,000
Non-controlling interest $(1.25 \times 60,000)$	75,000
Less: Fair value of net assets at acquisition (W1)	(196,000)
Goodwill on acquisition	5,000

(b) Penketh – Consolidated statement of profit or loss and other comprehensive income for the year ended 31 March 20X4

	$000
Revenue $(620,000 + (310,000 \times {}^6/_{12}) - 20,000$ intra-group sales)	755,000
Cost of sales (W2)	(457,300)
Gross profit	297,700
Distribution costs $(40,000 + (20,000 \times {}^6/_{12}))$	(50,000)
Administrative expenses $(36,000 + (25,000 \times {}^6/_{12}) + (5,000/5 \times {}^6/_{12}$ re customer list))	(49,000)
Investment income $(5,000 + (1,600 \times {}^6/_{12}))$	5,800
Finance costs $(2,000 + (5,600 \times 6/12) + (126,000 \times 10\% \times {}^6/_{12}$ re deferred consideration))	(11,100)
Profit before tax	193,400
Income tax expense $(45,000 + (31,000 \times {}^6/_{12}))$	(60,500)
Profit for the year	132,900
Other comprehensive income	
Loss on revaluation of land $(2,200 - 1,000$ gain for Sphere)	(1,200)
Total comprehensive income for the year	131,700

Profit attributable to:	
Owners of the parent (balance)	117,700
Non-controlling interest (W2)	15,200
	132,900

Total comprehensive income attributable to:	
Owners of the parent (balance)	116,100
Non-controlling interest (W3)	15,600
	131,700

Workings

(W1) Net assets of Sphere at acquisition

	$000
Share capital	75,000
Retained earnings (70,000 b/f + 40,000 pre-acquisition)	110,000
Fair value adjustment – plant	6,000
Fair value adjustment – customer relationships	5,000
	196,000

(W2) Cost of sales

	$000
Penketh	400,000
Sphere (150,000 × $^6/_{12}$)	75,000
Intra-group purchases	(20,000)
Additional depreciation of plant (6,000/2 years × $^6/_{12}$)	1,500
Unrealised profit in inventory (20,000 × $^1/_5$ × $^{25}/_{125}$)	800
	457,300

(W3) Non-controlling interest in profit for the year

	$000
Sphere's profit (80,000 × $^6/_{12}$)	40,000
Fair value depreciation – plant	(1,500)
Fair value amortisation – customer list	(500)
Sphere adjusted profit	38,000
Non-controlling interest at 40%	15,200

Non-controlling interest in total comprehensive income

	$000
Non-controlling interest in statement of profit or loss (above)	15,200
Other comprehensive income (1,000 × 40%)	400
	15,600

Marking scheme		Marks
(a)	Goodwill	
	Consideration paid	1
	NCI at acquisition	1
	Net assets at acquisition (½ share capital, 1½ RE, 1 FV adjustments)	3
(b)	Consolidated statement of profit or loss and other comprehensive income	
	Revenue	2
	Cost of sales	3
	Distribution costs	½
	Administrative expenses	1½
	Investment income	1
	Finance costs	1½
	Income tax expense	1
	Other comprehensive income	1½
	Non-controlling interest in profit for year	2
	Non-controlling interest in other comprehensive income	1
Total		20

382 PLASTIK

(a) **Plastik – Extracts from consolidated statement of profit or loss for the year ended 30 September 20X4**

		$000
(i)	Revenue $(62,600 + (30,000 \times {}^9/_{12}) - (300 \times 9$ months intra-group sales))	82,400
(ii)	Cost of sales $(45,800 + (24,000 \times {}^9/_{12}) - 2,700$ intra-group sales $+ 120$ PUP (W7) $+ 100$ FV dep'n)	(61,320)
(iii)	Finance costs $(200 + 135$ (W5))	(335)

(b) **Plastik – Consolidated statement of financial position as at 30 September 20X4**

Assets

Non-current assets	$000
Property, plant and equipment $(18,700 + 13,900 + 4,000$ FV $- 100$ FV dep'n $+ 600$ revaluation)	37,100
Intangible asset: goodwill (W3)	5,700
	42,800
Current assets	
$(9,000 + 4,000 - 120$ (W5) $- 400$ cash in transit $- 800$ intra-group)	11,680
Total assets	54,480

Equity and liabilities

Equity shares of $1 each (10, 000 + 4,800)	14,800
Other component of equity (share premium)	9,600
Revaluation surplus (2,000 + (600 × 80%))	2,480
Retained earnings (W5)	7,165
Non-controlling interest (W4)	4,900

Total equity	38,945

Non-current liabilities

10% loan notes (2,500 + 1,000 – 1,000 intra-group)	2,500

Current liabilities

Trade payables (7,900 + 4,400 – 400 cash in transit – 800 intra-group)	11,100
Deferred consideration (1,800 + 135 (W5))	1,935

	13,035

Total equity and liabilities	54,480

Workings (note figure in brackets are in $000)

(W1) Group structure

Plastik

80% – owned for 9 months

Subtrak

(W2) Net assets

	Acquisition	Reporting date	Post-acquisition
	$000	$000	$000
Share capital	9,000	9,000	–
Retained earnings	2,000	3,500	1,500
Fair value – property	4,000	4,000	–
Fair value depreciation		(100)	(100)
	15,000	16,400	1,400
	W3		W4/W5

(W3) Goodwill

	$000
Shares (9,000 × 80% × $^2/_3$ × $3)	14,400
Deferred consideration (9,000 × 80% × $0.275 × $^1/_{1.1}$)	1,800
Non-controlling interest (9,000 × 20% × $2.50)	4,500
Less: Fair value of net assets at acquisition (W2)	(15,000)
	———
Goodwill on acquisition	5,700
	———

The 4.8 million shares issued by Plastik represents share capital of $4.8 million (4,800 × $1) and share premium of $9.6 million (4,800 × $2).

(W4) Non-controlling interest (SFP)

	$000
At date of acquisition (W3)	4,500
NCI % × S post acquisition (20% × 1,400 (W2))	280
NCI % × S post acquisition revaluation (20% × 600)	120
	———
	4,900
	———

(W5) Group retained earnings

	$000
Plastik's retained earnings	6,300
Subtrak's post-acquisition (1,400 (W2) × 80%)	1,120
Unwinding discount on deferred consideration (1,800 × 10% × $^9/_{12}$)	(135)
PUP 600 x $^{25}/_{125}$	(120)
	———
	7,165
	———

Marking scheme		
		Marks
(a)	Consolidated statement of profit or loss and other comprehensive income:	
	Revenue	1½
	Cost of sales	2½
	Finance costs	1
		___
	Maximum	5
		___
(b)	Consolidated statement of financial position:	
	Property, plant and equipment	2
	Goodwill	2
	Current assets	2
	Equity shares	1
	Other component of equity (share premium)	1
	Revaluation surplus	1
	Retained earnings	1½
	Non-controlling interest	1
	10% loan notes	1
	Current liabilities	1½
	Deferred consideration	1
		___
	Maximum	15
		___
Total		**20**
		___

383 BYCOMB

(a) **Bycomb: Goodwill on acquisition of Cyclip as at 1 July 20X4**

	$000
Investment at cost:	
Shares ($12,000 \times 80\% \times {}^2/_3 \times \$3.00$)	19,200
Deferred consideration ($12,000 \times 80\% \times {}^{\$1.54}/_{1.1}$)	13,440
Non-controlling interest ($12,000 \times 20\% \times \$2.50$)	6,000
	———
	38,640
Net assets at date of acquisition (W1)	(26,845)
	———
Consolidated goodwill	11,795
	———

(b) **Extracts from Bycomb consolidated statement of profit or loss for the year ended 31 March 20X5**

		$000
(i)	Revenue ($24,200 + (10,800 \times {}^9/_{12}) - 3,000$ intra-group sales)	29,300
(ii)	Cost of sales (W2)	(20,830)
(iii)	Finance costs (W3)	(1,558)
(iv)	Profit for year attributable to non-controlling interest ($1,015 \times 20\%$ (W4)) or see (W5)	203

(c) IFRS 3 *Business Combinations* allows as an option a non-controlling interest to be valued at its proportionate share of the acquired subsidiary's identifiable net assets. This carries forward the only allowed method in the previous version of this Standard. Its effect on the statement of financial position is that the resulting carrying amount of purchased goodwill only relates to the parent's element of such goodwill and as a consequence the non-controlling interest does not reflect its share of the subsidiary's goodwill. Some commentators feel this is an anomaly as the principle of a consolidated statement of financial position is that it should disclose the whole of the subsidiary's assets that are under the control of the parent rather than just the parent's share. This principle is applied to all of a subsidiary's other identifiable assets, so it seems logical to extend that treatment to goodwill.

Any impairment of goodwill under this method would only be charged against the parent's interest, as the non-controlling interest's share of goodwill is not included in the consolidated financial statements.

The second, more recent, method of valuing the non-controlling interest at its fair value would normally increase the value of the goodwill calculated on acquisition. This increase reflects the non-controlling interest's ownership of the subsidiary's goodwill and has the effect of 'grossing up' the goodwill and the non-controlling interests in the statement of financial position by the same amount. It is argued that this method reflects the whole of the subsidiary's goodwill/premium on acquisition and is thus consistent with the principles of consolidation.

Under this method any impairment of the subsidiary's goodwill is charged against both the parent and non-controlling interest in proportion to their shareholding in the subsidiary.

Workings

(W1) Net assets of Cyclip at acquisition

	$000
Share capital	12,000
Retained earnings 1 April 20X4	13,500
Earnings 1 April 20X4 to acquisition:	
$((2,400 + 100) \times {}^3/_{12})$ – see note below	625
Fair value adjustment – plant	720
	26,845

Note: The profit for the year for Cyclip would be increased by $100,000 due to interest capitalised, in accordance with IAS 23 *Borrowing Costs*.

Alternatively, the profit for the year could have been calculated as:

$(2,400 \times {}^3/_{12}) + 25$. As the interest to be capitalised has accrued evenly throughout the year, $25,000 would relate to pre-acquisition profits and $75,000 to post-acquisition profits.

(W2) Cost of sales

Bycomb	17,800
Cyclip (6,800 × $^9/_{12}$)	5,100
Intra-group purchases	(3,000)
URP in inventory (420 × 20/120)	70
Impairment of goodwill per question	500
Additional depreciation of plant (720 × $^9/_{18}$ months)	360
	20,830

(W3) Finance costs

Bycomb per question	400
Unwinding of deferred consideration (13,440 × 10% × $^9/_{12}$)	1,008
Cyclip ((300 – 100 see below) × $^9/_{12}$)	150
	1,558

The interest capitalised in accordance with IAS 23 *Borrowing Costs* of $100,000 would reduce the finance costs of Cyclip for consolidation purposes.

(W4) Post-acquisition profit of Cyclip

Profit plus interest capitalised and time apportioned ((2,400 + 100) × $^9/_{12}$) – see note in (W1)	1,875
Impairment of goodwill (per question)	(500)
Additional depreciation of plant (W2)	(360)
	1,015

(W5) Alternative working for non-controlling interest share of profit

NCI share of profit ((2,400 + 100) × $^9/_{12}$ × 20%)	375
NCI share of impairment (500 × 20%)	(100)
NCI share of FV depreciation of plant (360 × 20%)	(72)
	203

Marking scheme			Marks
(a)		Goodwill at acquisition	6
(b)	(i)	Revenue	1
	(ii)	Cost of sales	3
	(iii)	Finance costs	2½
	(iv)	Profit or loss attributable to non-controlling interests.	2½
			9
(c)		One mark per point made	5
Total			**20**

384 PALISTAR

Palistar – Consolidated statement of financial position as at 30 June 20X5

	$000
Assets	
Non-current assets:	
Property, plant and equipment (55,000 + 28,600)	83,600
Goodwill (W3)	3,000
Game rights (12,000 – 1,200 (W2))	10,800
Financial asset equity investments (13,200 + 7,900)	21,100
	118,500
Current assets	
Inventory (17,000 + 15,400 + 800 GIT – 600 (W6))	32,600
Trade receivables (14,300 + 10,500 – 2,400 intra-group)	22,400
Bank (2,200 + 1,600)	3,800
	58,800
Total assets	177,300
Equity and liabilities	
Equity attributable to owners of the parent	
Equity shares of $1 each (20,000 + 6,000 (W3))	26,000
Other components of equity (share premium) (4,000 + 18,000 (W3))	22,000
Retained earnings (W5)	52,425
	100,425
Non-controlling interest (W4)	15,675
Total equity	116,100
Current liabilities	
Deferred consideration (18,000 + 900 finance cost (W5))	18,900
Other current liabilities (25,800 + 18,100 – (2,400 intra-group – 800 GIT))	42,300
	61,200
Total equity and liabilities	177,300

Workings

(W1) Group structure

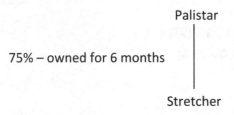

Palistar

75% – owned for 6 months

Stretcher

(W2) Net assets

	Acquisition	Reporting date	Post-acquisition
	$000	$000	$000
Share capital	20,000	20,000	–
Retained earnings (see below)	18,000	24,000	6,000
Fair value: game rights	12,000	12,000	–
Amortisation $\times \frac{1}{5} \times \frac{6}{12}$		(1,200)	(1,200)
Fair value investments	1,000	1,900	900
	51,000	56,700	5,700
	W3		W4/W5

Stretcher makes 60% of its profit in the period from 1 June. Therefore the post-acquisition retained earnings is $6 million (60% × $10 million), making the retained earnings at acquisition $18 million ($24 million less $6 million).

(W3) Goodwill in Stretcher

	$000
Share exchange (20,000 × 75% × $\frac{2}{5}$) = (6,000 × $4)	24,000
Deferred consideration (20,000 × 75% × $^{\$1.32}/_{1.1}$)	18,000
Non-controlling interest (20,000 × 25% × $3)	15,000
	57,000
Net assets at acquisition	(51,000)
Goodwill on acquisition	6,000
Impairment	(3,000)
Goodwill at 30 June 20X5	3,000

The shares issued by Palistar (6 million at $4 – see above) would be recorded as share capital of $6 million (6,000 × $1) and share premium in other components of equity of $18 million (6,000 × $3).

(W4) Non-controlling interest

	$000
Fair value on acquisition (W3)	15,000
Post-acquisition profit (5,700 × 25% (W2))	1,425
NCI share of impairment (3,000 × 25%)	(750)
	15,675

(W5) Consolidated retained earnings:

	$000
Palistar's retained earnings (26,200 + 24,000)	50,200
Stretcher's adjusted post-acquisition profit (5,700 (W2) × 75%)	4,275
Palistar's share of impairment (3,000 × 75%)	(2,250)
Finance cost on deferred consideration (18,000 × 10% × $^6/_{12}$)	(900)
URP in inventory (W6)	(600)
Gain on equity investments (13,200 – 11,500)	1,700
	52,425

(W6) Provision for unrealised profit (PUP)

The inventory of Stretcher at 30 June 20X5 (adjusted for goods-in-transit (GIT) sale of $800,000) is $2.6 million (1,800 + 800). The unrealised profit on this will be $600,000 ($2.6m × $^{30}/_{130}$).

Marking scheme	Marks
Consolidated statement of financial position:	
Property, plant and equipment	½
Goodwill	5
Game rights	1
Financial asset investments	1
Inventory	2
Receivables	1
Bank	½
Equity shares	1
Other component of equity	1
Retained earnings	4
Non-controlling interest	1
Deferred consideration	1
Other current liabilities	1
Total	**20**

385 LAUREL

(a) Laurel: Consolidated goodwill on acquisition of Rakewood

	$000	$000
Investment at cost		
Shares (15,000 × 60% × $^3/_5$ × $7.00)		37,800
Deferred consideration (9,000 × $1.62/1.08)		13,500
Non-controlling interest (15,000 × 40% × $2.00)		12,000
		63,300
Net assets (based on equity) of Rakewood as at 1 January 20X6		
Equity shares	15,000	
Retained earnings at 1 October 20X5	25,000	
Earnings 1 October 20X5 to acquisition (10,400 × $^3/_{12}$)	2,600	
Fair value adjustments:		
plant	4,000	
inventory	200	
Net assets at date of acquisition		(46,800)
Consolidated goodwill		16,500

(b) Laurel consolidated statement of profit or loss for the year ended 30 September 20X6

	$000
Revenue (84,500 + (52,000 × $^9/_{12}$) – (1,200 × 9 months) intra-group sales)	112,700
Cost of sales (see working below)	(74,900)
Gross profit	37,800
Distribution costs (2,000 + (1,600 × $^9/_{12}$))	(3,200)
Administrative expenses (4,100 + (2,800 × $^9/_{12}$))	(6,200)
Investment income (400 × $^9/_{12}$)	300
Income from associate (2,400 × 25% based on underlying earnings)	600
Finance costs (300 + (13,500 × 8% × $^9/_{12}$ re deferred consideration))	(1,110)
Profit before tax	28,190
Income tax expense (4,800 + (3,600 × $^9/_{12}$))	(7,500)
Profit for the year	20,690
Profit for year attributable to:	
Equity holders of the parent	18,370
Non-controlling interest	
((10,400 × $^9/_{12}$) – 200 re inventory – 1,500 depreciation – 300 PUP) × 40%))	
	2,320
	20,690

Working

Cost of sales

	$000
Laurel	58,200
Rakewood (34,000 × $^9/_{12}$)	25,500
Intra-group purchases (1,200 × 9 months)	(10,800)
Fair value inventory adjustment	200
PUP in inventory at 30 September 20X6 (1,800 × $^{20}/_{120}$)	300
Additional depreciation (4,000/2 years × $^9/_{12}$)	1,500
	74,900

ACCA Marking scheme			
			Marks
(a)	Consolidated goodwill:		
	Consideration – share exchange		1
	– deferred consideration		1
	– NCI		1
	Net assets – equity shares		½
	– retained earnings at acquisition		1½
	– fair value adjustments		2
			7
(b)	Consolidated statement of profit or loss:		
	Revenue		1½
	Cost of sales		4½
	Distribution costs		½
	Administrative expenses		½
	Investment income		1½
	Finance costs		1½
	Income tax expense		1
	NCI		2
			13
Total			**20**

386 DARGENT CO

Consolidated statement of financial position as at 31 March 20X6

Assets	$000	$000
Non-current assets:		
Property, plant and equipment (75,200 + 31,500 + 4,000 mine – 200 dep)		110,500
Goodwill (W3)		11,000
Investment in associate (4,500 + 1,200 (W5))		5,700
		127,200
Current assets		
Inventory (19,400 + 18,800 + 700 GIT – 800 PUP (W6))	38,100	
Trade receivables (14,700 + 12,500 – 3,000 intra group)	24,200	
Bank (1,200 + 600)	1,800	
		64,100
Total assets		191,300
Equity and liabilities		
Equity shares of $1 each (50,000 + 10,000 (W3))		60,000
Other equity reserves (share premium) (W3)		22,000
Retained earnings (W5)		37,390
		119,390
Non-controlling interest (W4)		9,430
Total equity		128,820
Non-current liabilities		
8% loan notes (5,000 + 15,000 consideration (W3))	20,000	
Accrued loan interest (W5)	300	
Environmental provision (4,000 + 80 interest (W2))	4,080	
		24,380
Current liabilities (24,000 + 16,400 + 700 GIT – 3,000 intra group)		38,100
Total equity and liabilities		191,300

Workings (figures in brackets are in $000)

(W1) Group structure

Dargent

75%

Latree

(1 Jan 20X6)

(W2) Net assets of Latree Co

	Acquisition	Reporting date	Post-acquisition
	$000	$000	$000
Equity shares	20,000	20,000	
Retained earnings at 1 April 20X5	19,000	19,000	
Earnings 1 April to acquisition (8,000 × 9/12)	6,000	8,000	2,000
Fair value adjustment: Mine asset	4,000	4,000	
Mine depreciation (4,000 × 1/5 × 3/12)		(200)	(200)
Mine provision	(4,000)	(4,000)	
Interest on provision (4,000 × 8% × 3/12)		(80)	(80)
	45,000	46,720	1,720

Applying the group policy to the environmental provision would mean adding $4 million to the carrying amount of the mine and the same amount recorded as a provision at the date of acquisition. This has no overall effect on the net assets at acquisition, but it does affect the consolidated statement of financial position and post-acquisition profit.

(W3) Goodwill in Latree Co

	$000
Controlling interest	
Share exchange (20,000 × 75% × 2/3 × $3.20)	32,000
8% loan notes (20,000 × 75% × $100/100)	15,000
Non-controlling interest (20,000 × 25% × $1.80)	9,000
	56,000
Net assets at acquisition (W2)	(45,000)
	11,000

The share exchange of $32 million would be recorded as share capital of $10 million (10,000 × $1) and share premium of $22 million (10,000 × ($320 – $1)).

(W4) Non-controlling interest

		$000
Value at acquisition (W3)		9,000
Post-acquisition profit (1,720 (W2) × 25%)		430
		9,430

(W5) Retained earnings

	$000
Dargent Co retained earnings	36,000
Latree Co post-acquisition profit (1,720 (W2) × 75%)	1,290
Amery unrecorded share of profit ((6,000 – 2,000) × 30%)	1,200
Unpaid loan interest (15,000 (W3) × 8% × 3/12)	(300)
PUP (W6)	(800)
	37,390

(W6) Provision for Unrealised Profit (PUP)

	$000
Inventory held by Latree	2,100
Goods in transit	700
Total intra-group inventory held	2,800
Profit included (2,800 × 40/140)	800

ACCA Marking scheme	
	Marks
Property, plant and equipment	2
Goodwill: consideration	2½
Goodwill: fair value net assets	2
Investments in associate	1
Inventory	1½
Receivables	1
Bank	½
Equity shares and share premium	1
Retained earnings: post-acquisition sub	2
Retained earnings: other	2
Non-controlling interests	1½
8% loan notes	½
Environmental provision	1½
Current liabilities	1
Total	**20**

387   PARTY CO

(a)   **Consolidated statement of financial position for Party Co as at 30 September 20X5**

		$000
Assets		
Non-current assets:		
Property, plant and equipment	(392,000 + 84,000)	476,000
Investments	(120,000 – 92,000 –– 28,000)	0
Goodwill		32,396
		508,396
Current assets:	(94,700 + 44,650 + 60 FV – 250 PUP)	139,160
Total assets		647,556
Equity and liabilities		
Equity:		
Share capital		190,000
Retained earnings	(W5)	209,398
Revaluation surplus		41,400
		440,798
Non-controlling interest	(W4)	15,392
		15,392
Total equity		456,190
Non-current liabilities:		
Deferred consideration	(23,996 + 1,920)	25,916
Current liabilities:	(137,300 + 28,150)	165,450
Total equity and liabilities		647,556

Working 1 – Group structure

Party Co owns 80% of Streamer Co.

Party Co has owned Streamer Co for one year.

Working 2 – Net assets

	Acquisition	SOFP date	Post acq
	$000	$000	$000
Share capital	60,000	60,000	0
Retained earnings	34,000	36,500	2,500
Revaluation surplus	4,000	4,000	0
Fair value adj inventory	600	60	(540)
	98,600	100,560	1,960

Working 3 – Goodwill

	$000
Cash	92,000
Deferred cash (28m × 0.857)	23,996
NCI at acquisition	15,000
Less: Net assets at acquisition	(98,600)
Goodwill at acquisition	32,396

Working 4 – Non-controlling interest

	$000
NCI at acquisition	15,000
NCI % of Streamer post acquisition (1,960 × 20%)	392
	15,392

Working 5 – Retained earnings

	$000
Party Co	210,000
P's % of Streamer post acquisition RE (1,960 × 80%)	1,568
Unwinding discount on deferred consideration (23,996 × 8%)	(1,920)
Unrealised profit (1,000 × 25%)	(250)
	209,398

(b) The consolidated financial statements of the Party Group are of little value when trying to assess the performance and financial position of its subsidiary, Streamer Co. Therefore the main source of information on which to base any investment decision would be Streamer Co's individual financial statements. However, where a company is part of a group, there is the potential for the financial statements (of a subsidiary) to have been subject to the influence of related party transactions. In the case of Streamer Co, there has been a considerable amount of post-acquisition trading with Party Co and, because of the related party relationship, there is the possibility that this trading is not at arm's length (i.e. not at commercial rates). Indeed from the information in the question, Party Co sells goods to Streamer Co at a much lower margin than it does to other third parties. This gives Streamer Co a benefit which is likely to lead to higher profits (compared to what they would have been if it had paid the market value for the goods purchased from Party Co). Had the sales of $8m been priced at Party Co's normal prices, they would have been sold to Streamer Co for $10.9 million (at a margin of 25% these goods cost $6m; if sold at a normal margin of 45% they would have been sold at $6m/55% × 100). This gives Streamer Co a trading 'advantage' of $4.9 million ($10.9 million – $6 million).

There may also be other aspects of the relationship where Party Co gives Streamer Co a benefit which may not have happened had Streamer Co not been part of the group, e.g. access to technology/research, cheap finance, etc.

The main concern is that any information about the 'benefits' Party Co may have passed on to Streamer Co through related party transactions is difficult to obtain from published sources. It may be that Party Co has deliberately 'flattered' Streamer Co's financial statements specifically in order to obtain a high sale price and a prospective purchaser would not necessarily be able to determine that this had happened from either the consolidated or entity financial statements.

ACCA marking guide			
			Marks
(a)	Property, plant and equipment		½
	Goodwill		4
	Current assets		2½
	Share capital		½
	Retained earnings		3½
	Revaluation surplus		½
	NCI		1½
	Deferred consideration		1½
	Current liabilities		½
			–––
			15
			–––
(b)	Limitations of interpretation using consolidated financial statements		5
			–––
Total			**20**
			–––

Examiner's comments

Part (a) required the preparation of a consolidated statement of financial position with a series of routine adjustments supporting the consolidation process. The overall performance on this question, from a well-tried part of the syllabus, was very good. That said there were a number of common errors and weaknesses.

The fair value adjustment required at consolidation was $600,000 but this needed to be split by recognising that 90% of this had been sold since acquisition ($540,000 of this profit has been realised) and only 10% ($60,000) should be adjusted for at the date of consolidation by increasing the value of current assets.

Many candidates scored full marks for the goodwill calculation. Other than the fair value adjustment, the deferred consideration was the most common problem. The $28 million (payable on 1 July 20X8 – in two years' time) needed to be discounted at 8% to its present value at 1 July 20X6, for which the discount rate was given. Candidates who correctly made their own factor calculations and/or rounded the sum to $24 million were not penalised. A few candidates omitted the NCI (or tried to calculate the amount at acquisition for themselves) or tried to calculate the parent's share of goodwill only.

Some candidates incorrectly included the pre-acquisition amount of the revaluation surplus in the consolidated revaluation surplus – it should of course have been included in the goodwill calculation.

Most candidates, using the "own figure" rule, gained full marks for the NCI as this was the value at the date of acquisition plus 20% of post-acquisition profits (including the revaluation surplus).

The deferred consideration was also an issue for retained earnings and liabilities. As noted above, the amount needed to be discounted for the goodwill calculation as it was payable in two years' time. For the consolidated statement of financial position one year later the discount (at 8%) needed to be "unwound" for a year with a deduction from the parent's retained earnings and an increase in the discounted non-current liability. The majority of candidates who recognised this amount only adjusted retained earnings.

Although many candidates provided full and clear workings, the importance of explaining where all numbers not already given in the question have come from cannot be over-emphasised. This allows markers to determine whether an incorrect figure has been used in a calculation or whether the final total is wrong but the supporting figures are correct.

In part (b) of the question, most candidates were able to identify that the individual financial statements of Streamer Co would be a better source of information on which to base any investment decisions. However, the main point to be made was that the subsidiary's post-acquisition results had been improved due to favourable pricing of the intra-group trading originated by the parent based on the terms stated in the question. This is an example of the possible effect of related party transactions but very little of this was mentioned by the vast majority of candidates. Only a very small proportion of answers made reference to any numbers in this part of the question.

ANALYSING FINANCIAL STATEMENTS

388 HARDY *Walk in the footsteps of a top tutor*

Key answer tips

This question requires an appraisal of a business that is experiencing problems as a result of a global recession, so do not be surprised when some profitability ratios produce negative results. A weak answer will simply refer to ratio movements as having increased or decreased, whereas a strong answer will refer to improvements or deteriorations in the ratios and will aim to relate it to the scenario provided by the examiner, explaining possible causes for the movements.

Note: references to 20X5 and 20X6 should be taken as being to the years ended 30 September 20X5 and 20X6 respectively.

Profitability:

Statement of profit or loss performance:

Hardy's statement of profit or loss results dramatically show the effects of the downturn in the global economy. Revenues are down by 18% (6,500/36,000 × 100), gross profit has fallen by 60% and a healthy after tax profit of $3.5 million has reversed to a loss of $2.1 million. These are reflected in the profit (loss) margin ratios shown in the appendix (the 'as reported' figures for 20X6). This in turn has led to a 15.2% return on equity being reversed to a negative return of 11.9%. However, a closer analysis shows that the results are not quite as bad as they seem. The downturn has directly caused several additional costs in 20X6: employee severance, property impairments and losses on investments (as quantified in the appendix). These are probably all non-recurring costs and could therefore justifiably be excluded from the 20X6 results to assess Hardy's 'underlying' performance. If this is done the results of Hardy for 20X6 appear to be much better than on first sight, although still not as good as those reported for 20X5. A gross margin of 27.8% in 20X5 has fallen to only 23.1% (rather than the reported margin of 13.6%) and the profit for period has fallen from $3.5 million (9.7%) to only $2.3 million (7.8%). It should also be noted that as well as the fall in the value of the investments, the related investment income has also shown a sharp decline which has contributed to lower profits in 20X6.

Given the economic climate in 20X6 these are probably reasonably good results and may justify the Chairman's comments. It should be noted that the cost saving measures which have helped to mitigate the impact of the downturn could have some unwelcome effects should trading conditions improve. It may not be easy to re-hire employees and a lack of advertising may cause a loss of market share.

Statement of financial position:

Perhaps the most obvious aspect of the statement of financial position is the fall in value ($8.5 million) of the non-current assets, most of which is accounted for by losses of $6 million and $1.6 million respectively on the properties and investments. Ironically, because these falls are reflected in equity, this has mitigated the fall in the return of the equity (from 15.2% to 13.1% underlying) and contributed to a perhaps unexpected improvement in asset turnover from 1.6 times to 1.7 times.

Liquidity:

Despite the downturn, Hardy's liquidity ratios now seem at acceptable levels (though they should be compared to manufacturing industry norms) compared to the low ratios in 20X5. The bank balance has improved by $1.1 million. This has been helped by a successful rights issue (this is in itself a sign of shareholder support and confidence in the future) raising $2 million and keeping customer's credit period under control. Some of the proceeds of the rights issue appear to have been used to reduce the bank loan which is sensible as its financing costs have increased considerably in 20X6. Looking at the movement on retained earnings (6,500 − 2,100 − 3,600) it can be seen that Hardy paid a dividend of $800,000 during 20X6. Although this is only half the dividend per share paid in 20X5, it may seem unwise given the losses and the need for the rights issue. A counter view is that the payment of the dividend may be seen as a sign of confidence of a future recovery. It should also be mentioned that the worst of the costs caused by the downturn (specifically the property and investments losses) are not cash costs and have therefore not affected liquidity.

The increase in the inventory and work-in-progress holding period and the trade receivables collection period being almost unchanged appear to contradict the declining sales activity and should be investigated. Although there is insufficient information to calculate the trade payables credit period as there is no analysis of the cost of sales figures, it appears that Hardy has received extended credit which, unless it had been agreed with the suppliers, has the potential to lead to problems obtaining future supplies of goods on credit.

Gearing:

On the reported figures debt to equity shows a modest increase due to statement of profit or loss losses and the reduction of the revaluation surplus, but this has been mitigated by the repayment of part of the loan and the rights issue.

Conclusion:

Although Hardy's results have been adversely affected by the global economic situation, its underlying performance is not as bad as first impressions might suggest and supports the Chairman's comments. Hardy still retains a relatively strong statement of financial position and liquidity position which will help significantly should market conditions improve. Indeed the impairment of property and investments may well reverse in future. It would be a useful exercise to compare Hardy's performance during this difficult time to that of its competitors – it may well be that its 20X6 results were relatively very good by comparison.

Appendix:

An important aspect of assessing the performance of Hardy for 20X6 (especially in comparison with 20X5) is to identify the impact that several 'one off' charges have had on the results of 20X6. These charges are $1.3 million redundancy costs and a $1.5 million (6,000 – 4,500 previous surplus) property impairment, both included in cost of sales and a $1.6 million loss on the market value of investments, included in administrative expenses. Thus in calculating the 'underlying' figures for 20X6 (below) the adjusted cost of sales is $22.7 million (25,500 – 1,300 – 1,500) and the administrative expenses are $3.3 million (4,900 – 1,600). These adjustments feed through to give an underlying gross profit of $6.8 million (4,000 + 1,300 + 1,500) and an underlying profit for the year of $2.3 million (−2,100 + 1,300 + 1,500 + 1,600).

Note:it is not appropriate to revise Hardy's equity (upwards) for the one-off losses when calculating equity based underlying figures, as the losses will be a continuing part of equity (unless they reverse) even if/when future earnings recover.

	20X6		20X5
	underlying	as reported	
Gross profit % (6,800/29,500 × 100)	23.1%	13.6%	27.8%
Profit (loss) for period % (2,300/29,500 × 100)	7.8%	(7.1)%	9.7%
Return on equity (2,300/17,600 × 100)	13.1%	(11.9)%	15.2%
Net asset (taken as equity) turnover (29,500/17,600)	1.7 times	same	1.6 times
Debt to equity (4,000/17,600)	22.7%	same	21.7%
Current ratio (6,200:3,400)	1.8:1	same	1.0:1
Quick ratio (4,000:3,400)	1.2:1	same	0.6:1
Receivables collection (in days) (2,200/29,500 × 365)	27 days	same	28 days
Inventory and work-in-progress holding period (2,200/25,500 × 365)	31 days	same	27 days

Note: the figures for the calculation of the 20X6 'underlying' ratios have been given, those of 20X6 'as reported' and 20X5 are based on equivalent figures from the summarised financial statements provided.

Alternative ratios/calculations are acceptable, for example net asset turnover could be calculated using total assets less current liabilities.

Marking scheme	
	Marks
Comments – 1 mark per valid point, up to	13
Ratio calculations – up to	7
Total	20

389 PINTO

(a) Comments on the cash management of Pinto

Operating cash flows:

Pinto's operating cash inflows at $940,000 (prior to investment income, finance costs and taxation) are considerably higher than the equivalent profit before investment income, finance costs and tax of $430,000. This shows a satisfactory cash generating ability and is more than sufficient to cover finance costs, taxation (see later) and dividends. The major reasons for the cash flows being higher than the operating profit are due to the (non-cash) increases in the depreciation and warranty provisions. Working capital changes are relatively neutral, with a large increase in inventory appearing to be being financed by a substantial increase in trade payables and a modest reduction in trade receivables. The reduction in trade receivables is perhaps surprising as other indicators point to an increase in operating capacity which has not been matched with an increase in trade receivables. This could be indicative of good control over the cash management of the trade receivables (or a disappointing sales performance).

An unusual feature of the cash flow is that Pinto has received a tax refund of $60,000 during the current year. This would indicate that in the previous year Pinto was making losses (hence obtaining tax relief). Whilst the current year's profit performance is an obvious improvement, it should be noted that next year's cash flows are likely to suffer a tax payment as a consequence.

Investing activities:

There has been a dramatic investment/increase in property, plant and equipment. The carrying amount at 31 March 20X8 is substantially higher than a year earlier. It is difficult to be sure whether this represents an increase in operating capacity or is the replacement of the plant disposed of. (The voluntary disclosure encouraged by IAS 7 *Statement of Cash Flows* would help to assess this issue more accurately). However, judging by the level of the increase and the (apparent) overall improvement in profit position, it seems likely that there has been a successful increase in capacity. It is not unusual for there to be a time lag before increased investment reaches its full beneficial effect and in this context it could be speculated that the investment occurred early in the accounting year (because its effect is already making an impact) and that future periods may show even greater improvements.

The investment property is showing a good return, generating rental income of $40,000 in the year.

Financing activities:

It would appear that Pinto's financial structure has changed during the year. Debt of $400,000 has been redeemed (for $420,000) and there has been a share issue raising $1 million. The share issue has covered the cost of redemption and contributed to the investment in property, plant and equipment. The remainder of the finance for the property, plant and equipment has come from the very healthy operating cash flows. If ROCE is higher than the finance cost of the loan note at 6% (nominal) it may call into question the wisdom of the early redemption especially given the penalty cost (which has been classified within financing activities) of the redemption.

Cash position:

The overall effect of the year's cash flows is that they have improved the cash position dramatically. A sizeable overdraft of $120,000, which may have been a consequence of the (likely) losses in the previous year, has been reversed to a modest bank balance of $10,000 even after the payment of a $150,000 dividend.

Summary

The above analysis indicates that Pinto has invested substantially in renewing and/or increasing its property, plant and equipment. This has been financed largely by operating cash flows, and appears to have brought a dramatic turnaround in Pinto's fortunes. All the indications are that the future financial position and performance will continue to improve.

(b) The accruals/matching concept applied in preparing a statement of profit or loss has the effect of smoothing cash flows for reporting purposes. This practice arose because interpreting 'raw' cash flows can be very difficult and the accruals process has the advantage of helping users to understand the underlying performance of a business. For example if an item of plant with an estimated life of five years is purchased for $100,000, then in the statement of cash flows for the five year period there would be an outflow in year 1 of the full $100,000 and no further outflows for the next four years. Contrast this with the statement of profit or loss where by applying the accruals principle, depreciation of the plant would give a charge of $20,000 per annum (assuming straight-line depreciation). Many would see this example as an advantage of a statement of profit or loss, but it is important to realise that profit is affected by many items requiring judgements. This has led to accusations of profit manipulation or creative accounting, hence the disillusionment of the usefulness of the statement of profit or loss.

Another example of the difficulty in interpreting cash flows is that counter-intuitively a decrease in overall cash flows is not always a bad thing (it may represent an investment in increasing capacity which would bode well for the future), nor is an increase in cash flows necessarily a good thing (this may be from the sale of non-current assets because of the need to raise cash urgently).

The advantages of cash flows are:

- it is difficult to manipulate cash flows, they are real and possess the characteristic of objectivity (as opposed to profits affected by judgements).

- cash flows are an easy concept for users to understand, indeed many users misinterpret statement of profit or loss items as being cash flows.

- cash flows help to assess an entity's liquidity, solvency and financial adaptability. Healthy liquidity is vital to a going concern.

- many business investment decisions and valuations are based on projected cash flows.

- the 'quality' of profit is said to be confirmed by closely correlated cash flows. Some analysts take the view that if a business shows a healthy profit from operations, but has low or negative operating cash flows, there is a suspicion of profit manipulation or creative accounting.

390 HARBIN *Walk in the footsteps of a top tutor*

Key answer tip

Be aware that the examiner specifically asks you to draw your attention to the chief executives report and the purchase of Fatima – if you do not discuss this at all you will be limited in the overall marks that you can achieve. You may choose to calculate further ratios to support your analysis (marks would be awarded where relevant). The highlighted words are key phrases that markers are looking for.

Note: Figures in the calculations of the ratios are in $million

(a)

	20X7	Workings
Return on year end capital employed	11.2%	24/(114 + 100) × 100
Current ratio	0.86	38/44
Closing inventory holding period	46 days	25/200 × 365
Trade receivables' collection period	19 days	13/250 × 365
Gearing	46.7%	100/214 × 100

(b) Analysis of the comparative financial performance and position of Harbin for the year ended 30 September 20X7

Note: References to 20X7 and 20X6 should be taken as the years ended 30 September 20X7 and 20X6.

Introduction

The figures relating to the comparative performance of Harbin 'highlighted' in the Chief Executive's report may be factually correct, but they take a rather biased and one dimensional view. They focus entirely on the performance as reflected in the statement of comprehensive income without reference to other measures of performance, notably the ROCE. There is no reference to the purchase of Fatima at the beginning of the year which has had a favourable effect on profit for 20X7. Due to this purchase, it is not consistent to compare Harbin's statement of comprehensive income results in 20X7 directly with those of 20X6 because it does not match like with like. Immediately before the $100 million purchase of Fatima, the carrying amount of the net assets of Harbin was $112 million. Thus the investment represented an increase of nearly 90% of Harbin's existing capital employed. The following analysis of performance will consider the position as shown in the reported financial statements (based on the ratios required by part (a) of the question) and then go on to consider the impact the purchase has had on this analysis.

Profitability

The ROCE is often considered to be the primary measure of operating performance, because it relates the profit made by an entity (return) to the capital (or net assets) invested in generating those profits. On this basis the ROCE in 20X7 of 11.2% represents a 58% improvement (i.e. 4.1% on 7.1%) on the ROCE of 7.1% in 20X6. Given there were no disposals of non-current assets, the ROCE on Fatima's net assets is 18.9% (22m/100m + 16.5m). **Note:** The net assets of Fatima at the year-end would have increased by profit after tax of $16.5 million (i.e. 22m × 75% (at a tax rate of 25%)). Put another way, without the contribution of $22 million to profit before tax, Harbin's 'underlying' profit would have been a loss of $6 million which would give a negative ROCE. The principal reasons for the beneficial impact of Fatima's purchase is that its profit margins at 42.9% gross and 31.4% net (before tax) are far superior to the profit margins of the combined business at 20% and 6.4% respectively. It should be observed that the other contributing factor to the ROCE is the net asset turnover and in this respect Fatima's is actually inferior at 0.6 times (70m/116.5m) to that of the combined business of 1.2 times.

It could be argued that the finance costs should be allocated against Fatima's results as the proceeds of the loan note appear to be the funding for the purchase of Fatima. Even if this is accepted, Fatima's results still far exceed those of the existing business.

Thus the Chief Executive's report, already criticised for focussing on the statement of comprehensive income alone, is still highly misleading. Without the purchase of Fatima, underlying sales revenue would be flat at $180 million and the gross margin would be down to 11.1% (20m/180m) from 16.7% resulting in a loss before tax of $6 million. This sales performance is particularly poor given it is likely that there must have been an increase in spending on property plant and equipment beyond that related to the purchase of Fatima's net assets as the increase in property, plant and equipment is $120 million (after depreciation).

Liquidity

Harbin's liquidity position as measured by the current ratio has deteriorated dramatically during the period. A relatively healthy 2.5:1 is now only 0.9:1 which is rather less than what one would expect from the quick ratio (which excludes inventory) and is a matter of serious concern. A consideration of the component elements of the current ratio suggests that increases in the inventory holding period and trade payables payment period have largely offset each other. There is a small increase in the collection period for trade receivables (up from 16 days to 19 days) which would actually improve the current ratio. This ratio appears unrealistically low, it is very difficult to collect credit sales so quickly and may be indicative of factoring some of the receivables, or a proportion of the sales being cash sales. Factoring is sometimes seen as a consequence of declining liquidity, although if this assumption is correct it does also appear to have been present in the previous year. The changes in the above three ratios do not explain the dramatic deterioration in the current ratio, the real culprit is the cash position, Harbin has gone from having a bank balance of $14 million in 20X6 to showing short-term bank borrowings of $17 million in 20X7.

A statement of cash flow would give a better appreciation of the movement in the bank/short term borrowing position.

It is not possible to assess, in isolation, the impact of the purchase of Fatima on the liquidity of the business.

Dividends

A dividend of 10 cents per share in 20X7 amounts to $10 million (100m × 10 cents), thus the dividend in 20X6 would have been $8 million (the dividend in 20X7 is 25% up on 20X6). It may be that the increase in the reported profits led the Board to pay a 25% increased dividend, but the dividend cover is only 1.2 times (12m/10m) in 20X7 which is very low. In 20X6 the cover was only 0.75 times (6m/8m) meaning previous years' reserves were used to facilitate the dividend. The low retained earnings indicate that Harbin has historically paid a high proportion of its profits as dividends, however in times of declining liquidity, it is difficult to justify such high dividends.

Gearing

Harbin has gone from a position of nil gearing (i.e. no long-term borrowings) in 20X6 to a relatively high gearing of 46.7% in 20X7. This has been caused by the issue of the $100 million 8% loan note which would appear to be the source of the funding for the $100 million purchase of Fatima's net assets. At the time the loan note was issued, Harbin's ROCE was 7.1%, slightly less than the finance cost of the loan note. In 20X7 the ROCE has increased to 11.2%, thus the manner of the funding has had a beneficial effect on the returns to the equity holders of Harbin. However, it should be noted that high gearing does not come without risk. Any future downturn in the results of Harbin would expose the equity holders to much lower proportionate returns and continued poor liquidity may mean payment of the loan interest could present a problem. Harbin's gearing and liquidity position would have looked far better had some of the acquisition been funded by an issue of equity shares.

Conclusion

There is no doubt that the purchase of Fatima has been a great success and appears to have been a wise move on the part of the management of Harbin. However, it has disguised a serious deterioration of the underlying performance and position of Harbin's existing activities which the Chief Executive's report may be trying to hide. It may be that the acquisition was part of an overall plan to diversify out of what has become existing loss making activities. If such a transition can continue, then the worrying aspects of poor liquidity and high gearing may be overcome.

Marking scheme		
		Marks
(a)	One mark per required ratio	5
(b)	For consideration of Chief Executive's report	3
	Remaining issues 1 mark per valid point	12
Total		**20**

391 VICTULAR *Walk in the footsteps of a top tutor*

Key answer tips

This style of question is naturally time consuming – ensure you answer all parts of the question and do not spend too much time calculating ratios. Part (c) offers easy marks and is independent of the rest of the question – try doing part (c) first to ensure you do not miss out on such easy marks. When interpreting the results in part (b) be wary of making generalisations – you must ensure that you relate it to the information given in the question. Presentation is also crucial in part (b), so make it easy for the marker to read by being as neat as possible, with short paragraphs and spaces between paragraphs. The highlighted words are key phrases that markers are looking for.

(a) **Equivalent ratios from the financial statements of Merlot (workings in $000)**

Return on year end capital employed (ROCE)	20.9%	$(1,400 + 590)/(2,800 + 3,200 + 500 + 3,000) \times 100$
Pre-tax return on equity (ROE)	50%	$1,400/2,800 \times 100$
Net asset turnover	2.3 times	$20,500/(14,800 - 5,700)$
Gross profit margin	12.2%	$2,500/20,500 \times 100$
Operating profit margin	9.8%	$2,000/20,500 \times 100$
Current ratio	1.3:1	$7,300/5,700$
Closing inventory holding period	73 days	$3,600/18,000 \times 365$
Trade receivables' collection period	66 days	$3,700/20,500 \times 365$
Trade payables' payment period	77 days	$3,800/18,000 \times 365$
Gearing	71%	$(3,200 + 500 + 3,000)/9,500 \times 100$
Interest cover	3.3 times	$2,000/600$
Dividend cover	1.4 times	$1,000/700$

As required by the question, Merlot's lease liabilities (3,200 + 500) have been treated as debt when calculating the ROCE and gearing ratios.

(b) **Assessment of the relative performance and financial position of Grappa and Merlot for the year ended 30 September 20X8**

Introduction

This report is based on the draft financial statements supplied and the ratios shown in (a) above. Although covering many aspects of performance and financial position, the report has been approached from the point of view of a prospective acquisition of the entire equity of one of the two entities.

Profitability

The ROCE of 20.9% of Merlot is far superior to the 14.8% return achieved by Grappa. ROCE is traditionally seen as a measure of management's overall efficiency in the use of the finance/assets at its disposal. More detailed analysis reveals that Merlot's superior performance is due to its efficiency in the use of its net assets. It achieved a net asset turnover of 2.3 times compared to only 1.2 times for Grappa. Put another way, Merlot makes sales of $2.30 per $1 invested in net assets compared to sales of only $1.20 per $1 invested for Grappa. The other element contributing to the ROCE is profit margins. In this area Merlot's overall performance is slightly inferior to that of Grappa, gross profit margins are almost identical, but Grappa's operating profit margin is 10.5% compared to Merlot's 9.8%. In this situation, where one entity's ROCE is superior to another's it is useful to look behind the figures and consider possible reasons for the superiority other than the obvious one of greater efficiency on Merlot's part.

A major component of the ROCE is normally the carrying amount of the non-current assets. Consideration of these in this case reveals some interesting issues. Merlot does not own its premises whereas Grappa does. Such a situation would not necessarily give a ROCE advantage to either entity as the increase in capital employed of an entity owning its factory would be compensated by a higher return due to not having a rental expense, and vice versa. If Merlot's rental cost, as a percentage of the value of the related factory, was less than its overall ROCE, then it would be contributing to its higher ROCE. There is insufficient information to determine this. Another relevant point may be that Merlot's owned plant is nearing the end of its useful life (carrying amount is only 22% of its cost) and they seem to be replacing owned plant with leased plant. Again this does not necessarily give Merlot an advantage, but the finance cost of the leased assets at only 7.5% is much lower than the overall ROCE (of either entity) and therefore this does help to improve Merlot's ROCE. The other important issue within the composition of the ROCE is the valuation basis of the entities' non-current assets. From the question, it appears that Grappa's factory is at current value (there is a property revaluation surplus) and note (ii) of the question indicates the use of historical cost for plant. The use of current value for the factory (as opposed to historical cost) will be adversely impacting on Grappa's ROCE. Merlot does not suffer this deterioration as it does not own its factory.

The ROCE measures the overall efficiency of management. However, as Victular is considering buying the equity of one of the two entities, it would be useful to consider the return on equity (ROE) – as this is what Victular is buying. The ratios calculated are based on pre-tax profits, which takes into account finance costs, but does not cause taxation issues to distort the comparison. Clearly Merlot's ROE at 50% is far superior to Grappa's 19.1%. Again the issue of the revaluation of Grappa's factory is making this ratio appear comparatively worse than it would be if there had not been a revaluation. In these circumstances it would be more meaningful if the ROE was calculated based on the asking price of each entity (which has not been disclosed) as this would effectively be the carrying amount of the relevant equity for Victular.

Gearing

From the gearing ratio it can be seen that 71% of Merlot's assets are financed by borrowings (39% is attributable to Merlot's policy of leasing its plant). This is very high in absolute terms and double Grappa's level of gearing. The effect of gearing means that all of the profit after finance costs is attributable to the equity even though (in Merlot's case) the equity represents only 29% of the financing of the net assets. Whilst this may seem advantageous to the equity shareholders of Merlot, it does not come without risk. The interest cover of Merlot is only 3.3 times whereas that of Grappa is 6 times. Merlot's low interest cover is a direct consequence of its high gearing and it makes profits vulnerable to relatively small changes in operating activity. For example, small reductions in sales, profit margins or small increases in operating expenses could result in losses and mean that interest charges would not be covered.

Another observation is that Grappa has been able to take advantage of the receipt of government grants, Merlot has not. This may be due to Grappa purchasing its plant (which may then be eligible for grants) whereas Merlot leases its plant. It may be that the lessor has received any grants available on the purchase of the plant and passed some of this benefit on to Merlot via lower lease finance costs (at 7.5% per annum, this is considerably lower than Merlot has to pay on its 10% loan notes).

Liquidity

Both entities have relatively low liquid ratios of 1.2 and 1.3 for Grappa and Merlot respectively, although at least Grappa has $600,000 in the bank whereas Merlot has a $1.2 million overdraft. In this respect Merlot's policy of high dividend payouts (leading to a low dividend cover and low retained earnings) is very questionable. Looking in more depth, both entities have similar inventory days. Merlot collects its receivables one week earlier than Grappa (perhaps its credit control procedures are more active due to its large overdraft), and of notable difference is that Grappa receives (or takes) a significantly longer credit period from its suppliers (108 days compared to 77 days). This may be a reflection of Grappa being able to negotiate better credit terms because it has a higher credit rating.

Summary

Although both entities may operate in a similar industry and have similar profits after tax, they would represent very different purchases. Merlot's sales revenues are over 70% more than those of Grappa, it is financed by high levels of debt, it rents rather than owns property and it chooses to lease rather than buy its replacement plant. Also its remaining owned plant is nearing the end of its life. Its replacement will either require a cash injection if it is to be purchased (Merlot's overdraft of $1.2 million already requires serious attention) or create even higher levels of gearing if it continues its policy of leasing. In short although Merlot's overall return seems more attractive than that of Grappa, it would represent a much more risky investment. Ultimately the investment decision may be determined by Victular's attitude to risk, possible synergies with its existing business activities, and not least, by the asking price for each investment (which has not been disclosed to us).

(c)   The generally recognised potential problems of using ratios for comparison purposes are:

- inconsistent definitions of ratios

- financial statements may have been deliberately manipulated (creative accounting)

- different entities may adopt different accounting policies (e.g. use of historical costs compared to current values)

- different managerial policies (e.g. different entities offer customers different payment terms)

- statement of financial position figures may not be representative of average values throughout the year (this can be caused by seasonal trading or a large acquisition of non-current assets near the year-end)

- the impact of price changes over time/distortion caused by inflation.

When deciding whether to purchase a business, Victular should consider the following additional useful information:

- in this case the analysis has been made on the draft financial statements. These may be unreliable or change when being finalised. Audited financial statements would add credibility and reliance to the analysis (assuming they receive an unmodified Auditors' Report)

- forward-looking information such as profit and financial position forecasts, capital expenditure and cash budgets and the level of orders on the books

- the current (fair) values of assets being acquired

- the level of risk within a business. Highly profitable businesses may also be highly risky, whereas a less profitable business may have more stable 'quality' earnings

- not least would be the expected price to acquire the entity. It may be that a poorer performing business may be a more attractive purchase because it is relatively cheaper and may offer more opportunity for improving efficiencies and profit growth.

392 QUARTILE

(a) Below are the specified ratios for Quartile and (for comparison) those of the business sector average:

		Quartile	Sector average
Return on year-end capital employed			
$((3,400 + 800)/(26,600 + 8,000) \times 100)$		12.1%	16.8%
Net asset turnover	$(56,000/34,600)$	1.6 times	1.4 times
Gross profit margin	$(14,000/56,000 \times 100)$	25%	35%
Operating profit margin	$(4,200/56,000 \times 100)$	7.5%	12%
Current ratio	$(11,200:7,200)$	1.6:1	1.25:1
Average inventory $(8,300 + 10,200/2) = 9,250)$ turnover			
	$(42,000/9,250)$	4.5 times	3 times
Trade payables' payment period	$(5,400/43,900 \times 365)$	45 days	64 days
Debt to equity	$(8,000/26,600 \times 100)$	30%	38%

(b) **Assessment of comparative performance**

Profitability

The primary measure of profitability is the return on capital employed (ROCE) and this shows that Quartile's 12.1% is considerably underperforming the sector average of 16.8%. The main cause of this seems to be a much lower gross profit margin (25% compared to 35%). A possible explanation for this is that Quartile is deliberately charging a lower mark-up in order to increase its sales by undercutting the market. There is supporting evidence for this in that Quartile's average inventory turnover at 4.5 times is 50% better than the sector average of three times. An alternative explanation could be that Quartile has had to cut its margins due to poor sales which have had a knock-on effect of having to write down closing inventory.

Quartile's lower gross profit percentage has fed through to contribute to a lower operating profit margin at 7.5% compared to the sector average of 12%. However, from the above figures, it can be deduced that Quartile's operating costs at 17.5% (25% − 7.5%) of revenue appear to be better controlled than the sector average operating costs of 23% (35% − 12%) of revenue. This may indicate that Quartile has a different classification of costs between cost of sales and operating costs than the entities in the sector average or that other entities may be spending more on advertising/selling commissions in order to support their higher margins.

The other component of ROCE is asset utilisation (measured by net asset turnover). If Quartile's business strategy is indeed to generate more sales to compensate for lower profit margins, a higher net asset turnover would be expected. At 1.6 times, Quartile's net asset turnover is only marginally better than the sector average of 1.4 times. Whilst this may indicate that Quartile's strategy was a poor choice, the ratio could be partly distorted by the property revaluation and also by whether the deferred development expenditure should be included within net assets for this purpose, as the net revenues expected from the development have yet to come on stream. If these two aspects were adjusted for, Quartile's net asset turnover would be 2.1 times (56,000/(34,600 − 5,000 − 3,000)) which is 50% better than the sector average.

In summary, Quartile's overall profitability is below that of its rival businesses due to considerably lower profit margins, although this has been partly offset by generating proportionately more sales from its assets.

Liquidity

As measured by the current ratio, Quartile has a higher level of cover for its current liabilities than the sector average (1.6:1 compared to 1.25:1). Quartile's figure is nearer the 'norm' of expected liquidity ratios, often quoted as between 1.5 and 2:1, with the sector average (at 1.25:1) appearing worryingly low. The problem of this 'norm' is that it is generally accepted that it relates to manufacturing rather than retail entities, as applies to Quartile (and presumably also to the sector average). In particular, retail entities have very little, if any, trade receivables as is the case with Quartile. This makes a big difference to the current ratio and makes the calculation of a quick ratio largely irrelevant. Consequently, retail entities operate comfortably with much lower current ratios as their inventory is turned directly into cash. Thus, if anything, Quartile has a higher current ratio than might be expected. As Quartile has relatively low inventory levels (deduced from high inventory turnover figures), this means it must also have relatively low levels of trade payables (which can be confirmed from the calculated ratios). The low payables period of 45 days may be an indication of suppliers being cautious with the credit period they extend to Quartile, but there is no real evidence of this (e.g. Quartile is not struggling with an overdraft). In short, Quartile does not appear to have any liquidity issues.

Gearing

Quartile's debt to equity at 30% is lower than the sector average of 38%. Although the loan note interest rate of 10% might appear quite high, it is lower than the ROCE of 12.1% (which means shareholders are benefiting from the borrowings) and the interest cover of 5.25 times ((3,400 + 800)/800) is acceptable. Quartile also has sufficient tangible assets to give more than adequate security on the borrowings, therefore there appear to be no adverse issues in relation to gearing.

Conclusion

Quartile may be right to be concerned about its declining profitability. From the above analysis, it seems that Quartile may be addressing the wrong market (low margins with high volumes). The information provided about its rival businesses would appear to suggest that the current market appears to favour a strategy of higher margins (probably associated with better quality and more expensive goods) as being more profitable. In other aspects of the appraisal, Quartile is doing well compared to other businesses in its sector.

393 BENGAL

Note: references to 20X1 and 20X0 refer to the periods ending 31 March 20X1 and 20X0 respectively.

It is understandable that the shareholder's observations would cause concern. A large increase in sales revenue has not led to a proportionate increase in profit. To assess why this has happened requires consideration of several factors that could potentially explain the results.

Perhaps the most obvious would be that Bengal has increased its sales by discounting prices, and thereby cutting profit margins. Interpreting the ratios rules out this possible explanation as the gross profit margin has in fact increased in 20X1 (up from 40% to 42%).

Another potential cause of the disappointing profit could be overheads (distribution costs and administrative expenses) getting out of control, perhaps due to higher advertising costs or more generous incentives to sales staff. Again, when these expenses are expressed as a percentage of sales, this does not explain the disparity in profit as the ratio has remained at approximately 19%.

What is evident is that there has been a very large increase in finance costs which is illustrated by the interest cover deteriorating from 36 times to only 9 times.

The other 'culprit' is the taxation expense: expressed as a percentage of pre-tax accounting profit, the effective rate of tax has gone from 28.6% in 20X0 to 42.9% in 20X1. There are a number of factors that can affect a period's effective tax rate (including under- or over-provisions from the previous year), but judging from the figures involved, it would seem likely that either there was a material adjustment from an under-provision of tax in 20X0 or there has been a considerable increase in the rate levied by the taxation authority.

As an illustration of the effect, if the same effective tax rate in 20X0 had applied in 20X1, the after-tax profit would have been $3,749,000 (5,250 × (100% – 28.6%) rounded) and, using this figure, the percentage increase in profit would be 50% ((3,749 – 2,500)/2,500 × 100) which is slightly higher than the percentage increase in revenue.

Thus an increase in the tax rate and increases in finance costs due to much higher borrowings more than account for the disappointing profit commented upon by the concerned shareholder.

The other significant observation in comparing 20X1 with 20X0 is that Bengal has almost certainty acquired another business. The increased expenditure on property, plant and equipment of $6,740,000 and the newly acquired intangibles (probably goodwill) of $6.2 million are not likely to be attributable to organic or internal growth.

Indeed the decrease in the bank balance of $4.2 million and the issue of $7 million loan notes closely match the increase in non-current assets. This implies that the acquisition has been financed by cash resources (which Bengal looks to have been building up) and issuing debt (no equity was issued).

It may be that these assets were part of the acquisition of a new business and are 'surplus to requirements', hence they have been made available for sale.

They are likely to be valued at their 'fair value less cost to sell' and the prospect of their sale should be highly probable (normally within one year). That said, if the assets are not sold in the near future, it would call into question the acceptability of the current ratio which may cause short-term liquidity problems.

In summary, although reported performance has deteriorated, it may be that future results will benefit from the current year's investment and show considerable improvement. Perhaps some equity should have been issued to lower the finance costs and if the dividend of $750,000 had been postponed for a year there would be a better liquid position.

Appendix

Calculation of ratios (figures in $000):	20X1	20X0
Gross profit margin (10,700/25,500 × 100)	42.0%	40.0 %
Operating expenses % (4,800/25,500 × 100)	18.8%	19.1%
Interest cover ((5,250 + 650)/650)	9 times	36 times
Effective rate of tax (2,250/5,250)	42.9%	28.6%
Net profit (before tax) margin (5,250/25,500 × 100)	20.6%	20.3%

The figures for the calculation of 20X1's ratios are given in brackets, the figures for 20X0 are derived from the equivalent figures.

394 WOODBANK

Key answer tips

This style of question is naturally time consuming – ensure you answer all parts of the question and do not spend too much time calculating ratios. When interpreting the results in part (b) be wary of making generalisations – you must ensure that you relate it to the information given in the question. Presentation is also crucial in part (b), so make it easy for the marker to read by being as neat as possible, with short paragraphs and spaces between paragraphs. The highlighted words are key phrases that markers are looking for.

(a)   Note: Figures in the calculations of the ratios are in $million

	20X4 Excluding Shaw	20X3	20X4
Return on capital employed (ROCE)	13%	10.5%	12.0%
(profit before interest and tax/year-end total assets less current liabilities)	(13/100)		
Net asset (equal to capital employed) turnover	1.2 times (120/100)	1.16 times	1.0 times
Gross profit margin	20% (24/120)	22.0%	22.0%
Profit before interest and tax margin	10.8% (13/120)	9.1%	12.0%
Current ratio	–	1.7:1	1.08:1
Gearing (debt/(debt + equity))	–	5.3%	36.7%

(b) **Analysis of the comparative financial performance and position of Woodbank for the year ended 31 March 20X4**

Introduction

When comparing current performance and position with the previous year (or years), using trend analysis, it is necessary to take into account the effect of any circumstances which may create an inconsistency in the comparison. In the case of Woodbank, the purchase of Shaw is an example of such an inconsistency.

20X4's figures include, for a three-month period, the operating results of Shaw, and Woodbank's statement of financial position includes all of Shaw's net assets (including goodwill) together with the additional 10% loan notes used to finance the purchase of Shaw. None of these items were included in the 20X3 financial statements.

The net assets of Shaw when purchased were $50 million, which represents one third of Woodbank's net assets (capital employed) as at 31 March 20X4. It therefore represents a major investment for Woodbank and any analysis necessitates careful consideration of its impact.

Profitability

ROCE is considered by many analysts to be the most important profitability ratio. A ROCE of 12.0% in 20X4, compared to 10.5% in 20X3, represents a creditable 14.3% (12.0 – 10.5)/10.5) improvement in profitability.

When ROCE is calculated excluding the contribution from Shaw, at 13.0%, it shows an even more favourable performance. Although this comparison (13.0% from 10.5%) is valid, it would seem to imply that the purchase of Shaw has had a detrimental effect on Woodbank's ROCE.

However, caution is needed when interpreting this information as ROCE compares the return (profit for a period) to the capital employed (equivalent to net assets at a single point in time).

In the case of Woodbank, the statement of profit or loss only includes three months' results from Shaw whereas the statement of financial position includes all of Shaw's net assets, which is inconsistent.

It would be fair to speculate that in future years, when a full year's results from Shaw are reported, the ROCE effect of Shaw will be favourable.

Indeed, assuming a continuation of Shaw's current level of performance, profit in a full year could be $20 million. On an investment of $50 million, this represents a ROCE of 40% (based on the initial capital employed) which is much higher than Woodbank's pre-existing business.

The cause of the improvement in ROCE is revealed by consideration of the secondary profitability ratios: asset turnover and profit margins. For Woodbank this reveals a complicated picture.

Woodbank's results, as reported, show that it is the increase in the profit before interest and tax margin (12.0% from 9.1%) which is responsible for the improvement in ROCE, as the asset turnover has actually decreased (1.0 times from 1.16 times) and gross profit is exactly the same in both years (at 22.0%).

When the effect of the purchase of Shaw is excluded the position changes. The overall improvement in ROCE (13.0% from 10.5%) is caused by both an increase in profit margin (at the before interest and tax level, at 10.8% from 9.1 %), despite a fall in gross profit (20.0% from 22.0%) and a very slight improvement in asset turnover (1.2 times from 1.16 times). This means that the purchase of Shaw has improved Woodbank's overall profit margins, but caused a fall in asset turnover.

Again, as with the ROCE, this is misleading because the calculation of asset turnover only includes three months' revenue from Shaw, but all of its net assets. When a full year of Shaw's results are reported, asset turnover will be much improved (assuming its three-months performance is continued).

Liquidity

The liquidity position, as measured by the current ratio, has fallen considerably in 20X4 and is a cause for concern.

At 1.67:1 in 20X3, it was within the acceptable range (normally between 1.5:1 and 2.0:1) but the 20X4 ratio of 1.08:1 is very low, indeed it is more like that which would be expected for the quick ratio (acid test).

Without needing to calculate the component ratios of the current ratio (for inventory, receivables and payables), it can be seen from the statements of financial position that the main causes of the deterioration in the liquidity position are the reduction in the cash (bank) position and the dramatic increase in trade payables. The bank balance has fallen by $4.5 million (5,000 – 500) and the trade payables have increased by $8 million.

An analysis of the movement in the retained earnings shows that Woodbank paid a dividend of $5.5 million (10,000 + 10,500 – 15,000) or 6.88 cents per share. It could be argued that during a period of expansion, with demands on cash flow, dividends could be suspended or heavily curtailed.

Had no dividend been paid, the 20X4 bank balance would be $6.0 million and the current ratio would have been 1.3:1 ((27,000 + 5,500):25,000). This would be still on the low side, but much more reassuring to credit suppliers than the reported ratio of 1.08:1.

Gearing

Woodbank has gone from a position of very modest gearing at 5.3% in 20X3 to 36.7% in 20X4. This has largely been caused by the issue of the additional 10% loan notes to finance the purchase of Shaw.

Arguably, it might have been better if some of the finance had been raised from a share issue, but the level of gearing is still acceptable and the financing cost of 10% should be more than covered by the prospect of future high returns from Shaw, thus benefiting shareholders overall.

Conclusion

The overall operating performance of Woodbank has improved during the period (although the gross profit margin on sales other than those made by Shaw has fallen) and this should be even more marked next year when a full year's results from Shaw will be reported (assuming that Shaw can maintain its current performance). The changes in the financial position, particularly liquidity, are less favourable and call into question the current dividend policy. Gearing has increased substantially, due to the financing of the purchase of Shaw but it is still acceptable and has benefited shareholders. It is interesting to note that of the $50 million purchase price, $30 million of this is represented by goodwill. Although this may seem high, Shaw is certainly delivering in terms of generating revenue with good profit margins.

(c) Below are a number of issues/items of information in relation to the acquisition of Shaw which would be useful in producing a better analysis of Woodbank.

- Did the acquisition of Shaw include any consideration payable dependent on Shaw's results? If so, this should be recorded as a liability at its fair value.

- Shaw's statement of financial position would be useful. This would be useful in assessing the working capital cycle of Shaw compared to Woodbank, as the Woodbank group has a low cash balance as at 31 March 20X4.

- Shaw's statement of cash flows would be useful (as would the statement of cash flow for Woodbank). This would help assess the reasons for the significant fall in cash during the year.

- Any one-off costs associated with the acquisition of Shaw, such as professional fees. These will have been expensed and will have affected the profit margins in the year.

- Whether there are any potential savings to be made following the acquisition of Shaw, such as reduction in staff costs or shared properties. These may involve one-off costs such as redundancies or lease termination costs but could lead to improved margins in future periods.

- The nature of Shaw's business should be looked at in comparison to Woodbank. It will be useful to know if Shaw was a competitor of Woodbank, or maybe a supplier of goods to Woodbank. This would help with further analysis regarding market share or the potential future cost of goods if Shaw was either of these.

- A breakdown of Shaw's major customers would be useful, to see if any have left following the change of ownership in Shaw.

Marking scheme		
		Marks
(a)	1 mark per ratio Maximum	4
(b)	1 mark per relevant point to maximum	12
(c)	1 mark per relevant point to maximum	4
Total		**20**

395 HYDAN

(a) **For comparison**

	Hydan adjusted	Hydan as reported	Sector average
Return on equity (ROE)	21.7%	47.1%	22.0%
Net asset turnover	1.75 times	2.36 times	1.67 times
Gross profit margin	28.6%	35.7%	30.0%
Net profit margin	9.3%	20.0%	12.0%

Hydan's adjusted ratios

On the assumption that after the purchase of Hydan, the favourable effects of the transactions with other businesses owned by the family would not occur, the following adjustments to the statement of profit or loss should be made:

	$000
Cost of sales (45,000/0.9)	50,000
Directors' remuneration	2,500
Loan interest (10% × 10,000)	1,000

These adjustments would give a revised statement of profit or loss:

Revenue	70,000
Cost of sales	(50,000)
Gross profit	20,000
Operating costs	(7,000)
Directors' remuneration	(2,500)
Loan interest	(1,000)
Profit before tax	9,500
Income tax expense	(3,000)
Profit for the year	6,500

In the statement of financial position:

Equity would be the purchase price of Hydan (per question)	30,000
The commercial loan (replacing the directors' loan) would now be debt	10,000

From these figures the adjusted ratios above are calculated as:

Return on equity	((6,500 /30,000) × 100)	21.7%
Net asset turnover	(70,000/(30,000 + 10,000))	1.75 times
Gross profit margin	((20,000)/70,000) × 100)	28.6%
Net profit margin	((6,500/70,000) × 100)	9.30%

(b) An analysis of Hydan's ratios based on the financial statements provided reveals a strong position, particularly in relation to profitability when compared to other businesses in this retail sector. Hydan has a very high ROE which is a product of higher-than-average profit margins (at both the gross and net profit level) and a significantly higher net asset turnover. Thus, on the face of it, Hydan is managing to achieve higher prices (or reduced cost of sales), has better control of overheads and is using its net assets more efficiently in terms of generating revenue.

However, when adjustments are made for the effects of its favourable transactions with other businesses owned by the family, the position changes somewhat. The effect of purchasing its inventory from another family-owned supplier at favourable market prices means that its reported gross profit percentage of 35.7% is flattering. Had these purchases been made at market prices, it would fall to 28.6% which is below the sector average of 30.0%. The effects of the favourable inventory purchases carry through to net profit. Based on Xpand's estimate of future directors' remuneration, it would seem the existing directors of Hydan are not charging commercial rates for their remuneration. When Xpand replaces the board of Hydan, it will have to increase directors' remuneration by $1.5 million. Additionally, when the interest free directors' loans are replaced with a commercial loan, with interest at 10% per annum, this would reduce net profit by a further $1 million. The accumulation of these adjustments means that the ROE which Xpand should expect would be 21.7% (rather than the reported 47.1%) which is almost exactly in line with the sector average of 22.0%.

In a similar vein, when the asset turnover is calculated based on the equity purchase price and the commercial loan (equating to net assets), it falls from 2.36 times to 1.75 times which is above, but much closer to, the sector average of 1.67 times. In summary, Hydan's adjusted results would still be slightly ahead of the sector averages in most areas and may well justify the anticipated purchase price of $30 million. However, Hydan will be nowhere near the excellently performing business suggested by the reported figures and Xpand needs to exercise a degree of caution in its negotiations.

(c) The consolidated financial statements of Lodan are of little value when trying to assess the performance and financial position of its subsidiary, Hydan. Therefore the main source of information on which to base any investment decision would be Hydan's own entity financial statements. However, where an entity is part of a group, there is the potential for the financial statements to have been subject to the influence of related-party transactions. In the case of Hydan, there has been a considerable amount of post-acquisition trading with Lodan and, because of the related-party relationship, it appears that this trading is not at arm's length (i.e. not at commercial rates).

There may be other aspects of the relationship where Lodan gives Hydan a benefit that may not have happened had Hydan not been part of the group, e.g. access to technology/research, cheap finance.

The operations of Hydan may now be centralised and run by Lodan. If Lodan doesn't allocate some of these costs to Hydan then Hydan's expenses will be understated. It could also be difficult for a purchaser to assess whether additional property would be required if Hydan share this with other group entities.

The main concern is that any information about the 'benefits' Lodan may have passed on to Hydan through related party transactions is difficult to obtain from published sources. It may be that Lodan would deliberately 'flatter' Hydan's financial statements specifically in order to obtain a high sale price and a prospective purchaser would not necessarily be able to determine that this had happened from either the consolidated or entity financial statements. There are suggestions of this in the fact that Hydan's directors are not charging market rates for their remuneration and are giving interest-free loans.

Marking scheme		Marks
(a)	1½ marks per ratio	6
(b)	1 mark per valid point. A good answer must emphasise the different interpretation when using adjusted figures	9
(c)	1 mark per valid point, emphasising potential distortion of true trading performance	5
Total		20

396 YOGI

Note: References to 20X5 and 20X4 refer to the periods ended 31 March 20X5 and 20X4 respectively.

(a) Calculation of equivalent ratios (figures in $000):

	(i) 20X4 excluding division	(ii) 20X5 as reported	20X4 per question
Gross profit margin ((20,000 – 8,000)/(50,000 – 18,000) × 100)	37.5%	33.3%	40.0%
Operating profit margin ((11,800 – 5,800)/32,000 × 100)	18.8%	10.3%	23.6%
Return on capital employed (ROCE) ((11,800 – 5,800)/(29,200 – 7,200 – 7,000 see below) × 100)	40.0%	21.8%	53.6%
Net asset turnover (32,000/15,000)	2.13 times	2.12 times	2.27 times

Note: The capital employed in the division sold at 31 March 20X4 was $7 million ($8 million sale proceeds less $1 million profit on sale).

The figures for the calculations of 20X4's adjusted ratios (i.e. excluding the effects of the sale of the division) are given in brackets, the figures for 20X5 are derived from the equivalent figures in the question. However, the operating profit margin and ROCE calculations exclude the profit from the sale of the division (as stated in the requirement) as it is a 'one-off' item.

(b)   The most relevant comparison is the 20X5 results (excluding the profit on disposal of the division) with the results of 20X4 (excluding the results of the division), otherwise like is not being compared with like.

Profitability

Although comparative sales have increased (excluding the effect of the sale of the division) by $4 million (36,000 – 32,000), equivalent to 12.5%, the gross profit margin has fallen considerably (from 37.5% in 20X4 down to 33.3% in 20X5) and this deterioration has been compounded by the sale of the division, which was the most profitable part of the business (which earned a gross profit margin of 44.4% (8/18)). The deterioration of the operating profit margin (from 18.8% in 20X4 down to 10.3% in 20X5) is largely due to poor gross profit margins, but operating expenses are proportionately higher (as a percentage of sales) in 20X5 (23.0% compared to 18.8%) which has further reduced profitability. This is due to higher administrative expenses (as distribution costs have fallen), perhaps relating to the sale of the division.

Yogi's performance as measured by ROCE has deteriorated dramatically from 40.0% in 20X4 (as adjusted) to only 21.8% in 20X5. As the net asset turnover has remained broadly the same at 2.1 times (rounded), it is the fall in the operating profit which is responsible for the overall deterioration in performance. Whilst it is true that Yogi has sold the most profitable part of its business, this does not explain why the 20X5 results have deteriorated so much (by definition the adjusted 20X4 figures exclude the favourable results of the division). Consequently, Yogi's management need to investigate why profit margins have fallen in 20X5. It may be that customers of the sold division also bought (more profitable) goods from Yogi's remaining business and they have taken their custom to the new owners of the division, or it may be related to external issues which are also being experienced by other businesses such as an economic recession. A study of industry sector average ratios could reveal this.

Other issues

It is very questionable to have offered shareholders such a high dividend (half of the disposal proceeds) to persuade them to vote for the disposal. At $4 million (4,000 + 3,000 – 3,000, i.e. the movement on retained earnings or 10 million shares at 40 cents) the dividend represents double the profit for the year of $2 million (3,000 – 1,000) if the gain on the disposal is excluded. Another effect of the disposal is that Yogi appears to have used the other $4 million (after paying the dividend) from the disposal proceeds to pay down half of the 10% loan notes. This has reduced finance costs and interest cover, but, as the finance cost at 10% is much lower than the 20X5 ROCE of 21.8%, it will have had a detrimental effect on overall profit available to shareholders.

Summary

In retrospect, it may have been unwise for Yogi to sell the most profitable part of its business at what appears to be a very low price. It has coincided with a remarkable deterioration in profitability (not solely due to the sale) and the proceeds of the disposal have not been used to replace capacity or improve long-term prospects. By returning a substantial proportion of the sale proceeds to shareholders, it represents a downsizing of the business.

(c) Although the sports club is a not-for-profit organisation, the request for a loan is a commercial activity that should be decided on according to similar criteria as would be used for other profit-orientated entities.

The main aspect of granting a loan is how secure the loan would be. To this extent a form of capital gearing ratio should be calculated, say existing long-term borrowings to net assets (i.e. total assets less current liabilities). Clearly if this ratio is high, further borrowing would be at an increased risk. The secondary aspect is to measure the sports club's ability to repay the interest (and ultimately the principal) on the loan. This may be determined from information in the statement of comprehensive income. A form of interest cover should be calculated, say the excess of income over expenditure (broadly the equivalent of profit) compared to (the forecast) interest payments. The higher this ratio the less risk of interest default. The calculations would be made for all four years to ascertain any trends that may indicate a deterioration or improvement in these ratios. As with other profit-oriented entities the nature and trend of the income should be investigated: for example, are the club's sources of income increasing or decreasing, does the reported income contain 'one-off' donations (which may not be recurring) etc? Also matters such as the market value of, and existing prior charges against, any assets intended to be used as security for the loan would be relevant to the lender's decision-making process. It may also be possible that the sports club's governing body (perhaps the trustees) may be willing to give a personal guarantee for the loan.

Marking scheme			
			Marks
(a)	(i) and (ii)	Gross profit margin	1
		Operating profit margin	1½
		Return on capital employed	1½
		Net asset turnover	1
			___
			5
			___
(b)	1 mark per point (a good answer must consider the effect of the sale of the division)		10
(c)	1 mark per point		5
			___
Total			**20**
			___

397 XPAND

(a) **Missing ratios for Kovert:**

Return on year-end capital employed (ROCE)   31.0%
(4,900/(5,600 + 9,200 + 1,000 × 100)

Profit margin (before interest and tax) (4,900/40,000 × 100)   12.3%

Trade payables' payment period (2,100/32,800 × 365)   23 days

Gearing (debt/(debt + equity)) (10,200/15,800 × 100)   64.6%

(b) **Assessment of the comparative performance and financial position of Kandid and Kovert for the year ended 30 September 20X5**

Introduction

This assessment of the two entities will look at the areas of profitability, liquidity and gearing with reference to some differences which may make the comparison of the reported figures potentially invalid.

Profitability

ROCE is usually considered as the most important measure of profitability and is often described as a measure of management's overall efficiency in the use of the assets at its disposal. The ROCE of 62.5% of Kandid is far superior (more than double) to the 31.0% return achieved by Kovert. This superior return of Kandid can be analysed into its component parts of profit margin and asset turnover and in both of these areas Kandid's performance is better than that of Kovert. Kandid is generating $3.30 for every dollar invested, compared to only $2.50 per dollar invested in Kovert and earning a profit margin of 19.0% compared to just 12.3% by Kovert. Additionally, Kandid's gross profit margin at 24% is a third (6%/18%) higher than the 18% of Kovert. This may be, at least in part, due to marketing policy. Kovert may be deliberately charging lower selling prices in order to generate greater revenue. This is evidenced by Kovert's turnover of $40 million compared to only $25 million for Kandid. The superior gross margin of Kandid continues into the operating profit level indicating that Kandid has better control of its overheads.

There are, however, a number of areas relating to the capital employed which may bring this superiority into question. Kandid has deducted the receipt of a government grant directly from the carrying amount of the related plant, which is allowed but is rather unusual. Normally, plant is shown gross less accumulated depreciation and related government grants are shown as a separate deferred credit. It also appears that Kandid rents its property whereas Kovert has purchased its property (and indeed revalued it which has increased its capital employed). Kandid also holds proportionately less inventory and receivables than Kovert. Whilst these factors may not necessarily result in a higher profit for Kandid (e.g. property rental may be higher than the equivalent depreciation of property), they would act to give Kandid lower net assets, and thus lower capital employed and in turn a higher ROCE than Kovert.

Bearing in mind these differences, it may be more helpful if Xpand were to calculate a return on its potential equity investment (ROE) of $12 million as this would be more relevant should it acquire either of the entities. Using profit after tax, Kandid's ROE would be 30% (3,600/12,000 × 100) whereas Kovert's ROE would be 25% (3,000/12,000). This still supports Kandid's superior return, but this introduces further differences. Both entities have $5 million in loan notes but the interest rate on Kandid's loan is only 5% compared to 10% for Kovert, presumably this reflects the difference in the creditworthiness of the two entities which is something that Xpand should take note of. There also appears to be a favourable tax discrepancy with Kandid paying a nominal rate of tax on its profit of 20% compared with 25% paid by Kovert. This may be due to be adjustments relating to previous years' profits or other tax issues. If Kandid had a comparable finance cost and tax rate to Kovert, its ROE would be nearer that of Kovert.

Liquidity

The given ratios show that both entities have healthy liquidity positions. Kandid's current ratio is slightly higher than Kovert's, perhaps too high. This seems to be down to holding more cash than Kovert as it has better inventory and receivables control, though arguably the current lease liability of Kovert should not be included in this ratio for comparative purposes. The individual components of the current ratio could suggest that Kovert holds a greater range of inventory, perhaps enabling it to achieve more sales, and the relatively high receivables collection period could be indicative of an uncollectable customer balance which should have been written off, or may just be due to poor credit control.

Gearing

At around 65%, both entities are highly geared. The relatively low equity, particularly retained earnings, may be due to the entities having a policy of paying most of their earnings as dividends. Kovert's high gearing is in part due to its policy of using leases to acquire its plant. Xpand should be aware that, for both entities, the $5 million loans are due for repayment in the near future which will represent a substantial further cash outlay on top of the purchase price it may pay.

Summary

Although both entities operate in a same industry sector and have a similar level of after-tax profits, and indeed have the same indicative valuation, they would represent very different investments. Kovert's revenue is over 60% (15,000/25,000 × 100) higher than that of Kandid, it is financed by high levels of debt (loans and leases), and it also owns, rather than rents, its property. Another point of note is that Kovert's plant is 80% depreciated and will need replacement in the near future, with consequent financing implications. Ultimately, the investment decision may be determined by Xpand's attitude to risk and how well each investment would fit in with existing activities and management structure.

(c) Basing an investment decision solely on one year's summarised financial statements is fraught with danger. Below are a number of issues and items of information to which Xpand may wish to seek clarification before making an offer.

General:

- in addition to using different strategies (e.g. buying property or renting it, targeting low mark-up/high volume sales), the two entities may use different accounting policies

- the availability of non-published forward-looking information such as profit forecasts, capital commitments and the size of orders on the books (providing this information should not be unreasonable if the shareholders are receptive to a takeover)

- is either entity established or a relatively young and growing entity, with more risk, but potentially more reward?

Specific:

- as noted above, the owned assets of Kovert are nearing the end of their useful life. Will these need replacing soon, or have they already been replaced by the leased assets?

- how much of the profit is due to the reputation or contacts of the current management and would they continue in their role after a takeover (and indeed would Xpand want this or would it prefer to use its own managers)?

- the fair value of the assets, compared to their carrying amounts, which will impact on the calculation of goodwill.

Marking scheme		Marks
(a)	1 mark per ratio	4
(b)	1 mark per value point up to	12
(c)	1 mark per valid point up to	4
Total		**20**

398 SCHRUTE

Ratios for Schrute for the year ended 30 September 20X3

			20X2
Gross profit margin	51.1%	(48,000/94,000) × 100	59.1%
Operating profit margin	1.3%	(1,200/94,000) × 100	8.5%
Return on Capital Employed	1.0%	(1,200/(99,010 + 20,000)) × 100	7.4%
Current ratio	2.6:1	(24,110/9,100)	4.6:1
Inventory turnover period	52 days	(6,500/46,000) × 365	60 days
Receivables collection period	66 days	(17,000/94,000) × 365	83 days

Performance

Revenue and expenses have all increased during the year, due to the acquisition of Howard, the new subsidiary. Howard would have contributed a full year's results to 20X3 that would not have been included within 20X2.

Whilst revenue has increased significantly, it can be seen that higher expenses have meant that the Schrute group has made less profit than in previous years.

It is also worth noting that the new hotel was only opened in March, so a full year's revenue has not yet been generated by the hotel.

The gross profit margin has fallen. It may well be that the hotel business generates much lower margins than the farming side of things. It may also be that the new hotel had to offer low room rates to attract new business as it was set up, or to bring customers back with special offers following the poor feedback. As the hotel establishes itself, the need to cut prices will hopefully not be a common issue.

The improvement in online feedback should lead to increased future bookings, so it may be that the new hotel generates a significantly improved return in the next year.

The operating profit margin has also deteriorated in the year. In addition to this fall, there is a significant one-off $4.5 million income relating to the disposal of investments, which shows a false position.

Without this gain on disposal, Schrute would have made a worrying loss from operations of $3.3 million. Analysing this further, it can be seen that the reason for the loss would be due to a significant increase in administrative expenses, which would be $30.1 million if the investment disposal is ignored.

Some of these expenses may be linked to the acquisition of Howard, such as professional fees, which will not be incurred in future years. There may also be some redundancy costs included if Schrute has merged administrative departments with Howard such as human resources.

A number of expenses are likely to be linked to the new hotel project in the year.

A large amount of these administrative expenses will hopefully relate to set up costs for the hotel and can be regarded as one-off expenses. Schrute has undertaken a significant marketing campaign to reverse their reputation.

Whilst these could be classed as one-off expenses, there will be many expenses included that will remain high in future periods. Staff numbers will have increased due to the hotel, and costs such as heating, lighting, and repairs will continue to be incurred each year.

There has not been a significant increase in distribution costs in the year. This could suggest that Schrute has done significantly less business from the farming side of the business, or that Howard has extremely low distribution costs.

While the distribution costs may have been saved, it is questionable whether it is wise to have diversified to avoid the impact of fuel prices. Howard appears to have smaller margins, and will incur significant heating and lighting costs, which are likely to rise in a similar manner to fuel costs.

The return on capital employed (ROCE) has also deteriorated in the year. This would actually be negative if the gain on investments had not been included, as Schrute would have been loss-making.

As well as making less profit, the capital employed by Schrute has also increased significantly. New shares have been issued by Schrute, and a new loan has been taken out. All of this seems to have been due to the acquisition of Howard and the new hotel, which has not been operational for a full year.

It actually appears that Howard is a loss-making entity, as the non-controlling interest share of the profit is negative. This could mean that the rest of the Schrute group has remained profitable, with Howard generating a loss.

It could also be that there has been a significant impairment in the goodwill of Howard since acquisition. If Schrute uses the fair value method for valuing the non-controlling interest, the non-controlling interest will have an allocation of the impairment.

It may well be that in 20X4 the performance improves significantly as the new hotel has a full year's operation in the results and many of the set up costs will not be included.

Cash flow

The cash balance has fallen to $0.6 million. It should be noted that Schrute has undertaken a number of activities to raise cash in the year. Investments were sold for $15.5 million, $19 million was raised from a share issue and $20 million has been raised from debt finance. It seems that the vast majority of these funds were spent on the acquisition of Howard and the new hotel.

Looking at the other areas and their impact on cash flow, it can be seen that receivable days have decreased significantly in the year. With no indication of changes in customer terms for the farms, it is likely that this is the effect of Howard being largely cash based and having a positive impact on cash flow.

The inventory turnover period has reduced, which is likely to be due to Howard not having the same level of inventory, as inventory in a hotel may be limited to food and drink. A period of 52 days still seems potentially high for a business involved in the farming industry, and the inventory should be investigated to ensure that none of the produce has perished.

Conclusion

It is difficult to judge the success of the business as a whole in this transitional year. There are concerns over the acquisition of Howard. Whilst the revenue has increased significantly, Howard appears to have made a loss and put pressure onto the cash flow of the Schrute group.

The individual results of Howard need to be obtained for a more meaningful comparison to be made. It would then be possible to better understand the impact of the new hotel.

399 PITCARN

(a) **Ratios for the year ended 31 March 20X6**

Gross profit margin	30%	$(28,200/94,000) \times 100$
Operating margin	6%	$(5,600/94,000) \times 100$
Interest cover	2.9 times	$(5,600/(1,900)$

In producing the consolidated information, Sitor must be added in for the year, with adjustments made to remove the intra-group sale, rent, interest and dividend.

	20X6
	$000
Revenue (86,000 + 16,000 – 8,000 intra-group)	94,000
Cost of sales (63,400 + 10,400 – 8,000 intra-group)	(65,800)
Gross profit	28,200
Other income (3,400 – 300 rent – 1,000 dividend – 500 interest)	1,600
Operating expenses (21,300 + 3,200 – 300 rent)	(24,200)
Profit from operations	5,600
Finance costs (1,500 + 900 – 500 intra-group)	(1,900)

(b)   Looking at the figures calculated for the Pitcarn group, it seems that performance has deteriorated in terms of revenue, margins and interest cover.

This would suggest that the disposal of Sitor is a mistake, as the group appear to be performing worse without Sitor than when Sitor was included as a subsidiary.

Looking at Sitor's individual results appears to confirm this, as Sitor has profit margins which are higher than the rest of the group, both in terms of gross and operating margin.

A closer examination of Sitor's results highlights an issue to be aware of. Half of Sitor's revenue is made by selling to Pitcarn, and this is done at an extremely high margin of 40%. This is much higher than the margin of 35% made overall, and means that the other half of Sitor's sales must be made at a margin of 30%. This means that the external sales of Sitor are actually made at the same gross margin as the rest of the group.

It is possible that Pitcarn deliberately purchased goods from Sitor at an inflated price in order to demonstrate a stronger performance in Sitor in order to achieve a good selling price.

While this allowed, it highlights the problem with analysing an entity's performance based on its individual financial statements if it is part of a group, as prices can be manipulated within the group to artificially inflate the performance of one part.

A similar fear arises in respect of the operating margin. Sitor uses Pitcarn's properties, and is paying a lower rate than the market rate of rent. This will again artificially inflate the margin made by Sitor, as Pitcarn bear the majority of the property costs without recharging an accurate rate of rent.

It appears that Pitcarn have suffered lower margins in order to make the margins look better in Sitor by paying a high price for goods and not charging a market rate of rent. Pitcarn has taken a further $1.5 million cash out of Sitor during the year, through the receipt of a $1 million dividend and $500,000 interest. The loan agreement should be investigated further in order to assess if the interest charged was at market rates or not.

Following the disposal of Sitor, Pitcarn will lose at least $1.3 million of income through no longer obtaining a dividend or rent from the properties. For a more detailed analysis of future prospects, it will be important to speak to Pitcarn regarding the excess office space and whether there are plans to utilise it themselves or to rent it to a third party. The loan agreement with Sitor should also be examined to see if this will change following the sale. It may be that the interest rate increases now Sitor is no longer in the group, or the loan may need repaying by the new Sitor owners.

The one area where Sitor underperformed relative to the rest of the Pitcarn group is in terms of interest cover, with profits able to cover interest less times. Again, a review of the loan agreement with Pitcarn will be able to assess if this interest rate is at market rate, as Pitcarn may be charging a higher rate of interest than market rates in exchange for the cheaper rent and higher priced goods.

Examination should also be made as to whether Pitcarn will still need Sitor to supply goods. If so, supplies may be harder to obtain now that Sitor is no longer in the group.

Overall, the sale of Sitor appears to be a reasonable move. Whilst Sitor does appear to be making good profits, when the goods and rent with Pitcarn are adjusted to market values it is likely that Sitor would not be making significant profits. As long as Pitcarn is not reliant on Sitor as a supplier, this seems to be a reasonable move and one which may free up space in the premises to pursue more lucrative options.

(c) **Gain/loss on disposal**

	$000	$000
Proceeds		25,000
Net assets at disposal	17,000	
(10,000 share capital + 7,000 retained earnings)		
Goodwill at disposal (W1)	7,000	
Non-controlling interest at disposal (W2)	(3,800)	
		(20,200)
Gain on disposal		**4,800**

Workings

(W1) Goodwill

	$000
Consideration	17,000
NCI at acquisition	3,000
Net assets at acquisition	(13,000)
(10,000 share capital + 3,000 retained earnings)	
Goodwill at acquisition	7,000

(W2) Non-controlling interest at disposal

	$000
NCI at acquisition	3,000
NCI share of Sitor's post acquisition retained earnings	
(20% × (7,000 – 3,000))	800
Non-controlling interest at disposal	3,800

400 GREGORY

(a) **Note: References to 20X6 and 20X5 are to the years ending 31 March 20X6 and 20X5 respectively.**

Comment (1)

"I see the profit for the year has increased by $1m which is up 20% on last year, but I thought it would be more as Tamsin was supposed to be very profitable."

There are two issues with this statement: first, last year's profit is not comparable with the current year's profit because in 20X5 Gregory was a single entity and in 20X6 it is now a group with a subsidiary. A second issue is that the consolidated statement of profit or loss for the year ended 31 March 20X6 only includes six months of the results of Tamsin, and, assuming Tamsin is profitable, future results will include a full year's profit. This latter point may, at least in part, mitigate the CEO's disappointment.

Comment (2)

"I have calculated the EPS for 20X6 at 13 cents (6, 000/46, 000 × 100 shares) and at 12.5 cents for 20X5 (5,000/40, 000 × 100) and, although the profit has increased 20%, our EPS has barely changed."

The stated EPS calculation for 20X6 is incorrect for two reasons: first, it is the profit attributable to only the equity shareholders of the parent which should be used and second the 6 million new shares were only in issue for six months and should be weighted by $^6/_{12}$. Thus, the correct EPS for 20X6 is 13.3 cents (5,700/43,000 × 100). This gives an increase of 6% (13.3 − 12.5)/12.5) on 20X5 EPS which is still less than the increase in profit. The reason why the EPS may not have increased in line with reported profit is that the acquisition was financed by a share exchange which increased the number of shares in issue. Thus the EPS takes account of the additional consideration used to generate profit, whereas the trend of absolute profit does not take additional consideration into account. This is why the EPS is often said to be a more accurate reflection of performance than the trend of profits.

Comment (3)

"I am worried that the low price at which we are selling goods to Tamsin is undermining our group's overall profitability."

Assuming the consolidated financial statements have been correctly prepared, all intra-group trading has been eliminated, thus the pricing policy will have had no effect on these financial statements. The comment is incorrect and reflects a misunderstanding of the consolidation process.

Comment (4)

"I note that our share price is now $2.30, how does this compare with our share price immediately before we bought Tamsin?"

The increase in share capital is 6 million shares, the increase in the share premium is $6m, thus the total proceeds for the 6 million shares was $12m giving a share price of $2 at the date of acquisition of Tamsin. The current price of $2.30 presumably reflects the market's favourable view of Gregory's current and future performance.

(b)

		20X6	20X5
(i)	Return on capital employed (ROCE) (7,500/74,300 × 100)	10.1%	11.3%
(ii)	Net asset turnover (46,500/74,300)	0.63 times	0.53 times
(iii)	Gross profit margin (9,300/46,500 × 100)	20.0%	25.7%
(iv)	Operating profit margin (7,500/46,500 × 100)	16.1%	21.4%

Looking at the above ratios, it appears that the overall performance of Gregory has declined marginally. The ROCE has fallen from 11.3% to 10.1%, which has been caused by a substantial fall in the gross profit margin (down from 25.7% in 20X5 to 20% in 20X6), over a 22% (5.7%/25.7%) decrease. The group have relatively low operating expenses (at around 4% of revenue), so the poor gross profit margin feeds through to the operating profit margin. The overall decline in the ROCE due to the weaker profit margins has been mitigated by an improvement in net asset turnover, increasing from 0.53 times to 0.63 times. Despite the improvement in net asset turnover, it still seems very low, with only 63 cents of sales generated from every $1 invested in the business, although this will depend on the type of business Gregory and Tamsin are engaged in.

On this analysis, the effect of the acquisition of Tamsin seems to have had a detrimental effect on overall performance, but this may not necessarily be the case, as there could be some distorting factors in the analysis. As mentioned above, the 20X6 results include only six months of Tamsin's results, but the statement of financial position includes the full amount of the consideration for Tamsin. [The consideration has been calculated (see comment (4) above) as $12m for the parent's 75% share plus $3.3m (3,600 – 300 share of post-acquisition profit) for the non-controlling interest's 25%, giving total consideration of $15.3m.] The above factors disproportionately increase the denominator of ROCE which has the effect of worsening the calculated ROCE. This distortion should be corrected in 20X7 when a full year's results for Tamsin will be included in group profit. Another factor is that it could take time to fully integrate the activities of the two entities and more savings and other synergies may be forthcoming such as bulk buying discounts.

The non-controlling interest share in the profit for the year in 20X6 of $300,000 allows a rough calculation of the full year's profit of Tamsin at $2.4m (300,000/25% × $^{12}/_6$, i.e. the $300,000 represents 25% of $^6/_{12}$ of the annual profit). This figure is subject to some uncertainty such as the effect of probable increased post-acquisition depreciation charges. However, a profit of $2.4m on the investment of $15.3m represents a return of 16% (and would be higher if the profit was adjusted to a pre-tax figure) which is much higher than the current year ROCE (at 10.1%) of the group. This implies that the performance of Tamsin is much better than that of Gregory as a separate entity, and that Gregory's performance in 20X6 must have deteriorated considerably from that in 20X5 and this is the real cause of the deteriorating performance of the group.

Another issue potentially affecting the ROCE is that, as a result of the consolidation process, Tamsin's net assets, including goodwill, are included in the statement of financial position at fair value, whereas Gregory's net assets appear to be based on historical cost, as there is no revaluation surplus. As the values of property, plant and equipment have been rising, this effect favourably flatters the 20X5 ratios. This is because the statement of financial position of 20X5 only contains Gregory's assets which, at historical cost, may considerably understate their fair value and, on a comparative basis, overstate 20X5 ROCE.

In summary, although on first impression the acquisition of Tamsin appears to have caused a marginal worsening of the group's performance, the distorting factors and imputation of the non-controlling interest's profit in 20X6 indicate the underlying performance may be better than the ratios portray and the contribution from Tamsin is a very significant positive. Future performance may be even better.

Without information on the separate financial statements of Tamsin, it is difficult to form a more definite view.

Marking scheme		
		Marks
(a)	2 marks for each reply to the CEO's observations	8
(b)	1 mark for each pair of ratios	4
	1 mark per relevant comment on performance up to	8
		12
Total		**20**

Examiner's comments

This is the first time a question combining interpretation with an element of consolidation has been examined and candidates did find this a challenging question.

For part (a) the comments required in response to the Chief Executive Officer (CEO)'s observations were not at the expected standard. Most candidates launched into irrelevant detail regarding ratio movements and did not consider the reason for the difference between the two years' financial statements, specifically that the statement of profit or loss for the second year included the consolidated results of the newly-acquired subsidiary but, crucially, only for six months.

The low margin on intra-group sales was seen by many candidates as, correctly, not affecting the consolidated financial statements or the overall profitability of the group. Some candidates did mention the impact of any unrealised profit on inventories held from such trading, but this was not likely to have a material effect.

For part (b) the four ratio calculations were generally well done although for ROCE, capital employed should include the non-controlling interest as this is part of equity (those who took total assets less current liabilities had no problem with this) and the calculation of net asset turnover (revenue/capital employed) was either omitted or the figures inverted. A minority of candidates attempted to adjust for the intra-group transactions before calculating ratios which was not required as we must assume that intra-group transactions had already been correctly eliminated on consolidation.

For the comments on comparative performance, the usual observations on past papers continue to apply. To suggest ratios have increased or decreased does not qualify as analysis; suggesting the change is better or worse begins to show understanding, but more than this is required. In many cases the impact of the acquisition (as answered in part (a)) was completely ignored and candidates compared this year and last year results as if they were directly comparing like with like.

The relationship between gross and operating profit margin was often misunderstood. Many candidates stated that the decrease in the operating margin was caused by increased operating costs when in fact operating costs were a lower % of revenue in the second year (despite any one-off costs of the acquisition) and the cause of the decrease was the reduction in the gross profit margin. Very few candidates used the information in the question regarding the non-controlling interest in the subsidiary's profit to determine the subsidiary's possible contribution to the group's profit for the year and thus determine that there could have been a decline in the profit earned by the parent alone in the second year.

401 LANDING

(a) Archway's restated figures

On the assumption that Landing purchases Archway, the following adjustments relate to the effects of notes (i) to (iii) in the question and the property revaluation:

	$000
Revenue (94,000 × 95%)	89,300
Cost of sales (see below)	76,000
Loan interest (10,000 × 8%)	800
Equity (10,000 + 2,300 RE + 3,000 revaluation)	15,300
Non-current liabilities: 8% loan notes	10,000

The cost of sales should be first adjusted for the annual licence fee of $1m, reducing this to $72m. Half of these, $36m, are net of a discount of 10% which equates to $4m (36,000/90% – 36,000). Adjusted cost of sales is $76m (73,000 – 1,000 + 4,000).

(b) These figures would give the following ratios:

Annual sales per square metre of floor space	(89,300/12,000)	$7,442
ROCE	(13,300 – 10,000)/(15,300 + 10,000) × 100)	13%
Net asset turnover	(89,300/(15,300 + 10,000))	3.5 times
Gross profit margin	((89,300 – 76,000)/89,300 × 100)	15%
Operating profit margin	((13,300 – 10,000)/89,300 × 100)	3.7 %
Gearing (debt/equity)	(10,000/15,300)	65.4%

(c) Performance

	Archway as reported	Archway as adjusted	Sector average
Annual sales per square metre of floor space	$7,833	$7,442	$8,000
ROCE	58.5%	13%	18.0%
Net asset turnover	5.0 times	3.5 times	2.7 times
Gross profit margin	22.3%	15%	22.0%
Operating profit margin	11.7%	3.7%	6.7%
Gearing (debt/equity)	nil	65.4%	30.0%

A comparison of Archway's ratios based upon the reported results compares very favourably to the sector average ratios in almost every instance. ROCE is particularly impressive at 58.5% compared to a sector average of 18%; this represents a return of more than three times the sector average. The superior secondary ratios of profit margin and asset utilisation (net asset turnover) appear to confirm Archway's above average performance. It is only sales per square metre of floor space which is below the sector average. The unadjusted figure is very close to the sector average, as too is the gross profit margin, implying a comparable sales volume performance. However, the reduction in selling prices caused by the removal of the brand premium causes sales per square metre to fall marginally.

As indicated in the question, should Archway be acquired by Landing, many figures particularly related to the statement of profit or loss would be unfavourably impacted as shown above in the workings for Archway's adjusted ratios. When these effects are taken into account and the ratios are recalculated, a very different picture emerges. All the performance ratios, with the exception of net asset turnover, are significantly reduced due to the assumed cessation of the favourable trading arrangements. The most dramatic effect is on the ROCE, which, having been more than three times the sector average, would be 27.8% (18.0 – 13.0)/18.0 × 100) below the sector average (at 13% compared to 18.0%). Analysing the component parts of the ROCE (net asset turnover and profit margins), both aspects are lower when the reported figures are adjusted.

The net asset turnover (although adjusted to a lower multiple) is still considerably higher than the sector average. The fall in this ratio is due to a combination of lower revenues (caused by the loss of the branding) and the increase in capital employed (equal to net assets) due to classifying the loan notes as debt (non-current). Gross margin deteriorates from 22.3% to only 15.0% caused by a combination of lower revenues (referred to above) and the loss of the discount on purchases. The distribution costs and administrative expenses for Archway are less than those of its retail sector in terms of the percentage of sales revenue (at 11.3% compared to 15.3%), which mitigates (slightly) the dramatic reduction in the profit before interest and tax. The reduction in sales per square metre of floor space is caused only by the reduced (5%) volume from the removal of the branded sales.

Gearing

The gearing ratio of nil based on the unadjusted figures is not meaningful due to previous debt being classified as a current liability because of its imminent redemption. When this debt is replaced by the 8% loan notes and (more realistically) classified as a non-current liability, Archway's gearing is much higher than the sector average. There is no information as to how the increased interest payable at 8% (double the previous 4%) compares to the sector's average finance cost. If such a figure were available, it may give an indication of Archway's credit status although the doubling of the rate does imply a greater degree of risk in Archway seen by the lender.

Summary and advice

Based upon Archway's reported figures, its purchase by Landing would appear to be a good investment. However, when Archway's performance is assessed based on the results and financial position which might be expected under Landing's ownership, the recalculated ratios are generally inferior to Archway's retail sector averages. In an investment decision such as this, an important projected ratio would be the return on the investment (ROI) which Landing might expect. The expected net profit after tax can be calculated as $2m ((3,300 before interest and tax − 800 interest) × 80% post-tax), however, there is no information in the question as to what the purchase consideration of Archway would be. That said, at a (probable) minimum purchase price based on Archway's net asset value (with no goodwill premium), the ROI would only be 7.9% (2,000/25,300 × 100) which is very modest and should be compared to Landing's existing ROI. A purchase price exceeding $25.3m would obviously result in an even lower expected ROI. It is possible that under Landing's management, Archway's profit margins could be improved, perhaps coming to a similar arrangement regarding access to branded sales (or franchising) as currently exists with Cardol, but with a different entity. If so, the purchase of Archway may still be a reasonable acquisition.

ACCA Marking scheme		
		Marks
(a)	Revenue	½
	Cost of sales	2
	Loan interest	½
	Equity	1½
	Non-current liabilities	½
		5
(b)	1 mark per ratio	6
(c)	1 mark per relevant comment up to	9
Total		**20**

402 FUNJECT CO

(a) **Restated financial information**

Statement of profit or loss

	20X4
	$000
Revenue (54,200 – 2,100 (note (i)))	52,100
Cost of sales (21,500 – 1,200 (note (i)))	(20,300)
Gross profit	31,800
Operating expenses (W1)	(12,212)
Profit before tax	19,588

(W1) Restatement of operating expenses

	20X4
	$000
As per question	11,700
Less: expenses relating to non-core division	(700)
Less: loss on disposal of non-core division	(1,500)
Less: Gamilton management charge (54,200 × 1%)	(542)
Add: Funject management charge (31,800 × 10%)	3,180
Less: rent charged by Gamilton	(46)
Add: commercial rent	120
Restated operating expenses	12,212

(b) Profit has decreased from $21,000,000 to $19,588,000 and the resulting journal entry will be ($000s):

Dr Retained earnings (21,000 – 19,588)	$1,412
Cr Cash	$1,412

Ratio calculations

		20X4
Gross profit margin	31,800/52,100 × 100	61%
Operating profit margin	19,588/52,100 × 100	38%
Receivables collection period (days)	(5,700/52,100) × 365	40 days
Current ratio	(12,900 – 1,412)/(11600)	1:1
Acid test (quick)ratio	(12,900 – 4,900 – 1,412)/(11,600)	0.57:1
Gearing (debt/equity)	16,700/(9,000 – 1,412)	220%

(c)   **Commentary on performance**

Profitability

The discontinued operation had a gross profit % (GP%) of 43% (900/2,100 × 100) and an operating profit % (OP%) of 10% (200/2,100 × 100). Before adjusting for the disposal, Aspect Co had a GP% of 60%. After an adjustment has been made to reflect the disposal, Aspect Co's GP% is 61%, which is higher than the industry average of 45%. Thus, it would appear that the disposal of the non-core division has had a positive impact on the GP% of Aspect Co. Such a positive comparison of the GP% to the industry average would suggest that Aspect Co has negotiated a very good deal with its suppliers for the cost of goods in comparison to its competitors, as the GP% is 16% (61 – 45) higher than the industry average.

However, when considering the OP%, the financial statements have been adjusted to reflect: (i) the disposal of the discontinued operation, (ii) a new management charge which would be imposed by Funject Co, and (iii) commercial rent charges. These adjustments result in an OP% of 38%. So, although the OP% is still 10% (38 – 28) higher than the industry average, it would appear that some of the advantage of having such a good deal with its suppliers is lost when operating costs are incurred. The OP% does not outperform the industry average to the same extent that GP% did. Although the management charge will be eliminated as an intra-group transaction on consolidation, it will still have an impact in the individual financial statements of Aspect Co. However, there is no indication of what this charge represents, and whether or not it reflects a market value for these costs. The rent of $120,000 is deemed to be a fair market value which would indicate that the previous rent charge of $46,000 was artificially low. If Funject Co acquires Aspect Co, it may wish to capitalise on the relationship which Aspect Co has with its supplier of goods but it might also need to investigate the composition of operating costs other than those described above to see if any of these can be avoided or reduced.

Liquidity

Aspect Co's receivables collection period appears to be comparable with the KPIs provided (40 days in comparison to 41 days). Terms of trade of 30 days are quite reasonable (though this usually depends on the type of business) and so there appear to be no causes for concern here.

Given that Aspect Co's receivables collection period is comparable to the industry average, the difference in the current ratio (1:1 in comparison to 1.6:1) can only be explained by either lower current assets other than receivables (for example, cash) or higher current liabilities. As Aspect Co's cash balance does not appear to be low ($2.3m), this suggests that its liabilities might be higher than average. Perhaps Aspect Co's favourable relationship with its suppliers also extends to longer than average credit terms. As Aspect Co's acid (quick) ratio (0.57:1) is much less than the industry average (1.4:1), this would also suggest that Aspect Co is holding a higher than average level of inventory. This may raise a concern about Aspect Co's ability to sell its inventory. There is also a current tax bill to consider. Indeed, if Aspect Co were asked to settle its current liabilities from merely its receivables and bank, it would be unable to do so. Perhaps Funject Co may wish to further investigate the procedures associated with the purchase and holding of Aspect Co's inventory prior to a takeover. As a parent company, Funject Co should be able to influence these procedures and have more control over the levels of inventory held.

Gearing

Aspect Co appears to be highly-geared but perhaps this is not a huge cause for concern because it appears to be a highly-geared industry (220% compared to 240%). It may be that the proceeds from the sale of the non-core division can be or perhaps were used to repay loans. As the gearing for the industry is higher than that of Aspect Co, it may be that Aspect Co could still increase borrowings in future. If so, Aspect Co may need to increase working capital efficiency and reduce costs in order to generate enough cash to service higher borrowings.

Conclusion

Overall, Aspect's statement of financial position gives little cause for concern: the profit margins appear to be healthy, although further investigation of operating costs and working capital efficiency may be required. More information also needs to be obtained about the nature of the business and perhaps the financial statements of several years (as opposed to one) would also be beneficial.

ACCA Marking scheme		Marks
(a)	Adjustment to revenue and cost of sales	1
	Disposal of non-core division	1
	Management charge (remove old, add new)	2
	Rent expense (remove current, add commercial)	1
		5
(b)	1 mark per ratio	5
(c)	1 mark per relevant comment:	
	Profitability	5
	Liquidity	3
	Gearing	1
	Conclusion	1
		10
Total		**20**

403 FLASH CO

(a)

		20X4		20X3
Gross profit margin	(37,000/92,600)	40%	(29,400/81,700)	36%
Operating profit margin	(22,600/92,600)	24.4%	(17,100/81,700)	20.9%
Interest cover	(22,600/5,100)	4.4 times	(17,100/4,200)	4.1 times
Cash generated from operations/profit from operations	(29,900/22,600)	132.3%	(18,000/17,100)	105.3%

(b) **Performance**

Flash Co's revenue has increased significantly in 20X4. This increase is likely to be due to Flash's geographical expansion during 20X4.

The loss of a competitor during the year will have benefitted Flash Co, as the competitor's customers seek alternative supply. There is likely to be much less impact in 20X4 from the new stores, as these only opened in February 20X4, but we would expect that the effect of the new stores will prove much more significant in future years, once a full year's income is recognised from the new locations.

Flash Co's gross profit margin has increased from 36% to 40%, and there may be a number of reasons for this. Flash Co are likely to have been able to charge higher prices for solar panels following the increased demand for that product.

Secondly the improved terms with major suppliers are also likely to have contributed to lower purchase prices. This will also have improved the gross profit margin.

The operating margin has also increased, although slightly less than the increase in gross profit, which suggests that operating costs have increased. A quick analysis shows that operating costs have increased by 17% compared to an increase in revenue of 13%. This increase is likely to incorporate various one-off costs associated with the geographical expansion and acquisition of new stores. In the year of acquisition and opening, there would be expected to be numerous set-up and marketing costs, but these have not led to an excessive increase in costs. In future years these costs will not be repeated and we should see an improvement in operating margins.

Interest cover has improved in the year, despite the increase in finance costs which will have arisen as a result of the new loan notes. This demonstrates that Flash Co is generating sufficiently robust profits to meet its interest obligations.

It is likely that the 8% loan notes were issued to fund the acquisition of the new stores, and may therefore not have been in existence for the entire period. The annual interest payable on these new loan notes will be $0.8m, so Flash Co will easily be able to cover this based on 20X4's performance.

Cash flow

Flash Co is generating excellent cash from operations in comparison to the profit from operations in both years, and there is a significant improvement in this from 20X3 to 20X4. The cash generated in 20X4 easily covers the interest and tax payments, as well as a dividend. This shows that sufficient cash exists for the expansion of the business.

In addition to this, Flash Co's working capital management seems to be strong. Inventories have fallen during the year despite the increased sales level. This is likely to be due to the high demand for solar panels.

There is a significant increase in trade receivables, which is likely to be as a result of acquiring new customers following the demise of the competitor.

The increase in trade payables is likely to result from the increased trading levels, together with an increased payment period following the negotiated improved terms with major suppliers.

The major reason for the net cash outflow during the year is the large amount spent on the purchase of property, plant and equipment. This is likely to be linked to the acquisition of the new stores, and related geographical expansion.

Of the $31.6m spend on new assets, $22.5m is funded from the cash generated from Flash Co's operating activity, demonstrating the sustainable strength of Flash Co's performance.

Flash Co has raised $10m through the issue of 8% loan notes in the year. These are likely to have been issued to fund the acquisition of the new stores, which is an appropriate use of long-term financing. As stated previously, Flash Co is easily capable of covering the interest payments on this, although it is worth noting that the finance costs are greater than the interest paid. This suggests that the effective rate of interest on their overall funding is above that being paid, and may mean that a redemption premium will be payable in the future.

Conclusion

To reassure the sales director it is worth pointing out that cash inflows and outflows arise as a result of the three different activities that an entity undertakes: operating, investing and financing. The increased levels of profit mentioned by the sales director are reflected within the cash generated from operating activities. The net reduction in cash balances during the year is due to significant levels of investing activity as a result of the business expansion, but this should lead to increased levels of revenue and profits in the future.

	ACCA marking guide	
		Marks
(a)	Ratios	4
(b)	Revenue and margins	7
	Interest cover	2
	Cash flow	6
	Conclusion	1
		16
Total		**20**

404 MOWAIR CO

(a)

	20X7	Workings	20X6	Workings
Operating profit margin	8.0%	12,300/154,000	11.7%	18,600/159,000
Return on capital employed	3.6%	12,300/(192,100 + 130,960 +19,440)	8.7%	18,600/(44,800 + 150,400 +19,440)
Net asset turnover	0.45 times	154,000/(192,100 + 130,960 +19,440)	0.74 times	159,000/(44,800 + 150,400 +19,440)
Current ratio	0.53:1	15,980/29,920	1.22:1	28,890/23,690
Interest cover	1.3 times	12,300/9200	1.8 times	18,600/10,200
Gearing (Debt/Equity)	78.3%	(130,960+19,440)/ 192,100	379.1%	(150,400 + 19,440)/44,800

(b)   Performance

Mowair Co's revenue has declined in the year. As Mowair Co has had exactly the same number of flights in the year, the decline must be due to either lower numbers of passengers or from Mowair Co reducing the price on certain flights. To substantiate this, it would be helpful to see the number of passengers who have flown on Mowair Co flights during the year.

In addition to the decline in revenue, there has been a decline in the operating profit margin in the year. As the number of flights operated by Mowair Co has remained the same, it would appear that a number of the costs incurred by Mowair Co on operating the airline will be relatively fixed and may not have changed significantly during the year. It has been noted that there has been an increase in cost of licences charged by airports during the year, which would again cause the operating profit margin to fall as amortisation would be higher. This only occurred in April 20X7, so the full impact will not actually be felt until next year.

In addition to this, it important to note that there are numerous contracts up for renewal in the next year. This could lead to higher prices for using the airports, and may even result in Mowair Co being unable to use those airports in future. If this was the case, it may have a significant impact on the revenue for the business, as these are described as major airports, which will have the higher levels of demand.

Return on capital employed has declined significantly in the year. There are two major reasons for this. First, there has been a decline in the profit from operations, as discussed above. In addition to this, Mowair Co has revalued its non-current assets in the year. This means that there is a large revaluation surplus in 20X7 which was not present in 20X6. This will have the effect of reducing the return on capital employed due to there being a much larger total balance in equity. If the return on capital employed is calculated without this, it would be 6.2%, which still represents a decline in performance.

Looking at the net asset turnover, this has declined dramatically from 0.74 times to 0.45 times. This will again be affected by the revaluation surplus, making the two years incomparable. If this is removed from the calculation, the net asset turnover increases to 0.78 times. This is a slight increase in performance. This increase has not come from increased revenue, as it can be seen that revenue has fallen by $5 million. Rather, this increase has come from the decrease in capital employed. This arises from the reduction in the loan notes, which appear to have a significant amount repaid annually.

Position

The value of non-current assets has risen sharply in the year, by $147 million. A large proportion of that will be due to the revaluation which has taken place, leading to an increase of $145 million. This suggests that Mowair Co has acquired some new assets in the year, but it is unclear what these are. They may be replacement components on aircraft, as it is unlikely to be significant enough to be an actual new aircraft itself.

The level of debt in the business is a concern, as this makes up a significant portion of the entity's financing, and appears to incur a large annual repayment. The reduction in the current ratio can be attributed to the large decrease in cash, which is likely to be due to the debt repayments made.

It is worth noting that Mowair Co is almost completely funded by debt, with a relatively small amount held in share capital. Therefore, there is an opportunity for a new investor to consider putting more money into the business in the form of shares and the company then repaying some of the loans held by Mowair Co. As Mowair Co is currently repaying $19 million a year on the loans, it may be more sensible to repay these if possible, freeing up a lot more cash for growing the business or to be returned annually in the form of dividends, also saving $9 million a year in interest.

Areas of concern for the future

There are a number of things to consider regarding the future performance of Mowair Co. The first of these is the ten major licences which are due for renegotiation with airports. If the price is raised on these, then this will lead to reduced profits being made by Mowair Co in future periods.

The debt appears to be being repaid in annual instalments of $19 million, meaning that Mowair Co needs to generate sufficient cash to repay that each year, before returning any profit to the owner. In addition to this, the $9 million interest means that the business appears currently unable to return any cash to investors.

Finally, Mowair Co's business model is heavily dependent on large, expensive items of non-current assets. It has been noted that there has been criticism of under-investment in these, so this could lead to large potential outlays in the near future to replace assets.

Conclusion

Mowair Co has not shown a weakened performance in the current year, but appears to be a profitable business at its core. The major issue with the business is the level of debt, which is resulting in $19 million annual repayments and $9 million annual interest. Any new investor who was able to reduce these amounts as part of any future purchase, would put the business in a much stronger cash position.

ACCA marking guide		
		Marks
(a)	Ratio calculations	6
		—
(b)	Performance	6
	Position	4
	Future issues of concern	3
	Conclusion	1
		—
		14
		—
Total		**20**
		—

Examiner's Comments

This was a standard ratios and analysis question built around summary financial statements and a brief scenario for an airline. As in many previous diets, the majority of answers provided for the interpretation were superficial and lacked depth. This commentary shows how these answers might have been improved.

Candidates are reminded to provide workings to support all ratio calculations as these are helpful to markers. Appropriate workings allow markers to see what adjustments have been made, and to ensure that any obvious arithmetic errors are not penalised. This approach also allows markers to easily apply the "own figure" rule where candidates have interpreted ratios that have been calculated incorrectly.

For part (b), the structure of candidates' responses could have been improved had they been presented in three (headed) sections: performance, position and conclusion. This approach was consistent with the requirements of the question and the marking grid. Additionally, there was a specific requirement to highlight issues that the company should consider in the near future. Few candidates gave any separate consideration to these issues at all; very good scripts identified this as a separate heading and reflected on their analysis of the company's recent past and looked forward.

Candidates were expected to use the information provided in the scenario which gave useful clues as to why the company's performance in 20X7 was weaker than in 20X6. (A few candidates got the years the wrong way round, however, markers continued to give due credit in such circumstances)

Many candidates noted if the ratios in part (a) were higher or lower, the percentage increase or decrease from the past year and whether they represented an improvement or a worsening of the financial performance or position. Whilst this approach is acceptable as an introductory sentence, it does not answer the question and does not comment on the company's performance or position using of all the information available.

A key criticism of the company was its under-investment in its non-current assets. However, there was a substantial increase in the carrying amount of its property, plant and equipment (PPE) which led many candidates to say that such investment had taken place without appreciating that these assets had been revalued, for the first time, by almost the same amount as the increase in carrying amount. Removing the effect of the revaluation from the 20X7 carrying amount shows a small reduction in PPE, thus confirming (subject to depreciation charges) that no substantial investment had taken place. Well-prepared candidates pointed out that this distorted comparison between the two years (particularly for key ratios such as ROCE, net asset turnover and gearing).

Revenue and operating profit margin had both declined (one is not an inevitable consequence of the other) although the number of flights and destinations remained the same. This invited comments as to the company's pricing policies, number of passengers carried, cost control, the incidence of fixed costs (for an airline these would be significant) and the part-year effect of increased licence costs.

ROCE declined significantly but was, as noted above, materially influenced by the impact of the PPE revaluation and the decline in profit from operations in both absolute and relative terms. Candidates were given credit if their answer included a revised 20X7 ROCE calculation, excluding the effect of the revaluation, for a better comparison between the two years. In this case, this showed a decline but not as significant as the initial calculations. A similar approach could have been taken to net asset turnover which showed a very slight increase in 20X7. This was caused by a combination of the decline in revenue and a decrease in capital employed evidenced by the decrease in cash and cash equivalents and/or non-current liabilities.

The cost of the licences acquired late in the financial year was responsible for the increase in intangible assets. It was not possible for candidates to assess the impact of increased depreciation charges caused by the revaluation of PPE or amortisation of the intangible assets, but a good answer referred to these charges having a further impact on 20X7 margins and thereby limiting a valid comparison between the two years.

With respect to the current ratio, many candidates insisted that as this ratio was below 2:1, this was a significant financial problem. There are no "ideal" ratios and no sector averages were provided on this occasion so answers should have concentrated on the reasons for the decline which were a combination of the increase in trade payables and the decrease in cash and cash equivalents (influenced by the repayment of loan notes).

Interest cover had declined, even though finance costs had decreased (because of the repayment of some loan notes). This was primarily because of the decline in the profit from operations noted earlier. The decline in cash flow from operations provided further evidence of potential liquidity problems for the company.

Unless the revaluation surplus was excluded from the 20X7 equity, the decrease in gearing was not a valid comparison or evidence of a stronger financial position. The main reason for the decrease was the impact of the revaluation. If this was removed it shows that gearing was still worryingly high – especially for a company that will need to invest in new non-current assets in the near future (to address the issue of recent under-investment).

The above commentary on performance and position is intended to offer those working through the question an insight into the sort of issues that should be taken from the question (especially the written narrative and candidate's own ratios) and applied to support analysis of the company's (in this case) financial weaknesses.

The question asked candidates to "highlight any issues that Mowair Co should be considering in the near future". As this was specifically asked, markers were looking for responses – ideally as a separately headed section in answers. Very few candidates made any reasonable attempt at this although observations from the question were repeated in different parts of answers. Good answers could have mentioned, under one heading, such impending issues as: the impact of the negotiations with airports for more new licences which will put further strain on profitability and cash flow and may even prevent the company from using those airports if renewal costs are prohibitive; the high levels of existing debt and the company's limited ability to continue to pay this off; the possible difficulties of paying dividends with little available profit and cash; the need to invest in non-current assets and how this investment will be financed.

A conclusion, drawing together key issues (present and future in this case) in a short final paragraph was expected.

405 PERKINS

(a) **Gain on disposal in Perkins group consolidated statement of profit or loss**

	$000
Proceeds	28,640
Less: Goodwill (W1)	(4,300)
Less: Net assets at disposal	(26,100)
Add: NCI at disposal (W2)	6,160
	4,400

(W1) Goodwill

	$000
Consideration	19,200
NCI at acquisition	4,900
Less: Net assets at acquisition	
	4,300

(W2) NCI at disposal

	$000
NCI at acquisition	4,900
NCI% × S post acquisition	
20% × (26,100 – 19,800)	1,260
	6,160

(b) **Adjusted P/L extracts:**

	$000
Revenue (46,220 – 9,000 (S × 8/12) + 1,000 (intra-group))	38,220
Cost of sales (23,980 – 4,400 (S × 8/12)) [see note]	(19,580)
Gross profit	18,640
Operating expenses (3,300 – 1,673 (S × 8/12) + 9,440 profit on disposal)	(11,067)
Profit from operations	7,573
Finance costs (960 – 800 (S x 8/12))	(160)

Note: Originally, the intra-group sale resulted in $1m turnover and $0.7m costs of sales. These amounts were recorded in the individual financial statements of Perkins Co. On consolidation, the $1m turnover was eliminated – this needs to be added back. The corresponding $1 m COS consolidation adjustment is technically made to Swanson Co's financial statements and so can be ignored here.

(c) **Ratios of Perkins Co, eliminating impact of Swanson Co and the disposal during the year**

	20X7 recalculated	Working (see P/L above)	20X7 original	20X6
Gross profit margin	48.8%	18,640/38,220	48.1%	44.8%
Operating margin	19.8%	7,573/38,220	41%	16.8%
Interest cover	47.3 times	7,573/160	19.7 times	3.5 times

(d) **Analysis of Perkins Co**

Gross profit margin

In looking at the gross margin of Perkins Co, the underlying margin made by Perkins Co is higher than in 20X6.

After the removal of Swanson Co's results, this continues to increase, despite Swanson Co having a gross margin of over 50%. It is possible that Swanson Co's gross profit margin was artificially inflated by obtaining cheap supplies from Perkins Co. Perkins Co makes a margin of 48.8%, but only sold goods to Swanson at 30%.

Operating margin

The operating margin appears to have increased significantly on the prior year. It must be noted that this contains the profit on disposal of Swanson Co, which increases this significantly.

Removing the impact of the Swanson Co disposal still shows that the margin is improved on the prior year, but it is much more in line.

Swanson Co's operating margin is 32.6%, significantly higher than the margin earned by Perkins Co, again suggesting that a profitable business has been sold. This is likely to be due to the fact that Swanson Co was able to use Perkins Co's facilities with no charge, meaning its operating expenses were understated compared to the market prices.

It is likely that the rental income earned from the new tenant has helped to improve the operating margin, and this should increase further once the tenant has been in for a full year.

Interest cover

Initially, the interest cover has shown good improvement in 20X7 compared to 20X6, as there has been a significant increase in profits. Even with the profit on disposal stripped out, the interest cover would still be very healthy.

Following the removal of Swanson Co, the interest cover is improved further. This may be because the disposal of Swanson Co has allowed Perkins Co to repay debt and reduce the interest expense incurred.

Conclusion

Swanson Co seems to have been a profitable company, which raises questions over the disposal. However, some of these profits may have been derived from favourable terms with Perkins Co, such as cheap supplies and free rental. It is worth noting that Perkins Co now has rental income in the year. This should grow in future periods, as this is likely to be a full year's income in future periods.

<table>
<tr><td colspan="3" align="center">**ACCA marking guide**</td></tr>
<tr><td></td><td></td><td align="right">*Marks*</td></tr>
<tr><td>(a)</td><td>Proceeds</td><td align="right">½</td></tr>
<tr><td></td><td>Goodwill</td><td align="right">2½</td></tr>
<tr><td></td><td>Net assets</td><td align="right">½</td></tr>
<tr><td></td><td>NCI</td><td align="right">1½</td></tr>
<tr><td></td><td></td><td align="right">5</td></tr>
<tr><td>(b)</td><td>Revenue and COS</td><td align="right">2</td></tr>
<tr><td></td><td>Other costs</td><td align="right">2</td></tr>
<tr><td></td><td></td><td align="right">4</td></tr>
<tr><td>(c)</td><td>Ratios</td><td align="right">2</td></tr>
<tr><td>(d)</td><td>Gross profit margin</td><td align="right">2</td></tr>
<tr><td></td><td>Operating profit margin</td><td align="right">5</td></tr>
<tr><td></td><td>Interest cover</td><td align="right">1</td></tr>
<tr><td></td><td>Conclusion</td><td align="right">1</td></tr>
<tr><td></td><td></td><td align="right">9</td></tr>
<tr><td>**Total**</td><td></td><td align="right">**20**</td></tr>
</table>

406 DUKE CO

(a)   Calculation of NCI and retained earnings:

	$000
Non-controlling interest (W1)	3,740
Retained earnings (W2)	14,060

(W1) Non-controlling interest

	$000	
NCI at acquisition	3,400	
NCI% × S post acq	700	20% × ($7m × 6/12)
NCI% × FV depn	(60)	20% × ($3m/5 × 6/12)
NCI% × URP	(300)	20% × $1.5m
Total	3,740	

Alternative presentation:

		$000	
NCI at acquisition		3,400	
Profit	3,500		($7m × 6/12)
FV depn	(300)		($3m/5 × 6/12)
URP	(1,500)		($4,500 – $2,500 = $1.5m)
	1,700		
	× 20%	340	
		3,740	

(W2) Retained earnings

	$000	
100% × P RE	13,200	
P% × S post acq	2,800	80% × ($7m × 6/12)
P% × FV depn	(240)	80% × ($3m/5 × 6/12)
P% × URP	(1,200)	80% × $1.5m
Professional fees	(500)	
Total	14,060	

Alternative presentation:

		$000	
NCI at acquisition		13,200	
Professional fees		(500)	
Profit	3,500		($7m × 6/12)
FV depn	(300)		($3m/5 × 6/12)
URP	(1,500)		($4,500 – $2,500 = $1.5m)
	1,700		
× 80%		1,360	
		14,060	

(b)   Ratios:

	20X8	Working	20X7	Working
Current	1.4:1	30,400/21,300	1.8:1	28,750/15,600
ROCE	31.3%	14,500/(11,000 + 6,000 + 14,060 + 3,740 + 11,500)	48.1%	12,700/(19,400 + 7,000)
Gearing	33%	(11,500/11,000 + 6,000 + 14,060 + 3,740)	36.1%	(7,000/19,400)

(c)   Analysis

Performance

The ROCE has declined significantly from 20X7. However, rather than being due to a reduction in profit from operations which has increased slightly ($14.5m from $12.7m), it is due to a significant increase in capital employed which has gone from $26.4m to nearly $50m. This will be partly due to the fact that Smooth Co was acquired through the issue of shares in Duke Co.

The ROCE will look worse in the current period as it will only contain six months' profit from Smooth, but the entire liabilities and non-controlling interest at the reporting period.

As Smooth Co made a profit after tax of $7m in the year, six months of this would have made a significant increase in the overall profit from operations. If excluded from the consolidated SOPL, it suggests that there is a potential decline (or stagnation) in the profits made by Duke Co.

Position

The current ratio has decreased in the year from 1.8:1 to 1.4:1. Some of this will be due to the fact that Smooth Co is based in the service industry and so is likely to hold very little inventory. The large fall in inventory holding period would also support this.

An increase in trade receivables is perhaps expected given that Smooth Co is a service based company. This is likely to be due to Smooth Co's customers having significant payment terms, due to their size.

This increase in receivables collection period could mean that Smooth Co has a weaker cash position than Duke Co. While the size of the customers may mean that there is little risk of irrecoverable debts, Smooth Co may have a small, or even overdrawn, cash balance due to this long collection period.

The gearing has reduced in the year from 36.1% to 33%. This is not due to reduced levels of debt, as these have actually increased during the year. This is likely to be due to the consolidation of the debt held by Smooth Co, as Duke Co has not taken out additional loans in the year.

This increase in debt has been offset by a significant increase in equity, which has resulted from the share consideration given for the acquisition of Smooth Co.

Conclusion

Smooth Co is a profitable company and is likely to have boosted Duke Co profits, which may be slightly in decline. Smooth Co may have more debt and have potentially put pressure on the cash flow of the group, but Duke Co seems in a stable enough position to cope with this.

ACCA marking guide		Marks
(a)	Non-controlling interests	3
	Retained earnings	3
		6
(b)	Ratios	4
(c)	Performance	4
	Position	5
	Conclusion	1
		10
Total		**20**

Examiner's Comments

This question required three tasks to be completed with most of the marks being awarded for the calculation of some standard ratios and an analysis of financial statement extracts for a newly formed, two company group.

Part (a) required a calculation of non-controlling interests and group retained earnings to complete the financial statement extracts. Overall, this section of the question was well received by most candidates with some achieving full marks. For those who did not achieve full marks, this was generally due to some common mistakes noted below.

Many candidates treated the professional fees incurred by Duke Co as an expense in Smooth Co's calculation of profit. Professional fees (acquisition costs) per IFRS 3 are not to be included within the calculation of goodwill but should instead be expensed as incurred. This cost would need to be deducted from Duke Co's profit within the retained earnings working.

When looking at the detail in the question, Duke Co acquired Smooth Co on 1 January 20X8. The acquisition therefore took place six months into the accounting year. As a result, when looking to identify Smooth Co's post-acquisition profit, the profit for the year of $7 million needed to be time apportioned 6/12. Similarly, fair value depreciation on the brand also needed to be time apportioned and this was often omitted by candidates.

Finally, for those candidates who calculated unrealised profit on the non-current asset transfer correctly, many included this as a deduction against Duke Co. It was Smooth Co that transferred the asset and made the profit on disposal and therefore the unrealised profit needed to be split between both non-controlling interests and retained earnings according to the percentage of ownership.

For part (b) candidates were asked to calculate three ratios for both 20X7 and 20X8 using some of the information that been calculated in part (a). Most candidates correctly calculated current ratio for both 20X7 and 20X8, but for many calculating return on capital employed and gearing correctly proved to be more challenging.

Candidates, as always, are reminded to provide workings for their ratio calculations. This is because an incorrect answer that has no supporting workings will be awarded no marks. However, the same response may have been awarded full marks if the incorrect balance was found using the candidates 'own figures' from part (a).

Finally, part (c) to this question required candidates to comment on the comparative performance and position over the two-year period and to specifically comment on the impact that the acquisition had on the analysis. Despite the requirement being very clear, many candidates failed to refer to the acquisition at all. This was disappointing for the marking team as group interpretation is no longer a new area to the syllabus and there are numerous examiner commentaries and several past practice questions that have similar requirements.

For some candidates, the analysis was very weak with many simply noting that a ratio had increased or decreased in the year. This approach will continue to secure limited marks as it is not providing an analysis of why there was a change in performance during the year.

Well-prepared candidates discussed liquidity and noted that the change in current ratio was likely to be due to Smooth Co being in the service industry and therefore holding limited (if any) inventory. Few candidates went on to support this comment with evidence from the decrease in the inventory holding period. Only a few candidates noted that Duke Co's liquidity would have reduced due to the acquisition of Smooth Co in part being due to a cash element.

Many candidates stated that the current ratio was very poor, and that the company faced going concern issues as the ratio was below the 'norm' of 2:1. These comments received few, if any marks, and candidates are discouraged from making statements such as this. Instead, candidates are encouraged to use the scenario to suggest possible reasons for the change in the ratio.

Return on capital employed (ROCE) had deteriorated significantly in 20X8. Indeed, the scenario provided candidates with clues as to why ROCE may have deteriorated which included an increase in share capital and share premium because of the share exchange on acquisition of Smooth Co. Also, there had been an increase in long-term loans which must have been due to the acquisition, given that the scenario said that Duke Co had no new loans during the year. In addition, it was worth noting that Smooth Co's profit had only been consolidated for six months and therefore ROCE may improve in the following year. Very few candidates discussed all of these issues.

There had been very little change in gearing during the year with a small decrease in gearing being recognised. Many candidates suggested that this was due to a reduction in loans, when in fact long-term loans had increased following the acquisition (as previously mentioned this was solely due to the acquisition of Smooth Co). Well-prepared candidates were able to identify that the fall in gearing was due to the increase in equity following the acquisition of Smooth Co resulting in increased share capital and share premium.

Candidates are encouraged to provide a conclusion for any analysis requirement, pulling together the key findings from the scenario and the analysis performed.

Section 7

SPECIMEN EXAM QUESTIONS

This exam is divided into three sections:

Section A

- 15 objective test (OT) questions, each worth 2 marks.
- 30 marks in total.

Section B

- Three OT cases, each containing a scenario which relates to five OT questions, each worth 2 marks.
- 30 marks in total.

Section C

- Two constructed response questions, each containing a scenario which relates to one or more requirement(s).
- Each constructed response question is worth 20 marks in total.
- 40 marks in total.

Please note that the live exam is worth a total of 110 marks, 10 marks of which are for questions that do not count towards your final result and are included for quality assurance purposes. This specimen exam is worth a total of 100 marks, reflecting the element of the live exam on which your result will be based.

All questions are compulsory.

Click **Next** to start your exam.

F7 Financial Reporting - Specimen Exam

Section A

This section of the exam contains **15 objective test (OT) questions**.

Each question is worth **2 marks** and is compulsory.

This exam section is worth **30 marks** in total.

Select **Next** to continue.

Q1

Match the tokens to the appropriate category based on whether or not the costs should be capitalised in the initial carrying amount of an item of plant.

Tokens

The cost of transporting the plant to the factory

The cost of a three-week training course for staff to operate the plant

The cost of installing a new power supply required to operate the plant

The cost of a three-year plant maintenance agreement

The initial carrying amount of plant should include:

The initial carrying amount of plant should NOT include:

Q2

When a parent is evaluating the assets of a potential subsidiary, certain intangible assets can be recognised separately from goodwill, even though they have not been recognised in the subsidiary's own statement of financial position.

Which of the following is an example of an intangible asset of the subsidiary that may be recognised separately from goodwill when preparing consolidated financial statements?

- ○ A new research project which the subsidiary has correctly expensed to profit or loss but the directors of the parent have reliably assessed to have a substantial fair value

- ○ A global advertising campaign which was concluded in the previous financial year and from which benefits are expected to flow in the future

- ○ A contingent asset of the subsidiary from which the parent believes a flow of future economic benefits is possible

- ○ A customer list which the directors are unable to value reliably

Q3

On 1 October 20X4, Flash Co acquired an item of plant under a five-year lease agreement. The present value of the total lease payments was $25m. The agreement had an implicit finance cost of 10% per annum and required an immediate deposit of $2m and annual rentals of $6m paid on the 30 September each year for five years.

Calculate the current liability of the lease in Flash Co's statement of financial position as at 30 September 20X5.

$ [   ]

Q4

Financial statements represent transactions in words and numbers. To be useful, financial information must represent faithfully these transactions in terms of how they are reported.

Only one of the following four statements regarding faithful representation is true. Identify that statement, by clicking on the relevant box in the table below, and mark all of the others as false.

Charging the rental payments for an item of plant to profit or loss where the rental agreement meets the criteria for a right of use asset is an example of faithful representation	TRUE	FALSE
Including a convertible loan note in equity on the basis that the holders are likely to choose the equity option on conversion is an example of faithful representation	TRUE	FALSE
Derecognising factored trade receivables sold without recourse is an example of faithful representation	TRUE	FALSE
Treating redeemable preference shares as part of equity in the statement of financial position is an example of faithful representation	TRUE	FALSE

Q5

On 1 October 20X4, Kalatra Co commenced drilling for oil from an undersea oilfield. Kalatra Co is required to dismantle the drilling equipment at the end of its five-year licence. This has an estimated cost of $30m on 30 September 20X9. Kalatra Co's cost of capital is 8% per annum and $1 in five years' time has a present value of $0.68.

What is the provision which Kalatra Co would report in its statement of financial position as at 30 September 20X5 in respect of its oil operations?

- ⚪ $32,400,000

- ⚪ $22,032,000

- ⚪ $20,400,000

- ⚪ $1,632,000

Q6

When a single entity makes purchases or sales in a foreign currency, it will be necessary to translate the transactions into its functional currency before the transactions can be included in its financial records.

In accordance with IAS 21 The Effect of Changes in Foreign Currency Exchange Rates, which TWO of the following foreign currency exchange rates may be used to translate the foreign currency purchases and sales?

- ☐ The rate that existed on the day that the purchase or sale took place

- ☐ The rate that existed at the beginning of the accounting period

- ☐ An average rate for the year, provided there have been no significant fluctuations throughout the year

- ☐ The rate that existed at the end of the accounting period

Q7

On 1 October 20X4, Hoy Co had $2.5m of equity share capital (shares of $0.50 each) in issue. No new shares were issued during the year ended 30 September 20X5, but on that date, there were outstanding share options which had a dilutive effect equivalent to issuing 1.2 million shares for no consideration.

Hoy Co's profit after tax for the year ended 30 September 20X5 was $1,550,000.

The graph below represents a trend in both basic and diluted earnings per share (EPS) since 20X3. Complete the EPS trend analysis by calculating the diluted EPS for the year ended 30 September 20X5 for Hoy Co and click on the graph to identify its position.

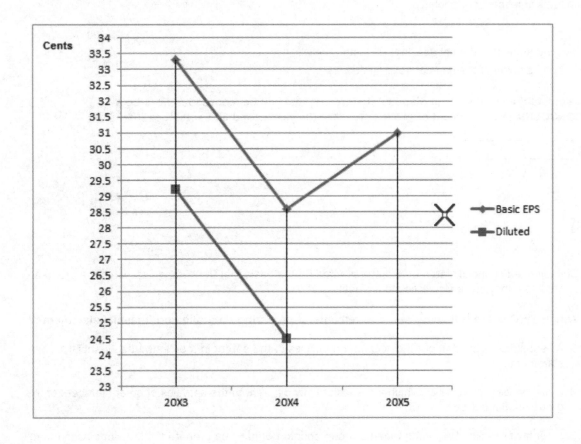

Q8

Fork Co owns an 80% investment in Spoon Co which it purchased several years ago. The goodwill on acquisition was valued at $1,674,000 and there has been no impairment of that goodwill since the date of acquisition.

On 30 September 20X4, Fork Co disposed of its entire investment in Spoon Co details of which are as follows:

	$'000
Sales proceeds of Fork Co's entire investment in Spoon Co	5,580
Cost of Fork Co's entire investment in Spoon Co	3,720

Immediately before the disposal, the consolidated financial statements of Fork Co included the following amounts in respect of Spoon Co:

	$'000
Carrying amount of the net assets (excluding goodwill)	4,464
Carrying amount of the non-controlling interests	900

Calculate the profit/loss on disposal (before tax) that will be recorded in Fork Co's CONSOLIDATED statement of profit or loss for the year ended 30 September 20X4.

$ [   ]

Q9

Consolidated financial statements are presented on the basis that the companies within the group are treated as if they are a single economic entity.

Which TWO of the following are requirements of preparing consolidated financial statements?

☐ All subsidiaries must adopt the accounting policies of the parent in their individual financial statements

☐ Subsidiaries with activities which are substantially different to the activities of other members of the group should not be consolidated

☐ All entity financial statements within a group should normally be prepared to the same accounting year end prior to consolidation

☐ Unrealised profits within the group must be eliminated from the consolidated financial statements

Q10

A parent sells goods to its 80% owned subsidiary during the financial year, some of which remains in inventory at the year end.

Match the tokens to the appropriate item in the statement of financial position (SOFP) to reflect the adjustment required in the consolidated statement of financial position to eliminate any unrealised profit in inventory.

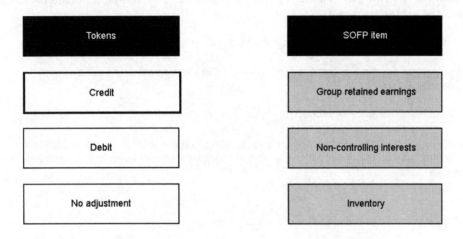

Tokens	SOFP item
Credit	Group retained earnings
Debit	Non-controlling interests
No adjustment	Inventory

Q11

Caddy Co acquired 240,000 of Ambel Co's 800,000 equity shares for $6 per share on 1 October 20X4. Ambel Co's profit after tax for the year ended 30 September 20X5 was $400,000 and it paid an equity dividend on 20 September 20X5 of $150,000.

On the assumption that Ambel Co is an associate of Caddy Co, what would be the carrying amount of the investment in Ambel Co in the consolidated statement of financial position of Caddy Co as at 30 September 20X5?

◯ $1,515,000

◯ $1,560,000

◯ $1,395,000

◯ $1,690,000

Q12

Quartile Co is in the jewellery retail business which can be assumed to be highly seasonal. For the year ended 30 September 20X5, Quartile Co assessed its operating performance by comparing selected accounting ratios with those of its business sector average as provided by an agency.

Assume that the business sector used by the agency is a meaningful representation of Quartile Co's business.

Which TWO of the following circumstances may invalidate the comparison of Quartile Co's ratios with those of the sector average?

☐ In the current year, Quartile Co has experienced significant rising costs for its purchases

☐ The sector average figures are compiled from companies whose year ends are between 1 July 20X5 and 30 September 20X5

☐ Quartile Co does not revalue its properties, but is aware that other entities in this sector do

☐ During the year, Quartile Co discovered an error relating to the inventory count at 30 September 20X4. This error was correctly accounted for in the financial statements for the current year ended 30 September 20X5

Q13

Which of the following criticisms does NOT apply to historical cost financial statements during a period of rising prices?

○ They contain mixed values; some items are at current values and some are at out of date values

○ They are difficult to verify because transactions could have happened many years ago

○ They understate assets and overstate profit

○ They overstate gearing in the statement of financial position

Q14

The following information has been taken or calculated from Fowler Co's financial statements for the year ended 30 September 20X5:

Cash cycle as at 30 September 20X5	70 days
Inventory turnover	6 times
Year-end payables at 30 September 20X5	$230,000
Credit purchases for the year ended 30 September 20X5	$2,000,000
Cost of sales for the year ended 30 September 20X5	$1,800,000

Complete the following table, by dragging and dropping the tokens into the appropriate place, in order to reflect the correct calculation for Fowler Co's cash cycle at 30 September 20X5.

Tokens	Add/subtract		Days
Subtract			
		Inventory turnover days	C
Add			
42 days	A	Receivables collection period	D
51 days			
	B	Trade payables period	E
61 days			
		Fowler Co's cash cycle at 30 September 20X5	70

Q15

On 1 October 20X4, Pyramid Co acquired 80% of Square Co's 9 million ($1) equity shares. At the date of acquisition, Square Co had an item of plant which had a fair value of $3m in excess of its carrying amount. At the date of acquisition it had a remaining life of five years.

Pyramid Co's policy is to value non-controlling interests at fair value at the date of acquisition. For this purpose, Square Co's shares had a value of $3.50 each at that date. In the year ended 30 September 20X5, Square Co reported a profit of $8m.

At what amount should the non-controlling interests of Square Co be valued in the consolidated statement of financial position of Pyramid Co as at 30 September 20X5?

Select... ▼
Select...
$26,680,000
$7,900,000
$7,780,000
$12,220,000

Section B

This section of the exam contains **three OT cases**.

Each OT case contains a scenario which relates to **five OT questions**.

Each question is worth **2 marks** and is compulsory.

This exam section is worth **30 marks** in total.

Select **Next** to continue.

Telepath Co has a year end of 30 September and owns an item of plant that it uses to produce and package pharmaceuticals. The plant cost $750,000 on 1 October 20X0 and, at that date, had an estimated useful life of five years. A review of the plant on 1 April 20X3 concluded that the plant would last for a further three and a half years and that its fair value was $560,000. Telepath Co adopts the policy of revaluing its non-current assets to their fair value but does not make an annual transfer from the revaluation surplus to retained earnings to represent the additional depreciation charged due to the revaluation.

On 30 September 20X3, Telepath Co was informed by a major customer that it would no longer be placing orders with Telepath Co. As a result, Telepath Co revised its estimates that net cash inflows earned from the plant for the next three years will be:

Year ended 30 September:	$'000
20X4	220
20X5	180
20X6	200

Telepath Co's cost of capital is 10% which results in the following discount factors:

Value of $1 at 30 September:	$
20X4	0.91
20X5	0.83
20X6	0.75

Telepath Co also owns Rilda Co, a 100% subsidiary, which is treated as a cash generating unit. On 30 September 20X3, there was an impairment to Rilda Co's assets of $3,500,000. The carrying amount of the assets of Rilda Co immediately before the impairment were:

	$'000
Goodwill	2,000
Factory building	4,000
Plant	3,500
Receivables and cash (at recoverable amount)	2,500
	12,000

Q16

Use the tokens to complete the following definitions in accordance with IAS 36 Impairment of Assets.

An asset is impaired if its [   ] is [   ]

than its recoverable amount. In turn, the recoverable amount

of an asset is defined as the higher of its fair value less costs

of disposal and its [   ]

TOKENS		
carrying amount	historical cost	less
replacement cost	greater	value in use

Q17

Prior to considering any impairment, what is the carrying amount of Telepath Co's plant and the balance on the revaluation surplus at 30 September 20X3?

○ The carrying amount of the plant is $480,000 and the balance on the revaluation surplus is $185,000

○ The carrying amount of the plant is $300,000 and the balance on the revaluation surplus is $0

○ The carrying amount of the plant is $480,000 and the balance on the revaluation surplus is $0

○ The carrying amount of the plant is $300,000 and the balance on the revaluation surplus is $185,000

Q18

Calculate the value in use of Telepath Co's plant at 30 September 20X3.

$ [   ]

Q19

Which of the following are TRUE in accordance with IAS 36 Impairment of Assets?

(1) A cash generating unit is the smallest identifiable group of assets for which individual cash flows can be identified and measured

(2) When considering the impairment of a cash generating unit, the calculation of the carrying amount and the recoverable amount does not need to be based on exactly the same group of net assets

(3) When it is not possible to calculate the recoverable amount of a single asset then that of its cash generating unit should be measured instead

- ⦿ 1 only

- ⦿ 2 and 3

- ⦿ 3 only

- ⦿ 1 and 3

Q20

Calculate the carrying amount of Rilda Co's plant at 30 September 20X3 after the impairment loss has been correctly allocated to its assets.

$ [   ]

At a board meeting in June 20X3, Neutron Co's directors made a decision to close down one of its factories by 30 September 20X3 and market both the building and the plant for sale. The decision had been made public, was communicated to all affected parties and was fully implemented by 30 September 20X3.

The directors of Neutron Co have provided the following information relating to the closure:

(1) Of the factory's 250 employees, 50 will be retrained and deployed to other subsidiaries within the Neutron group during the year ended 30 September 20X4, at a cost of $125,000. The remainder accepted redundancy at an average cost of $5,000 each.

(2) The factory's plant had a carrying amount of $2.2m, but is only expected to sell for $500,000, incurring $50,000 of selling costs. The factory itself is expected to sell for a profit of $1.2m.

(3) The company also rented a number of machines in the factory under operating leases which have an average of three years to run after 30 September 20X3. The present value of these future lease payments at 30 September 20X3 was $1m, however, the lessor has stated that they will accept $850,000 if paid on 30 October 20X3 as full settlement.

(4) Penalty payments, due to the non-completion of supply contracts, are estimated to be $200,000, 50% of which is expected to be recovered from Neutron Co's insurers.

Q21

Which TWO of the following must exist for an operation to be classified as a discontinued operation in accordance with IFRS 5 Non-current Assets Held for Sale and Discontinued Operations?

☐ It represents a separate major line of business or geographical area

☐ It is a subsidiary

☐ It has been sold or is classified as held for sale

☐ It is considered not to be capable of making a future profit following a period of losses

Q22

IFRS 5 Non-current Assets Held for Sale and Discontinued Operations prescribes the recognition criteria for non-current assets held for sale. For an asset or a disposal group to be classified as held for sale, the sale must be highly probable.

Which TWO of the following must apply for the sale to be considered highly probable?

☐ A buyer must have been located

☐ The asset must be marketed at a reasonable price

☐ Management must be committed to a plan to sell the asset

☐ The sale must be expected to take place within the next six months

Q23

Calculate the employee cost associated with the closure and sale of
Neutron Co's factory that should be charged to profit or loss for the year
ended 30 September 20X3.

$ [   ]

Q24

What is the profit or loss on discontinued operations relating to property, plant and
equipment for the year ended 30 September 20X3?

○ $1.75m loss

○ $1.75m profit

○ $550,000 loss

○ $550,000 profit

Q25

In respect of the operating leases and penalty payments, what provision is
required in the statement of financial position of Neutron Co as at 30 September
20X3?

○ $1,100,000

○ $1,050,000

○ $1,200,000

○ $950,000

Speculate Co is preparing its financial statements for the year ended 30 September 20X3. The following issues are relevant:

(1) Financial assets

Shareholding A - a long-term investment in 10,000 of the equity shares of another company. These shares were acquired on 1 October 20X2 at a cost of $3.50 each. Transaction costs of 1% of the purchase price were incurred. On 30 September 20X3 the fair value of these shares is $4.50 each.

Shareholding B – a short-term speculative investment in 2,000 of the equity shares of another company. These shares were acquired on 1 December 20X2 at a cost of $2.50 each. Transaction costs of 1% of the purchase price were incurred. On 30 September 20X3 the fair value of these shares is $3.00 each.

Where possible, Speculate Co makes an irrevocable election for the fair value movements on financial assets to be reported in other comprehensive income.

(2) Taxation

The existing debit balance on the current tax account of $2.4m represents the under/over provision of the tax liability for the year ended 30 September 20X2. A provision of $28m is required for income tax for the year ended 30 September 20X3.

The existing credit balance on the deferred tax account is $2.5m and the provision required at 30 September 20X3 is $4.4m.

(3) Revenue

On 1 October 20X2, Speculate Co sold one of its products for $10m. As part of the sale agreement, Speculate Co is committed to the ongoing servicing of its product until 30 September 20X5 (ie three years after the sale). The sale value of this service has been included in the selling price of $10m. The estimated cost to Speculate Co of the servicing is $600,000 per annum and Speculate Co's gross profit margin on this type of servicing is 25%. Ignore discounting.

Q26

Match the financial instrument to its appropriate classification in accordance with IFRS 9 Financial Instruments.

Financial instrument	Classification
A contract to exchange financial instruments with another entity under conditions that are potentially unfavourable	A financial asset
Any contract that evidences a residual interest in the assets of an entity after deducting all of its liabilities	A financial asset
Cash	An equity instrument
An equity instrument of another entity	A financial liability

Q27

In respect of the financial assets of Speculate Co, what amount will be included in other comprehensive income for the year ended 30 September 20X3?

○ $9,650

○ $10,600

○ $10,000

○ $0

Q28

Calculate the total amount that will be charged to the statement of profit or loss for the year ended 30 September 20X3 in respect of taxation.

$ [   ]

Q29

What is the amount of deferred income which Speculate Co should recognise in its statement of financial position as at 30 September 20X3 relating to the contract for supply and servicing of products?

○ $1.2 million

○ $0.6 million

○ $1.5 million

○ $1.6 million

Q30

Only two of the following statements in respect of Speculate Co's deferred income at 30 September 20X3 are true. Identify these statements, by clicking on the relevant box in the table below and mark all the others as false.

The deferred income will be split evenly between the current and non-current liabilities in Speculate Co's statement of financial position as at 30 September 20X3	TRUE	FALSE
The costs associated with the deferred income of Speculate Co should be recognised in the statement of profit or loss at the same time as the revenue is recognised	TRUE	FALSE
The deferred income can only be recognised as revenue by Speculate Co when there is a signed written contract of service with its customer	TRUE	FALSE
When recognising the revenue associated with the service contract of Speculate Co, the stage of its completion is irrelevant	TRUE	FALSE

Section C

This section of the exam contains **two constructed response questions**.

Each question contains a scenario which relates to one or more requirement(s) which may be split over multiple question screens.

Each question is worth **20 marks** and is compulsory.

This exam section is worth **40 marks** in total.

Important: In your live exam please show all notes/workings that you want the marker to see within the spreadsheet or word processing answer areas. Remember, any notes/workings made on the Scratch Pad or on your workings paper will not be marked.

Select **Next** to continue.

Q31

This scenario relates to three requirements.

After preparing a draft statement of profit or loss for the year ended 30 September 20X5 and adding the current year's draft profit (before any adjustments required by notes (1) to (3) below) to retained earnings, the summarised trial balance of Kandy Co as at 30 September 20X5 is:

	$'000	$'000
Equity shares of $1 each		20,000
Retained earnings as at 30 September 20X5		15,500
Proceeds of 6% loan note (note (1))		30,000
Investment properties at fair value (note (2))	20,000	
Land ($5 million) and buildings – at cost (note (2))	35,000	
Plant and equipment – at cost (note (2))	58,500	
Accumulated depreciation at 1 October 20X4:		
buildings		20,000
plant and equipment		34,500
Current assets	68,700	
Current liabilities		43,400
Deferred tax (notes (2) and (3))		2,500
Interest paid (note (1))	1,800	
Current tax (note (3))		1,100
Suspense account (note 2)		17,000
	184,000	**184,000**

The following notes are relevant:

(1) The loan note was issued on 1 October 20X4 and incurred issue costs of $1 million which were charged to profit or loss. Interest of $1·8 million ($30 million at 6%) was paid on 30 September 20X5. The loan is redeemable on 30 September 20X9 at a substantial premium which gives an effective interest rate of 9% per annum. No other repayments are due until 30 September 20X9.

(2) Non-current assets:
On 1 October 20X4, Kandy Co owned two investment properties. The first property had a carrying amount of $15 million and was sold on 1 December 20X4 for $17 million. The disposal proceeds have been credited to a suspense account in the trial balance above. On 31 December 20X4, the second property became owner occupied and so was transferred to land and buildings at its fair value of $6 million. Its remaining useful life on 31 December 20X4 was considered to be 20 years. Ignore any deferred tax implications of this fair value.

The price of property has increased significantly in recent years and so the directors decided to revalue the land and buildings. The directors accepted the report of an independent surveyor who, on 1 October 20X4, valued the land at $8 million and the buildings at $39 million on that date. This revaluation specifically excludes the transferred investment property described above. The remaining life of these buildings at 1 October 20X4 was 15 years. Kandy Co does not make an annual transfer to retained profits to reflect the realisation of the revaluation gain; however, the revaluation will give rise to a deferred tax liability. The income tax rate applicable to Kandy Co is 20%.

Plant and equipment is depreciated at 12.5% per annum using the reducing balance method. No depreciation has yet been charged on any non-current asset for the year ended 30 September 20X5.

Plant and equipment is depreciated at 12.5% per annum using the reducing balance method. No depreciation has yet been charged on any non-current asset for the year ended 30 September 20X5.

(3) A provision of $2·4 million is required for income tax on the profit for the year to 30 September 20X5. The balance on current tax in the trial balance is the under/over provision of tax for the previous year. In addition to the temporary differences relating to the information in note (2), Kandy Co has further taxable temporary differences of $10 million as at 30 September 20X5.

Required:

(a) Prepare a schedule of adjustments required to the retained earnings of Kandy Co as at 30 September 20X5 as a result of the information in notes (1) to (3).

(8 marks)

(b) Prepare the statement of financial position of Kandy Co as at 30 September 20X5.

Note: The notes to the statement of financial position are not required

(9 marks)

(c) Prepare the extracts from Kandy Co's statement of cash flows for operating and investing activities for the year ended 30 September 20X5 which relate to property, plant and equipment.

(3 marks)

(20 marks)

Q32

This scenario relates to three requirements.

The summarised consolidated financial statements for the year ended 30 September 20X5 (and the comparative figures) for the Tangier group are shown below.

Consolidated statements of profit or loss for the year ended 30 September:

	20X5	20X4
	$m	$m
Revenue	2,700	1,820
Cost of sales	(1,890)	(1,092)
Gross profit	**810**	**728**
Administrative expense	(345)	(200)
Distribution costs	(230)	(130)
Finance costs	(40)	(5)
Profit before taxation	**195**	**393**
Income tax expense	(60)	(113)
Profit for the year	**135**	**280**

Consolidated statements of financial position as at 30 September:

	20X5	20X5	20X4	20X4
	$m	$m	$m	$m
Non-current assets				
Property, plant and equipment		680		310
Intangible asset: manufacturing licence		300		100
goodwill		230		200
		1,210		**610**
Current assets				
Inventory	200		110	
Trade receivables	195		75	
Bank	0	**395**	120	**305**
Total assets		**1,605**		**915**

Equity and liabilities				
Equity shares of $1 each		330		250
Other components of equity		100		0
Retained earnings		375		295
		805		**545**
Non-current liabilities				
5% secured loan notes	100		100	
10% secured loan notes	300	**400**	0	**100**
Current liabilities				
Bank overdraft	110		0	
Trade payables	210		160	
Current tax payable	80	**400**	110	**270**
Total equity and liabilities		**1,605**		**915**

At 1 October 20X4, the Tangier group consisted of the parent, Tangier Co, and two wholly owned subsidiaries which had been owned for many years. On 1 January 20X5, Tangier Co purchased a third 100% owned investment in a subsidiary called Raremetal Co. The consideration paid for Raremetal Co was a combination of cash and shares. The cash payment was partly funded by the issue of 10% loan notes. On 1 January 20X5, Tangier Co also won a tender for a new contract to supply aircraft engines which Tangier Co manufactures under a recently acquired long-term licence. Raremetal Co was purchased with a view to securing the supply of specialised materials used in the manufacture of these engines. The bidding process had been very competitive and Tangier Co had to increase its manufacturing capacity to fulfil the contract.

Required:

(a) Comment on how the new contract and the purchase of Raremetal Co may have affected the comparability of the consolidated financial statements of Tangier Co for the years ended 30 September 20X4 and 20X5.

(5 marks)

(b) Calculate appropriate ratios and comment on Tangier Co's profitability and gearing. Your analysis should identify where the new contract and the purchase of Raremetal Co have limited the usefulness of the ratios and your analysis.

Note: Your ratios should be based on the consolidated financial statements provided and you should not attempt to adjust for the effects of the new contract or the consolidation. Working capital and liquidity ratios are not required.

(12 marks)

(c) Explain what further information you might require to make your analysis more meaningful.

(3 marks)

(20 marks)

Section 8

ANSWERS TO SPECIMEN EXAM QUESTIONS

SECTION A

Q1

The correct answer is that the initial carrying amount of plant should include:
(1) the cost of transporting the plant to the factory; and
(2) the cost of installing a new power supply required to operate the plant.

Q2

The correct answer is the new research project.

Q3

Current liability = 19,300,000-15,230,000 = $4,070,000

	$'000s
FV 1 Oct 20X4	25,000
Deposit	(2,000)
	23,000
Interest 10%	2,300
Payment 30 Sep 20X5	(6,000)
	19,300
Interest 10%	1,930
Payment 30 Sep 20X6	(6,000)
Liability at 30 Sep 20X6	15,230

Q4

The correct answer is:
Derecognising factored trade receivables sold without recourse to the seller is an example of faithful representation.

Q5

Dismantling provision at 1 October is $20.4 million (30,000 x 0.68) discounted. This will increase by an 8% finance cost by 30 September 20X5 = $22,032,000

Q6

The correct answer is the rate that existed on the day that the purchase or sale took place or an average rate for the year may be used.

Q7

$(1,550/(2,500 \times 2 + 1,200)) = \$0.25$

Q8

		$'000
Sales proceeds		5,580
Net assets at disposal	4,464	
Goodwill at disposal	1,674	
Less: carrying amount of NCI	(900)	(5,238)
		342

Q9

The correct answer is that all entity financial statements within a group should normally be prepared to the same accounting year end prior to consolidation and unrealised profits within the group must be eliminated.

Q10

The correct answer is:
DEBIT   Group retained earnings
CREDIT Inventory

Q11

	$'000
Cost (240,000 x $6)	1,440
Share of associate's profit (400 x 240/800)	120
Less dividend received (150 x 240/800)	(45)
	1,515

Q12

The correct answers are:
- The sector average figures are compiled from companies whose year ends are between 1 July 20X5 and 30 September 20X5
- Quartile Co does not revalue its properties, but is aware that other entities in this sector do

Q13

The correct answer is:
They are difficult to verify because transactions could have happened many years ago - this is not a vald criticism of historic cost financial statements

Q14

Inventory turnover is 61 days (365/6)
Trade payables period is 42 days (230,000 x 365/2)
Therefore, receivables collection period is 51 days (70-61 +42)

Q15

	$'000s
FV NCI at 1/10/14 (9000 x 20% x $3.50)	6,300
Post acq'n profit (8000-(3000/5)) = 7,400@20%	1,480
	7,780

Q16

The correct answer is:
An asset is impaired if its carrying amount is greater than its recoverable amount. In turn, the recoverable amount of an asset is defined as the higher of its fair value less costs of disposal and its value in use.

Q17

Annual depreciation prior to the revaluation is $150,000 (750/5). At the date of revaluation (1 April 20X3) the carrying amount is $375,000 (750-(150x2.5yrs)). Revalued to $560,000 with a remaining life of 3.5 years results in a depreciation charge of $160,000 per annum which means $80,000 for 6 mths. The carrying amount at 30 September 20X3 is therefore $480,000 (560-80). An alternative calculation is $560,000 - ($560,000/3.5 x 6/12) = $480,000 Revaluation surplus : $560,000-$375,000=$185,000

Q18

	cflow	10%discount	present value
	$'000	$'000	$'000
30-Sep-X4	220	0.91	200.2
30-Sep-X5	180	0.83	149.4
30-Sep-X6	200	0.75	150
			499.6

Q19

The correct answers are:
- A cash generating unit is the smallest identifiable group of assets for which individual cash flows can be identified and measured; and
- When it is not possible to calculate the recoverable amount of a single asset then that of its cash generating unit should be measured instead

Q20

	Carrying amt before	Impairment loss	Carrying amt after
Goodwill	2,000	2,000	Nil
Property	4,000	800	3,200
Plant	3,500	700	2,800
Cash and receivables	2,500	nil	2,500
	12,000	3,500	8,500

Q21

The correct answers are:
- It represents a separate major line of business or geographical area
- It has been sold or is classified as held for sale

Q22

The correct answers are:
- The asset must be marketed at a reasonable price
- Management must be committed to a plan to sell the asset

Q23

The correct answer is:
200 employees at $5,000 = $1,000,000 redundancy costs. The retraining costs are a future cost.

Q24

The impairment loss on plant is $1,750,000 (2,200,000 - (500,000 - 50,000))

Q25

Onerous contract $850,000 + penalty payments $200,000 = $1,050,000. The possible insurance receipt should be ignored as there is no certainty that it would be received and it would not be netted off against the provision anyway.

Q26

The correct answer is:
- Cash = a financial asset
- An equity instrument of another entity = a finacial asset
- A contract to exchange financial instruments with another entity under conditions that are potentially unfavourable = a financial liability
- Any contract that evidences a residual interest in the assets of an entity after deducting all of its liabilities = an equity instrument

Q27

The correct answer is:
Shareholding A is not held for trading as an election made - FVTOCI
Shareholding B is held for trading and so FVTPL (transaction costs are not included in carrying amount)
Cost of shareholding A is 10,000 x $3.50 x 1.01 = $35,350
FV at 30 September 20X3 10,000 x $4.50 = $45,000
Gain - 45,000 - 35,350 = $9,650

Q28

	$'000s
DT provision required at 30 Sep 20X3	4,400
DT provision at 1 October 20X2	(2,500)
	1,900
Underprovision for the y/e 30 Sep 20X2	2,400
Income tax for the year ended 30 Sep 20X3	28,000
Charge for the year ended 30 Sep 20X3	32,300

Q29

At 30 September 20X3 there are two more years of servicing work, thus $1.6 million ((600,000 x 2) x 100/75) must be treated as deferred income

Q30

The correct answers are:

- the deferred income will be split evenly between the current and non-current liabilities in Speculate Co's statement of financial position as at 30 September 20X3; and

- The costs associated with the deferred income of Speculate Co should be recognised in the statement of profit or loss at the same time as the revenue is recognised

Q31

Note: this spreadsheet is preformatted so that all numbers use a comma separator for $'000s and all negatives are expresse

Kandy Co – Schedule of adjustments to retained earnings as at 30 September 20X5

	$'000
Retained earnings per trial balance	15,500
Adjustments re:	
Issue costs of loan note (w(i))	1,000
Loan finance costs [(30,000-1,000)@9%] (w(i))	(2,610)
Gain on disposal of investment property (17,000-15,000)	2,000
Gain on revaluation of investment property prior to transfer (6,000-5,000)	1,000
Depreciation of buildings (w (ii))	(2,825)
Depreciation of plant and equipment(w(ii))	(3,000)
Income tax expense (w(iii))	(800)
Adjusted retained earnings	10,265

Kandy Co – Statement of Financial Position as at 30 September 20X5

	$'000	$'000
ASSETS		
Non-current assets		
Property, Plant and Equipment(50,175 + 21,000) (w(ii))		71,175
Current assets		
Per trial balance		68,700
Total Assets		139,875

EQUITY AND LIABILITIES
Equity

Equity Shares of $1 each	20,000
Revaluation Surplus(32,000 - 6,400) (w (ii) and (iii))	25,600
Retained Earnings Part (a)	10,265
	55,865

Non-current liabilities

6% loan note (w(i))	29,810	
Deferred Tax (w(iii))	8,400	38,210

Current liabilities

Per trial balance	43,400	
Current Tax	2,400	45,800

Total Equity and Liabilities	**139,875**

Kandy Co – Extracts from the Cash Flow Statement for the year ended 30 September 20X5

	$'000
Cash flows from operating activities:	
Add back depreciation	5,825
Deduct gain on revaluation of investment property	(1,000)
Deduct gain on disposal of investment property	(2,000)
Cash flows from investing activities:	
Investment property disposal proceeds	17,000

Workings (monetary figures in brackets in $'000)
w(i) Loan note

The issue costs should be deducted from the proceeds of the loan note and not charged as an expense. The finance cost of the loan note, at the effective rate of 9% applied to the carrying amount of the loan note of $29 million (30,000 - 1,000) is $2,610,000. The interest actually paid is $1.8 million. The difference between these amounts of $810,000 (2,610 - 1,800) is added to the carrying amount of the loan note to give $29,810,000 (29,000 + 810) for inclusion as a non-current liability in the statement of financial position.

w(II) Non-current assets
Land and Buildings

The gain on revaluation and carrying amount of the land and buildings will be:

	$'000
Carrying amount at 1 October 20X4 (35,000 – 20,000)	15,000
Revaluation at that date (8,000 + 39,000)	47,000
Gain on revaluation	32,000

Buildings depreciation for the year ended 30 September 20X5:

L&B existing at 1 October 20X4 (39,000/15 years)	2,600
Transferred investment property (6,000/20 x 9/12)	225
	2,825

Carrying amount at 30 September 20X5 (47,000 + 6,000 – 2,825)	50,175

Plant and Equipment

Carrying amount at 1 October 20X4 (58,500 – 34,500)	24,000
Depreciation for the year ended 30 September 20X5 (12.5% reducing balance	(3,000)
	21,000

w(III) Taxation
Income Tax Expense

Provision for year ended 30 September 20X5	2,400
Over-provision in previous year	(1,100)
Deferred tax (see below)	(500)
	800

Deferred Tax

Provision required at 30 September 20X5 ((10,000 + 32,000) x 20%)	8,400
Provision at 1 October 20X4	(2,500)
Movement in provision	5,900
Charge to revaluation of land and buildings (32,000 x 20%) - SOCIE	(6,400)
Balance – credit to profit or loss	(500)

Marking scheme		
Part (a) Schedule of adjustments to retained earnings at 30 Sep 20X5		
	Maximum Ma	Awarded
retained earnings per trial balance	½	
issue costs	1	
loan finance costs	1	
gains on investment properties	1	
depreciation charges	3	
income tax expense	1½	
	8	
Part (b) Statement of financial position as at 30 September 20X5		
property, plant and equipment	2	
current assets	½	
equity shares	½	
revaluation surplus	2	
deferred tax	1	
6% loan note	1½	
current liabilities (per trial balance)	½	
current tax payable	1	
	9	
Part (c) Extracts from the statement of cash flows for the year ended 30 September 20X5		
Cash flows from operating activities:		
add back depreciation	1	
less gain on revaluation of investment property	½	
less gain on disposal of investment prop	½	
Cash flows from investing activities:		
Investment property disposal proceeds	1	
	3	

Q32

(a) Note: References to '20X5' are in respect of the year ended 30 September 20X5 and '20X4' refers to the year ended 30 September 20X4.

The key matter to note is that the ratios for 20X4 and 20X5 will not be directly comparable because two significant events, the acquisition of Raremetal Co and securing the new contract, have occurred between these dates. This means that the underlying financial statements are not comparable. For example, the 20X4 statement of profit or loss (SOPL) will not include the results of Raremetal Co or the effect of the new contract. However, the 20X5 SOPL will contain nine months of the results of Raremetal Co (although intra-group transactions will have been eliminated) and nine months of the effects of the new contract (which may have resulted in either a net profit or loss). Likewise, the 20X4 statement of financial position does not contain any of Raremetal Co's assets and liabilities, whereas that of 20X5 contains all of the net assets of Raremetal Co and the cost of the licence. This does not mean that comparisons between the two years are not worthwhile, just that they need to be treated with caution. For some ratios, it may be necessary to exclude all of the subsidiaries from the analysis and use the single entity financial statements of Tangier Co as a basis for comparison with the performance of previous years. Similarly, it may still be possible to compare some of the ratios of the Tangier group with those of other groups in the same sector although not all groups will have experienced similar acquisitions.

Assuming there has been no impairment of goodwill, the investment in Raremetal Co has resulted in additional goodwill of $30 million which means that the investment has cost more than the carrying amount of Raremetal Co's net assets. Although there is no indication of the precise cost, it is known to have been achieved by a combination of a share exchange (hence the $180 million new issue of shares) and a cash element (funded from the proceeds of the loan issue and the decrease in the bank balance). Any intra-group sales have been eliminated on consolidation and it is not possible to determine in which individual company any profit on these intra-group sales will be reported; it is therefore difficult to measure any benefits of the investment. Indeed, the benefit of the investment might not be a financial one but merely to secure the supply of raw materials. It would be useful to establish the cost of the investment and the profit (if any) contributed by Raremetal Co so that an assessment of the benefit of the investment might be made.

(b)

Relevant ratios:	20X5	20X4
Gross profit margin % (810/2,700 x 100)	30·0%	40·0%
Operating profit margin (235/2,700 x 100)	8·7%	21·9%
ROCE (235/(805 + 400))	19·5%	61·7%
Net asset turnover 2,700/(805 + 400)	2·24 times	2·82 times
Debt/equity (400/805)	49·7%	18·3%
Interest cover (235/40)	5·9 times	79·6 times

All of the issues identified in (a) make a comparison of ratios difficult and, if more information was available, then some adjustments may be required. For example, if it is established that the investment is not generating any benefits, then it might be argued that the inclusion of the goodwill in the ROCE and asset turnover is

unjustified (it may be impaired and be written off). Goodwill has not been excluded from any of the following ratios.

The increase in revenues of 48·4% (880/1,820 x 100) in 20X5 will be partly due to the consolidation of Raremetal Co and the revenues associated with the new contract. Yet, despite these increased revenues, the company has suffered a dramatic fall in its profitability. This has been caused by a combination of a falling gross profit margin (from 40% in 20X4 to only 30% in 20X5) and markedly higher operating overheads (operating profit margin has fallen from 21.9% in 20X4 to 8.7% in 20X5). Again it is important to note that some of these costs will be attributable to the consolidation of Raremetal Co and some to the new contract. It could be speculated that the 73% increase in administrative expenses may be due to one-off costs associated with the tendering process (consultancy fees, etc) and the acquisition of Raremetal Co and the 77% increase in higher distribution costs could be due to additional freight/packing/insurance cost of the engines, delivery distances may also be longer (even to foreign countries) (although some of this increase may also be due to consolidation).

This is all reflected in the ROCE falling from an impressive 61·7% in 20X4 to only 19·5% in 20X5 (though even this figure is respectable). The fall in the ROCE is attributable to a dramatic fall in profit margin at operating level (from 21·9% in 20X4 to only 8·7% in 20X5) which has been compounded by a reduction in the asset turnover, with only $2·24 being generated from every $1 invested in net assets in 20X5 (from $2·82 in 20X4).

The information in the question points strongly to the possibility (even probability) that the new contract may be responsible for much of the deterioration in Tangier Co's operating performance. For example, it is likely that the new contract may account for some of the increased revenue; however, the bidding process was 'very competitive' which may imply that Tangier Co had to cut its prices (and therefore its profit margin) in order to win the contract.

The costs of fulfilling the contract have also been heavy: investment in property, plant and equipment has increased by $370 million (at carrying amount), representing an increase of 61% (no doubt some of this increase will be due to the acquisition of Raremetal Co). The increase in licence costs to manufacture the new engines has cost $200 million plus any amortisation (which is not identified in the question) and there is also the additional goodwill of $30 million.

An eight-fold increase in finance cost caused by the increased borrowing at double the interest rate of the borrowing in 20X4 and (presumably) some overdraft interest has led to the dramatic fall in the company's interest cover (from 79·6 in 20X4 to only 5·9 in 20X5). The finance cost of the new $300 million 10% loan notes to partly fund the investment in Raremetal Co and any other non-current assets has also increased debt/equity (one form of gearing measure) from 18·3% in 20X4 to 49·7% in 20X5 despite also issuing $180 million in new equity shares. At this level, particularly in view of its large increase from 20X4, it may give debt holders (and others) cause for concern as there is increased risk for all Tangier Co's lenders. If it could be demonstrated that the overdraft could not be cleared for some time, this would be an argument for including it in the calculation of debt/equity, making the 20X5 gearing

level even worse. It is also apparent from the movement in the retained earnings that Tangier Co paid a dividend during 20X5 of $55 million (295,000 + 135,000 − 375,000) which may be a questionable policy when the company is raising additional finance through borrowings and leaves Tangier Co with a substantial overdraft.

Overall, the acquisition of Raremetal Co to secure supplies appears to have been an expensive strategy, perhaps a less expensive one might have been to enter into a long-term supply contract with Raremetal Co.

(c) Further information which would be useful to obtain would therefore include:

(i) The cost of the investment in Raremetal Co, the carrying amount of the assets acquired and whether Tangier Co has carried out a goodwill impairment test as required under IFRS.

(ii) The benefits generated from the investment; for example, Raremetals Co's individual financial statements and details of sales to external customers (not all of these will be measurable in financial terms).

(iii) The above two pieces of information would demonstrate the investment in Raremetal Co had been worthwhile.

(iv) The amount of intra-group sales made during the year and those expected to be made in the short to medium term.

(v) The pricing strategy agreed with Raremetal Co so that the effects on the profits reported in the individual financial statements of Raremetal Co and Tangier Co can be more readily determined.

(vi) More information is needed to establish if the new contract has been detrimental to Tangier Co's performance. The contract was won sometime between 1 October 20X4 and 1 January 20X5 and there is no information of when production/sales started, but clearly there has not been a full year's revenue from the contract. Also there is no information on the length or total value of the contract.

Marking Scheme		
	Maximum Marks	**Awarded**
Part (a) comparability		
A like for like comparison taking account of the consolidation and the contract	5	
Part (b) Analysis of results		
up to 5 marks for ratio calculations	5	
Profitability	4½	
Gearing and interest cover	2½	
	12	
Part (c) additional information		
Any three of the six suggestions provided	3	

Section 9

REFERENCES

The Board (2018) *Conceptual Framework for Financial Reporting*. London: IFRS Foundation.

The Board (2018) *IAS 1 Presentation of Financial Statements*. London: IFRS Foundation.

The Board (2018) *IAS 2 Inventories*. London: IFRS Foundation.

The Board (2018) *IAS 7 Statement of Cash Flows*. London: IFRS Foundation.

The Board (2018) *IAS 8 Accounting Policies, Changes in Accounting Estimates and Errors*. London: IFRS Foundation.

The Board (2018) *IAS 10 Events after the Reporting Period*. London: IFRS Foundation.

The Board (2018) *IAS 12 Income Taxes*. London: IFRS Foundation.

The Board (2018) *IAS 16 Property, Plant and Equipment*. London: IFRS Foundation.

The Board (2018) *IAS 20 Accounting for Government Grants and Disclosure of Government Assistance*. London: IFRS Foundation.

The Board (2018) *IAS 21 The Effects of Changes in Foreign Exchange Rates*. London: IFRS Foundation.

The Board (2018) *IAS 23 Borrowing Costs*. London: IFRS Foundation.

The Board (2018) *IAS 27 Separate Financial Statements*. London: IFRS Foundation.

The Board (2018) *IAS 28 Investments in Associates and Joint Ventures*. London: IFRS Foundation.

The Board (2018) *IAS 32 Financial Instruments: Presentation*. London: IFRS Foundation.

The Board (2018) *IAS 33 Earnings per Share*. London: IFRS Foundation.

The Board (2018) *IAS 36 Impairment of Assets*. London: IFRS Foundation.

The Board (2018) *IAS 37 Provisions, Contingent Liabilities and Contingent Assets*. London: IFRS Foundation.

The Board (2018) *IAS 38 Intangible Assets*. London: IFRS Foundation.

The Board (2018) *IAS 40 Investment Property*. London: IFRS Foundation.

The Board (2018) *IAS 41 Agriculture*. London: IFRS Foundation.

The Board (2018) *IFRS 3 Business Combinations*. London: IFRS Foundation.

The Board (2018) *IFRS 5 Non-current Assets Held for Sale and Discontinued Operations*. London: IFRS Foundation.

The Board (2018) *IFRS 7 Financial Instruments: Disclosure*. London: IFRS Foundation.

The Board (2018) *IFRS 9 Financial Instruments*. London: IFRS Foundation.

The Board (2018) *IFRS 10 Consolidated Financial Statements*. London: IFRS Foundation.

The Board (2018) *IFRS 13 Fair Value Measurement*. London: IFRS Foundation.

The Board (2018) *IFRS 15 Revenue from Contracts with Customers*. London: IFRS Foundation.

The Board (2018) *IFRS 16 Leases*. London: IFRS Foundation.